MW01283195

THE DAILY LESSON

366 Essays to Challenge Your Status Quo

HONEROD

ALSO BY HONEROD

The NO-BS Self-Help Book

701 LIFE LESSONS

101 LIFE QUOTES

Visit **www.honerod.com** to follow **Honerod** and
stay up to date on future book releases

All contact email can be sent to: **phonerodb@gmail.com**

ISBN eBook: 978-82-693372-8-0

ISBN Paperback: 978-82-693372-7-3

ISBN Hardcover: 978-82-693372-6-6

 www.honerod.com

"The unexamined life is not worth living, for it is within the profound introspection and interrogation of our own actions, beliefs, and desires that we truly understand the essence of our existence."

SOCRATES, PHILOSOPHER

CONTENTS

ix

xvi

xvii

INTRODUCTION

"ARE YOU READY TO CHANGE YOUR LIFE?"

"YES!"

And everyone screams as the self-help guru steps on stage, and the whole scene goes off like a giant, glittery, over-the-top party. It's like being in the middle of the chorus at a Taylor Swift concert, with everyone bouncing up and down like they've got springs for legs. Maybe you've been at it firsthand, or maybe you know someone who constantly posts those "blessed" and motivational statuses on *Facebook*, they have definitely been there. I'm talking about those crazy self-help seminars, the ones that promise you the moon and the stars and every good thing in between.

Their pitch is always the same. Tired of your current life? Want to get more out of life? Tired of being tired? Want more joy, more cash, more... of everything? Well, that's where the journey begins. It's like you've just signed up for an adventure into a world promising a better you. And it makes sense, doesn't it? After all, if you're not totally thrilled with where you're at right now, you'd naturally want to shake things up.

But here's the thing. When you're feeling low and looking for a way out, it's easy to get swept up in the grand promises of self-development. It's quite tempting, isn't it? A world full of people striving to be better, taking charge of their lives, and feeling like they're moving forward. It's like you've joined a secret VIP club where everyone's focused on personal growth while the rest of the world's busy partying.

Breaking free from a tough place feels pretty awesome, like you've climbed a mountain or something. You've bit the bullet and let a new voice guide you, which is great. But that's also when you've got to watch out for the pitfalls you might not see coming. So as you journey through this self-help world, keep your eyes wide open and remember: not everything that glitters is gold.

I'M AS GUILTY AS YOU

I can still picture it, clear as day, how it all started over a decade ago. Back then, I was your typical kid. Anxious, not quite fitting in anywhere, but my dreams and ambitions—they were big. Then I stumbled on this catchy book—*Think And Grow Rich* by Napoleon Hill. Even the guy's name was kind of appealing like it promised something cool. So, I jumped online and ordered it from *Amazon*, but let me tell you, that book was thick. I put off reading it for a while, kind of intimidated by its size.

But when I finally cracked it open and started reading? Man, I was hooked! It was like I'd been caught by a huge fisherman, and before I knew it, I was neck-deep in the self-help world. I started hitting the gym, watching what I ate, and filling up my calendar with all sorts of things. And the books—I was reading one after the other like there was no tomorrow.

I followed every guru's advice, started meditating, took ice-cold showers (talk about wake-up calls), read affirmations, and visualized my goals. I was reading more, working out more, and going after my dreams harder than ever before. I was on cloud nine, feeling super confident and motivated. "This is it," I thought to myself, "I've finally cracked the code." Life seemed perfect, absolutely perfect.

While I was busy inhaling all this self-help stuff, what I didn't realize was that I was getting hooked. Yep, I was turning into a self-help junkie. I've become addicted to this industry.

THE ADDICTIVE SIDE OF SELF-HELP

There's a certain undeniable charm about the self-help universe. It leaves you basking in a cozy feeling that seems to come from every single page of all the self-help books you ooze down. Just like a gamer reaching new heights and unlocking new levels in a video game, each book, each nugget of wisdom appears to unlock a new level of self-improvement.

Each video you watch, every book you read, sends a surge of dopamine straight to the brain, a pleasure hormone that leaves the mind with a feeling of accomplishment. This sensation, akin to the thrill of achievement, seems to propel them into the cycle over and over again. Finish one book, feel the rush of motivation, order a bunch more on *Amazon*, and do it all over again.

If one doesn't spot the problem here, let's delve a bit deeper into the addictive nature of dopamine. The thing with addiction is that it's never about the substance, or the activity, but rather, it's about the impact on the brain. It's not the drug itself that causes addiction, but what the drug does to the neurotransmitters.

And just like that, it's alarmingly easy to get hooked on self-help. This world, whether by design or by accident, can draw you into a grand illusion—the illusion of constant progress. After finishing a book, you feel accomplished. After attending a seminar, you feel enlightened. After watching a self-help video, you feel transformed. You get the feeling that you've climbed a mountain, conquered a significant chunk of your journey. This motivation keeps brewing within you, prompting you to reach for the next book, sign up for the next seminar, click on the next video.

It's only when you pause, catch your breath, and really evaluate your situation that you might realize that despite all the activity, despite all the perceived progress, not much has actually changed. And that's when you realize you could be a victim of "action faking," tricked by the illusion of advancement without real growth. This is the complex illusion of the self-help industry.

ACTION FAKING

You might have been a victim without even realizing it. Picture this—it's the crafty urge to reorganize your garage when a critical report is due. It's the illusion of a full day's work after merely crafting a comprehensive to-do list. It's the thrill of researching every element of writing a book, yet never putting pen to paper. It's the distraction of designing the perfect logo for your business while avoiding the real challenge—never take the time to make one, or call the first potential client.

Action faking is a strong form of procrastination. It's lethal because it fools you into thinking you're moving forward, while you're actually standing still. And that's the lesson to be learned from this. You don't have to read every self-help book out there, attend endless seminars, accumulate online courses, or binge-listen to motivational podcasts. There's a point where consuming advice can overwhelm taking actual steps. It's a trap, and many of us get caught in it, with serious consequences.

The aftermath can be quite harsh and unpleasant. Picture an empty wallet, a brief surge of motivation, and a nagging realization hidden in the back of your mind—you haven't made any progress from where you began. You've merely become an expert at fooling yourself. A master of the illusion of progress. This is the unpleasant truth about the world of self-help—it's a circus of the mind, and one that we all too readily buy tickets for.

THE PROBLEM WITH THE SELF-HELP INDUSTRY

Here's a fun little secret the self-help industry won't tell you. When you think about it, the usual advice—the positive feel-good messages, the traditional life advice, the motivational speeches we hear all the time—really focus on what you lack. They focus on what you don't have, the things you think are missing in your life, and the faults you believe you have. They take what you believe are your failures and worries, and your own feelings of not being good enough, and make them appear bigger and more important than they actually are in your mind.

Think about it. You seek out endless productivity hacks because you believe you're not efficient enough already. You pore over books on building confidence, convinced you're not confident enough as you are. You watch videos on being happier because you feel you're not happy enough. Or when you feel like your love life isn't fulfilling, you find yourself reading countless relationship advice articles or books, because you feel you're not loved enough.

Funny thing is, all this positive vibe stuff they're selling, all this "be better, be superior" noise, only keeps reminding us of what we're not. Truth is, if you're really happy, you don't need to convince yourself that you are in front of a mirror. You just are, end of story.

WHY READ THIS BOOK?

Now, that I've got you hooked—I know what you are thinking, "This is terrifying stuff, Honerod. I grabbed this book for my daily shot of motivation, to juice up my positivity, to learn to be a money magnet, a communication whizz, productivity powerhouse. And now I'm here, wondering if I should even keep going?"

Hold on, though. This book isn't about making you "more." This book isn't just another self-help read or the last one (maybe) you'll read. This book is not about getting you hooked on a product or trying to give you a sense of artificial motivation. This book was thoughtfully crafted with the intent to disrupt established norms, challenge the current societal status quo, and provoke thought on various topics, while integrating elements of philosophy. Each essay addresses a unique topic that, until now, we have struggled to put into words. You may have found yourself stirred by certain emotional one-liners or motivational quotes, yet struggled to put your reaction into words. This book aims to bridge that gap, providing the words and understanding necessary to explore these deep, often elusive, concepts.

The essays within this book are prepared to tackle subjects frequently covered in silence, considered taboo, or difficult to articulate. You'll confront the harsh unpreparedness we always face upon our parents' eventual departure, the blink-and-you-miss-it speed of our kids' childhood, explore the paradoxical increase in loneliness even if we are more connected than ever, and why love is a beautiful pain.

The primary objective of this book is to inspire introspection and encourage readers to reevaluate their values and priorities, springing from the diverse themes explored within the essays. Admittedly, change is a challenging process yet an inevitable certainty. As creatures of curiosity and reflection by nature, this book is here to ignite the change. Each day provides an opportunity to reflect on a unique essay, underlining this hands-on approach to life, amplified with a dose of philosophy, with the main goal of helping readers enhance their quality of life.

However, it's vital to remember that this book, despite its insights, serves only as a catalyst. Knowledge, without action, is merely potential energy and useless. With this understanding, the narrative unfolds. **Let the book begin.**

— DAY 1 —

You are the author of your own story

ISN'T it fascinating that we're all the main characters in our own life stories, with the unique power to write each chapter? Not the one dictated by others, but the one where you're not just the protagonist, but also the author. It's a perspective worth exploring, trust me.

Think of your life as a blank canvas, waiting to be painted with the strokes of your choices, actions, and beliefs. You hold the pen, and with every decision you make, you write a new line, a new scene, in the grand theatre of your existence. You are the architect of your dreams, the creator of your destiny.

The beauty lies in the fact that you have the power to choose the direction of your story. You can choose to embrace challenges as opportunities for growth, to seek joy in the simplest moments, and to create a narrative that aligns with your values and aspirations. Your story is unique, shaped by your experiences, beliefs, and the dreams that reside within your heart.

But being the author of your own story also comes with responsibility. It requires self-awareness, introspection, and the willingness to take ownership of your choices. It's about realizing you hold the power over your life and that you can consciously make choices that shape your journey.

While external factors may influence our circumstances, it's ultimately our perception, attitude, and actions that determine the narrative we weave. Even in the face of adversity, we can choose resilience, courage, and a steadfast belief in our ability to overcome.

But let's not forget the power of collaboration in our storytelling. Just as authors may have editors, mentors, or fellow writers to provide guidance and support, we too can seek the wisdom and encouragement of those around us. Surrounding ourselves with a nurturing community can enrich our narrative, offering diverse perspectives and new insights that enhance our personal growth.

You are the author here. You can change the course, introduce a plot twist, or transform the villain into an ally. You write the story of your life. Make it a page-turner. Make it a tale worth telling. Remember, every day is a blank page, so write your story well.

— DAY 2 —

Challenge the status quo

ISN'T it incredible how we, as humans, have this innate desire to make sense of the world around us? We crave order, predictability, and a sense of belonging. While these aspects undoubtedly offer comfort, they can also lead to self-satisfaction and stagnation. What if, instead of merely accepting the status quo, we dared to challenge it? The idea might seem daunting, but the truth is that when we question the established norms, we unleash our true potential and contribute to the evolution of society.

Our world is peppered with tales of individuals who dared to defy convention. Galileo Galilei, who, against a backdrop of rigid geocentric belief, stood by his heliocentric view of our Solar System. Or Rosa Parks, who, with one protest, catalyzed the civil rights movement. They are the testimonies to the power of challenging the status quo.

But why challenge the status quo? Isn't it easier to just fall in line and follow the crowd? Well, it may be more comfortable, but will it lead to progress, growth, or innovation? History gives us a clear "No!" Innovations, be they in technology, society, or thought, stem from the courage to question, challenge, and change the prevailing norms.

I'm sure you've faced times when you've been expected to conform. I certainly have. It's like walking on a tightrope, where one misstep could lead to criticism or rejection. Yet, think about the times you've dared to take a different stance. Challenging, wasn't it?

So, let's keep pushing, questioning, and innovating. When we see something that doesn't feel right or could be improved, let's have the courage to speak up. Yes, it's daunting, and yes, it might ruffle a few feathers. But in the end, it is through challenging the status quo that we drive forward progress.

The next time you're standing at the crossroads of the familiar and the unknown, remember this: the status quo is simply a reflection of the past, and it's in our hands to shape the future. Let's dare to step off the well-trodden path and forge our own. After all, every revolutionary change in our world began with a challenge to the status quo.

— DAY 3 —

Don't go broke trying to impress broke

T HIS statement hides a profound exploration of human psychology, consumerism, and the relentless pursuit of social validation. At its core, this statement delves into the paradox of sacrificing our authentic selves and financial security in the pursuit of impressing others who are equally, if not more, financially and emotionally insecure.

The modern world thrives on appearances, and social media intensifies this obsession. Platforms such as *Instagram* and *Facebook* provide selected views into the lives of others, where material possessions and experiences serve as yardsticks for success and happiness. We often find ourselves trapped in an endless cycle of comparison, unable to escape the gnawing pressure to "keep up with the Joneses," even if it means sacrificing our financial stability and mental well-being. This desire to impress stems from the innate human need for validation and belonging, which, when twisted together with consumerism, results in a vicious cycle of debt and dissatisfaction.

This phenomenon is not merely a reflection of personal choices; rather, it is a systemic issue perpetuated by societal norms and expectations. Advertisements and marketing campaigns capitalize on our insecurities, creating a false narrative of happiness linked to material success. As we strive to impress those around us, we often fail to recognize that they too are caught in the same trap, continuing a cycle of mutual disillusionment and self-deception.

To break free from this self-destructive cycle, we must first recognize the transient nature of material possessions and external validation. True happiness and self-worth cannot be derived from the fleeting opinions of others, nor can they be measured by the accumulation of objects that lose value over time. Instead, we must direct our attention inward and seek validation from within, cultivating self-awareness, self-acceptance, and self-respect.

We must challenge the societal norms that promote superficiality and redefine success on our terms. Success should not be measured by our ability to impress others, but rather by the fulfillment of our unique potential, the pursuit of our passions, and the positive impact we leave on the world.

— DAY 4 —

What is the meaning of life?

THE question of life's meaning has fascinated humanity for centuries. Philosophers, theologians, and curious minds alike have sought to unravel this profound mystery. Yet, despite countless examinations and theories, the answer remains difficult to find. So, what's the meaning of life?

Picture, for a moment, a world where there was a singular, universally accepted meaning of life. How uniform, how monotone would that world be? If life's purpose were carved in stone, we would lose our freedom, and our individuality, living instead on autopilot, locked in an endless race towards a singular, predetermined end. Each person's unique journey would be reduced to just an imitation, a persistent echo of someone else's narrative. A universal meaning of life would strip away the dynamism, diversity, and wonder that make our world so compellingly beautiful.

In the pursuit of life's meaning, you might eventually face something called *Agrippa's Trilemma*, which presents three philosophical dead-ends, named after the philosopher Agrippa the Sceptic. [1]First, there's the infinite regress, where every proof demands another, creating an endless chain. For instance, when asking why an event happened, each answer might lead to another question of "why" in a never-ending sequence. Second, there's circular reasoning, where evidence for a claim relies on the claim itself. An example might be when someone says a book is true because the book itself claims to be true. Lastly, axiomatic acceptance, wherein a premise is deemed "true" without solid evidence, much like accepting the rules of a game without questioning them, simply acting as a foundational assumption.

Yet, despite this seemingly pointless pursuit, the beauty of life's meaning may just be that it remains elusive, subjective, and deeply personal. It bends a spectrum of colorful interpretations, each as unique and beautiful as the individual perceiving it. Perhaps life's true meaning is not a definitive answer to be unearthed but rather a question that inspires us to seek, to wonder, and to grow. It is this unending search, this continuous desire for understanding that fuels our creativity, our empathy, and our humanity.

— DAY 5 —

Cheating is a choice, loyalty is a duty

WHEN it comes to relationships, cheating is often seen as the ultimate betrayal. It can destroy trust, break hearts, and leave lasting scars. On the other hand, loyalty is seen as a key component of a healthy relationship. But why is it that some people choose to cheat, while others remain loyal?

Cheating is a choice. It's a conscious decision to break a commitment that was made to another person. Whether it's a physical affair or emotional unfaithfulness, the act of cheating shows a lack of respect and disregard for the feelings of one's partner.

Loyalty is a duty. When we enter into a committed relationship, we are making a promise to be faithful and supportive to our partner. It's a responsibility that we have to the person we love.

So why do some people choose to cheat? It's often a complex combination of factors, including dissatisfaction in the relationship, a desire for validation or attention, or even a lack of self-control. But ultimately, it comes down to a lack of respect for one's partner and a disregard for the commitment that was made.

In a world where we are constantly bombarded with messages that encourage us to prioritize our own desires and needs, it can be easy to lose sight of the importance of loyalty. But the truth is, loyalty is the foundation of a healthy relationship. It creates a sense of security and trust that allows both partners to grow and thrive.

Ultimately, the paradox of choice and duty reveals the complexity of the human experience. While cheating may offer the illusion of freedom and excitement, it is a fleeting and empty joy that fades in comparison to the richness and depth of true loyalty. In choosing to fulfill our duty to be loyal, we not only honor the trust and faith that others have placed in us, but we also elevate ourselves to a higher plane of integrity and self-respect. Thus, in the ever-changing landscape of human relationships, let us strive to embrace the duty of loyalty, for it is in this sacred commitment that we discover the true essence of love, trust, and commitment.

— DAY 6 —

Your children only get one childhood

CHILDHOOD, a precious and momentary phase of life. It's a time of wonder, curiosity, and boundless imagination. As adults, we have the power to shape and influence our children's experiences during this crucial period.

Imagine for a moment the significance of this idea. Childhood is a foundation upon which a lifetime is built. It's a canvas waiting to be painted with colorful memories, meaningful connections, and valuable lessons. It's a time of innocence and discovery, a time that shapes the very essence of who we become.

As parents, guardians, or mentors, we hold the key to unlocking the potential of our children's childhood. We have the opportunity to create a nurturing and enriching environment that allows them to explore, learn, and grow. Our actions, words, and presence leave a lasting imprint on their young hearts and minds.

Yet, in the middle of the countless responsibilities of parenthood, it's crucial to remember that childhood is not just about growth and learning. It is also about the joy of unfettered play, the wonder of insatiable curiosity, the thrill of uncharted exploration. It is a time of endless summers and magic realism, where imaginations are boundless and every new day is an adventure. Let's allow children to revel in their childhood, cherish its purity and innocence, and navigate its challenges at their own pace. Let's create memories that they can look back upon with warmth and joy.

Time is a precious commodity, and childhood slips away in the blink of an eye. It's easy to get caught up in the busyness of life, and to prioritize work or other responsibilities. The truth is that our children's childhoods will never come again. They deserve our undivided attention.

Make sure to let every moment count. Let's be present for their laughter, their tears, and their milestones. Let's create space for exploration, imagination, and play. Let's listen to their stories, validate their emotions, and offer guidance when needed. Let's be their safe haven in a world full of uncertainties.

— DAY 7 —

Spend time with old people

I MAGINE sitting across from an elderly person, their eyes sparkling with a lifetime of experiences, their wrinkled hands holding the wisdom of years gone by. They may be physically weak, but their spirit is strong, resilient, and filled with stories waiting to be shared. In a world that often celebrates youth and the pursuit of the new, we often overlook the invaluable treasure that lies within our elders.

Remember that day when you complained about a minor inconvenience like slow Wi-Fi? Well, let's chat about this for a moment. When you sit with an elder, you're sitting with someone who witnessed the world without the internet, without color television, and they survived, even thrived. They can share what real patience felt like, waiting for letters in the mail, not texts in an instant.

They're not just about the past though. They've bridged the gap between then and now. So, they see the world through a different lens, colored by experiences we can't even understand or comprehend. They've weathered storms we only read about. They've danced at the victories we consider historical moments.

I mean, how cool would it be to hear firsthand what it was like to witness mankind's first steps on the moon? Or how communities came together during a world war? Each wrinkle, a story, each gray hair, a lesson learned.

And let's flip the script here. When we spend time with them, we're not just receiving. We're giving them something precious. Our time, our ear, our respect. We're reminding them that they still matter, that they are an important part of the existence of life.

Look, time is the most valuable currency. Once spent, it's gone. But here's the thing: spending it with the elderly, it's an investment, not an expenditure. The returns? Immeasurable. Stories you won't find on *Google*, wisdom that doesn't come from a self-help book, and the sort of genuine human connection that money just can't buy.

So, pause *Netflix*, and put down the smartphone. Seek out the company of an elder. Trust me, you won't regret it. It's time well spent, it's life well lived.

— DAY 8 —

Suffering is inevitable

I MAGINE sitting at a cafe, the sunlight filtering through the trees, a fresh brew ´ in hand, and an old friend across from you. This friend leans in and says, "You know, I've been thinking... suffering, it's just part of the package, isn't it?" You raise an eyebrow, intrigued by the sudden depth to your coffee talk. "What do you mean?"

Well, life's a roller coaster, right? One moment, you're scaling the heights of joy, hands raised in triumph, and the next, you're plummeting into the depths of despair. It's not just you; it's everyone. From the billionaire in his skyscraper to the artist painting sunsets, everyone faces the ebb and flow of life. What's funny is, the universe doesn't really discriminate; it just serves everyone a slice of the "suffering pie."

Your friend continues, "I mean, think about diamonds." Now you're really curious. "Diamonds?" "Yeah! They're just chunks of carbon that went through a ton of pressure. And yet, look how they shine!" They're not just hinting at the age-old wisdom of adversity forging strength; they're nudging you towards appreciating that maybe, just maybe, the challenges and heartaches we face are nature's way of polishing us.

You sip your coffee, pondering. "But why?" you ask. "Why is suffering so universal?" Your friend shrugs, "Maybe it's life's way of ensuring we never take things for granted. Or perhaps, in a world where we're more connected than ever but feel lonelier by the day, it's our shared language, our communal experience."

Right, because when was the last time you felt a deep connection with someone over shared joys? It's almost always shared struggles that bind us closer. That time when both of you faced career lows or battled personal demons—it's in these shared valleys of suffering that the most profound human connections often emerge.

As you both get ready to part, your friend offers one final thought: "Life's not about avoiding the storm, but dancing in the rain." You smile, knowing that perception can transform inevitable suffering.

— DAY 9 —

Truth has three sides

D EBATES are a fundamental part of human interaction, and they play an important role in shaping our understanding of the world. We often perceive truth as a singular entity, an absolute that is either right or wrong. But upon closer examination, we discover that truth is multi-dimensional, encompassing various perspectives and interpretations.

Picture this: you and I are both witnesses to the same event. It's pretty likely that we'll both come away from that experience with our own version of what happened, right? That's because our individual truths are shaped by our unique experiences, beliefs, and values. What seems true to me might be different from what seems true to you, but that doesn't mean either of us is wrong. That's the first two sides of truth, your truth and my truth.

Now, let's talk about the third side—the objective truth. This is the truth that exists outside of our own perspectives, the one that's not colored by our personal biases or experiences. It's the truth that, in theory, is the same for everyone, regardless of their individual viewpoints. The thing is, though, it's almost impossible to pin down that objective truth, because our understanding of it is always filtered through our own perspectives.

But here's the amazing part: when we recognize that truth has these three sides, it can actually bring us closer together. By accepting that our own truth might not be the whole story and being open to understanding someone else's truth, we open ourselves up to empathy, compassion, and deeper connections with others. Plus, in our pursuit of that elusive objective truth, we might just learn something new and grow as individuals.

Next time you find yourself in a disagreement or facing a tough decision, remember that there's more than one side to the truth. Embrace your truth, but also be open to the truths of others. And who knows? In the process, you might just find yourself a little closer to that ever-elusive objective truth that brings us all together. Gain a deeper understanding of the world around you, and become a better communicator and problem-solver.

— DAY 10 —

You are forever a student in life

JUST when we thought our school days were over, here comes this statement, reminding us that learning never really ends. And you know what? That's the beauty of life.

The world around us is overflowing with lessons, waiting to be learned. It's like a colossal, open-air classroom, with experiences serving as our teachers and moments as our textbooks. And, just like a student, we're here to learn, to grow, to evolve.

See, life isn't static, it's dynamic. It's a constant ebb and flow, constantly changing. And to keep up, we need to be on our toes, ever-ready to learn and adapt. This could mean learning a new skill for work, understanding a different culture while traveling, or even just figuring out how to assemble that flat-pack furniture. Every day brings a new lesson, and we're the everlasting students.

But there's more to it than just practical lessons. As students of life, we also get to delve into the deep, existential stuff. We grapple with questions of love and loss, joy and pain, purpose and meaning. These are not lessons that can be taught in a conventional classroom. They're the lessons that come from living, from experiencing, and from feeling.

Consider the complexity of human relationships. Every person we encounter is a walking, talking textbook filled with chapters of their own unique experiences and perspectives. Our interactions provide an opportunity to learn about empathy, patience, and understanding, thereby enriching our own emotional intelligence.

Further, each challenge we face serves as a rigorous practical exam. These tests of life push us beyond our comfort zones, compelling us to adapt and evolve. They teach us resilience, perseverance, and the importance of maintaining hope amidst adversity.

Life urges us to delve into the philosophical realm, posing questions about purpose, meaning, and our roles in the grand theatre of existence. These abstract lessons provoke examination, sparking the process of self-realization and spiritual growth.

— DAY 11 —

Wealth feeds ego

THERE is a common belief that runs through the existence of humanity, as constant as the sun's rise and set. Wealth, a material emblem of success and power, is frequently regarded as the pinnacle objective in one's life. However, an often overlooked but critical aspect of accumulating riches is the deep impact it can have on our ego.

Wealth can be seen as a medium, a substance that feeds the ego, much as air fuels fire. The ego, that part of us which is associated with our sense of self-esteem and self-importance, can rapidly expand under the impact of wealth. When individuals acquire significant wealth, the ego often experiences an intoxicating increase in self-worth, self-confidence, and a sense of superiority over others. This can lead to a distorted perception of reality, where one's value is closely tied to their financial standing.

The problem begins when wealth becomes the primary measure of a person's worth. As the ego grows with each financial gain, the individual's understanding of self becomes more tied to their material possessions and less tied to their inherent qualities. This misconstrued sense of identity can lead to a cascade of negative behaviors such as arrogance, entitlement, and lack of empathy, as the wealthy individual becomes increasingly detached from the reality of those less fortunate.

When the ego is fed by wealth, it becomes reliant on it, creating a dependency that is as harmful as it is powerful. The pursuit of wealth shifts from being a means to an end, to an end in itself. This cycle of accumulation and ego-boosting can become a dangerous loop that drives individuals to prioritize wealth over relationships, ethics, and sometimes, even their own well-being.

However, it's crucial to remember that wealth itself isn't the villain; it is the unchecked growth of ego that wealth can sometimes facilitate. Like any powerful tool, wealth can be used to build or destroy, uplift or suppress, empower, or manipulate. It all depends on the hands that hold it, or more accurately, the mind that wields it.

— DAY 12 —

Tame your anger and temper

Y OU'RE stuck in traffic, late for an important meeting, and the driver in front of you is moving at a snail's pace. Instantly, the fires of anger ignite within you, ready to consume your sanity.

Anger is a primal instinct, a natural response to perceived threats or injustices. It can be a catalyst for change, motivating us to stand up for ourselves or others. However, when left unchecked, anger can become a destructive force that harms not only those around us but also ourselves.

Taming anger requires an understanding of its roots and triggers. It's about delving into the depths of our emotions and learning to navigate them with grace and self-awareness. It's recognizing that anger is not the problem itself, but rather how we choose to express and manage it.

One crucial aspect of taming anger is developing emotional intelligence. It's about recognizing the signs of escalating anger and taking proactive steps to defuse the situation. It involves cultivating empathy and seeking healthier ways to communicate and resolve conflicts.

Mindfulness also plays a crucial role in taming anger. By practicing mindfulness, we learn to observe our thoughts and emotions without judgment, creating space for self-reflection and conscious choice.

Understanding the underlying causes of anger is crucial for its effective management. Anger often stems from unmet needs, unresolved conflicts, or deeply rooted pain.

It's important to remember that taming anger is not about suppressing or denying our emotions. It's about channeling them in productive and healthy ways. It's about finding constructive outlets for our anger, such as engaging in physical activity, writing, or seeking professional guidance when needed.

To tame our anger and temper is to embrace our full humanity. It's about taking the wild, untamed parts of ourselves and cultivating them with understanding and patience. The process is not easy, but the rewards—stronger relationships, personal growth, and a deeper understanding of ourselves—are truly priceless.

— DAY 13 —

Are you using technology, or is it using you?

S OUNDS like something out of a sci-fi movie, doesn't it? But when you chew on it for a moment, it's a question that hits right at the heart of our digitized lives.

See, there's no doubt that technology is a game-changer. It's connected us in ways we could never have imagined. A tap on a screen and voila! We can chat with someone halfway across the globe, navigate unknown cities, and access a wealth of knowledge. It's like having superpowers at our fingertips!

But here's where it gets tricky. Sometimes, it feels like we're dancing to technology's tune, doesn't it? Your phone buzzes and, like Pavlov's dog, you instantly reach for it. We scroll, swipe, and click, led on by algorithms that seem to know us better than we know ourselves. And how about the way we can lose hours hooked to our screens, while time just slips away?

So, is technology using us? Are we becoming puppets, with technology pulling the strings? That's where this question leads us. It's about being aware of the invisible ways technology might be controlling our actions, our thoughts, and perhaps even shaping who we are.

At the end of the day, it's not just about whether we're using technology, but how we're using it. It's about knowing when to switch off, tune out, and reclaim our time. It's about using technology as a tool, not letting it become the master.

Are you using technology, or is it using you? It's a mirror held up to our modern lives, a call to think about our relationship with the tech in our pockets. It's an invitation to be more conscious, more mindful, in this digitized world we live in. Now, isn't that a thought worth exploring?

The power lies within you. You have the ability to use technology as a tool rather than allowing it to control you. Embrace mindful practices, such as setting boundaries, engaging in purposeful use, and fostering a healthy relationship with technology.

— DAY 14 —

Love is a beautiful pain

W HEN we think of love, we often envision the idyllic scenes of romance, the moments of tenderness and connection. We imagine the warm embrace, the gentle touch, and the sweet whispers of affection. Love fills our hearts with euphoria, with a sense of completeness and belonging. It makes us feel alive, vibrant, and invincible.

But love also has its darker side. It exposes our vulnerabilities, lays bare our insecurities, and confronts us with our deepest fears. It brings uncertainty, heartbreak, and disappointment. It challenges us to confront our own shortcomings, question our worthiness, and to face the painful truth that love can be fleeting and fragile.

Consider this. You meet someone, and suddenly, the world seems brighter, more vibrant. You laugh louder, smile wider, and live fuller. Their happiness becomes your joy, their pain, your sorrow. You share moments, memories, and dreams. It's beautiful, isn't it? This merging of souls, this interconnection of lives, this dance of love.

But then, there's the pain. Oh, the pain. The heartache when they're away, the tears when they're hurt, the fear when they're in danger. Love opens you up, makes you vulnerable, and exposes your heart. And that, my friends, can hurt. It's a pain that burns through your soul, a hurt that echoes in your heart, a wound that leaves a scar.

Here's where it gets exciting. This pain, as painful as it may be, is beautiful. Yes, you heard that right—beautiful. It's a testament to the depth of your love, the strength of your bond, and the intensity of your connection. It's a reflection of your courage, your resilience, your capacity to love.

Love isn't just about the butterflies in your stomach or the stars in your eyes. It's also about the tears on your pillow, the ache in your heart, the fear in your soul. And yet, we wouldn't have it any other way, would we? Because love, in all its beautiful, painful glory, is worth it.

— DAY 15 —

Life is a costume party

I MAGINE life as a giant costume party. Each day, when we wake up, it's like we're standing in front of a vast wardrobe, filled with endless costumes to choose from. These aren't just clothes, but roles we slip into. One day, we might pick out the costume of a brave hero, ready to tackle any challenge. Another day, we might choose to be the quiet listener, offering a shoulder to lean on for friends in need.

This costume party is quite an adventure. We're all guests here, trying on different looks and lives. Sometimes, we choose costumes because they feel right; they match who we think we are or who we want to be. Other times, we pick a role because it's what others expect of us, like being the perfect student, the reliable coworker, or the caring family member.

But the most magical part of this party doesn't happen when we're perfectly dressed for the role. It happens in those unexpected moments when the mask slips, and our true selves peek through. Maybe it's a burst of laughter, a tear shed during a movie, or a genuine smile at a simple kindness. In these moments, the costumes fall away, and we connect as the real, wonderfully complex people we are.

Navigating this costume party can be tricky. With all these roles and expectations, it's easy to feel lost, wondering which costume is really "you." You might feel like you're changing costumes so often, trying to find the right fit, that you lose sight of what's underneath all those layers.

Remember that this costume party of life is about more than just fitting in. It's about finding those moments and those roles that feel genuinely right, where the costume feels like a second skin because it aligns so closely with your inner self. It's about discovering that, beneath the various roles, there's a core "you" that's always there, steady and true.

Don't be afraid to change costumes, try on new roles, and explore all the different facets of who you are. Cherish those moments when the costumes come off, when you're just you, in all your imperfect, authentic glory.

— DAY 16 —

Books are mental workouts

PICTURE your brain as a muscle. Now, you wouldn't neglect your gym time, would you? Your brain, much like the muscles in your body, needs regular exercise to stay in shape. Books are the ultimate mental barbells, my friends.

Each book we pick up to read is like a new mountain we set out to climb. With every page, we ascend, pulling ourselves up through ideas and stories, learning, absorbing, and constantly stretching our cognitive capacity. Every new word we encounter, every complex plot twist, every emotional roller-coaster within the pages, it's all a part of this intense workout regimen.

Imagine running a marathon without training, sounds impossible right? Similarly, attempting to navigate life without mentally conditioning our minds with books is like setting sail in a storm with no compass. Books equip us with knowledge and wisdom that prepare us for the unanticipated challenges life throws our way.

Furthermore, books provide us with a cognitive agility course, challenging our perspectives, pushing us to question, explore, and expand our understanding of the world. This mental flexibility is similar to the elasticity a seasoned yogi develops over time. Reading is to the mind what yoga is to the body.

While you're lifting these mental barbells, not only are you building cognitive muscle, but you're also increasing your emotional intelligence. As we walk in the shoes of the characters, feel their joys, their sorrows, we become more empathetic, and more understanding.

Every genre, every author, and every story presents a unique mental workout, building your cognitive endurance, enhancing your analytical prowess, and enriching your imagination. Reading is the ultimate brain gym, with no membership fees, no closing hours, available anytime, anywhere.

Flex your cognitive muscles and go on a mental workout. I promise, by the end of it, you'll be intellectually ripped. Now, isn't that a thrilling thought? Turn the key, and open that gate. Happy training!

— DAY 17 —

Go the f*** to sleep

ALRIGHT, folks, let's chat about something we all love but often neglect: Sleep. You know, that magical state where we recharge, dream, and escape the whirlwind of daily life. Now, I hear you saying, "But I'm a night owl," or "I do my best work at night." My friend, I'm going to cut to the chase—go the f*** to sleep.

See, your body is like a sophisticated piece of machinery. It runs on a clock—a circadian rhythm, if you want to get technical. This internal metronome orchestrates everything from your digestion to your brainwaves, all synced to the rotation of this beautiful blue planet we call home. Ignore it at your own risk!

Sleep deprivation is no joke. It's not a badge of honor to see how long you can function on as little sleep as possible. It's not cool, and let's face it, you're not as "fine" as you think you are. That's your sleep-deprived brain playing tricks on you. Believe me, you're not fooling anyone with those dark circles and that third cup of coffee before noon.

What happens when you don't sleep? You're damaging your cognitive functions, impacting your mood, and increasing risks of serious health issues. Heck, even one night of poor sleep can make you feel like a zombie. Now, imagine that, day after day. Not so fun, huh?

Let's make this really simple. You need to work? Your body needs to sleep. You want to play? Your body still needs to sleep. You want to live a long, healthy, and vibrant life? You guessed it—go the f*** to sleep!

In a world that never sleeps, be the rebel who does. Embrace sleep not as a necessary evil but as the key to an energetic, productive, joyful life. Do it for your health, your sanity, your loved ones. Trust me, everything else can wait. You're not going to miss out on anything by getting some shut-eye. So turn off the gadgets, fluff up the pillows, and for heaven's sake, go the f*** to sleep.

—— DAY 18 ——

Life's too short to sweat everything

IN our pursuit of perfection, we often lose sight of what truly matters. We become consumed by trivial matters, worrying about every little decision, every minor setback. We allow ourselves to be overwhelmed by the fear of failure, the fear of judgment, and the fear of the unknown.

Every tick of the clock, every beat of our hearts, signifies the continual, unstoppable march of time. Each moment, once passed, is lost to the books of history, irretrievable and irreplaceable. In this light, the concept of sweating the small stuff seems rather pointless and unproductive, doesn't it?

We live in a world circulating with expectations, deadlines, and responsibilities. The flood of tasks can often make us feel like we're drowning, losing sight of the shore, and forgetting the sweetness of the sun's warmth. But isn't it ironic? We waste our fleeting moments stressing over what could go wrong, over what needs to be done, instead of cherishing the beauty of what is.

There's an art in differentiating what's worth our sweat and what isn't. It's about recognizing that some battles are not ours to fight, some burdens not ours to carry. It's about understanding that we can't control every ripple in the water, every gust of wind. It's about choosing our battles wisely, and sometimes, the wisest battle is the one we walk away from.

When we are on our deathbeds, will we worry about the report that was submitted late or the promotion we missed? Will we be upset about the party we couldn't attend or the vacation that didn't go as planned? Or will we ponder the missed sunsets, the unspoken words of love, the opportunities for laughter and joy we let slip through our fingers because we were too preoccupied with sweating the small stuff?

Let's take a deep breath. Let's remember the temporariness of our existence and the beautiful transience of every moment. Let's strive not for perfection, but for fulfillment. Let's stop sweating everything and start enjoying life, for it's too short to be anything but vibrant, adventurous, and joyously unpredictable.

— DAY 19 —

Reading 200 self-help books won't do it

S ELF-HELP books have become a staple in our society, promising to offer the secrets to happiness, success, and fulfillment. And with so many books on the market, it's easy to believe that reading 200 of them will finally do it—finally give us the answers we've been searching for. But the truth is, reading 200 or 2000 self-help books won't do it. In fact, it might not do much at all.

Don't get me wrong, self-help books can be a great source of inspiration and guidance. They can offer new perspectives, provide practical advice, and help us understand ourselves better. But the problem is that reading a book, no matter how good it is, won't change your life. Real change comes from taking action, not from reading about it.

It's important to remember that self-help books are just that—a means of helping yourself. They can provide guidance and support, but they can't do the work for you. Only you have the power to make the changes you want to see in your life. And that requires more than just reading a book. It requires taking responsibility for your own life, and being proactive in making the changes you want to see.

Consider the advice of Richard Branson, the entrepreneurial maverick, who professed, "You don't learn to walk by following rules. You learn by doing, and by falling over." The road to self-improvement is a series of stumbles and recoveries. It is a labyrinth of introspection, struggle, failure, resilience, and ultimately, growth.

So, read those books, soak up the wisdom, but remember to close the book and open the door to real-world experience. Test theories in the cauldron of life. Discard what doesn't work. Iterate on what does. Reflect. Adapt. Grow. This, my friend, is the true path to self-improvement.

The next time you pick up a self-help book, remember: Reading isn't the end of your journey, it's merely the spark that lights the merge. Your task is to transform that spark into a blazing fire of personal development and change.

— DAY 20 —

All silent truths become poisonous

H AVE you ever held a truth so close, wrapped it in layers of silence until it felt like a secret poison coursing through your veins? It's about those truths we keep buried, the ones we think we're hiding for the greater good or perhaps to spare ourselves and others from pain. They don't just fade into the background. Nope, they fester, grow, and start to seep into every crack of our being.

Think about it. Ever kept something from a friend thinking it's for the best, only to find that unspoken truth creating a rift as wide as a canyon between you? Or what about families, where things left unsaid build walls so high, that no one remembers how to reach over them? It's not just personal; it's everywhere. Societies bury truths under layers of history and wonder why the ground is so unstable.

Recognizing that silence can poison us is like finding a map out of a maze. It's not about blurting out every thought or secret; it's about understanding the power of bringing truth into the light. It's scary, sure. Saying out loud what we've kept silent can feel like stepping off a cliff. But it's also where healing starts. It's where connections are mended and where we start to build something real.

Breaking the silence doesn't mean we'll always get the outcome we hope for. People might get hurt, and things might change. But, more often than not, it's the only way to stop the poison from spreading. It's how we start to fix the cracks, bridge the gaps, and maybe, just maybe, find a way to turn those silent truths into something that can bring us together instead of tearing us apart.

The next time you find yourself guarding a silent truth, ask yourself this: Is the silence worth the poison? Or is it time to let the truth breathe, no matter how daunting that may seem? Because on the other side of that fear might just be the antidote we've all been searching for.

— DAY 21 —

Big house, big troubles

A big house stands as an emblem of achievement, whispering tales of luxury and social standing. The grandeur, the space, the promise of plentiful room for every imagined comfort—it's undeniably appealing.

We live in a world that often equates success with material possessions, and a big house is often seen as a symbol of achievement and status. However, what we don't often consider are the hidden costs and responsibilities that come with it.

Having a big house means more space to fill, more rooms to clean, and more maintenance to oversee. It can become a constant source of stress and time-consuming tasks. Suddenly, the dream of a grand residence can turn into a never-ending cycle of upkeep and financial burden.

A big house can also come with emotional and psychological challenges. It can create a sense of isolation and distance within a family. Each person retreats to their own corners, and the shared spaces lose their sense of warmth and connection. The pursuit of a larger house can unintentionally lead to a loss of intimacy and togetherness.

Moreover, a big house often comes with a higher price tag, which can lead to financial strain and limited flexibility. It may require sacrificing other important aspects of life, such as travel, experiences, or even the ability to pursue meaningful passions. The pursuit of a big house can unknowingly trap us in a cycle of working harder and longer to maintain a lifestyle that may not bring us the true happiness we seek.

It's not about the size of the house, but the quality of the life lived within its walls. It's about creating a home that fosters love, connection, and a sense of belonging. A smaller house, filled with warmth, laughter, and cherished memories, can bring far greater joy than a big, empty house that lacks a sense of love and community

— DAY 22 —

Seize opportunities when you can

OPPORTUNITIES are like gifts—they come in all shapes and sizes, and we should never take them for granted. In life, we are presented with various opportunities, both big and small. Some of them may be life-changing, while others may be small moments that can have a profound impact on our lives. Regardless of their nature, it's important to seize opportunities when you can.

When I think of seizing opportunities, I think about the quote by Seneca, "Luck is a matter of preparation meeting opportunity." This quote resonates with me because it highlights the importance of being prepared for opportunities when they arise. We never know when an opportunity will present itself, so we should always be ready to take action.

I can think of several moments in my life when I seized an opportunity and it led to something amazing. One such moment was when I decided to take a leap of faith and pursue a career change. I had been working in the same field for several years and felt unfulfilled, but I was hesitant to make a change. One day, I saw a job posting that aligned with my passions and skills, and I decided to apply. Long story short, I got the job and it has been a game-changer.

Seizing opportunities requires us to be proactive and open-minded. We need to be willing to step outside our comfort zones and take calculated risks. We should approach life with a mindset of curiosity and a willingness to learn. This can open doors to new experiences and opportunities we may never have considered before.

It's also important to recognize that opportunities don't always come at convenient times. We may need to make sacrifices or take a leap of faith in order to seize an opportunity. But the rewards can be worth it. Seizing opportunities can lead to personal growth, career advancement, and even life-changing experiences.

Life's beauty is found in its ever-changing nature and the abundance of opportunities that it presents us. Embrace the mantra of "carpe diem" and seize opportunities when we can, for it is in these moments that we truly come alive.

— DAY 23 —

Enjoy your youth without ruining your future

I MAGINE you're on a road trip. You're young, the windows are down, the music's up, and the world is a blur of color and life. It's electrifying, isn't it? As young individuals, we often find ourselves caught between the desire to live in the moment and the pressure to plan for the future. It's easy to get swept up in the thrill of instant gratification and forget about the consequences of our actions. However, it is in these shaping years that the decisions we make can deeply influence our future.

Let's take a moment to consider youth as a banquet. It's a feast of experiences, a buffet of tastes and flavors, all laid out for your enjoyment. You're encouraged to eat, drink, and enjoy. But here's the catch: what if some dishes, as delicious as they might seem, give you a terrible stomachache the next day? Would you still reach out and take a bite?

The art of living youth to its fullest isn't about avoiding the banquet. It's about choosing wisely from the spread. It's about savoring the flavors and experimenting with the new, but also recognizing which dishes might leave you with a hangover. It's about understanding that the choices you make today—the bites you take—directly impact how you feel tomorrow.

Dance under the moonlight, but be ready to rise with the sun. Fall in love, but don't lose sight of who you are. Take the road less traveled, but keep a map handy. Make memories, but don't forget to dream.

See, it's all about balance. It's about understanding that the excitement of the dive isn't worth the risk if the pool is empty. It's about enjoying the journey without forgetting your destination.

Remember, youth is a one-time offer, but it's not a free pass to jeopardize your future. It's a chance to learn, grow, make mistakes, and figure out how to correct them. It's about making memories that you'll look back on warmly, not ones that you'll regret.

Enjoy your youth and live it to the fullest. But do so while planting seeds that will grow into a fruitful future. Your future self will thank you. After all, the goal is to look back at your life and say, "What a ride!" not "What a wreck!"

— DAY 24 —

Live in the present

H AVE you ever held a snow globe, covered by the flurry of glittering snow suspended in a miniature world? As the snow settles, you're brought back to reality, a reminder of the transient nature of moments. This fascinating experience is a metaphor for life itself, underlining the deep wisdom of living in the present.

Let's visualize life as a grand play. The past is an act that's already been performed, the future is the unwritten script, and the present is the live stage. While we often find ourselves lost in the echoes of past performances or the anticipation of future acts, the only true moment we can live, breathe, and enact is the one happening right now.

Living in the present is about immersing yourself in the concert of life. It's about feeling the beat, moving with the rhythm, absorbing the lyrics. It's about experiencing life in high-definition, with all the color, sound, and texture it has to offer.

Imagine the present moment as a snapshot. It's a freeze-frame of life that exists for a split second before it melts into the past. Now, imagine if you could fully inhabit each of these snapshots, live them, breathe them, and savor them. That's the magic of living in the present.

In the present, we find freedom from the burdens of the past. We release ourselves from the grip of regret and resentment, understanding that dwelling on what was or what could have been only robs us of the present moment. We forgive ourselves and others, allowing healing and transformation to take place.

Living in the present requires practice and mindfulness. It requires cultivating a deep awareness of our thoughts, our actions, and our surroundings. It means quieting the chatter of the mind and tuning in to the rhythm of our breath, grounding ourselves in the present moment.

Because, in the end, life isn't about capturing moments, it's about experiencing them. It's about being present, here and now. And trust me, there's no better time or place to live than right where you are, right now. Go ahead, take a deep breath, look around, and dive into the river of "Now."

—— DAY 25 ——

Your job funds your life, not defines it

PICTURE this: an individual, let's call him Joe, invests his heart and soul into his work, clocking in long hours and sacrificing personal time, all in pursuit of a big career. Joe is often praised for his dedication and soon enough, his job title becomes synonymous with his identity. We live in a world that's quick to ask, "What do you do?" It's almost as if our job title is our passport to social acceptance. But isn't it high time we challenged this deeply rooted idea?

Sure, our jobs are important. They put food on the table, pay the bills, and often allow us to satisfy ourselves in the finer things in life. They can give us a sense of purpose, stimulate our minds, and even enable us to make a positive difference. But do they really define us? Should they?

You see, each one of us is a fascinating, intricate spectrum of experiences, ideas, talents, passions, and dreams. We're artists, adventurers, dreamers, lovers, friends, and so much more. Can a job title capture all that? Hardly! So why let it define us?

It's so easy to get caught up in the rat race, to become so consumed by our work that we start believing that our job is who we are. But what happens when that job is no more? Do we cease to exist? Of course not!

My friend, your job is important, no doubt. It provides stability, financial security, and a sense of purpose. But remember that it is just a piece of the puzzle. Your true identity goes far beyond your job title. Embrace the fullness of who you are—the passions, relationships, and dreams that make your heart sing.

Find a balance that allows you to thrive both personally and professionally. Pursue work that aligns with your values and brings you joy. And never forget that your worth extends far beyond the boundaries of your job. Your job funds life, but it does not define it. It's up to you to paint a masterpiece that encompasses all the colors and experiences that make you uniquely you.

— DAY 26 —

Experimentation is the ultimate teacher

IN the grand classroom of life, there are many teachers, but none quite as impactful as *Experimentation*. This humble maestro, armed with a baton of trial and error, conducts the symphony of our growth. It turns our lives into a laboratory, where we're both the scientist and the experiment.

Remember when we were kids, fearlessly exploring the world around us? Poking an anthill, tasting a lemon, touching a hot surface—each action, an experiment; each reaction, a lesson. This innate curiosity, this daring spirit of experimentation, is the bedrock of learning.

Consider the marvels of our world. The lightbulb, the airplane, the smartphone in your hand—none would exist without a series of bold experiments. Life-changing innovations are born not from certainty but from the audacity to question, challenge, and venture into the unknown.

But let's bring it closer to home. Think about your own life. Remember that time when you took a leap of faith, leaving the well-trodden path for the road less traveled? Maybe it was a new job, a new city, or even a new recipe. It was scary, wasn't it? Yet, you learned, you grew, and you emerged stronger and wiser.

Life, in all its complexity, is an experiment. Each decision we make, each path we take, adds a new data point to the graph of our existence. Sometimes our hypotheses are proven, and sometimes they're debunked, but they always teach us something new.

Embrace the scientist within you. Question, hypothesize, experiment, observe, and learn. Step into the unknown, for it is there that the greatest lessons are discovered. It's in the melting pot of experimentation that resilience is forged, adaptability is learned, and courage is kindled.

In the laboratory of life, experimentation is our guiding light, shedding light on the path to greatness. It is a beacon that reminds us to never stop questioning, never stop exploring, and never stop daring to imagine a world beyond our wildest dreams.

— DAY 27 —

Jealousy is insecurity poisoning love

L OVE, what a beautiful and complicated dance it is. When we find ourselves caught in its embrace, we expect joy, passion, and a connection that outlasts time itself. But lurking in the shadows of love, there is a poisonous presence that can diminish its beauty and erode its foundations. That presence is jealousy—an insidious emotion that stems from our own insecurities and has the power to corrode even the strongest bonds of love.

Jealousy, at its core, is a reflection of our own fears and doubts. It arises when we question our worth, our desirability, and our place in the hearts of those we love. Like a toxic brew, it seeps into our thoughts and distorts our perception, making us view every interaction as a threat, every gesture as a betrayal. In this state of mind, love becomes a battlefield, and the very thing that should nurture us becomes a source of pain.

You see, when jealousy sneaks into the heart's grand celebration, it doesn't dance to the rhythm of love. Instead, it beats to the beat of insecurity, casting shadows of doubt and fear. It whispers tales of imaginary rivals, summons visions of loss, and breeds a monstrous creature of uncertainty.

Here's the thing, folks. Jealousy isn't the wicked witch we often make it out to be. Instead, it's more of a strict teacher, although one with unconventional teaching methods. It forces us to confront our deepest insecurities, question our self-worth, and face our fear of loss.

Consider it from this perspective. You know those fire drills at school or work? They're not meant to scare you but to prepare you for emergencies. Similarly, jealousy isn't there to ruin your love life. Instead, it's signaling that there are insecurities you need to address.

Instead of shoving jealousy into a dark corner, why not invite it for a chat over coffee? Ask it, "What are you trying to tell me?" You might find that it's pointing you toward deep-seated fears you didn't even know existed. Fears of not being good enough, fears of being replaced, or fears stemming from past heartbreaks.

— DAY 28 —

Life's not a rehearsal. Every choice counts

I MAGINE life as a series of crossroads, each presenting us with countless possibilities. At every intersection, we stand before a choice—a choice that will steer the course of our journey. It's easy to become overwhelmed and paralyzed by the magnitude of the decisions before us. But remember my friend, every choice counts.

Each morning, the moment you open your eyes, you step onto the stage. The choices you make, as insignificant as picking a blue or white shirt, or as significant as choosing a career path, all contribute to the scenes of your life's performance.

However, life's lack of rehearsal often places us at crossroads, shrouded in foggy uncertainty, questioning our decisions, doubting our choices, wondering if we're making the right move. This is where life demands courage. It requires us to embrace the unknown, to trust our instincts, to make decisions with the understanding that they count, that they're shaping the narrative of the grand play.

The choices that we often label as missteps or blunders are not errors in our performance. They're unique twists and turns that add depth to our character, create suspense in our plot, and eventually lead to an unexpected yet memorable finale. Our choices and decisions are not just mere crossroads; they're the milestones that shape our journey, the brush strokes that color our canvas, the notes that compose our symphony.

Embrace this reality, revel in the freedom it brings, and take pride in your ability to shape your destiny. Each choice, each decision, is a testament to your individuality, a tribute to your resilience, a celebration of your life.

As the curtain rises on each new day, let's savor every moment, for they are fleeting. Let's embrace the freedom and responsibility of choice, knowing that every decision we make has the potential to transform our lives and leave an enduring legacy. Remember, life's not a rehearsal. Let's seize the opportunity to make each choice count and craft a life that resonates with our heart's deepest desires.

— DAY 29 —

Injustice is inevitable, prepare for it

MY friend, let's set off on a journey to explore a harsh reality of our world—a reality that can be disheartening and unsettling. Injustice, that steadfast force that persists despite our deepest hopes and desires for a fair and equitable world. It is a bitter pill to swallow, but acknowledging its inevitability allows us to prepare ourselves and respond with resilience and determination.

The world isn't perfect. There's inequality, unfairness, and discrimination. We see it in the news, we experience it in our lives. It's like a bitter pill that's part of the human experience. But this inevitability of injustice doesn't have to break us. In fact, it can make us stronger, wiser, and more resilient.

Imagine yourself as a seasoned sailor. You know the seas are unpredictable. Calm waters can turn stormy in an instant. But does that stop you from sailing? No. You prepare for it. You learn to navigate the storm, ride the waves, and find your way even in the darkest night. That's the approach we need to take towards life's injustices.

The key is to develop a mindset of resilience and adaptability. To understand that injustices, as painful as they are, can be stepping stones to growth. They can teach us empathy, fortitude, and courage. They can push us to stand up, speak out, and make a difference. They can inspire us to fight for justice and to strive for a better world.

Preparing for injustice doesn't mean accepting it passively; it means taking action. It means standing up against injustice, raising our voices, and advocating for change. By building inclusive communities, educating ourselves and others, and engaging in collective action, we contribute to a ripple effect of transformation.

Injustice is inevitable, but don't let that scare you. Brace for it. Build your resilience. Grow from it. And remember, in the face of injustice, you're not a victim. You're a fighter. You're a survivor. You're a hero in your own story. And that, my friend, is a narrative worth living for.

— DAY 30 —

Memento mori

FROM ancient philosophers to modern thinkers, *Memento Mori* bluntly reminds us: "Remember, you're going to die," challenging us to confront life's fleeting nature and truly value our moments. It is a powerful tool that forces us to confront the transient nature of our lives and prioritize what truly matters. It encourages us to live in the present moment, to appreciate the beauty and wonder that surrounds us, and to make the most of the time we have.

In our fast-paced modern world, it's easy to get caught in the whirlwind of our daily lives, to bury ourselves in the pursuit of success, wealth, and recognition. But Memento Mori, with its frightening shortness, forces us to pause, to step back and look at the big picture.

Death, as unsettling as it may be, is the great equalizer. It doesn't discriminate based on wealth, status, or power. It puts life into perspective and reveals the fleeting nature of worldly achievements and possessions. You may own a grand mansion or drive a fancy car, but at the end of your journey, you can't take these with you. In this light, does it not seem wise to invest in the intangible—in relationships, experiences, and personal growth?

But Memento Mori doesn't only prompt us to reassess our priorities, it's also a catalyst for change. Knowing that our time is finite can drive us into action, pushing us to chase our dreams, make up for past actions, say those unsaid words, and to live authentically.

And so, Memento Mori serves as a compass, guiding us towards a life of purpose and fulfillment. It's not a call to obsess over death, but to celebrate life. To live each day with intention, passion, and gratitude, to love fiercely, to learn continuously, and to contribute meaningfully. After all, isn't the most significant testament to our lives how we live and how we touch the lives of others?

Memento Mori, while seemingly grim, is indeed a powerful philosophy. It frees us from the shackles of superficiality, encourages profound self-reflection, and motivates us to lead a meaningful life. For a life well-lived, infused with love, learning, and purpose, is perhaps the best preparation for death.

— DAY 31 —

Value everyone's presence

EVERY person we encounter, whether they are family, friends, colleagues, or even strangers, brings something unique to our lives. Each individual has their own experiences, perspectives, and contributions that shape our world in profound ways.

Imagine the conversations, stories, laughter, and yes, the disagreements we encounter. Above all, imagine the sheer variety of experiences and perspectives. It's a rainbow of human existence, where every shade matters. Each person, regardless of where they come from, what language they speak, or what dreams they harbor, adds a unique flavor to this melting pot. Every voice echoes a unique melody in this symphony of life.

Let's not forget, however, that in enormous gatherings, it's easy for someone to feel lost, unnoticed, their voice drowned in the discord. Imagine if we, as fellow guests, took a moment to turn towards them, to genuinely value their presence. Picture their faces lighting up as they're heard, seen, and appreciated. That's the power each one of us holds.

The concept of valuing everyone's presence isn't just about warm, fuzzy feelings. It's a powerful statement that can shift how we interact with our world. It alters conversations, builds bridges across canyons of misunderstanding, and forms a more inclusive, empathetic society. Isn't that the kind of world you'd want to live in?

Life is a story authored by billions, and everyone adds a word, a sentence, or a chapter. The narrative unfolds unpredictably, but the ink that writes it is our collective presence. Our individual existence is a powerful testament to the idea that no one is insignificant; we are all stardust with a purpose.

The choice is ours. Will we continue to walk through life with our vision narrowed, unmindful of the brilliance that surrounds us? Or will we open our eyes, our hearts, and our minds to the symphony of souls that enriches our lives? When we truly see others, when we acknowledge their inherent worth, we tap into a wellspring of empathy and kindness. We become catalysts for change, spreading love and acceptance in a world often starved of it.

— DAY 32 —

True investment lies in emotions and memories

I bet when you hear the word "investment," the first things that pop up in your mind are stocks, real estate, or perhaps even cryptocurrency. But let's hit the pause button on the traditional thought train for a moment and think outside the vault. What if I told you that the best investments you could make wouldn't cost a dime but would yield a wealth that is priceless?

The world echoes around with the phrase, "Time is money." Yet, in a more profound sense, time is a canvas on which we paint with the connection of our emotions, crafting memories that remain engraved in our hearts long after the moment has passed. We find the value of these emotional investments not in ledgers or balance sheets, but in the laughter ringing through a family gathering, in the pride swelling from a friend's accomplishment, in the warmth enveloping a shared sunset.

Every shared smile, every heartfelt conversation, every tear shed in empathy, and every hand held in solidarity are investments we make. They yield dividends not of monetary wealth, but of an emotional richness that saturates our existence, turning life from a mere passage of time into a vibrant, resonating melody. This currency of emotions and memories, once invested, multiplies exponentially, yielding joy, compassion, love, and a sense of interconnectedness that binds us together as humans.

But how does one quantify the worth of a mother's lullaby, a lover's gaze, or a friend's comforting silence? How does one measure the return on investment of a hearty laugh, a shared adventure, or the understanding expressed in a single glance? They are invaluable, exceeding the boundaries of conventional metrics, and that is where their true wealth lies.

True investment lies in emotions and memories because they make us rich in ways money never can. They grant us the ability to cherish, empathize, and find joy in the simple nuances of the human experience. These emotional bonds and shared memories form the priceless capital of our lives, the real wealth that remains resistant to market fluctuations. They are the treasures we carry within us, the investments that truly enrich our journey through life.

—— DAY 33 ——

Act now, delay means never

HAVE you ever found yourself caught in the web of indecision, waiting for the perfect moment to take action? We all have, at some point in our lives. We convince ourselves that we need more time, more resources, or more confidence before we can pursue our dreams or make a change. We tell ourselves that I'll start tomorrow, next week, or next month. But as time goes by, that initial spark fades, and the idea becomes a distant memory.

The power of now is something we often take for granted. We're always planning for the future or pondering over the past, forgetting that our true power resides in the present. Every moment that passes by is an opportunity—to act, to change, to grow. Delay, my friend, is the silent killer of these opportunities.

You see, the tricky thing about delay is that it disguises itself as "tomorrow." It gives us a false sense of security, making us believe that there's always a "later." But let's be honest. How many "later" turned into "never"? How many dreams were delayed, ideas discarded, and opportunities missed, all because we believed in the illusion of "later"? It's a harsh reality, but "later" is often a synonym for "never."

And it's not just about big dreams or life-changing decisions. Even the smallest actions, when delayed, can create a ripple effect. The text you were supposed to send, the help you wanted to offer, the kind word you meant to say, the healthy habit you wanted to start—when you delay these, you don't just postpone actions, but you also defer the positive impact they could have had on your life and the lives of others.

What's the solution? Act now! Yes, it's that simple. If you have an idea, start working on it. If you want to say something, speak up. If you want to learn a skill, start learning. Act, not because you're afraid of time running out, but because you respect the potential of every moment.

Let's make a pact. Let's replace "later" with "now." Let's challenge delays, and let's harness the power of the present. Because when we act now, we affirm life, and in the process, we turn "never" into "now."

— DAY 34 —

Loneliness is a state of mind

Y OU know, loneliness is a feeling that we've all experienced at some point in our lives. It's that sense of isolation, of longing for connection, that can weigh heavily on our hearts. But what if I told you that loneliness is not merely a consequence of external circumstances? What if I told you that loneliness is, in fact, a state of mind?

It's true. Loneliness is not just about being physically alone. You can be surrounded by people and still feel that deep sense of disconnection. On the other hand, you can be by yourself and feel a deep sense of inner peace and contentment. Loneliness, my friend, is a product of our perception, a state of mind that can be changed.

At its core, loneliness stems from a lack of meaningful connection. It's that feeling of being misunderstood, unseen, or unaccepted. Because we have the power to overcome loneliness. It starts with shifting our perspective, with recognizing that loneliness is not a fixed state, but a temporary experience that can be transformed.

The first step in overcoming loneliness is to cultivate a deep connection with ourselves. We often neglect our own inner world, caught up in the external distractions of life. But true connection begins within. It requires self reflection, self-acceptance, and self-love. When we develop a strong sense of self-awareness and self-compassion, we create a foundation of inner connection that can shield us from the pangs of loneliness.

Equally important is our connection to others. Loneliness thrives in isolation, but it dissipates in the presence of genuine human connection. It's not about the number of friends or followers we have; it's about the quality of our relationships. Meaningful connections are built on empathy, vulnerability, and shared experiences. It's about finding our tribe, those who accept us for who we are, and with whom we can be our most authentic selves.

My friend, let us remember that loneliness is a state of mind. It is within our power to overcome it, cultivate deep connections, and foster a profound sense of belonging.

— DAY 35 —

Comparison is the thief of joy

A N opinion credited to Theodore Roosevelt, rings strikingly true in today's hyper-connected world. We'll navigate this principle's depths, casting light on the dark corners where joy is frequently taken, and shedding light on how comparison robs us of the happiness that is rightfully ours.

Picture this: You're scrolling through your social media feed, and what do you see? Perfectly assembled lives, filtered moments, and seemingly flawless individuals. It's easy to get swept up in the appeal of comparison.

We live in a world that constantly encourages us to measure ourselves against others. We compare our achievements, our appearances, and our lifestyles. We fall into the trap of believing that our worth is dependent upon how we stack up against others. But the truth is, comparison is an illusion. It distorts our perception and creates an unattainable standard of perfection.

When we constantly compare ourselves to others, we set ourselves up for disappointment. There will always be someone who appears more successful, more attractive, or more accomplished. But what we fail to realize is that comparison is like comparing apples to oranges.

Comparison breeds unhappiness and dissatisfaction. It blinds us to the blessings in our own lives, the progress we've made, and the beauty of our individuality. We become so obsessed with what we lack that we lose sight of what we already have. Our joy becomes conditional, dependent on external validation and the approval of others.

The path to reclaiming our joy lies in shifting our focus from comparison to self-acceptance and gratitude. We must recognize our own worth, our own journey, and the progress we've made. We must celebrate our accomplishments, big and small, and find satisfaction in the present moment.

Instead of comparing ourselves to others, let's cheer each other on. Let's celebrate the successes of others as a testament to what is possible. Let's support and uplift one another, knowing that our journeys are interconnected. We can find inspiration in the achievements of others without diminishing our own worth.

— DAY 36 —

Keep your mind clean and clear

OUR minds are like sponges, absorbing everything we encounter. We are bombarded with information from the media, social media, advertisements, and the opinions of others. It's no wonder that our thoughts become confused and our minds become cluttered with unnecessary noise.

Imagine your mind like a window. When it's clean and clear, the world outside is vivid. Every leaf, every speck of dust, is visible in high definition. This clarity is not just about having a panoramic view of the world. It's about understanding yourself, making decisions that align with your true nature, and achieving peace even in the face of chaos.

Now, consider the "clean" aspect. A clean mind, much like a clean body, is free from toxins. Negative emotions, harmful thoughts, and destructive habits are the toxins of the mind. They cloud our judgment, distort reality, and hinder growth. A clean mind, therefore, isn't one absent of negativity, but one that recognizes these toxins and consciously detoxifies itself, promoting mental health and happiness.

So, how can we maintain this cleanliness and clarity? It begins with mindfulness. By cultivating an awareness of our thoughts and feelings, we can identify the "dirt" and "clouds" obstructing our mental clarity. A mindful pause can help us separate fact from fiction, reality from perception, and truth from illusion.

Next, comes the cleaning. Just like how a daily shower washes off physical dirt, certain practices can help cleanse our minds. Meditation, gratitude, acts of kindness, positive affirmations—these are the soap and water for our minds, washing away the muck of negativity and restoring clarity.

Lastly, we must strive to maintain this cleanliness and clarity. Nourishing our minds with positive thoughts, learning new things, challenging our beliefs, and questioning our assumptions—these are all part of keeping our mental waters clear and toxin-free.

— DAY 37 —

Parents deserve respect for selflessness

T HE selflessness of parents is evident in the sacrifices they make. From sleepless nights to endless days, they give their all to provide for their children.

Firstly, parents dedicated their lives to our well-being. From the moment we came into this world, they selflessly prioritized our needs above their own. They gave up their sleep, their personal time, and their own dreams to ensure that we had the best opportunities in life. It's remarkable to think about how they put their own desires aside to nurture and support us.

Consider all the times they stayed up all night, comforting us when we were sick or scared. Remember the sacrifices they made to provide for us, working long hours to ensure that we had food on the table and a safe place to call home. Their selflessness knows no bounds.

Parents are our guiding lights. They teach us life's most valuable lessons, foster ethical values, and share the wisdom gained through their own experiences. Their love is unconditional and unwavering, providing a strong foundation for us to grow and thrive. It's remarkable to think about the impact their guidance has on our lives.

Even as we grow older, our parents continue to support us. They celebrate our achievements, offer a helping hand during challenging times, and provide a listening ear when we need it most. Their love remains a constant presence as we navigate the ups and downs of adulthood.

Respecting our parents is a testament to their selflessness, but it's also a reflection of our own character. It's about acknowledging their sacrifices and expressing gratitude for their steadfast support. It's about honoring the pillars of strength who have shaped us into the individuals we are today.

That's why I say, parents deserve respect for their selflessness. They're the silent warriors, the unsung heroes who shape the world one child at a time. They do it without fanfare, without seeking awards or honors. They do it because they love us. And for that, they deserve our utmost respect.

— DAY 38 —

Be kind, stay true, respect boundaries

IN a world that often feels chaotic and overwhelming, there are three guiding principles that can bring us back to a place of harmony: kindness, authenticity, and respect for boundaries. These principles may seem simple, but their impact is profound and far-reaching.

Let's start with kindness. Kindness is a superpower that has the ability to transform lives, including our own. When we choose kindness, we create a ripple effect of positivity and compassion. It's about treating others with empathy, understanding, and a genuine desire to uplift their spirits. Kindness costs us nothing, yet its value is boundless. It connects us to the humanity within ourselves and others, fostering a sense of unity and shared experience.

Staying true to ourselves is another essential principle. It's about embracing our authenticity, honoring our values, and expressing our true selves without fear of judgment. When we stay true, we align our thoughts, words, and actions with our core beliefs. We cultivate a sense of self-respect and inner peace, creating a world where individuality is celebrated, and everyone feels empowered to be their authentic selves.

Respecting boundaries is a crucial aspect of fostering healthy relationships and maintaining personal well-being. Boundaries are the invisible lines that define our comfort zones, our limits, and our sense of autonomy. Respecting boundaries means recognizing and honoring the boundaries of others while asserting our own. It's about cultivating open and honest communication, consent, and understanding. When we respect boundaries, we create an environment where trust and mutual respect can flourish.

"Be kind, stay true, respect boundaries" is more than just a mantra; it's a blueprint for personal growth and societal harmony. It advocates for a compassionate, authentic, and respectful way of life, fostering an environment that supports individual well-being and collective peace. It urges us to extend kindness, practice authenticity, and respect boundaries.

— DAY 39 —

You alone control your happiness

WE often fall into the trap of believing that external factors determine our happiness. We believe that if we achieve certain goals, acquire certain possessions, or receive recognition from others, then we will finally be happy. But the reality is that these external factors are temporary and fleeting. True and lasting happiness cannot be reliant on such variables.

See, we tend to outsource our joy, pinning it on circumstances, or people, or success. If this happens, we think, then I'll be happy. If this person changes, then I'll be satisfied. It's a dangerous game, one where we surrender our power, casting our well-being into the turbulent sea of external variables.

The truth is that happiness is not a consequence, it's a decision. It's the ability to find joy in the journey, not just the destination. It's the conscious choice to find bright spots in the middle of the stormiest clouds. It's the ability to be thankful for the present, rather than grieving over the absent.

Picture your mind as a garden. Negative thoughts, they're like weeds, creeping in uninvited, choking out the blooms of joy and peace. But you, you're the gardener. You decide what grows and what doesn't. You can remove the weeds, and water the flowers. You're not controlled by the garden; the garden is controlled by you. It's the same with happiness.

Circumstances, people, and even our own minds can play tricks on us, making us believe we're helpless. But we're not. We're the artists of our lives, and happiness is a color we choose to splash onto our canvas.

Now, this doesn't mean ignoring pain, hardship, or challenges. They're part of the human experience, inevitable and real. But even within their influence, we can choose resilience. We can choose hope. We can choose to cherish the good and learn from the rest.

The key to happiness is in your hand. Use it. You alone control your happiness, and that, my friend, is the most beautiful kind of power there is.

— DAY 40 —

Make no assumptions to life

A SSUMPTIONS are the silent saboteurs of truth, the barriers that blind us from seeing the world as it truly is. They trap us in a rigid framework of predetermined beliefs, preventing us from experiencing the richness and diversity that life has to offer. They become the lenses through which we view reality, distorting our perception and hindering our growth.

From the moment we open our eyes each morning to when we close them at night, our minds are busy writing narratives based on our perceptions, rather than the reality. It's like walking through a garden and assuming you know the scent of every flower, without really bending down to take a whiff. You see, when we assume, we're denying ourselves the opportunity to experience life in all its rawness and realness.

The truth is, that assumptions are an insidious illusion that can cloud our judgments, our relationships, and our understanding of the world. We assume we know someone's thoughts, we predict outcomes, and we jump to conclusions, all without hard evidence. This blind assumption is like a foggy windshield through which we navigate, often leading to misunderstandings, errors, and regret.

On the flip side, when we stop making assumptions, we crack open the door to infinite possibilities. We open our minds to the richness of uncertainty, the beauty of surprise, and the thrill of discovery. We begin to see people as they are, not who we assume they are. We see situations in their full depth and dimension, not just our skewed interpretation of them.

Living without assumptions is like being a continuous adventurer, always curious, always open, always ready to learn something new. It's about questioning more and presuming less. It's about living in the moment rather than being trapped in our prior assumptions.

To conclude, making no assumptions is about breaking free from the self-created constraints of our minds. It's about adopting a beginner's mindset and a lifelong learner's curiosity. Remember, life is a beautiful mystery, an unscripted journey. Let's not thin it out with our presumptions.

— DAY 41 —

Trust carefully

I N a world filled with complexities and uncertainties, it can be tempting to approach trust with caution, to guard our hearts and minds against potential betrayals. Yet, we must recognize that a life lacking trust is a life lived in isolation and fear. Trust opens the door to genuine connections, vulnerability, and growth.

In a world where deception and betrayal exist, trust can be both a powerful asset and a vulnerable state. It's natural to want to trust others, to believe in their intentions, and to open our hearts to them. However, trust requires us to be wise, discerning, and aware of the potential risks involved.

Trust carefully, for it is a precious commodity. It's not about being skeptical or closed off, but rather, it's about being mindful of who we choose to trust and the extent to which we place that trust in others. Trust is earned through consistent actions, honesty, and reliability. It's a fragile bond that should be nurtured and protected.

The act of trust also extends to ourselves. We must trust in our own judgment, intuition, and abilities. It's about honoring our own boundaries, needs, and values. Trusting ourselves empowers us to make confident decisions, to embrace vulnerability, and to navigate the uncertainties of life with courage.

But what happens when trust is broken? It's a painful reality that trust can be shattered, leaving us wounded and hesitant to extend it again. Yet, even in the face of betrayal, trust can be rebuilt. It takes time, honesty, and a willingness to engage in open communication and forgiveness.

Trust carefully, but don't let fear consume you. While there are risks involved, trust is also the foundation of deep connections, love, and personal growth. It's through trust that we build bridges, create meaningful relationships, and foster a sense of belonging.

Ultimately, trust is a personal choice, and we must honor our own instincts and experiences. It's about finding a balance between being cautious and being open-hearted. Trust is an ongoing process that requires us to be mindful and to make conscious decisions about whom we let into our inner circle.

— DAY 42 —

Release broken relationships, move forward

PICTURE relationships as bridges. Some are sturdy, built with care, and maintained with love, lasting a lifetime. Others are temporary, maybe a little shaky, serving a purpose for a time but not meant to stand forever. Now, imagine you're at a broken bridge, and the path ahead lies on the other side. You could stay, hoping to fix it. But what if the damage runs too deep?

We've all experienced relationships that have become stressful, toxic, or no longer serve our best interests. It's natural to hold onto what's familiar, even if it's hurting us. But there comes a time when we must gather our courage and release those broken relationships, giving ourselves the freedom to embrace the possibilities that lie ahead.

Letting go of a broken relationship is not a sign of failure or weakness. It's an act of self-love and self-preservation. We deserve to be surrounded by relationships that lift us up, support us, and bring joy to our lives. Holding onto what's broken only holds us back from experiencing the depth of connections that align with our true selves.

Moving forward requires us to let go of what no longer serves us. It's a journey of self-discovery, personal growth, and finding new paths that lead us to fulfillment. When we release broken relationships, we create space for new connections, fresh experiences, and the opportunity to redefine who we are.

Releasing a broken relationship doesn't mean we erase its significance or deny the lessons learned. It's about honoring the journey we shared, the memories created, and the growth that came from it. We carry those experiences with us as we step into the future with open hearts.

Yes, letting go can be challenging. It may trigger emotions of grief, sadness, or even guilt. But remember, that by releasing what's broken, we are giving ourselves permission to heal, to grow, and to create a life that aligns with our values and aspirations.

Moving forward means embracing the uncertainty and the discomfort that change brings. It's about trusting in our own resilience, knowing that we have the strength within us to navigate the unknown.

— DAY 43 —

Accepting imperfection is true self-care

TAKE a moment and close your eyes. Picture the most recent image you have seen in a magazine, a movie, or even on social media. Picture perfect, isn't it? Now, imagine stripping it of all the facade and staged glamour. What would you see? A human being, with imperfections, just like you and me.

In a world that's increasingly obsessed with crafting perfect narratives, it's easy to forget that imperfection is not our enemy. It's not something to be hidden away or corrected; rather, it's a testament to our individuality, our uniqueness. We are all works in progress, and each flaw, each imperfection, is a part of the journey that shapes us.

So why is accepting imperfection a form of true self-care? To understand that, we need to dig deeper into what self-care truly is. It's not merely about spa days or indulgent treats. At its core, self-care is about nurturing our mental, emotional, and physical well-being. It's about acknowledging our humanity, in all its flawed glory.

When we embrace our imperfections, we're choosing authenticity over pretense. We're learning to silence that nagging voice of self-doubt, that relentless critic that demands perfection. We're giving ourselves permission to make mistakes, fail, learn, and grow. We're allowing ourselves to experience the full range of human emotions, the highs, the lows, and the in-betweens, without judgment or fear.

This acceptance is freeing. It reduces stress, fosters resilience, and cultivates self-love because when we're no longer striving for an impossible standard, we have the energy to focus on what truly matters: our happiness, passions, and relationships.

Remember, acceptance is not about complacency. It's about recognizing our imperfections and understanding that we can always improve, but doing so from a place of love, not from a desire to fit into a cookie-cutter ideal.

You are perfectly imperfect, just as you should be. Embrace your flaws and cherish them, for they make you, you. And that, my friend, is the truest form of self-care.

— DAY 44 —

Endings open new beginnings

LIFE is a series of chapters, each one filled with experiences, emotions, and growth. Endings mark the completion of a chapter, whether it be a relationship, a job, a phase of life, or even a dream. They carry within them a mix of emotions— sadness, relief, nostalgia, and hope. It is in these moments of transition that we are called upon to reflect, learn, and evolve.

We're often reluctant to face endings. The final page of a beloved book, the last day at a job, the end of a cherished relationship, these are moments that could be saturated with sadness, a longing for what was. Yet, it's through these bittersweet goodbyes that we discover the strength within us. Endings strip us down to our most vulnerable selves, leaving us raw and exposed.

Imagine a seed's journey. Encased within its shell, it's safe and undisturbed. However, for it to transform into a majestic tree, it must first shed its protective casing, endure the harsh soil, and confront the uncertainty of growth. In the seed's journey, the end of its existence as a seed is the beginning of its life as a tree.

Each ending brings with it a lesson, a memory, an essence that adds to the symphony of our existence. They leave us with scars and stories, shaping our character, and refining our spirit. When one story ends, it sets the stage for a new one to begin, more vibrant because of the ending that came before it.

As the sun sets, the day ends, but the night, with its moonlit magic and starry silence, begins. As the melody of one song fades, it leaves room for a new tune to fill the air. Life, in its cyclical wisdom, teaches us that endings and beginnings are but two sides of the same coin, flipping continuously in the hand of time.

Remember, every ending carries within it the promise of a new beginning. And it's in this dance of endings and beginnings that we find the true rhythm of life. With every sunset, look forward to the dawn. Because, as the old phrase goes, "When one door closes, another opens." And it's through that open door that our next adventure awaits.

— DAY 45 —

Experience teaches the best lessons

T HINK about it—when have you learned the most? Was it from reading a book or sitting in a classroom? While those are valuable sources of knowledge, the most profound lessons often come from the firsthand encounters with life itself. It's the moments that push us out of our comfort zones, challenge our beliefs, and ignite the passions that truly shape us.

Experience has a way of leaving a lasting mark on our souls. It's in the face of adversity that we discover our strength and resilience. It's through heartbreak that we learn the power of healing and the importance of self-love. It's in pursuing our passions that we find purpose and fulfillment.

Experiences teach us not only about the world but also about ourselves. They reveal our values, strengths, and limitations. They challenge our assumptions and force us to question, reflect, and grow. Experience invites us to be active participants in our own lives, rather than mere observers.

The lessons learned through experience are often the ones that stay with us forever. They become ingrained in our being, shaping our beliefs, choices, and actions. It's through experience that we gain a depth of understanding that no textbook or lecture can provide.

It's important to remember that experience encompasses both triumphs and failures, joys and sorrows. Every experience, whether positive or challenging, offers an opportunity for growth and learning.

Experience is a unique teacher because it engages us completely—physically, emotionally, and intellectually. It immerses us in situations that demand our attention, provoke thought, and trigger emotions. When we make a mistake, the resulting negative emotions often reinforce the lesson learned, making it less likely for us to repeat the same error in the future.

Further, experience is the mother of wisdom. It pushes us out of our comfort zones, challenging us to adapt, evolve, and grow. It compels us to confront our fears, overcome obstacles, and develop resilience. It allows us to navigate the shades of gray that define the human experience, moving beyond black-and-white thinking to understand the nuances of life.

— DAY 46 —

Give what you expect to receive

OFTEN, we find ourselves caught up in a cycle of expectations, waiting for others to meet our needs, fulfill our desires, and make us happy. We long for love, understanding, and respect from those around us, yet we forget that we have the power to initiate and inspire these very qualities.

Our actions serve as cosmic echoes, bouncing off the walls of existence and ringing back to us, often when we least expect it. If you desire kindness, start by sowing seeds of compassion in your garden. If you hunger for respect, honor the dignity of others first. It's no coincidence we often hear the phrase, "Treat others how you want to be treated." It's a timeless truth that reflects the essential interplay of giving and receiving.

Imagine, if you will, a world where everyone truly absorbed this philosophy. A world where respect was universally given, where generosity was the norm, where love was as common as the air we breathe. It sounds like a perfect world, doesn't it? Yet, it all begins with a single step, a personal promise to give what we wish to receive.

However, let's not mistake this concept for a transactional exchange. Life isn't a marketplace, and actions aren't commodities. This isn't about giving with the expectation of an immediate return. Instead, it's about embracing an attitude, a lifestyle rooted in empathy and kindness. It's about understanding the power of our actions and realizing that our behavior shapes the world around us.

To conclude, it's worth remembering that change doesn't occur overnight. As we strive to give what we hope to receive, there will be days when the reflection isn't as clear, where our actions seem to go unnoticed. In these moments, hold tight. Patience, after all, is a virtue. Like ripples in a pond, our actions might take time to come back to us, but come back they will, often in ways we least expect but most need.

Let's be a little more generous, a little kinder, a little more understanding. Let's give what we hope to receive, and watch how our world changes. Now, doesn't that paint a beautiful picture?

— DAY 47 —

One mistake can outweigh many virtues

W E are all human, and making mistakes is part of our nature. We stumble, fall, and make choices that we later regret. But it is in those moments of imperfection that we face the true test of our character. How we respond to our mistakes defines who we are and shapes our future.

Now, imagine this—you're standing at a fork in the road. One path leads to regret and dwelling on the "what-ifs." It's an easy route, comfortable in its familiarity. The other path, though, that's where the challenge lies. It's paved with acceptance, lessons, and growth. It's a road less traveled but trust me, it's worth every step.

Remember that game *Jenga* we used to play as kids? Life's pretty much the same. Sometimes, just like in *Jenga*, one wrong move, and it feels like your whole world is tumbling down. But what did we do then? We didn't just leave the blocks scattered on the floor, right? We started over, learning from our previous mistakes, building again, block by block. The tower that emerged was often sturdier and higher.

Every wrong turn, every misstep, they're not the end of the world. They're opportunities disguised as roadblocks, catalysts pushing us to grow, evolve, and become better versions of ourselves. And sometimes, that growth can only be sparked by a mistake, a slip in judgment, or a momentary trip on the rocky road of life.

This is not to say that we should dismiss accountability or the consequences of our actions. It's essential to acknowledge the impact our mistakes may have on others and take responsibility for them.

So, next time you find yourself face down in the dirt because of a mistake, remember—it's not about the fall. It's about the rise. It's about dusting off the regret, learning the lesson, and stepping forward with newfound wisdom. Because we're human, we make mistakes, but we also learn, grow, and conquer. And that, my friend, is the real beauty of life.

— DAY 48 —

Resistance to change creates suffering

C HANGE is an undeniable force that shapes our lives. Why is it that we resist change? Perhaps it is the fear of the unknown, the uncertainty that lies beyond the boundaries of our comfort zones. We become comfortable in our routines and the familiarity of our lives, and the thought of disrupting that stability can be daunting. We fear the potential risks, the challenges, and the potential loss that change may bring.

We're hardwired to resist change. It's a biological safety net from our prehistoric past, helping our ancestors survive in a hostile and unpredictable world. This evolutionary coding, however, becomes a straightjacket in our modern lives where change is as inevitable as the rising and setting sun. Change unsettles, and interrupts the comfortable rhythm of our lives, but its inevitability doesn't promise doom; it's our resistance that causes discomfort.

Imagine wearing a pair of shoes that are a size too small. It's uncomfortable, even painful. But what if, instead of changing into a pair that fits, we hold on to them because they're familiar? That's what resistance to change looks like, a choice to suffer discomfort rather than confront the unknown. We become prisoners of familiarity, surrendering to a life of self-created suffering.

Resistance breeds fear, making molehills look like mountains. We inflate the perceived dangers of change, paralyzing ourselves into inaction. But resistance, like most fears, is often a paper tiger, posing no real threat. It's not change that's painful, but our resistance to it.

Embracing change is similar to flowing with the river, not against it. Acceptance isn't just acknowledging the inevitability of change but leveraging it for growth. It's about trading worn-out shoes for ones that fit, providing us with comfort and the ability to journey further.

To resist change is to resist life itself. It's to cling to a static picture in an ever-evolving film reel. The beauty of life lies in its dynamic nature. As we learn to embrace change, we unlock our potential for growth, adaptation, and evolution.

— DAY 49 —

Loyalty always pays off

LOYALTY, the steadfast commitment to a person, a cause, or a belief. It's a virtue that has stood the test of time, commonly honored and admired. But what if loyalty is not just a noble act, but also a source of personal reward and fulfillment? What if, in the grand theatre of life, loyalty always pays off?

When we talk about loyalty, we often think about our relationships with others. Loyalty is the glue that binds friendships, partnerships, and communities together. It's the steadfast support, trust, and commitment that we offer to those we hold dear.

But loyalty extends beyond external connections. It begins with the loyalty we show to ourselves—the commitment to honor our values, follow our passions, and stay true to our authentic selves. When we remain loyal to our inner voice, we cultivate a deep sense of self-worth and integrity that radiates into all aspects of our lives.

Loyalty also manifests in our work and endeavors. It's the dedication and perseverance we bring to our goals and aspirations. When we commit ourselves wholeheartedly, pouring our time and energy into our pursuits, we create a foundation for success.

Now, let's explore a challenging idea: loyalty in the face of adversity. It's during tough times that the power of loyalty shines brightest. When we stand by someone's side or remain committed to a cause despite the hardships, we not only display strength of character but also become catalysts for change and transformation.

The most profound form of loyalty is perhaps to oneself—staying true to your values, beliefs, and personal growth. This kind of loyalty is the compass that guides you through the foggy uncertainties of life. It lends consistency to your actions, authenticity to your persona, and clarity to your decisions. Even when you face setbacks and temporary failures, being true to your principles gives a sense of satisfaction and self-respect that outweighs any temporary loss. The return on loyalty here is the unshakeable peace of mind and self-esteem that are vital for long-term happiness.

— DAY 50 —

Grief can never be fully prepared

YOU might have stumbled across this thought before, and you're not alone. This little sentence carries a depth of truth that is often overlooked, but it is essential to comprehend.

Grief, oh grief, that shadowy figure that follows us when we lose something dear. We've all met it. We've all wished it away. But here's the thing about grief—it's not just a guest, it's a teacher. A hard one, sure, but invaluable nonetheless.

Grief is a powerful and deep emotion that arises from loss. It's a journey that every one of us will inevitably face at some point in our lives. We may try to prepare ourselves, mentally and emotionally, for the inevitable departure of a loved one, but the truth is, that grief can never be fully prepared for. Every departure, every ended chapter, every missed opportunity, births a pang of grief. We feel its imminent shadow, its inevitability, yet no amount of preparation can truly equip us for its arrival.

In the context of grief, we often associate it with the loss of a person. The death of a loved one can leave us feeling empty, shattered, and lost. We may try to anticipate the pain, telling ourselves that we are prepared for the inevitable, but the truth is, no amount of mental preparation can shield us from the overwhelming tidal wave of emotions that comes with grief.

Grief is a journey unique to each individual. It challenges any roadmap or timeline. We may experience shock, denial, anger, and deep sadness, often all at once. It's a rollercoaster of emotions that can leave us feeling drained, confused, and utterly vulnerable.

The thing about grief is that it is not just about the loss of a person; it encompasses the loss of dreams, hopes, and a future that will never be. It's a sorrow of the life we once knew and the void left behind.

But in the middle of the pain and the darkness, there is also a glimmer of hope. Grief, as devastating as it is, reminds us of the beauty and fragility of life. It teaches us to cherish our loved ones, to live fully in the present moment, and to embrace the complexities of human emotions.

— DAY 51 —

Overthinking is the enemy of solutions

S OUNDS a bit intense, doesn't it? But, trust me, it's one of those truths that kind of sneaks up on you. Let's take a moment to reflect on a common tendency that often hinders our progress and prevents us from finding solutions to our problems: overthinking. The more you let it marinate, the more you realize its great depth. It unlocks a paradox that seems counterintuitive to our rational selves yet resonates with the truth of many life experiences.

The capacity of the human mind for thought is enormous. Our ability to ponder, reason, and analyze has powered our survival and fostered our civilization's growth. However, when this same ability is not harnessed effectively, it transforms into a trap. Overthinking, thus, stands as an odd enemy—a selfconstructed labyrinth where solutions dissolve into a fog of uncertainty.

Overthinking fuels the myth that non-stop constant thinking is equivalent to action. It keeps us stuck in an illusionary state of productivity, when in reality, we are merely pacing back and forth in the same spot. It is like trying to navigate a river by predicting every current and undercurrent, every potential whirlpool, and each hidden rock. The result is stagnation, an inability to take the plunge and steer the course. Meanwhile, the river of life continues to flow, and the opportunity for action slowly disappears.

The irony is that overthinking, in its misguided mission to find the best solution, often prevents any solution at all. It amplifies fear, breeds doubt, and creates paralysis. Solutions, on the other hand, are born from courage—the courage to make decisions, make mistakes, learn, and adapt.

Therefore, it is not that we should cease thinking but that we should think effectively. Let us be navigators who consider the currents but also trust in our ability to swim. Let us be strategists who plan for battles but also have the courage to fight them. Only then can we break free from the chains of overthinking and embrace the liberating power of solutions. Indeed, the true enemy of solutions is not thinking but overthinking. For, in the space between thoughts, lie the answers you seek.

— DAY 52 —

Past actions determine future harvest

A phrase that, to me, feels like a guiding light of wisdom handed down from generation to generation. Every action we take, and every decision we make, leaves a lasting mark on our journey.

Consider a tiny acorn. Within its humble exterior lies the blueprint of a majestic oak. It simply needs the right conditions—nutrient-rich soil, sunlight, and water—to unleash its inherent potential. Similarly, every action we undertake has underlying potential, which, given the right conditions, can profoundly impact our future.

Our decisions and actions are seeds sown into the soil of time. They root, they germinate, and they grow, whether we are consciously aware of them or not. Sometimes, their effects are immediate, and at other times, they manifest years or even decades later. They may be as minor as a word spoken in haste that leaves a lasting imprint on a relationship, or as significant as a dedicated pursuit of knowledge that shapes our career path.

Each day, we make choices and take actions that are aligned with our beliefs, values, and ambitions. Are we planting seeds of hard work or laziness? Compassion or indifference? Courage or fear? Each seed, once planted, starts a chain reaction that sends ripples through our lives and, oftentimes, the lives of those around us.

However, it is crucial to remember that while we can sow any seeds we choose, we cannot influence the speed at which they grow. Nature does not hurry, yet everything is accomplished. Just as it takes time for a seed to grow into a tree, our actions may require time to fully manifest their outcomes.

Yet, the greatest lesson in understanding this principle is recognizing that every new moment presents a fresh opportunity to sow better seeds. No matter the nature of our past actions, every sunrise brings a new beginning, a chance to plant seeds of positivity, kindness, love, and courage.

The principle of cause and effect teaches us that the seeds we sow today will determine the fruits we harvest tomorrow. It reminds us that we have the power to create positive change, to cultivate a future filled with joy and fulfillment.

— DAY 53 —

Be yourself, be original

I N a world that constantly bombards us with images and messages of how we should look, act, and think, it can be easy to lose sight of our own unique identity.

We often lose ourselves in the noise of social influence, following a path that many people have walked before us. The matrix of societal expectations, family, peer pressure, and fear of judgment bind us in chains of imitation. We choose the safety of sameness, the comfort of the crowd.

There's a certain magic in originality. A magic that is born from the courage to dig deep into our being and embrace our unique traits, imperfections, and unique perspectives. When we free ourselves from the fear of being different and the desire to fit in, we experience the joy of self-discovery. Our thoughts, beliefs, passions, and dreams bloom brightly and colorfully when we allow them to be nurtured in the garden of our authenticity.

Consider the existence of human history. The most inspiring figures, those who left a lasting imprint on the sands of time, were they not originals? Whether it's the scientific genius of Einstein, the innovative spirit of Steve Jobs, or the soulful artistry of Frida Kahlo, it is their pure authenticity that made them who they were.

However, being original is not about being entirely different or alien. It's about finding your voice in the group of singers, about adding your unique note to the symphony of existence.

To "be yourself" is a journey, an exploration of the self that never ends. The road may be rocky and the journey difficult. It may feel lonely at times, frightening even. But with each step, each brave assertion of your individuality, you grow. You become more than just a reflection in the mirror of the world.

Dear reader, dare to be yourself, dare to be original. Embrace the beautiful chaos that is you. For in this dance of life, your steps are yours alone. And when you dance with authenticity, you inspire the world with the melody of your originality. Dance on, dear reader, dance on.

— DAY 54 —

Free yourself from external validation

Y OU know, it's easy to get lost in the whirlwind of "likes," "retweets," and "shares," isn't it? Let's face it, we all seek validation. We want to be liked, accepted and admired. But the question is, how much of it is healthy? How much is detrimental to our inner peace? Let's chat about this.

From a young age, we are conditioned to seek validation from others. We hunger for approval, praise, and recognition as a measure of our worth. We become trapped in a never-ending cycle, constantly seeking external sources to validate our existence and boost our self-esteem.

Imagine you're a puppet. Each string is controlled by a "like," a nod of approval, a look of appreciation. You dance to the rhythm set by others. Is this the dance you want? Probably not. But we've been so wired to seek external validation that we often forget the music within us.

See, the thing about external validation is it's fleeting. Here one moment, gone the next. It's like building a castle on shifting sands. You may feel on top of the world with a bit of praise, but a single criticism can shatter your confidence.

So, how about this? Let's break free from those puppet strings. Cut them off one by one. Start looking inward for validation. Your worth shouldn't be dictated by how many "likes" you get, or how many people applaud your choices. Instead, take pride in your actions, your values, and your growth. Embrace your authenticity, even if it's not "popular."

It's not going to be easy, I get it. The road to self-validation is less traveled, but trust me, it's worth the journey. It leads to a place where you're not a puppet, but a free spirit, dancing to the music within. A place of inner peace, self-confidence, and true happiness. A place where you're not chained by others' opinions, but free to be your own person.

Next time you feel the pull of those puppet strings, pause and remember: You are enough. Your worth is not defined by likes, shares, or nods of approval. You're a rockstar in your own right. Dance your own dance, my friend, free yourself from external validation.

— DAY 55 —

Reality is a mirror of perception

HERE'S a thought for you—what if I told you that everything you see, feel, touch, and experience, is not exactly as it seems? That what you consider as "reality" is not an absolute, but merely a reflection of your perception?

Consider the last time you encountered a situation or met someone new. How did you perceive it? How did your beliefs, biases, and past experiences influence your interpretation? The truth is, we all have our unique lenses through which we view the world. Our perception acts as a mirror, reflecting back to us the reality we believe to be true.

It's fascinating to realize that two people can witness the same event and yet have completely different interpretations. It's like looking into a mirror that shows different reflections depending on the observer.

Our thoughts, emotions, and beliefs act as filters through which we process information. They shape our understanding of reality and influence the meaning we assign to events. It's as if we are the authors of our own stories, crafting narratives based on our unique perspectives.

If reality is a mirror of perception, then we have the power to shift our perception and transform our experience of reality. We can choose to challenge our assumptions, question our biases, and broaden our perspectives. We can actively seek out different viewpoints, engage in meaningful conversations, and expand our understanding of the world.

This doesn't mean that we can simply wish away the challenges or hardships of life. It means that we have the ability to choose how we respond to them. We can choose to see obstacles as opportunities for growth, setbacks as lessons, and moments of adversity as catalysts for change.

Ultimately, the reality we live in is a reflection of the inner workings of our minds. It is a mirror that faithfully reflects our perceptions, beliefs, and attitudes. If we wish to change our reality, we must first change the way we perceive the world. For it is only through this inner transformation that we can begin to craft the reality we desire.

— DAY 56 —

Protect your time from energy vampires

HAVE you ever heard of energy vampires? I'm not talking about the mythical creatures from gothic lore or *The Twilight Saga*, but the people in your life who drain your emotional energy, leaving you feeling exhausted and used up.

Your time is a precious currency, and energy vampires as those who constantly seek to drain it. In a world filled with demands, distractions, and obligations, it's essential to guard your time from these energy vampires.

Energy vampires are everywhere. They could be that friend who loves basking in their misery, pulling you into their black hole of constant complaints. Or that colleague whose negative attitude seemingly sucks the joy out of every room they enter. Do these characters sound familiar? They are not evil, nor do they mean any harm. They are just, well, emotionally exhausting.

Now, I'm not saying to banish these people from your life. But remember this, time is our most precious commodity. Once spent, we can't get it back. So, it's crucial to protect it, especially from energy vampires.

Establishing boundaries is essential. It's crucial to recognize and understand your emotional limits, and then maintain them. Clearly express when certain interactions are not conducive to your well-being, or when personal time is necessary.

Another effective approach involves maintaining emotional detachment, especially when confronted by those who drain your energy. Engage with them without letting their negative sentiments affect you.

However, it's also vital to practice empathy. Many may be facing personal challenges. Offer understanding when appropriate, but prioritize your emotional well-being.

In the grand theater of life, remember you're the playwright. Choose carefully who gets the spotlight in your show. Make sure they're worth the time you're giving them. After all, we want a standing ovation when the curtains close, not a sigh of relief, right? Keep those energy vampires in check!

— DAY 57 —

A gentle heart is a rare and courageous trait

IN a world that often prizes strength, dominance, and competitiveness, it may seem counterintuitive to hail gentleness as a rare and courageous trait. We live in a society that often equates gentleness with weakness, as if kindness and empathy are somehow subpar to aggression and dominance.

Gentleness, often misunderstood as a sign of weakness, is a trait that demands tremendous strength. A gentle heart requires an unwavering resilience to remain soft amid adversity, to choose empathy over indifference, love over disdain, and understanding over judgment. It requires the bravery to respond to anger with kindness and to confront bitterness with compassion. In essence, it demands the courage to maintain our humanity when faced with the inhumane.

A gentle heart is a light in a storm, a tender touch in a world that often lacks the warmth of kindness. It soothes the hurt, the heartbroken, and the lost. It's the voice that whispers, "you are not alone," when the world seems to scream the opposite. In an era where individualism is increasingly celebrated, a gentle heart is a radical act of resistance. It is a testament to our shared humanity and an assertion that compassion and understanding can indeed coexist with ambition and individual success.

Being gentle doesn't mean being a pushover or neglecting one's own needs and boundaries. It is about mindful empathy, about nurturing a deep understanding and appreciation for the struggles of others while ensuring our self-respect remains intact. It is about being firmly grounded in one's values, fostering a tranquil spirit that can weather any storm.

Having a gentle heart in a tough world is a rarity, a light of hope, and a testament to the relentless fortitude of human beings. It's an act of courage, don't you think? Let us acknowledge and celebrate gentleness. Let us strive to nurture our hearts to be soft yet strong, kind yet firm, yielding yet steadfast. Because a gentle heart is indeed a rare and courageous trait, a quiet revolution against a tide of apathy and insensitivity, a light of hope that proclaims: even in the roughest of seas, our capacity for compassion shall remain undiminished.

— DAY 58 —

Silent battles are the hardest fought

S ILENT battles are indeed the hardest fought. They are the struggles that unfold within the depths of our hearts and minds, hidden from the world. They are the battles we fight without seeking external validation. In the age of social media, it has become commonplace for people to seek validation online to demonstrate their strength. But in reality, true strength does not need validation.

Social media platforms have become arenas where people display their triumphs, adventures, and moments of joy. The number of likes, comments, and followers has become a measure of success and strength. However, the true strength lies not in the recognition we receive from others, but in our ability to face adversity and overcome challenges without the need for external validation.

Silent battles are the unspoken struggles we face in our lives. They are the battles fought behind closed doors, where no one else sees the tears shed, the sleepless nights, or the internal battle within. These battles are fought with resilience, determination, and a deep inner strength that doesn't require public acknowledgement.

In a world consumed by social media, it is easy to fall into the trap of seeking validation from others. We begin to believe that our worth and strength are defined by the number of likes or comments we receive on a post. We measure our self-esteem based on the validation we receive online.

True strength, on the other hand, is born from within. It is not dependent on external validation or recognition. It is the quiet power that resides in our ability to persevere, to endure, and to rise above challenges. It is the resilience that allows us to face our silent battles with courage and grace, even when no one else is aware of the depths of our struggle.

The beauty of true strength lies in its authenticity. It doesn't seek validation or approval from others because it is rooted in self-acceptance and self-belief. It is the steadfast trust in our own abilities and the resolute commitment to our own values.

— DAY 59 —

Freedom is an illusion

I F you're reading this, you probably believe you're free. After all, you might have the freedom of speech, the freedom to vote, and the freedom to dream. But here's a provocative thought: you're living in a matrix of illusions, and true freedom is a lie we tell ourselves to sleep better at night.

Let's first dismantle democracy. Many hail it as the champion of freedom. Yet, is it not just a glorified popularity contest? The majority rules, which means the minority often gets sidelined. And let's not even dive into the murky waters of political campaigns, where money speaks louder than genuine concerns. Do we genuinely choose our leaders, or are we merely picking from a pre-selected roster presented by elites?

Now, capitalism is another darling of the "free" world. Sure, you can choose which brand of jeans to buy, but isn't it all just a mirage? Mega-corporations have monopolized markets, influencing not just our choices but even our desires. They decide the trends, and we, the "free" individuals, dutifully follow.

Society's "freedom of expression" is another minefield. Dress the way you want, love whom you desire, and follow your passion—until you realize that even these choices are dictated by forces larger than us. Social media, movies, literature—they all subtly tell us what's "in" and what's "out."

Biologically, our genes, hormones, and neural networks might be more in charge than our conscious selves. What if our choices are merely byproducts of biochemical reactions?

Now, more than ever, critical thinking emerges as the light of hope in this fog. In an age where information bombards us from every angle, the ability to break down, distinguish, and decide becomes essential. Critical thinking isn't just about intelligence or knowledge; it's the tool that helps us pierce the illusion, question the status quo, and seek the elusive truth beneath the layers of deception.

It's alarming to consider our prized freedom might be an illusion. Yet by promoting critical thinking and questioning given "freedoms," we may move towards a more genuine and unfiltered freedom.

— DAY 60 —

Always say less than necessary

I N a world where words flow unendingly and silence is often overlooked, there is deep wisdom in the art of saying less than necessary. It is a concept that challenges the societal norm of constant chatter and urges us to embrace the power of restraint and thoughtful communication.

We live in an era where everyone seems to have an opinion, where words overflow but lacking in depth of meaning. We are bombarded with information, messages, and noise that can overwhelm our senses and cloud our judgment. In such a chaotic environment, the power of saying less than necessary becomes even more significant.

Saying less than necessary does not imply withholding information or being cryptic. Instead, it is about choosing our words intentionally, carefully selecting what truly adds value to the conversation. It is about avoiding the temptation to speak merely for the sake of filling the void, but rather embracing the potency of silence and allowing it to amplify the impact of our words.

By saying less, we create space for active listening and deep understanding. We open ourselves up to truly hear others, empathize, and connect on a deeper level. In silence, we can truly absorb the essence of what is being said, rather than rushing to respond with our own thoughts.

Moreover, saying less than necessary encourages reflection and introspection. It prompts us to pause and consider the weight of our words before they escape our lips. It invites us to be intentional in our communication and to choose words that carry depth, meaning, and authenticity.

In a world where information overload is the norm, saying less than necessary also holds the power of intrigue and curiosity. It leaves room for interpretation and invites others to lean in, ask, and engage in meaningful dialogue. It sparks a sense of wonder and invites the exploration of different perspectives.

Saying less than necessary is an exercise in self-control. It allows us to manage our emotions and reactions, preventing hasty and regretful words from slipping through. It is an act of discipline that fosters better relationships, as we become mindful of how our words impact others.

— DAY 61 —

Self-interest is human nature's driving force

T HE heart of human existence beats to the rhythm of self-interest. From the moment we are born, we are wired to survive and thrive. Our instincts drive us to seek food, shelter, and security. It is this innate self-interest that pushes us to take action, to strive for success, and to improve our lives. It is the engine that propels us forward on our journey of self-fulfillment.

At first glance, self-interest might seem selfish, a byproduct of our survival instincts, but delve deeper and you find that it is a multifaceted complexity of motivations and needs that fuel our evolution. It is the engine that powers ambition, the desire to better oneself, and the will to achieve. Every invention, every discovery, every breakthrough that humanity has ever made can be traced back to the spark of self-interest.

The desire to be safe, the need to be loved, the wish to be understood—all are manifestations of self-interest. Our pursuit of knowledge and truth, our craving for meaning and purpose, and our quest for happiness and satisfaction, all stem from our natural tendency towards self-betterment. It's a thirst that propels us forward, that pushes us to explore the unknown, conquer our fears, and rise above our limitations.

However, self-interest is not a boundless license for selfishness or greed. It necessitates a balance, a recognition that our actions have repercussions beyond our individual selves. It encourages empathy, cooperation, and mutual growth.

Indeed, self-interest becomes a transformative power when it is guided by ethical values and social responsibility. It drives us to make a positive impact, contribute to our communities, and leave a lasting legacy. It compels us to look beyond our immediate needs and consider the greater good, encouraging us to strive for a better world, not just for ourselves but for future generations.

Embracing self-interest isn't about giving in to ruthless individualism; instead, it's recognizing and harnessing this inherent drive while staying empathetic and considerate to the world around us. Because after all, we are wired to be both "selfish" and "social" creatures, aren't we?

— DAY 62 —

See the beauty in boredom

B OREDOM, the often-avoided sensation, is a paradox that many of us struggle with in the high-speed, high-stimulation world of today. Boredom is often misunderstood. It is seen as a negative state, a void that needs to be filled with entertainment or busyness. However, boredom can be a gateway to creativity, self-reflection, and even deep insights. It is in these moments of emptiness that our minds have the space to wander, to explore new ideas and perspectives.

Consider boredom as the calm surface of a lake, seemingly still but packed with life underneath. It is in the quiet moments of boredom that our mind, uncluttered from the noise of daily stimuli, begins to echo the whispers of creativity. Fertile and rich, these are the moments when our best ideas take root and grow.

Did you know that many great thinkers, writers, and artists have often found inspiration in the lap of boredom? They understood that boredom isn't an empty void, but a space filled with the potential for insight and creativity. It's the blank canvas on which the colors of imagination and thought blend to create the masterpiece of cleverness.

Furthermore, boredom encourages self-reflection and mindfulness, turning our focus inward. It nudges us to reflect on our emotions, desires, and dreams. As we sit still, alone with our thoughts, we begin to understand ourselves better, appreciating the nuances of our complex nature.

Yet, the beauty in boredom extends beyond our mental and emotional realms. It lies in the simple, often overlooked aspects of life. The shifting patterns of clouds, the rhythmic fall of rain, the dance of shadows on a sunny afternoon, boredom inspires us to find joy and beauty in the everyday, enriching our lives with a profound sense of appreciation.

As we rush through life chasing goals and meeting expectations, let us pause and embrace the beauty of boredom. Not as an escape, but as a gateway to the endless field of creativity, self-awareness, and the majestic beauty of existence, hidden in plain sight.

— DAY 63 —

Failure is nature, regret is foolish

NATURE itself is a testament to the power of failure. The cycles of life and seasons demonstrate that growth often requires setbacks. In the spring, new buds emerge, but not all of them will blossom into flowers. Some will wither and fall, but that doesn't stop the beauty of nature from thriving. It is through these failures that the natural world evolves and adapts.

Similarly, in our own lives, failure is an inevitable part of the journey. It is in our failures that we learn valuable lessons, discover our resilience, and refine our paths. Failure is not a mark of incompetence or unworthiness, but rather a stepping stone towards success.

In our society, failure is often painted as an unwelcome monster, an imperfection an otherwise perfect record. We've all felt the sting of failure at some point. That job we didn't get, the relationship that didn't work out, the project that didn't go as planned. But if we step back and consider failure as nature does, not as an end but as a beginning, a seed of potential, we might see our setbacks in a new light.

But what about regret? Well, regret, in many ways, is like a ghost. It's a haunting presence tethered to the past, shadowing our steps, whispering "if only" into our ears. It's an emotional tax we pay for being human, for being capable of reflection and introspection. But does it serve us?

You see, regret is fundamentally at odds with the flow of life. It fixates on past mistakes, while life is continually moving forward. Regret says, "I wish I could change what happened," while life says, "Here's what's happening now. What are you going to do about it?"

In a universe where even stars, the long-standing guardians of the cosmos, explode into supernovae, creating elements that make life as we know it possible, isn't regretting failure rather foolish?

So, let's redefine our understanding. Failure? It's nature, a moment of transformation. Regret? It's a fool's game. Instead, let's strive for resilience, acknowledging our mistakes, learning from them, and then releasing them back into the history of time.

— DAY 64 —

Your dreams reveal your true desires

I F you delve into the depths of your subconscious mind, you will encounter a land unknown yet familiar, a realm that transcends the restrictions of reality, the dreamland. It's a place where time is adaptable, and the laws of physics bow to the impulses of the imagination. Yet, these seemingly random imaginations can be revealing signposts pointing towards our deepest, most authentic desires.

Dreams are the mind's playground, a meeting place for the conscious and the subconscious. While our conscious mind is occupied with daily tasks, deadlines, and societal pressures, our subconscious mind houses our deepest cravings, unfulfilled wishes, and unexplored potential. When we sleep, the conscious mind loosens its grip, and the subconscious mind rises, narrating stories, and spinning tales that often mirror our innermost desires.

These desires could be as simple as craving for an ice cream sundae or as complex as the pursuit of a lost love. Perhaps, your dreams frequently feature you playing the piano with ease and grace. You may wonder why, only to realize that deep down, you've always desired to learn it but never got around to doing so.

Sometimes, these desires aren't so readily identifiable. Dreams can be abstract, full of symbols that need decoding. They could be surrounded by metaphors, representing the aspirations you're too afraid to admit consciously. For instance, dreaming of flight might not mean you want to sprout wings literally. Instead, it could symbolize a desire for freedom, independence, or exploration.

Dreams, therefore, are like secret whispers from our subconscious mind. They reflect the raw, unfiltered versions of ourselves, stripped of societal norms, rules, and judgments. By exploring our dreams, we open a window into our deepest desires, giving us clues about who we are and what we genuinely crave. Understanding our dreams allows us to realize these desires, enabling us to create a reality aligned with our true selves.

— DAY 65 —

Letting go of the past frees the present

L ET me tell you a secret about the key to happiness. It's not wrapped in gold, nor is it hidden at the end of a rainbow. It's a mindset, an approach to life, a way of seeing the world. And it all begins with letting go of the past.

You see, the past is a relentless traveler, forever following behind us, whispering in our ears, and casting shadows over our present. Each memory, every misstep, mistake, heartbreak, and disappointment, like heavy chains, can keep us anchored, stuck in a time and place that no longer exists.

We often consider our past as a definitive narration of who we are. Our past mistakes become self-created labels, our past heartaches become blueprints for our future relationships, and our past failures become predictions of our potential. But in this retrospective obsession, we forget the most crucial element—the present. The now. The moment that actually has the power to influence the direction of our life's journey.

Let me paint a picture for you. Imagine you're holding onto a handful of sand. The more tightly you grasp it, the faster it slips through your fingers. The past is like that sand. The harder you try to hold onto it, the more it suffocates your present. But, if you open your palm and let the sand drift away with the wind, you free your hand for the new possibilities, experiences, and yes, even the new sand that awaits.

When we choose to release the past, we do not deny its significance or the lessons it has taught us. We acknowledge it, and respect it, but refuse to be enslaved by it. We understand that we are not the sum of our past mistakes, but the compound interest of our learned lessons.

Letting go of the past is not an act of removal but an act of evolution. It's about forgiving ourselves for not knowing better, appreciating how far we've come, and focusing on the journey ahead. When we let go, we transform our past from a restricting cage into a stepping stone, from a life sentence into a launchpad.

In the end, the present is all we truly have, right? Yesterday is gone, and tomorrow isn't promised. So why not make the most of the now?

— DAY 66 —

Masks can hide both good and evil

IN a world filled with masks, both literal and metaphorical, it is essential to recognize the profound truth that they have the ability to hide not only our true identities but also the spectrum of human nature itself.

At the heart of our societies, masks manifest as the personas we adopt in various situations. We adopt them to conform, protect ourselves, or sometimes, merely to belong. A friendly smile that disguises loneliness, a confident facade that hides insecurities, a quiet demeanor masking a storm of ideas—these are our everyday masks, the good and the evil hidden within us.

But why do we wear these masks? Why do we hide our authentic selves? Perhaps, we fear being vulnerable, being judged, or worse, being excluded. Maybe we believe that our masks make us more acceptable, more likable, more "normal." And so, we bury our authentic selves under layers of pretense and deception, eroding our individuality, and suppressing our spirit.

In our eager chase for uniformity, we miss an important truth—masks can hide the good as much as they can hide the evil. Behind a facade of arrogance, there might be a compassionate heart. Behind a wall of silence, there might be a wise observer. Just as masks can hide harmful intentions, they can also hide virtues, talents, and potentials that can contribute positively to our world.

So, what if we begin to look beyond the masks? What if we cultivate empathy, patience, and openness to understand what lies beneath? What if we encourage authenticity and celebrate uniqueness, fostering environments where masks become redundant?

Unmasking the good and the evil is not about exposing vulnerabilities but about revealing the authentic human being. It's about destroying illusions, breaking stereotypes, and enriching our collective consciousness.

Ultimately, masks do hide both good and evil. But it's our choice whether to live in a world ruled by masks or to create one where masks dissolve into irrelevance. It's our choice whether to accept the illusion or to seek the reality. And it's our choice whether to fear the hidden evil or to discover the concealed good. After all, every mask has a story. Are we ready to listen?

— DAY 67 —

You are not the center stage

HAVE you ever felt like the world revolves around you? Like you are the star of your own movie, with everyone else merely playing supporting roles? It's a common human tendency to place ourselves at the center stage of our own lives. We become so consumed with our own thoughts, desires, and ambitions that we forget there's an entire world unfolding around us.

In this grand universe, filled with billions of people and countless wonders, it's essential to recognize our place within the grand theatre of life. We are but one small part of a much larger whole, interconnected and interdependent. Each person has their own dreams, struggles, and stories unfolding simultaneously.

When we realize that we are not the center stage, it can be both humbling and liberating. It allows us to step back and gain a broader perspective, to see beyond our own limited scope. We begin to appreciate the diversity of experiences and perspectives that exist in the world.

Embracing this truth requires a shift in mindset. It means letting go of self-centeredness and cultivating empathy and compassion. It means acknowledging the importance of others' experiences and recognizing the impact we have on those around us. When we shift our focus from ourselves to the collective, we become more attuned to the needs of others, fostering deeper connections and a sense of shared humanity.

Moreover, understanding that we are not the center stage frees us from the burden of constant self-obsession. It relieves us from the pressure of always needing to be the protagonist in every story. We can find joy in supporting others, celebrating their successes, and contributing to their growth. We realize that collaboration and cooperation, rather than competition, lead to true fulfillment.

The beauty of life lies not in the illusion of a center stage but in the reality of a shared performance, a testament to the incredible symphony of existence. This illusion is crafted from our ego-driven perceptions. Don't let the *Spotlight Syndrome* ruin you. Turn it off, step into your own light, and live your life on your terms, not as a performance for an imaginary audience.

— DAY 68 —

There's no defense against stupidity

T ACKLING the challenge of willful ignorance, especially when it involves a conscious decision to disregard facts, highlights a significant issue within society. This problem goes beyond simple unawareness, which can typically be remedied through education.

For example, consider the dangerous trend of driving while texting. Despite widespread campaigns and clear evidence showing the risk it poses—not only to the driver but to everyone on the road—many continue this behavior. High-profile accidents and legal penalties have spotlighted the issue, yet the practice persists, underlining a refusal to accept personal responsibility and evidence based safety advice.

Another instance is the spread of dietary myths, such as the belief in quickfix detoxes and diets that promise rapid weight loss without scientific backing. Nutrition experts and medical professionals consistently debunk these myths, presenting evidence-based advice for healthy eating and living. However, the allure of an easy solution, often propelled by celebrity endorsements and social media influencers, leads many to ignore solid dietary guidance, sometimes to the detriment of their health.

The defense against such ignorance requires more than just debunking myths; it calls for a cultural shift towards valuing and understanding evidence, alongside a willingness to change behaviors based on new information.

Efforts to combat these tendencies include education that emphasizes critical thinking and media literacy, alongside societal norms that celebrate informed decision-making. It's also crucial for individuals with influence—educators, leaders, celebrities—to model evidence-based decision-making and to encourage their audiences to do the same.

For while stupidity may persist, it is ultimately no match for the unwavering resolve of the human intellect. As long as there are those willing to question, to learn, and to challenge the status quo, there will always be a defense against the darkness of ignorance.

— DAY 69 —

Forgive, accept, learn, move on

FIVE simple words strung together that form a powerful mantra for navigating life's winding path. This insightful philosophy serves as a compass, guiding us through the labyrinth of our experiences, both pleasant and painful, ultimately leading us toward inner growth and peace.

The first call to action is to forgive. It's about releasing the hold of past grievances and letting go of the grudge that ties us down. When we forgive, we liberate not only those who may have wronged us but more importantly, we free ourselves. It's a step towards severing the chains of past injuries, enabling us to navigate our journey unburdened.

Then comes acceptance. Life is an unpredictable blend of joy and sorrow, victories and setbacks. Acceptance means embracing this reality, absorbing the blows with grace, and savoring the wins with humility. It's about looking life in the eye and acknowledging it for what it is—a wild, beautiful, and sometimes heartbreaking adventure.

But forgiveness and acceptance are not enough if we do not extract wisdom from our experiences. Hence, we learn. Each encounter, each event, is a teacher in disguise, presenting us with lessons that shape our character, sharpen our understanding, and widen our perspective. By adopting a learner's mindset, we change life's war zone into a productive land for personal growth.

Finally, we move on. Life is a river, constantly flowing, constantly changing. To resist its current is to invite unnecessary struggle. Moving on signifies our willingness to adapt, to evolve with the ever-changing tide of life. It encapsulates the courage to step forward, to venture into the unknown, armed with the wisdom harvested from our past.

In this journey of forgiveness, acceptance, learning, and moving on, we find liberation and transformation. It's the code that guides us through life's labyrinth, ensuring that no matter what we face, we emerge stronger, wiser, and ready to embrace the beauty of our journey. We shed the heavy armor of resentment and embrace the freedom of forgiveness.

— DAY 70 —

Life's unpredictability adds to its beauty

LIFE is a symphony of chaos and harmony, a dance of uncertainty and blessing. It is in the unpredictable moments that the true essence of life reveals itself, adding depth, excitement, and beauty to our existence.

Similar to an unwritten book or an unpainted canvas, life's charm lies in its infinite possibilities. Imagine knowing exactly how every moment of your life would unfold. The thrill of anticipation, the joy of surprise, the sting of unexpected setbacks—all would be lost, making our existence monotonous, robotic even. Just like the surprising turns in an engaging book or the unexpected beauty beyond a hidden curve, life's unpredictability adds color and interest to our personal stories.

It is the unpredictability of life that breathes magic into mundane moments. The chance encounters that bloom into lifelong friendships, the sudden brainwaves that spark revolutionary ideas, and the unexpected challenges that reveal hidden strengths—all thrive in the fertile ground of uncertainty. They are the rare and beautiful wildflowers that spring up spontaneously in the wild fields of life's journey, their unexpectedness amplifying their beauty.

Moreover, unpredictability cultivates resilience and fosters growth. Life's uncertainties act as catalysts, propelling us out of our comfort zones and challenging us to adapt and evolve. They teach us that failure is not the opposite of success but an integral part of the journey. In the melting pot of uncertainty, we learn to weather life's storms, pick ourselves up after a fall, and view setbacks not as insurmountable hurdles but as stepping stones to growth and wisdom.

However, let us not forget, that while we navigate life's unpredictable waves, we are not just floating without purpose. We are sailors with the power to steer our ship. We can harness life's unpredictability, channeling it into a force of positive change and personal growth. By adopting an open mindset, we can transform life's uncertainties from daunting unknowns into intriguing mysteries waiting to be solved.

— DAY 71 —

Ego is the enemy

THE ego stands as a formidable force, shaping our thoughts, actions, and perceptions. It is the voice that whispers in our ears, constantly seeking validation and dominance. The ego is the enemy that hinders our growth and limits our potential.

The ego is like a self-created prison, a barrier that separates us from the beauty of life and the richness of genuine connections. It thrives on comparison, competition, and the need to be seen as superior. It clouds our judgment, distorts our perception, and creates conflicts within ourselves and with others.

But what if I told you that the ego is merely an illusion, a construct of the mind? What if I told you that beneath its loud and demanding presence lies the true essence of who we are? The ego is not our true self; it is a false identity we cling to out of fear and insecurity.

To overcome the ego, we must set off on a journey of self-awareness and introspection. We must peel back the layers of false narratives and societal expectations that have constructed our ego identity. We must confront our fears, insecurities, and attachments, and embrace the vulnerability and authenticity that lie beneath.

It is through humility that we can diminish the ego's power over us. Humility allows us to acknowledge our limitations and recognize the wisdom and strength in others.

By letting go of the ego's need for validation and control, we create space for growth and transformation. We can embrace our true potential, unleash our creativity, and pursue our passions with a sense of purpose and authenticity. We become open to learning from our mistakes, seeing them as opportunities for growth rather than personal failures.

The ego, my friend, is a double-edged sword. It can drive us to achieve great things, but it can also blind us to the beauty of life and the richness of our relationships. So, start peeling the onion of your ego, layer by tender layer, despite the tears it may bring, and uncover the strength and clarity that lie within.

— DAY 72 —

This too shall pass

A simple phrase that holds deep wisdom. It reminds us that no matter how challenging or painful our current circumstances may be, they are temporary. Time, like a river, flows relentlessly, carrying away our sorrows, struggles, and even our triumphs. It is a reminder of life's fleeting state, urging us to embrace the present moment and find solace in the knowledge that change is inevitable.

Life is a journey of highs and lows, of joys and sorrows. We are constantly navigating through the ebb and flow of experiences. In times of hardship, it is easy to become consumed by our pain and lose sight of the bigger picture. But "this too shall pass" reminds us that even the darkest nights give way to the dawn.

When we face adversity, it is important to remember that we are not alone in our struggles. Each of us has faced our own battles, our own moments of despair. In sharing our stories and connecting with others, we find solace and strength. We realize that our hardships are part of the human experience, and that others have overcome similar challenges.

"This too shall pass" invites us to practice patience and resilience. It encourages us to weather the storms of life with grace and to trust in our own inner strength. It reminds us that the obstacles we encounter are not unbeatable, and that growth and transformation often emerge from the most difficult circumstances.

On the other hand, when we are basking in the glory of success and happiness, we may become too satisfied or take things for granted. We may forget that life is ever-changing, and what we have today may not be here tomorrow.

These words not only apply to the external circumstances of life but also to our internal experiences and emotions. It reminds us that our pain, sorrow, and even our greatest joys are fleeting.

It's not just a phrase, it's a mantra, a mindset. It's a reminder that we're all just passing through, experiencing the ebb and flow of life. Remember, life is but a series of passing moments.

— DAY 73 —

Forgiving yourself for imperfection liberates growth

W E live in a world that often demands perfection from us. We strive to meet impossible standards and constantly compare ourselves to others. We beat ourselves up over every mistake, every flaw, every perceived imperfection. But here's the truth: we are all imperfect beings, and that imperfection is what makes us beautifully human.

So often, we find it easier to forgive others than to forgive ourselves. We hold ourselves to a higher standard, expecting perfection in everything we do. But the reality is, we are bound to make mistakes along the way. It's a natural part of life's journey. And in those moments when we stumble and fall, it's crucial that we extend the same compassion and forgiveness to ourselves that we would offer to a friend.

Forgiving ourselves for our imperfections is not an easy task. It requires us to let go of the self-criticism and self-judgment that holds us back. It means acknowledging that we are not defined by our mistakes, but rather by how we grow and learn from them. It means embracing our vulnerabilities and allowing ourselves to be human.

When we forgive ourselves, we create the space for growth and self-acceptance. We release the heavy weight of guilt and shame that hinders our progress. We free ourselves from the shackles of perfectionism and open ourselves up to new possibilities.

It's important to remember that growth and learning often stem from our imperfections. It is through our mistakes that we gain wisdom, resilience, and empathy. Each setback becomes an opportunity for self-reflection and personal growth. When we forgive ourselves, we give ourselves permission to learn from our mistakes and move forward with greater strength and understanding.

I encourage you to practice self-forgiveness. Embrace your imperfections as part of your unique journey. Embrace the growth that comes from acknowledging your mistakes and learning from them. See forgiveness as a transformative act that liberates you from the chains of self-doubt and allows you to step into your full potential.

— DAY 74 —

Build resilience to conquer brutality

LIFE is a complex and unpredictable journey, marked by moments of triumph and joy, as well as periods of adversity and hardship. In the face of these challenges, it is our resilience—our ability to adapt, persevere, and emerge stronger—that enables us to conquer the brutality that life can sometimes present.

The idea of building resilience to conquer brutality encourages us to reflect on the numerous ways our inherent strength protects us from life's storms. Resilience is not a static attribute but an ongoing process of engagement with our situation, enabling us to tackle adversity with courage, insight, and composure. This inner resilience emboldens us to confront our insecurities, extract lessons from our experiences, and transform life's harshness into avenues for personal growth and enlightenment.

Furthermore, resilience presents the prospect of transcending the confines created by our situation and accessing the reservoir of strength within each of us. In doing so, we can perceive life's challenges as stimulants for growth and transformation, fostering a deeper understanding of our true potential.

Resilience, in its essence, is the ability to bend without breaking. Like a mighty oak that sways in the face of a storm, resilient individuals remain rooted in their values and beliefs, drawing strength from within. They learn to embrace the lessons that come with adversity, using them as stepping stones to conquer the brutal forces that life throws at them. In this light, resilience is not a passive trait; rather, it is a proactive approach to dealing with life's challenges.

In an age where instant gratification and superficiality seem to dominate, cultivating resilience may appear to be a conservative idea. This traditional virtue holds the key to unlocking our true potential as individuals and as a society. By fostering resilience, we tap into a wellspring of inner strength that empowers us to face and overcome adversity.

As we cultivate resilience, we become unstoppable forces that not only weather life's storms but emerge stronger and wiser, ready to face whatever challenges lie ahead.

— DAY 75 —

Alone time can bring clarity and peace

IN the hustle and bustle of our modern lives, finding moments of solitude can be a rare luxury. We are constantly surrounded by noise, distractions, and the demands of our busy schedules. However, in the middle of this chaos, we often overlook the power of alone time—the moments when we disconnect from the world and find ourselves in the company of our own thoughts. Alone time is not just a mere break from social interactions; it is a transformative experience that can bring clarity, self-discovery, and deep peace.

When we are alone, away from the noise and opinions of others, we have the opportunity to connect with our true selves. We can delve deep into our thoughts, emotions, and desires, gaining insights into who we are and what truly matters to us. It is during these solitary moments that our minds are free to wander, explore the depths of our consciousness, and unlock our creativity. Alone time allows us to listen to our own inner voice and develop a stronger sense of self-awareness.

Moreover, in our solitude, we can reflect upon our experiences, both past and present. We can review our choices, evaluate our actions, and gain a clearer understanding of the path we wish to take. Alone time gives us the space to process our emotions, heal from past wounds, and find solace in the quiet corners of our hearts. It is in these moments of self-reflection that we can make important decisions, set new goals, and chart our course for the future.

In the solitude of our own company, we also find the opportunity to recharge and restore. Our minds and bodies are constantly bombarded with external stimuli, leaving us drained and overwhelmed. Alone time offers us a chance to step away from the chaos, to find stillness and peace within ourselves. It is in these moments that we can replenish our energy, find clarity in our thoughts, and return to the world with a renewed sense of purpose and perspective.

It is important to note that alone time does not mean isolation or loneliness. It is a deliberate choice to spend time with ourselves, to cultivate a deeper connection with our inner world. It is about nurturing our own well-being, without the need for external validation or distractions.

— DAY 76 —

Conquer fear to own your future

THE journey of life unravels like a tapestry woven from the threads of choices, opportunities, and experiences. As we navigate this labyrinth, we often encounter our most formidable adversary: fear. Fear has the power to paralyze us, to force us to retreat to the familiar, the comfortable, and the mundane. The key to unlocking our potential and owning our future lies in conquering this most primal of emotions.

Fear does not exist in a vacuum; it is born from the merging of uncertainty, vulnerability, and the innate desire to avoid pain. When we understand the roots of our fears, we can begin to dismantle them. This process begins with introspection, an honest examination of the self, and the willingness to confront our most deeply ingrained beliefs and assumptions.

The next step in this journey is to embrace failure. Failure, though often regarded as the forerunner of misery and disappointment, is actually the furnace in which character and resilience are forged. By reframing our perspective on failure and recognizing it as an essential component of growth and self-discovery, we can gradually strip away the anxiety that surrounds the unknown.

As we gain confidence in our ability to navigate uncharted territory, we must also cultivate gratitude. Gratitude is the humble recognition that life is momentary and that each moment, each experience, and each encounter is a gift. When we are grateful, we recognize that the challenges we face, the setbacks we endure, and the fears we conquer are all part of the grand theatre of existence. This perspective helps to dissolve the barriers that fear erects, allowing us to embrace our destiny with courage and grace.

To conquer fear and own our future, we must recognize the power that resides in our hands—the power to choose courage over fear, action over inaction, and growth over stagnation. It is in this ultimate triumph over fear that we truly claim ownership of our destinies, stepping boldly into the realm of infinite possibilities.

— DAY 77 —

You only control the effort, not the results

YOU have no control over the external factors that influence outcomes. You can't control how others perceive you, how they respond to your actions, or how the world unfolds around you. But what you can control is the effort you put into everything you do. You have the power to determine the amount of time, energy, and dedication you invest in pursuing your goals and dreams.

You and I, we're not all-powerful. We can't control everything, much as we might like to. We don't have command over how things will turn out, no matter how carefully we plot or how intensely we desire. Results, you see, are not entirely in our hands. They're shaped by an intricate collection of factors, many of which are as playful as a kitten in the sun.

But don't let that discourage you. In fact, let it liberate you. If you don't control the results, where does your power lie? It lies in the one thing you can control—your effort. Every moment you choose to act, try, or persevere, you're exercising your true power. The process is your kingdom, and you're the absolute monarch here.

Consider a seedling. It does what it can. It burrows its roots deep, stretches towards the sun, and it absorbs the nutrients it can find. It cannot ensure it will grow into a towering tree. Drought may come, or frost, or a browsing deer. But it can control its effort to grow, and it never stops trying. We should be like the seedling.

Imagine a world where we celebrated effort rather than outcome. The relentless persistence. The bold attempts. The unyielding endurance. The stumbles and the rises. The pure courage of trying, over and over again. Wouldn't that be a world filled with resilience, courage, and grit?

You only control the effort, not the results. It's a simple phrase with a substantial shift. It urges us to invest in the process, value persistence, and find satisfaction in knowing we have given our best. It challenges us to redefine success, not by the fruits of our labor, but by the labor itself. This is a radical, yet liberating approach to life, and a compelling call to action that echoes the wisdom of the ages.

— DAY 78 —

Ex-lovers return as tests of intelligence

I N the complex dance of human relationships, the spawn of an ex-lover can serve as a profound test of our emotional intelligence and personal growth. These encounters, often laden with unresolved emotions and a tangled web of memories, have the potential to challenge our understanding of ourselves, our values, and our ability to navigate the complexities of our emotions.

Picture this, you've grown, evolved, and moved on. Life has become brighter since you left a relationship that was wrong for you. Then, out of nowhere, an old lover reappears in your life. They seem to have changed, they say all the right things, and they seem like a new person. But is this a genuine evolution, or merely a facade?

This intelligence is not measured by IQ points or academic awards, but rather by emotional wisdom and the capacity to make rational decisions that support our well-being. It's about understanding patterns, recognizing destructive dynamics, and acknowledging that sometimes, what we want is not what we need. It's a critical thinking test, a challenge to determine whether we can recognize genuine transformation from manipulation, a true second chance from a repeated cycle of emotional unrest.

Ex-lovers returning as tests of intelligence also offer us a unique opportunity to measure our own growth. How we respond reflects the distance we've traveled since the relationship ended. Do we romanticize the past, ignore the red flags, and find ourselves falling into the same trap? Or do we stand firm in our growth, acknowledging the lessons learned?

The return of an ex-lover can indeed be a compelling test, but not just of intelligence. It's a test of self-love, a measure of self-respect, and a trial of our courage to prioritize our emotional health over momentary comfort.

In conclusion, when ex-lovers return, it isn't just about them or the possibility of rekindling old flames. It's about us—our growth, wisdom, and ability to make decisions that reflect our self-worth. It's about acknowledging that we are the authors of our stories, and we have the power to decide which characters get to play a role in them.

— DAY 79 —

Allow your children to struggle

A S parents, our natural instinct is to protect our children from any form of hardship or difficulty. We want to shield them from pain, disappointment, and failure. However, in our well-intentioned efforts to make their lives easier, we may inadvertently hinder their growth and development. It is essential to recognize the importance of allowing our children to struggle and face challenges, as it is through these experiences that they cultivate resilience, independence, and valuable life skills.

Firstly, let's clarify that advocating for our children to struggle does not involve abandoning them to the risks of life. It's about creating a supportive environment where they feel safe to face challenges, risk failures, and learn from their mistakes. It's about understanding that we cannot—and should not—walk their paths for them, but rather light the path, equipping them with the tools they need to navigate life's often tumultuous journey.

Struggle is an integral part of life. It's the grain of sand in the oyster that produces the pearl. By removing all obstacles from our children's paths, we unintentionally deny them opportunities to develop the ability to cope with adversity. The struggle is the master sculptor of character, shaving off feelings of entitlement and self-satisfaction, revealing hidden strengths, and fostering empathy through shared experiences of hardship.

Often, the most significant lessons we learn are born out of the melting pot of struggle. It's in our battles that we learn to strategize, persevere, and pick ourselves up after a fall. When we allow our children to experience these battles—within the context of a loving, supportive environment—we enable them to cultivate these vital life skills.

As heartbreaking as it may be, allowing our children to struggle is one of the most profound expressions of love. It's an understanding that our role as parents isn't to make the world a softer place for our children, but rather to prepare our children to thrive in an imperfect world.

— DAY 80 —

Underneath our differences, we are one

I N a world overflowing with diversity and seemingly overwhelming separations, it is all too easy to be consumed by the differences that separate us. We are bombarded with messages that highlight our contrasting beliefs, cultures, and appearances. Whether it be race, religion, or ideology, these distinctions often take center stage, hiding the fundamental truth of our shared humanity. However, when we strip away these superficial layers, we are confronted with the humbling realization that beneath it all, we are nothing more than a pile of flesh and bones strolling around on a large, lava-filled rock—all of us.

Each one of us, from the bus driver in New York to the Sherpa in Nepal, from the artist in Paris to the farmer in Kenya, is woven from the same fabric of existence. We share the same basic needs—food, shelter, and love. We are driven by the same fears and hopes, we laugh, we cry, we dream.

Our differences are not walls, but bridges, channels for shared understanding and growth. They provide a palette of experiences, a fabric of human existence that is as diverse as it is beautiful. These differences are not to be feared or fought against, but celebrated and learned from. They enrich our collective experience, challenge our perspectives, and push us towards growth.

Our shared human experience goes beyond the barriers of language, culture, and geography. In the end, we all marvel at a beautiful sunset, we all feel the sting of loss, and we all bask in the warmth of love. Regardless of our individual journeys, we are united by the human experience, bound by the common thread of life.

As humans, we are united by a shared biological foundation. Our bodies are composed of the same elements, our organs perform the same functions, and our minds grapple with the same existential questions.

We are not islands, isolated and disconnected. We are part of a larger whole, part of a symphony of existence that spans across the universe. We are, each one of us, a unique note in this grand composition, and beneath our differences, under the surface of variety, we are profoundly, deeply one.

— DAY 81 —

Embrace the reason you exist for

TOO often, we find ourselves caught up in the whirlwind of daily routines and societal expectations. Society teaches us to measure our worth by the yardstick of accomplishment, urging us to push forward on a never-ending quest for validation. We become consumed by the pursuit of external achievements, seeking validation and success in the eyes of others. But true fulfillment lies in aligning our actions and choices with our innermost passions and values.

The foundation of our existence lies in understanding our purpose. This purpose is not a singular goal, nor a predetermined destination; rather, it is the essence of our unique, individual journeys. The fabric of our lives is woven from the threads of our passions, talents, and relationships. By seeking to understand our intrinsic motivations, we unlock the key to our true selves.

As we begin to embrace our purpose, the world around us shifts. We discover a renewed sense of meaning and direction, grounded in the knowledge that our lives have intrinsic value. Our focus shifts from the relentless pursuit of external validation to cultivating an internal sense of worth. We learn to appreciate our lives not for the awards we accumulate, but for the moments of growth and understanding that define our existence.

In a world of relentless distractions, it is easy to lose sight of our unique purpose, swept up in the fleeting nature of life. However, it is only through a steadfast commitment to our purpose that we truly experience the "Aha" moments of self-realization. These moments of clarity, where the fog of uncertainty vanishes, allow us to gain perspective on the path we are meant to walk.

It may not be an easy task. Embracing your reason for existence requires courage, vulnerability, and perseverance. It often means going against the grain, challenging the status quo, and standing in your truth even when the world may not understand.

Dare to ask the hard questions, dare to explore the depths of your soul, dare to stand in your truth. Embrace the reason you exist, and remember, you're not just a drop in the ocean, you're the entire ocean in a drop.

— DAY 82 —

You are your best buddy

WITHIN the depths of our consciousness lies an unassuming truth that often remains unacknowledged: you are your best buddy. It is a simple concept with profound outcomes, an idea that challenges the very fabric of our social dependencies and preconceived beliefs about companionship. It is a journey that opens the doors to self-discovery, propelling us to build a strong foundation of self-love and acceptance.

In our journey of life, we often seek companionship, validation, and a sense of belonging from the external world. We forge bonds, create friendships, and cultivate relationships hoping to find that one person who'll understand us, support us, and stand by us through thick and thin. And yet, in the middle of this exhaustive search, we often overlook the one companion who is always there, always willing, always supportive— ourselves.

Being your own best buddy doesn't imply solitude or isolation. Rather, it signals a healthy relationship with oneself, similar to the rapport we share with a trusted confidante. It means treating ourselves with the same respect, kindness, and patience that we would offer to a beloved friend. It's about listening to our needs, honoring our feelings, and acknowledging our worth, even when the world fails to.

Imagine the strength that comes from knowing that you've got your own back, that you are your own cheerleader, your own confidante, your own shoulder to lean on. In moments of doubt and distress, it's this self-reliance that imparts resilience. In moments of triumph and joy, it's this self-love that heightens the elation.

The companionship we share with ourselves sets the tone for all other relationships in our lives. When we cherish our company, we foster a sense of self-worth that radiates outward, influencing how others perceive and treat us. It's a cycle of respect, dignity, and love that begins and ends with us.

Let's enjoy this beautiful journey of self-friendship. Let's engage in meaningful conversations with ourselves, appreciate our triumphs, learn from our failures, and above all, love ourselves unconditionally.

— DAY 83 —

Slow progress is still progress

IN an era of instant gratification, we have become a society obsessed with speed and efficiency, often dismissing the value of slow and steady progress. However, as we delve into the subtle nuances of growth, we discover that it is in the unhurried journey that true transformation lies. "Slow progress is still progress" serves as a reminder that the pace at which we evolve is not the defining factor of our success; rather, it is the steadfast commitment to personal development that leads us to our ultimate potential.

The Tortoise and the Hare, a timeless fable that resonates through generations, illustrates the importance of consistent effort, regardless of pace. The tortoise, unhurried and steadfast, emerges victorious against the swift hare, reminding us that speed is not always synonymous with triumph. It is the unyielding persistence in the face of adversity that defines true success, as we slowly and methodically navigate the path to self-improvement.

This appreciation for slow progress can be likened to the growth of a mighty oak, a testament to the beauty of gradual evolution. The oak tree begins its journey as a humble acorn, silently absorbing the nurturing elements of its surroundings. Over time, it ascends toward the sky, its roots extending deep into the earth, providing a stable foundation for its inevitable expansion. Much like the oak, our own progress is often invisible, occurring beneath the surface, and it is only through patience and perseverance that we begin to witness the fruits of our labor.

We are continuously bombarded with stories of overnight success, making it all too easy to forget the value of persistence and determination. Yet, beneath the surface of these seemingly instantaneous triumphs, countless hours of hard work, sacrifice, and dedication often lie hidden.

This perspective shift has the potential to transform our lives, as we begin to recognize the small victories that pave the path to our larger aspirations. By celebrating incremental advancements, we cultivate a mindset of gratitude and patience.

— DAY 84 —

Loneliness can be a side-effect of success

S UCCESS, a term often synonymous with happiness, fame, and fortune, has long been perceived as the ultimate aspiration. While society glorifies the triumphs of the accomplished, the darker aspects of achievement remain largely unexplored. We rarely acknowledge the other side of the coin—the solitude that often walks hand in hand with the pursuit of greatness. Yet, to truly understand the multifaceted nature of success, we must venture into this less-traveled path.

As individuals climb the ladder of success, the sacrifices made along the way often manifest as isolation. The pursuit of excellence demands a steadfast commitment to one's goals, leaving little time or energy for the cultivation of personal relationships. The resulting solitude can be both a driving force and an unintended consequence of ambition, as the need for connection is frequently overshadowed by the appeal of achievement.

Moreover, the attainment of success can create a perceived distance between oneself and others. As accomplishments compile, the gap between the triumphant individual and their peers widens, resulting in an increased sense of isolation. Friends and family may struggle to relate to the unique challenges faced by those who have reached the pinnacle of their fields, further amplifying the feeling of loneliness.

The loneliness that emerges as a side-effect of success also reveals a deeper truth about the human condition: the realization that external accomplishments cannot guarantee happiness or fulfillment. In a society that glorifies wealth, status, and power, it is all too easy to fall into the trap of believing that these markers of achievement will provide us with the happiness and satisfaction we seek. However, the experience of loneliness in the middle of success serves as an important reminder that true happiness lies beyond the realm of material gains.

Success and loneliness, though unlikely companions, together weave a narrative that is as insightful as it is transformative. A narrative that prompts us to redefine success, to see it not as a destination marked by wealth and recognition, but as a journey enhanced with growth, resilience, and self-discovery.

— DAY 85 —

Society values status over substance

FROM a young age, we are conditioned to believe that our worth is measured by external factors such as job titles, income levels, and social media followers. We are taught to strive for the highest positions, the biggest houses, and the latest trends, all in the pursuit of validation and acceptance from others. In this race for status, we may lose sight of our authentic selves and the values that truly define us.

Status is a powerful influencer. It taps into our innate desire for recognition and acceptance, weaving a captivating charm that pulls us into its shining sphere. The appeal of a high-powered job title, a luxurious mansion, a flashy car—they seem to bear the mark of success, offering a promise of happiness, respect, and fulfillment. And therein lies the paradox. Like a gilded mirage, status reflects not our genuine worth but the societal metrics we conform to.

Substance, on the other hand, is the silent hero of the narrative. It resides in our virtues, values, and competencies. It is the knowledge we amass, the kindness we extend, the resilience we embody. The substance may lack the immediate glamour of status, but it possesses a depth and authenticity that status often misses.

The consequence of such a societal disposition is a culture that continues superficiality and discourages depth. It compels us to build facades of achievement and perfection, thereby stifling our true selves. The relentless chase for status leaves little room for substance to bloom, building a society that's rich in pretense but poor in authenticity.

As individuals and as a collective, we can learn to recognize and celebrate substance over status. Let's admire people for their wisdom, not their wealth; their kindness, not their power; their resilience, not their rank. Let us not just aim to be successful but to be substantial, knowing that true value lies not in the awards and honors we gather, but in the difference we make, the legacy we leave behind.

For it is in this shift from status to substance that we can hope to find not just a more authentic society, but also a more authentic self.

— DAY 86 —

Social media fame doesn't equate to success

I N today's digital age, social media has become an integral part of our daily lives. From *Instagram* to *TikTok*, these platforms have given rise to a new form of fame, one that is measured in likes, followers, and viral videos. As our lives become increasingly interconnected with virtual realms, an odd phenomenon has taken root: the birth of social media fame with success. A dangerous misconception that has eroded the true essence of accomplishment and bent our perception of what it means to lead a fulfilling life.

The appeal of social media fame is, in part, a byproduct of our innate desire for validation and recognition. As humans, we crave to be seen, heard, and appreciated; a craving that social media platforms have expertly harnessed to foster a culture of instant gratification. Likes, shares, and followers have emerged as the new currency of esteem, the yardstick by which we measure our worth. And as this digital ecosystem continues to multiply, so too does the illusion that social media fame is synonymous with success.

Yet, this equation of social media fame with success is an insidious falsehood, one that obscures the multidimensional nature of human achievement. Success is not a one-size-fits-all phenomenon; rather, it is a complex tapestry woven from diverse threads of personal growth, meaningful relationships, and the pursuit of passion and purpose. It is the quiet triumphs, the small victories, and the steadfast resilience in the face of adversity that truly define a successful life.

Furthermore, social media fame can come at a cost. In our quest for likes and followers, we may find ourselves sacrificing our authenticity and integrity. We may become obsessed with projecting a certain image or persona, rather than being true to ourselves.

So how do we define success in the era of social media? Perhaps it is time to reevaluate our priorities and focus on the things that truly matter. We must remember that success is not solely measured by the number of likes or followers we have, True success is about finding happiness, pursuing our passions, and making a positive impact on the world.

— DAY 87 —

Physical attraction will be hedonically adapted

T HE complexities of human attraction have fascinated philosophers, poets, and scientists for centuries, as we endeavor to unravel the intricate dance of desire that fuels our relationships and shapes our destinies. Physical attraction plays a significant role. It enchants our senses, ignites our desires, and draws us towards one another. However, as time passes, we discover that physical attraction alone cannot sustain a deep and lasting connection. The truth is, that physical beauty is subject to the phenomenon known as hedonic adaptation.

Hedonic adaptation, a term coined by psychologists Brickman and Campbell in their seminal 1971 paper, refers to the human propensity to get used to new circumstances and return to a baseline level of happiness or satisfaction.[2] In the context of physical attraction, this suggests that the initial attraction we feel for a partner's physical appearance may gradually diminish as we grow accustomed to their presence in our lives.

This process of hedonic adaptation is deeply rooted in the evolutionary imperatives that have shaped our species. Our ancestors relied on novelty and change to survive in a dynamic and unpredictable environment, where selfsatisfaction and stagnation could prove fatal. Thus, the human brain evolved to derive pleasure from novel experiences and to adapt rapidly to new stimuli, ensuring that we remained ever vigilant and adaptable in the face of adversity.

While hedonic adaptation may have been advantageous to our ancestors, it also has deep implications for our understanding of physical attraction in the modern world. As we navigate the complex terrain of romantic relationships, it is essential to recognize that the initial spark of physical attraction may not be sustainable in the long term.

The realization that physical attraction is subject to hedonic adaptation serves as a reminder of the importance of cultivating relationships based on mutual respect, shared values, and emotional intimacy. It is these enduring qualities, rather than transient physical appeal, that will ultimately sustain and nourish our connections as we journey through the ever-shifting landscape of human experience.

— DAY 88 —

Life is either an exciting journey or nothing at all

L IFE is a funny thing. One moment we're here, full of dreams and aspirations, and the next, we're gone, leaving behind a legacy that will either be cherished or forgotten. But what if I told you that life is either an exciting journey or nothing at all? That's right! Our experience of life comes down to the choices we make and how we choose to see the world around us.

Consider this for a moment. We all have those friends who are always up for an adventure, ready to explore new places and experiences. They're the ones with the infectious energy and zest for life that makes us want to join them on their adventures. But then, there are also those who are satisfied with staying in their comfort zone, never daring to venture beyond the familiar. The difference between these two groups of people boils down to one thing: perspective.

You see, life is full of challenges, and we can choose to approach them with excitement and curiosity or cower away from them in fear. When we embrace the former, we're able to see the world as an endless playground, overflowing with opportunities for growth and self-discovery. It's this mindset that turns our lives into thrilling journeys, with every twist and turns revealing new possibilities and adventures.

On the flip side, when we choose to view life through a lens of fear and self-satisfaction, our world suddenly becomes smaller, confined to the narrow boundaries of our comfort zones. It's as if we've placed ourselves in a box, never allowing ourselves to see what lies beyond its walls. And when we live life this way, it can feel like nothing at all—devoid of meaning, purpose, or excitement.

The choice is yours. Will you choose to live life as an exciting journey, embracing the unknown with open arms and a spirit of adventure? Or will you settle for a life that feels like nothing at all?

In the end, it is those who view life as an exciting journey who are able to live life to the fullest. They can find joy and fulfillment in even the most mundane of tasks, and they approach each day with a sense of optimism and enthusiasm.

— DAY 89 —

Love and desire are not mutually exclusive

L OVE is a curious thing. We talk about it all the time, in songs, movies, and books, trying to capture its essence and understand its complexities. But love, like many things in life, is complex and multifaceted, often interconnected with other emotions and feelings. And that's where desire comes into play. People often wonder if love and desire are mutually exclusive, but let me tell you, they're not.

Picture this: you meet someone who lights up your world. Their presence sets your heart on fire, and you can't help but be drawn to them. That initial spark of attraction? That's desire, my friend. It's the magnetic pull that brings two people together, the force that ignites the flame of passion. But desire isn't just about physical attraction; it's also about the craving for emotional connection and intimacy with another person.

Now, let's talk about love. Love is that deep, lasting connection that we form with someone over time. It's the bond that grows stronger as we share our lives, dreams, and vulnerabilities with one another. Love is patient and kind, exceeding the superficial appeal of desire and rooting itself in the very core of our being.

So, how can love and desire coexist? Well, it's simple really. Love and desire complement each other, like two sides of the same coin. Desire is the spark that ignites the fire of love, providing the energy and excitement that fuels our relationships. Love, in turn, provides the framework and foundation upon which desire can flourish and thrive.

Love and desire need each other. A relationship without desire can feel stagnant and lifeless, devoid of the passion and excitement that make life worth living. And desire without love can feel empty and superficial, lacking the depth and substance that give meaning to our connections.

The key to a fulfilling relationship is finding the balance between love and desire, allowing them to coexist and enrich our lives. It's about nurturing the passion and excitement that brought us together while also cultivating the deep, emotional bond that sustains us through the ups and downs of life.

— DAY 90 —

Do one thing every day that scares you

IN the realm of self-improvement, where mantras and life hacks overflow, one rule stands out like a light of courage. It's not an invitation to court unnecessary danger, but a mantra that invites us to go beyond the confines of our comfort zones and engage with the world around us in more daring, fulfilling ways.

Each of us has fears, some minuscule and some monumental. They can be as tiny as the fear of cooking a complex dish or as immense as the fear of standing up for oneself in a challenging relationship. These fears, if left unchecked, erect invisible barriers that confine us, diminishing the radiance of our potential.

But what happens if we confront these fears? By doing one thing each day that frightens us, we begin to see that these fears, so daunting at first, often hide valuable opportunities for self-discovery and growth. Overcoming fear is an act of self-liberation, a defiance against the limitations we create upon ourselves.

Confronting fear is similar to standing on the brink of a steep cliff. It forces us to confront the reality of our vulnerability, and the inevitability of our ability to commit mistakes. But it's in this raw, deep-seated moment that we can truly appreciate the thrilling potential of our existence. Each fear overcome is a step towards expanding our boundaries, broadening our perspectives, and unleashing the latent power within us.

Furthermore, embracing this principle fosters a dynamic mindset that is versatile, adaptive, and resilient. Each day becomes a cauldron for courage, transforming fear from an obstacle to a driving force for change. It fosters a culture of experimentation and innovation, where failures are seen not as terminal endpoints but as critical waypoints on the journey of growth.

It's a philosophy of life, a testament to the transformative power of courage. It propels us to view each day not as a monotonous sequence of hours but as a vibrant canvas of opportunities. Opportunities to challenge ourselves, to learn, grow, and, most importantly, to live authentically, fully engaged with the thrilling, terrifying, and wondrous adventure that is life.

— DAY 91 —

Challenges are opportunities for growth

A S we journey through the scheme of life, we are continually met with an array of challenges that test our mettle, shake our resolve, and sometimes even bring us to our knees. Yet, within these moments of strife and struggle, there lies a hidden gift, a secret key that unlocks a treasure trove of growth and transformation.

The inherent beauty of challenges lies in their capacity to push us beyond the boundaries of our comfort zone, compelling us to confront our fears and insecurities and to question the very foundations of our beliefs. In this cauldron of adversity, we have forged anew, our mettle tempered by the fires of experience and our resolve strengthened by the winds of change. It is through this process of trial and tribulation that we are able to transcend the limitations of our former selves and emerge stronger, wiser, and more resilient than before.

One need only look to the annals of history to witness the transformative power of challenges. From the groundbreaking discoveries of pioneering scientists to the unstoppable spirit of those who have defied the odds and overcome seemingly insurmountable obstacles, the narrative of human progress is marked by countless instances of individuals who have risen to the occasion and embraced the opportunity for growth that lies within every challenge.

The key to harnessing the power of challenges as opportunities for growth lies in our mindset. When we approach adversity with an open mind and a willingness to learn, we are able to extract valuable lessons and insights from even the most difficult of circumstances. This perspective empowers us to reframe our challenges as stepping stones on the path to personal development, allowing us to embrace the uncertainty and struggle with grace and determination.

When we face change, we are forced to adapt and to learn new skills and behaviors. We may be forced to step outside of our comfort zones, confront our fears, and develop new coping strategies. Through this process, we can emerge stronger and more adaptable, better equipped to navigate the challenges of life.

— DAY 92 —

Progress thrives in new companies and mindsets

C HANGE, whether we like it or not, is the only constant in life. But when harnessed properly, change becomes progress, a transformative force capable of reshaping societies and individuals. In our current era, marked by rapid technological advancement and the rise of novel business models, progress thrives particularly in new companies and mindsets.

New companies are the flag bearers of progress in the modern world. They emerge from the belief that the status quo can, and should, be challenged. They venture into the unknown, fearlessly embracing risk, fueled by the potential of a novel idea. New companies disrupt existing paradigms, introduce innovations, and redefine industries, often ushering in a new era of prosperity and development.

Yet, the magic of new companies lies not in their innovative products or services, but rather in their progressive mindsets. Their success stems from their willingness to question, to experiment, to fail, and most importantly, to learn. They refuse to be confined by traditional thinking or outdated practices, opting instead to forge their own path. Their culture of continuous learning and improvement fosters a creative, dynamic environment that fuels progress.

But the journey towards progress isn't exclusive to new companies. It's a journey we can all embark on, individually and collectively. By adopting a progressive mindset—a mindset that embraces change, seeks growth, and is not afraid to challenge the status quo—we can become agents of progress in our own lives and communities.

To develop such a mindset, we must learn to value curiosity over comfort, flexibility over rigidity, and potential over familiarity. We must be willing to question our own beliefs, seek new perspectives, and embrace the discomfort that often accompanies growth.

The capacity for progress is not confined to new companies, but is within all of us, waiting to be unlocked by a shift in mindset. In the face of rapid change and uncertainty, let us embrace the spirit of progress, propelling ourselves and our society toward a brighter, more prosperous future.

— DAY 93 —

Shortcuts can lead to costly mistakes

T HE quest for success is a journey, not a sprint. It requires resilience, patience, and the ability to learn from failures. This is a universal truth, yet, in our fast-paced world, we are often tempted to seek shortcuts, overlooking the value of the process in the haste for quick results.

The realm of shortcuts often neglects the intrinsic value of learning that lies within the process of achieving a goal. When we bypass this process, we are essentially forgoing the lessons, experiences, and the skills it imparts. We become like sailors without a compass, our journey lacking the wisdom that the long road offers, making us vulnerable to errors we could have avoided had we opted for the diligent path.

Consider a pianist who seeks to master a concerto. Taking a shortcut might involve memorizing the key sequences without understanding the theory behind the composition. This method might result in a passable performance but any unexpected change, a slip of memory, or a shift in the composition, could lead to a disastrous outcome. However, if the pianist embraces the process, studying the theory, and practicing each bar individually, the depth of their performance increases exponentially, and they are equipped to navigate unexpected difficulties.

This doesn't mean we should disregard efficiency or innovative paths. The key is to distinguish between a shortcut that bypasses necessary learning and an efficient strategy that improves the process while preserving its instructive value. Implementing automation in an assembly line can be an efficient strategy. However, using a dubious "quick-fix" to pass a critical exam, instead of learning the material, is a shortcut that bypasses the critical learning process.

In the grand scheme of our lives, every thread, every decision contributes to the masterpiece we create. The shortcuts we take may seem to accelerate our journey, but they often leave us unprepared, creating weaknesses in our life. In contrast, when we choose to embrace the process, we weave resilience, knowledge, and wisdom into our lives, creating a robust and rich masterpiece that stands the test of time.

— DAY 94 —

People enter your life to teach lessons

L IFE has an interesting way of teaching us lessons. As we journey through this ever-evolving maze of experiences, we often encounter people who enter our lives for a reason, serving as catalysts for growth, change, and self-discovery. These individuals, whether they grace our existence for a brief moment or become lifelong companions, each carry with them invaluable insights and wisdom that can shape the very trajectory of our lives.

Remember that teacher who challenged you to push your boundaries and think outside the box? Or the friend who stood by your side during your darkest moments, offering steadfast support and encouragement? These people, and countless others, have left a lasting imprint on our lives, reminding us of the transformative power of human connection.

The beauty of these encounters lies in their unpredictability. Sometimes, these lessons come from the most unexpected sources, catching us off guard and forcing us to reevaluate our preconceived notions and beliefs. It could be a stranger we met on a train, a coworker with a vastly different perspective, or even a family member who suddenly revealed a side of themselves we never knew existed.

In order to fully embrace the lessons that these individuals have to offer, we must adopt a mindset of openness and curiosity. Be receptive to the wisdom that flows from the people who cross our paths, and listen to the subtle whispers of insight that echo through the conversations we share. When we approach life with an open heart and an open mind, we create a fertile ground for growth, allowing the seeds of knowledge and understanding to take root and flourish.

The next time you meet someone new, take a moment to pause and reflect on the potential lessons they may have to offer. The people we meet along our life's journey are not mere passengers, but are navigators guiding us towards our true selves. Their influence, direct or indirect, shapes us, molding us into the individuals we become. As we journey through life, it is essential to remain open to these lessons, for they hold the key to our personal growth and self-discovery.

— DAY 95 —

Society judges women and men differently

THE societal norms and expectations for women and men have always been different. This is a fact that we all know, but have we really stopped to think about why? Why is it that women are judged more harshly for their appearance and behavior than men? Why is it that men are praised for being assertive while women are labeled as aggressive? These are questions that need to be answered if we are to understand the deep-rooted gender biases that exist in our society.

Let's start with appearance. Women are constantly bombarded with messages telling them that they need to look a certain way in order to be considered attractive. They are expected to be thin, have clear skin, and wear makeup that enhances their features. Men, on the other hand, are not held to the same standard. In fact, men who put too much effort into their appearance are often ridiculed and labeled as being "feminine." This double standard is not only unfair, but it also prolongs harmful gender stereotypes.

The way society views women's behavior is also vastly different from how it views men's behavior. Women who speak their minds and assert themselves are often labeled as being "bossy" or "difficult," while men who do the same are praised for being assertive and confident. This double standard can make it difficult for women to succeed in male-dominated fields, where assertiveness is often necessary to get ahead.

But it's not just the way society views women's appearance and behavior that is different from how it views men's. Women are also judged more harshly for their personal choices. Women who choose to focus on their careers rather than having children are often seen as selfish or unnatural, while men who make the same choice are praised for their ambition. Similarly, women who choose to have children and take time off from work to raise them are often penalized in the workplace, while men who do the same are seen as responsible and family-oriented.

As we conclude our exploration, let us carry forward the insights gleaned from our journey, and strive to create a world where we judge each other not based on our gender, but on the content of our character.

— DAY 96 —

All emotions are temporary

IN the journey of life, our emotions come and go, coloring our experiences and shaping who we are. "All emotions are temporary" is a powerful truth that helps us understand the changing nature of our feelings and encourages us to explore the depths of our emotional world.

Picture this, you're at your favorite band's concert, singing along at the top of your lungs, feeling invincible. You think, "I could stay in this moment forever." But as the last chord fades, and the crowd scatters, the euphoria starts to evaporate. It's a bummer, I know, but hey, that's how it is.

Now, think about the last time you were really upset or scared. In the thick of it, it felt like you were stuck in a never-ending tunnel, right? But as time passed, the feeling gradually loosened its grip. You found a way out of that tunnel. The darkness wasn't forever.

See, that's the beauty of it. Emotions, as powerful as they can be, are fleeting. They're like visitors. They come, they stay a while, they leave. This doesn't belittle them, it's quite the contrary. The fleeting nature of emotions is what makes them precious. The joy of a shared laugh, the adrenaline rush of a new experience, the pang of heartbreak—they are the fabric of our life stories.

Knowing that all emotions are temporary is a game-changer. When you're down in the dumps, it offers a comforting whisper, "This too shall pass." When you're on cloud nine, it nudges you to soak up the joy, without clinging on too tight.

The more you get this, the more you'll see the balance it brings. The highs and lows, they're all parts of this beautiful, messy human experience. So why not ride this wave of emotions with acceptance and a touch of grace?

To wrap this up, let's keep this little nugget in mind: Emotions are transient guests in the inn of our hearts. Welcome them, learn from them, but don't cling. They are, after all, just passing through. Now, doesn't that perspective make life a whole lot more fascinating?

— DAY 97 —

Act your way to clarity

Y OU know that moment when you're faced with a tough decision? You weigh the pros and cons, sleep on it, ask your friends, your family, and maybe even your pet. But still, clarity seems as unattainable as a pot of gold at the end of a rainbow. While it may seem paradoxical at first glance, this phrase encourages us to plunge into action, as clarity often blooms not from passive contemplation, but active participation.

Think about learning to ride a bike. Did you figure it out by thinking really hard about it? Nope. You hopped on, wobbled a bit, and probably fell a few times, but with each attempt, things got clearer. Before you knew it, you were pedaling down the street, wind in your hair, a victorious grin on your face. That's the beauty of action—it clears the fog of uncertainty.

Consider life as a grand theatre. Each day, we play different roles and juggle different scripts. But the most memorable scenes, the ones where we truly find ourselves, aren't scripted. They're born out of improvisation. It's when we toss the script out the window and leap into the action that we bask in the spotlight of clarity.

Imagine a chef experimenting with a new recipe. Sure, he could spend hours researching, reading, and considering, but the real magic happens when he starts cooking, tasting, and adjusting. It's in the act of cooking that the recipe evolves, and that clarity emerges.

This "act your way to clarity" mantra doesn't just apply to learning new skills or creating masterpieces. It's relevant in all corners of our lives. Stuck in a career rut? Try a new role, even if it's temporary. Not sure if you should pursue that hobby? Dive in for a month and see how it feels.

When you find yourself stuck in the murky waters of indecision, remember, don't just sit on the dock, dive in! Embrace the splash of action. Each stroke might take you closer to the shore of clarity. And who knows? Along the way, you might discover that the journey to clarity, the action itself, is the real treasure, not the elusive pot of gold at the end of the rainbow. Now, how's that for a plot twist?

— DAY 98 —

Life always finds ways to surprise you

LIFE is a mystery. It can be beautiful and joyful one moment, and overwhelming and challenging the next. No matter how much we plan, how much we think we have it all figured out, life always finds ways to surprise us.

The surprises that life throws our way can come in many forms. They can be positive, like unexpected opportunities, chance encounters, or moments of sheer bliss. Or they can be negative, like sudden losses, unexpected obstacles, or moments of deep despair. Whatever form they take, these surprises have the power to shake us to our core and force us to re-evaluate our lives.

When we accept that life is full of surprises, we learn to approach each day with a sense of curiosity and wonder. This mindset allows us to appreciate the beauty in the unexpected and to find lessons in the challenges we face. By embracing the element of surprise, we become more adaptable and resilient, better equipped to navigate the unpredictable waters of life.

One of the most exciting aspects of life's surprises is the opportunity for personal growth and self-discovery. Through unexpected experiences, we learn more about ourselves and the world around us. Each surprise reveals new insights and perspectives, encouraging us to continually evolve and adapt to the ever-changing landscape of life.

The realization that life is full of surprises also fosters a deeper sense of gratitude and appreciation for the present moment. When we acknowledge that life can change in an instant, we learn to cherish the people, experiences, and emotions that make our lives unique and meaningful. And no matter what joys we may encounter, we have the capacity to fully embrace them and appreciate the beauty of the world around us.

Life always finds ways to surprise you. But it's up to us to embrace those surprises, to face them with open hearts and minds, and to use them as opportunities for growth and transformation. Because in the end, it's the surprises that make life worth living. They remind us of the fragility and beauty of life, and they give us the strength and courage to face whatever comes our way.

— DAY 99 —

Emotional dependence leads to loss of control

EMOTIONS are a fundamental part of our human experience. They allow us to feel and connect deeply with ourselves and others. In the world of human emotions, we often find ourselves dealing with a mix of needs, worries, and connections. But when we become emotionally dependent on others, we run the risk of losing control over our own lives.

Imagine a puppet with its strings attached, controlled by an invisible hand. Emotional dependence is similar, as our actions and choices become influenced by other people's feelings, leaving us feeling lost. Losing control in this way harms our emotional well-being and makes it harder to find our way through life's challenges.

When we depend too much on others emotionally, we give up our personal power, allowing outside forces to guide our lives. This not only stops us from growing but also creates a strong need for approval and help. This endless cycle continues to grow, slowly taking away our sense of self and making it hard to know what we truly want.

To break free from emotional dependence, we must learn to understand ourselves better and think deeply about our feelings. By looking at where our emotional connections come from, we can find and change the habits that keep us trapped. This journey of self-discovery helps us take back control and live our lives with purpose and intention.

The only way to regain control over our own lives is to take ownership of our own emotions. We need to learn how to validate ourselves, how to find our own sense of self-worth, and how to make our own choices and decisions. This means learning how to say "No" to others, setting boundaries, and being true to ourselves.

It's also important to seek help and support from others, but in a healthy way. We should surround ourselves with people who respect us and support us, but who also allow us to be our own person. We need to remember that we are the only ones who can truly control our own emotions and our own lives.

— DAY 100 —

Parental disappointment is inevitable

AS children, we all look up to our parents as the pillars of strength and guidance in our lives. In the journey of life, the relationship between a parent and a child is filled with expectations, dreams, and hopes. But the truth is, parental disappointment is inevitable. No matter how hard we try, we will inevitably disappoint our parents at some point in our lives.

Imagine a small flower, opening its petals under the warm sun, trying to catch the sunlight and grow. In the same way, children want the approval and support of their parents, working hard to live up to their hopes. But, just like the flower faces challenges from nature, children's lives have unexpected problems, changes, and new experiences. All these things can lead to parents feeling disappointed.

It's not that our parents set out to intentionally disappoint us. In fact, they often have the best intentions for us, hoping that we will achieve all of our dreams and goals. But when our lives don't go according to plan, or we make choices that don't align with our parents' values and expectations, disappointment can arise.

As children, we often feel the weight of our parents' disappointment. We may feel like we have let them down, or that we are not living up to their expectations. This can be a difficult and painful experience, but it is also a necessary part of growing up.

In fact, parental disappointment can be a catalyst for growth and self-discovery. It forces us to examine our own values and beliefs, and to make choices that align with our own sense of self. It can also be an opportunity for open and honest communication with our parents, allowing us to better understand each other and build a stronger relationship.

It's important to remember that parental disappointment is not a reflection of our worth or value as individuals. We are all unique, with our own dreams and aspirations, and it's impossible to please everyone all the time. It's okay to make mistakes and to deviate from the path of our parents' expectations. In fact, it's often necessary for our own growth and development.

— DAY 101 —

Your decisions shape your destiny

HAVE you ever stopped to consider how your decisions, big or small, have shaped your life? We are all the architects of our own destiny, and the decisions we make are the bricks and mortar that shape the path we walk. Every choice we make sets us on a different course, leading us towards different outcomes and destinations. It's up to us to make the decisions that will lead us to the life we want.

We all have moments of uncertainty and doubt, where we feel like we don't have control over our own lives. But the reality is that we have more control than we think. We have the power to shape our destiny through the decisions we make. The power of our decisions is often underestimated. It's easy to get caught up in the day-to-day minutiae of life, and to forget that every choice we make has the potential to change the course of our lives. From the smallest decisions, like what to eat for breakfast, to the biggest decisions, like where to live or who to marry, each one has an impact on our future.

Let's talk about something we all have in common—the people in our lives. Friends, partners, and even colleagues, all come into our world because of the choices we've made. Whether it's deciding to join a club, swiping right on a dating app, or simply striking up a conversation with a stranger, it's our decisions that bring these relationships into existence.

But it's not just about the people we meet. Our decisions impact every aspect of our lives, from our careers to our hobbies and even our overall happiness. Remember that time you decided to take up painting, or when you left that dead-end job to pursue your passion? Those choices led you down new paths and shaped the person you are today.

Now, don't get me wrong. Not every decision will be a game-changer, and that's perfectly okay. Sometimes we'll make mistakes, but even those missteps have value. They teach us valuable lessons and help us grow as individuals. The important thing is to keep making decisions, taking risks, and finding joy in the uncertainty that comes with it. Embrace the journey, my friend.

— DAY 102 —

Life has sad and beautiful moments

L ET'S kick back for a moment, you and I, and have a heart-to-heart about something we've all got in common, something that connects every living creature on this planet—life. Life, my friend, is a rollercoaster ride of epic proportions. It's got highs that can make you feel like you're soaring among the stars, and lows that can knock the wind right out of you. In other words, life has both sad and beautiful moments.

Now, we've all been there, haven't we? Moments when it feels like the universe is against us. We're knee-deep in the mud, struggling to take the next step, and it seems like the sky is falling. Everything around us feels gray and gloomy. But let me let you in on a secret—it's these very moments, these struggles and hardships that have the power to shape us into stronger, wiser, and more compassionate beings.

And then, there are those moments when life feels like a glorious, sun-kissed adventure. When everything aligns perfectly, we feel a kind of joy that can't be put into words. The taste of your favorite ice cream on a hot summer day, the sound of your favorite song on the radio, the feel of a loved one's hand in yours. These are the instances that make our hearts dance with pure, unfiltered joy.

But why this mixture of sadness and beauty, you might ask? Why can't life just be an endless summer? Well, imagine listening to a song that's all highs with no lows, or watching a movie that's all laughter and no tears. It would feel incomplete, wouldn't it? That's because it's the combination of highs and lows, the sad and beautiful moments, that make for a complete, fulfilling experience.

It's the balance, my friend, the Yin and Yang of life that make it so incredibly beautiful and rich. The sad moments teach us resilience, they show us our strength, and remind us of our humanity. The beautiful moments, on the other hand, they're the sweet reward, the light at the end of the tunnel, the sprinkle of magic that makes life worth living.

— DAY 103 —

Actions reveal true character

ACTIONS speak louder than words. It's a saying that we've all heard at some point in our lives, but have we truly understood the depth of its meaning? Words can be easily manipulated, but our actions showcase who we are and what we stand for.

We can talk all we want about our intentions, beliefs, and values, but it's our actions that truly reflect these things. We can claim to be kind, compassionate, and empathetic, but if we don't act on these qualities, then they are meaningless. Our actions reveal the truth about our character, and that is what people will remember about us.

Now, you might ask, "Why do actions matter more than intentions?" After all, aren't our intentions, the desires and motivations that drive us, the truest reflection of our character? Indeed, intentions are crucial, but they are not enough. They are merely the seeds of our character, while actions are the blossoming flowers that bear the fruits of our true nature. Actions give life to intentions, transforming them from mere thoughts into tangible realities. In this sense, actions are the definitive metric by which we measure the worth of our character.

Take a moment to consider the following scenario: Two people hold the intention of helping those in need. Person A acts upon this intention, volunteering at a homeless shelter, while Person B, despite having the same intention, never puts it into action. Who has demonstrated a stronger character? It is clear that Person A, through their actions, has brought their intentions to life, thus revealing their true character.

As we continue our introspective journey, we encounter the ever-interesting question of whether actions can change character. Are we static beings, or can our actions mold and shape the outlines of our character, carving out new facets and dimensions? The answer is an emphatic yes. Through our actions, we are constantly reinventing ourselves, refining our character, and growing into the person we strive to become.

— DAY 104 —

Don't manipulate emotions for lust

HAVE you ever been in a situation where someone tried to manipulate your emotions for their own benefit? Maybe it was a partner trying to convince you to do something you weren't comfortable with, or a friend trying to guilt trip you into doing them a favor. Whatever the situation, it's important to recognize when someone is trying to manipulate your emotions, especially for lust.

Manipulating someone's emotions for lust is a despicable act. It's a way of using someone's vulnerabilities against them to get what you want. It's a selfish and disrespectful way of treating someone, and it can have long-lasting negative effects.

Picture, for a moment, a world where emotions are the currency of connection, the threads that weave together the complex accumulation of human relationships. In such a world, the temptation to exploit these delicate emotional fibers for selfish, fleeting pleasure may become an intoxicating force.

So, why is it that we are compelled to manipulate emotions in the pursuit of lust? The answer lies in the intoxicating appeal of power—the power to bend another's will to our own, to elicit a response, a reaction, a surrender. But this power comes at a great cost. In manipulating emotions, we undermine the integrity of trust, eroding the foundations upon which authentic relationships are built. We become architects of our own destruction, fashioning a world of hollow connections and transient pleasures, devoid of the warmth and depth of true emotional intimacy.

As we navigate the murky waters of human desire, let us be ever mindful of the consequences of our actions. For every choice we make, every emotion we manipulate, and every lustful pursuit we undertake, we cast ripples upon the pond of our existence. These ripples, born of deceit and selfish desire, will eventually return to us, bearing the weight of their consequences. It is only through genuine, authentic connections, built on a foundation of trust and vulnerability, that we can hope to experience the full spectrum of human emotions and form lasting, meaningful relationships.

—— DAY 105 ——

One decision can change a life. Literally

L IFE is full of choices, both big and small. Some decisions are insignificant, while others can have a profound impact on our lives. In fact, it's often said that one decision can change your life. Literally. Think about it. A single decision can set us on a completely different path in life.

With each choice we make, we step onto a new path, leaving behind an infinite number of alternate realities in our wake. In this spectrum of potential, it becomes clear that a single decision—no matter how seemingly insignificant—can irrevocably alter the course of our lives, setting us on a journey toward a future we could never have foreseen.

A decision to take a different route to work could lead to a chance encounter that blossoms into a lifelong friendship. A decision to pursue a passion could ignite a fire that fuels our dreams and aspirations for years to come. Each decision, choice, and path we take has the potential to reshape our lives in unimaginable ways.

At this point, you might be thinking, "Wait, that's a lot of pressure!" But don't worry, here's the magical part: a decision doesn't just have the power to change your life's path, it has the power to create it. With every decision, we are not just passive riders on the journey of life; we become the architects, the builders, the sculptors of our destiny.

Let's take a step back and reflect upon some of the most influential figures in history. Consider Martin Luther King Jr., deciding to lead the civil rights movement, or Marie Curie, deciding to pursue a career in science despite societal norms. Their decisions, which might have seemed challenging and risky at the time, led to groundbreaking change and progress.

It's important to remember that the decisions we make don't just affect us. They also affect the people around us, from our family and friends to our coworkers and community. One decision can have a ripple effect that touches the lives of countless others.

— DAY 106 —

Love blinds us to flaws

L OVE is a powerful emotion that has the ability to make us feel both thrilled and vulnerable. It's a feeling that we all crave, and when we find it, it can be all-consuming. But love can also blind us to flaws, both in ourselves and in others.

When we're in love, we tend to see the best in our partners. We focus on their positive qualities and overlook their flaws. We may even justify or rationalize these flaws as minor inconveniences or even cute quirks. However, this can lead us to ignore red flags and warning signs that can cause problems later on in the relationship.

Love can cloud our judgment and make us believe that everything will be okay as long as we're together. We may think that our partner's flaws are not a big deal, or that they will eventually change. However, this is not always the case, and ignoring flaws can lead to disappointment and heartbreak.

But why is it that love, a force so pure and kind-hearted, has the power to blind us to the flaws of those we hold dear? The answer lies in the very nature of love itself. For love is not a mere emotion, but a force that transcends the confines of rational thought, an alchemical elixir that transforms the mundane into the extraordinary. It is through love that we glimpse the divine in the ordinary, the sacred in the profane, and the beauty in the imperfections that define our humanity.

And yet, this blindness to flaws is not a weakness, but a testament to the transformative power of love. For in loving another, we choose to see beyond the surface, to peer into the depths of their soul, and embrace the entirety of their being—flaws and all. It is this ability to accept and cherish the imperfections of another that forms the foundation of true love, a love that transcends the superficial and delves into the very essence of our humanity.

Acknowledging and accepting our own flaws and those of our partners can help us grow and improve. It's important to communicate and work on these flaws to create a healthy and successful relationship. Remember, love is not a cure-all, and it takes effort and work to make it successful.

— DAY 107 —

Life is a competitive game

L IFE is often compared to a game, and it's not hard to see why. From the moment we're born, we're competing for resources, attention, and success. It's a competitive game that requires us to constantly adapt and evolve to stay ahead.

Competition can be both motivating and challenging. On one hand, it can push us to work harder, think outside the box, and become the best versions of ourselves. On the other hand, it can also be frustrating, exhausting, and even demoralizing.

But the reality is that life is a competitive game, and we must learn how to navigate it to find success and fulfillment. This means learning how to deal with setbacks, failures, and disappointments, and finding the resilience to keep pushing forward.

Success in the game of life is often measured by our ability to compete and succeed in different areas, whether it's in our careers, relationships, or personal pursuits. But it's important to remember that success means different things to different people. For some, it may mean achieving financial stability, while for others, it may mean finding a sense of purpose and meaning.

It's also important to recognize that the game of life is not a zero-sum game. We don't have to tear others down to succeed. In fact, we often find greater success when we work together and support each other. Collaboration and cooperation can be just as important as competition in finding success and fulfillment in life.

Competition can be both motivating and challenging, but it's important to find the resilience to keep pushing forward and the support of others to help us along the way. As we continue to navigate the complex labyrinth of life, let us remain ever-conscious of the delicate balance between competition and collaboration, and the profound impact these forces can have on our lives. Remember, the game of life is not just about winning, but about finding purpose and meaning in our journey.

— DAY 108 —

Expect betrayals in life

IN discussions about life, the topic of betrayal might emerge as overly cynical or negative. However, this perspective isn't about anticipating deception at every turn; it's a recognition of life's multifaceted and unpredictable nature.

Picture this, you and me, we're each navigating our own universe of relationships, aren't we? Like explorers in a sea of personalities, desires, dreams, fears, every person an island unto themselves. And sometimes, the sea gets stormy, right? Betrayal, it's like a sudden tempest, unsettling but part of the journey.

Now, don't get me wrong. Betrayals are no fun fair. They sting. But, they bring powerful life lessons. Think of them as the toughest teachers you didn't sign up for, but who give you the most unforgettable lessons. They teach you about your relationships and, more importantly, about you.

You see, when betrayal happens, it's like someone turned on the harsh lights in the room of your relationship. You suddenly see the cracks, the strains. You figure out the bonds that are deep and those that are as thin as a spider's web.

But there's more. Betrayals, prompt you to do a bit of soul-searching, too. You start seeing your part in the grand scheme of things. This isn't about guilt or self-blame, it's about insight. It's about understanding your choices, your patterns, your blind spots.

To expect betrayals is not about building an emotional fortress. It's about realizing that life is a beautiful, imperfect mess. That people, just like us, can make mistakes. And that's okay. It's part of being human.

So here's what I'd suggest: let's walk into life with open eyes and open hearts. Let's understand that people may let us down. But let's also know that these experiences, as harsh as they may be, shape us into stronger, more discerning individuals.

Life is full of surprises, betrayals being one of them. But they're not just scars on your journey, they're more like badges of resilience, forgiveness, and authenticity. So, my friend, expect betrayals, but remember, they're just the universe's way of making us a little wiser, a little tougher.

— DAY 109 —

Relationships depend on mutual interest

R ELATIONSHIPS are a vital part of our lives, whether they be romantic, platonic, or professional. But what makes a relationship successful? One crucial element is mutual interest. In other words, both parties must have a genuine interest in the other person and what they bring to the relationship.

Mutual interest is a multifaceted concept that transcends mere shared hobbies or activities. At its core, it represents an alignment of our innermost desires, beliefs, and aspirations. This alignment creates a sense of harmony that resonates within our relationships, allowing us to feel seen, heard, and understood. When we find someone who shares our passions, it's as if a hidden force draws us together, creating a powerful emotional bond that transcends superficial connections.

This magnetic pull of mutual interest not only attracts us to one another but also fuels the growth of our relationships. As we share experiences, exchange ideas, and explore new horizons, our connections deepen, transforming from a mere commonality into a source of support, inspiration, and growth. Through the lens of mutual interest, we discover new facets of ourselves and the world around us, experiencing a profound sense of personal evolution and emotional fulfillment.

But what happens when the threads of mutual interest begin to fray as our interests evolve over time? Does this signal the demise of our connections? Not necessarily. The true power of mutual interest lies in its adaptability and flexibility. As we grow and change, so too can our relationships, provided both parties remain open to exploring new interests and finding common ground.

Without mutual interest, relationships can quickly become one-sided and unfulfilling. Remember, relationships are about what both parties can contribute, not just what one person can get out of it. Take the time to invest in the people in your life, and cultivate relationships that bring joy, fulfillment, and growth.

— DAY 110 —

Our biggest gift may be our toughest lesson learned

I MAGINE unwrapping a gift, and within it, you find a puzzle with a thousand pieces. The task before you is complex, complicated, and perhaps even a little daunting. But as you piece together each fragment, every tiny component, you gradually form a complete, vivid image. This is the exact nature of life's biggest gift—our toughest lessons learned.

Life, much like that puzzle, often appears as an elaborate, interconnected set of experiences. Each moment, each encounter, each triumph, and each failure is a puzzle piece, helping form the grand scheme of our existence. Yet, it's often the most challenging experiences, the most difficult challenges that add the most significant strokes to this masterpiece. These are the lessons that stretch us, pull us out of our comfort zones, and demand us to dig deep. They're the grueling nights, the uphill battles, the moments of doubt that leave us questioning our strength and ability.

Within this melting pot of challenges, something miraculous happens. We evolve. The fire of adversity, while it may scorch, also refines, purifies, and brings forth our most authentic selves. We grow resilient, resourceful, and in touch with our inner strength. We learn to persevere, to stand even when all else crumbles. We discover compassion—for ourselves and others—as we recognize the shared struggle that binds us all.

Through the lens of introspection, we understand our missteps weren't errors but opportunities, designed to initiate wisdom and growth. With each tumble, each fall, we get a chance to rise again, a little stronger, a little wiser. These hardships form the bedrock of our character, shaping us into the individuals we become.

Perhaps this is why life's biggest gift often comes concealed as our toughest lessons. It's a paradox, isn't it? But it is in the trenches of these challenges that we dig out our courage, our perseverance, our resilience. These lessons ask us not merely to survive, but to thrive—to transcend our perceived limitations and tap into our boundless potential.

— DAY 111 —

Don't cling to people just for history's sake

W E all have relationships in our lives that have stood the test of time. Whether it's a friend we've known since childhood, a sibling we've grown up with, or a romantic partner who has been with us for years, these relationships hold a special place in our hearts. However, there comes a time when we need to reevaluate these relationships and ask ourselves whether we are clinging to them just for history's sake.

Life is a dance, a symphony of fleeting moments and fleeting connections, and it is in the constant flux of relationships that we find the true beauty and richness of our human experience. To cling to people solely for history's sake is to suppress our growth and limit our potential, both individually and collectively. We must learn to gracefully let go of those relationships that no longer serve our evolution, cherishing the memories and lessons they offered, while opening ourselves to new connections and opportunities for growth.

Furthermore, holding onto relationships just for history's sake can prevent us from growing and evolving as individuals. We may feel that we need to stay in these relationships because of the history we share, even if they are no longer serving us or making us happy. This can cause us to feel trapped and unfulfilled.

It's important to remember that just because a relationship has a long history, it doesn't necessarily mean it's a healthy or positive relationship. We should evaluate our relationships based on how they make us feel in the present moment, not just based on our shared past.

The art of letting go is not an easy one, but it is an essential skill for a fulfilling and dynamic life. We must learn to embrace the temporariness of our relationships, recognizing that just as the river of life ebbs and flows, so too do the people who share our journey. By releasing those who no longer serve us, we create space for new connections, growth, and transformation.

In the dance of life, it is not the stability of our partners that defines our experience, but rather the fluidity of our movements and our willingness to embrace change and growth that truly sets us free.

— DAY 112 —

Emotions triumphs logic in relationships

Y OU know that feeling when you're just drawn to someone, and you can't put your finger on why? It's like a magnetic pull, and no matter how hard you try to rationalize it, the attraction remains. That's the thing about relationships; they're full of emotions that seem to defy logic. And yet, despite their central role in our lives, relationships are often characterized by a puzzling paradox: emotions, the driving force behind them, frequently defy logic.

From a young age, many of us are trained to prize logic over emotion, to see it as the compass guiding our decisions. The rationale, we are told, is safe. It is predictable. It provides order in the middle of the chaos. While true, this mindset may lead us off track when we enter the unclear domain of relationships. Our hearts, it appears, hold a language that our minds struggle to comprehend.

Love, passion, and intimate connections, the core of relationships, are fueled not by logic but by emotions. Emotions, with their raw intensity and abstract, colorful hues, are the music that sets relationships in motion. They create a unique rhythm, forming an extraordinary dance between two souls. And, in this dance, logic fades into the background, a silent observer of the emotional tango.

Here's the thing: relationships are not mathematics, solvable with a clear formula or algorithm. They're an art form, abstract, open to interpretation, and often defying explanation. They demand vulnerability, courage, and the willingness to dive into the deep end of emotions. The heart's wisdom often sounds illogical to the rational mind. It whispers to us to embrace risk, to allow ourselves to fall in love, and to believe in connections that logic may dismiss as irrational. Yet, it is precisely these "illogical" decisions that often lead to our deepest experiences of love and connection.

Does this mean that logic is irrelevant in relationships? Absolutely not. Logic has its place. It serves as a balance, a grounding force. Yet, it must not be allowed to drown out the symphony of emotions. In the end, it is emotions, not logic, that truly nourish and sustain our relationships.

— DAY 113 —

Age doesn't equate to wisdom

THE world often leads us to believe that age and wisdom go hand in hand, that as we grow older, our understanding of life deepens, and we become wiser. But is this idea truly valid? While it's true that age may afford us more life experiences, it's important to recognize that wisdom is not an automatic outcome of living through countless days and years.

Consider the various individuals we encounter in life—the elderly neighbor who shares stories of their youth, seemingly packed with wisdom, and the young prodigy who challenges conventional thinking with their innate understanding of complex concepts. These examples beg the question: Can we genuinely attribute wisdom to age alone?

The reality is that wisdom is a product of our ability to learn from our experiences, evaluate our actions, and adapt accordingly, regardless of our age. A young person with a curious mind and a desire for growth can be just as wise as someone who has lived through multiple decades. On the other hand, an older person who clings to outdated beliefs and refuses to change may lack the wisdom we often expect from their years.

Wisdom is not a linear or one-dimensional concept. It is a multidimensional interplay of experience, self-awareness, and emotional intelligence. It's possible for someone to be wise in certain aspects of life while demonstrating naivety in others. We must acknowledge that age alone does not guarantee a profound understanding of the world around us.

Rather than assuming that age and wisdom are inseparable, let's focus on cultivating wisdom through continuous learning, embracing personal growth, and valuing diverse perspectives. Wisdom can be found in individuals of all ages, and recognizing this can lead to more meaningful connections and a richer understanding of life.

Wisdom is not solely the domain of the aged. It is a product of how we choose to engage with our experiences, reflect on our actions, and empathize with others. Ultimately, it is not the number of years we've lived that defines our wisdom, but the depth of our understanding and the richness of our experiences.

— DAY 114 —

You can't please everyone

I N in a world driven by social approval and the desire to fit in, it's easy to get caught up in the endless pursuit of trying to please everyone.

As we navigate through life, we encounter countless individuals with diverse backgrounds, beliefs, and expectations. Each person we meet possesses their own unique set of values, shaped by their experiences and perspectives. You see, we live in a beautiful, vibrant, incredibly diverse world. Each of us carries a bundle of thoughts, beliefs, and preferences shaped by countless unique experiences. It's this wild diversity that makes our world so rich and fascinating. But it also means we're bound to cross paths with folks who simply won't see things the way we do, no matter how hard we try.

Now, I know what you're thinking: "But I want to be liked! I don't want any trouble!" Trust me, I get it. But let's consider what trying to please everyone truly entails. Imagine forming yourself into a different shape for every person you meet. Not only would it be exhausting, but you'd also lose sight of who you truly are in the process. Every "Yes" uttered to avoid conflict, every opinion silenced to fit in, takes away a bit of your authenticity, bit by bit. To be liked by all is to be genuinely loved by none.

Instead, let's focus on being true to ourselves, shall we? Because at the end of the day, pleasing everyone is like trying to catch all the stars in the sky—impossible and, quite frankly, not that useful. What matters more is being that one star, shining in its unique way.

Here's the bottom line. It's high time we stop fretting about winning everyone's approval. Instead, let's aim to respect ourselves, our values, and our unique perspectives. After all, you're the protagonist of your own story. Why waste time trying to fit into someone else's narrative?

Remember, it's okay to not please everyone. It's better to be true to yourself and let the right people appreciate you for who you truly are. So, let's celebrate our unique selves and let go of the impossible task of pleasing everyone. Because, in reality, the one person you should work hard to please is the one who stares back at you in the mirror every day.

— DAY 115 —

Better to be alone than in bad company

WE often find ourselves surrounded by a sea of faces, constantly seeking connections and companionship. We hunger for meaningful relationships, for bonds that lift us up and bring joy to our lives. In an era where our lives are often judged by the number of connections we have, this phrase offers a different perspective, emphasizing quality over quantity. Let's reflect on this a bit more.

We live in an era where the fear of being alone drives us to settle for toxic relationships. We cling to the familiarity of companionship, even if it means sacrificing our happiness and peace of mind. But here's the truth: solitude can be a powerful teacher. It is in the moments of being alone that we truly discover ourselves, our values, and our dreams.

Choosing solitude over bad company requires courage. It requires the willingness to walk away from toxic relationships, no matter how comfortable or familiar they may be. It means valuing our own well-being above the fear of being alone. It is a conscious decision to prioritize self-respect and self-love.

Being alone allows us the opportunity to explore our passions, to pursue our dreams without compromise. It is a time of self-discovery and growth, where we can nurture our own interests and cultivate a deep sense of self. We learn to rely on our own strength and resilience, becoming our own best friend.

In the solitude of our own company, we have the space to reflect, heal, and build a foundation of self-worth. We learn to set boundaries and surround ourselves with people who uplift and inspire us. We become more discerning about the energy we allow into our lives, realizing that our well-being is too precious to be compromised.

But let us not mistake solitude for loneliness, my friend. Solitude is a conscious choice, a refuge from the noise of the world. It is an opportunity to connect with our innermost selves, nourish our souls, and find satisfaction within.

It's not about isolating yourself from the world. It's about choosing relationships that lift you up, inspire you, and bring out the best in you. It's your life, your peace, and your happiness. Choose wisely.

— DAY 116 —

Maturity is choosing peace over argument

HAVE you ever found yourself in the middle of a heated argument, feeling the heat rise within you, your heart pounding, and your mind racing with a million thoughts and counter-arguments? It's in these moments that we truly understand the value of maturity and the power of choosing peace over engaging in endless arguments.

Maturity is not about being right all the time or proving your point at any cost. It's about recognizing that peace is more important than winning an argument. It's about understanding that arguments often lead to more conflict and damage than resolution. So, instead of getting caught up in the cycle of endless debates, a mature person knows when to step back and choose a different path.

Choosing peace over argument requires immense self-control and emotional intelligence. It's about being able to regulate your emotions and approach conflicts with a calm and rational mindset. It's about realizing that there is a time and place for discussions, but sometimes, it's better to let go and maintain harmony rather than fueling the fire of discord.

In a world filled with noise and opinions, choosing peace is a rare and courageous act. It takes strength to resist the urge to engage in arguments, to let go of the need to prove yourself right, and to prioritize the well-being of the relationship over being "right."

Maturity is not about avoiding difficult conversations or suppressing our thoughts and opinions. It's about choosing the right time, place, and approach to express ourselves. It's about realizing that not every disagreement needs to escalate into a full-blown argument, and that sometimes, the best way to communicate is through peaceful dialogue and active listening.

Choosing peace over argument is an act of wisdom and self-awareness. It allows us to preserve our relationships, maintain our mental well-being, and cultivate an atmosphere of respect and harmony. It is a reflection of our growth and understanding that true strength lies not in overpowering others with our words, but in fostering connection, empathy, and mutual understanding.

— DAY 117 —

One day or Day One

EVERY morning, as the sun rises, it's like the world is making a choice. Do we start on the dreams we've been talking about, or do we just talk a bit more? There are these two roads in front of us—one that's kind of foggy and leads off to a someday that never seems to come, and another that's right under our feet, waiting for us to take the first step.

The someday road is pretty comfortable. It's where we can imagine all the great stuff we're going to do without ever really getting started. We tell ourselves we've got all the time in the world, and so our big plans just stay plans. We think we're going to get around to it, but somehow we never do. It's like always planning the perfect party but never actually sending out the invites.

Then there's the road that starts right now. It's louder, messier, and a lot more real. This is where things begin. It's where you actually paint that picture, write that story, or play that tune you've been humming. Things don't always go smoothly, but that's part of the fun. The paint might go in the wrong spot, or the words might get mixed up, but that's how you end up making something nobody's ever seen or read or heard before.

Choosing to start now means we're okay with things not being perfect right off the bat. We know we might make a few wrong turns, but we also know that's how we learn and get better. It's in the doing and the trying that we start to see what we're really capable of.

When we look back, we realize it's not about when we get to the finish line but the fact that we decided to race at all. Each new day is a chance to say, "Here goes!" and dive into something—even if it's small.

In that moment of choosing to just begin, we find the real magic. That's when we move from dreaming to doing. It's not about waiting for everything to be perfect but about making a start, however simple, and seeing where it takes us. It's the real beginning of every adventure. And that's when we see that our stories don't start with a big bang or fanfare, but with the quiet determination to put one foot in front of the other and see where the path leads.

— DAY 118 —

Books are timeless sources of knowledge

J UST reflect upon it for a second. Isn't it fascinating that something as simple as a book, a collection of words bound together, can contain a universe within its covers?

Books aren't just about passing time or entertainment. They're much more than that. They're our gateways to different worlds, different times, and different minds. They allow us to engage in dialogue with the greatest thinkers, feel the emotions of fictional characters, or set out on journeys through realms beyond our wildest imagination. And isn't that simply extraordinary?

From the early days of mankind, when we first started painting our stories on cave walls, we've been on a relentless quest for knowledge and understanding. And books? Well, they're the fruits of that timeless quest. They're the distilled wisdom of generations, collected and preserved for future generations. They bridge the gap between the past and the present, letting us reach back in time to learn from our ancestors and project our knowledge into the future.

What makes a book truly magical is the unique experience it offers to each reader. It's like an intimate conversation, where the author speaks and the reader listens, but also responds with their interpretation, their emotions, their insights. It's this two-way interaction that makes each book a personal journey of discovery.

Even as our world races towards a digital future, where information is fleeting and often transient, books stand firm, holding their ground. They're like lighthouses in the storm, guiding us, and brightening our path. And the knowledge they hold? It's timeless, enduring, and ready to be discovered and rediscovered.

Let us turn their pages with admiration and gratitude, knowing that within them lie the keys to unlocking our potential and understanding the vast wonders of the world. Books are timeless, and in their pages, we find a treasure trove of wisdom that will continue to shape and enrich our lives for generations to come.

— DAY 119 —

Strive for excellence despite adversity

N OW, doesn't that get your gears grinding? It's an inspirational mantra for sure, but it's also so much more. It's an attitude, a philosophy, a lifestyle. Life has a curious way of testing our strength, doesn't it? Just when we think we have it all figured out, adversity comes knocking at our door, threatening to disrupt our plans and shatter our dreams.

Life has a funny way of throwing curveballs our way. Challenges, setbacks, and obstacles seem to pop up when we least expect them. But here's the thing: adversity doesn't define us. It's our response to adversity that truly matters. It's about how we choose to navigate those rocky roads and whether we allow them to throw us off course or become catalysts for growth.

When faced with adversity, it's natural to feel overwhelmed, discouraged, and even defeated. But let me tell you, those are the moments when our true strength and resilience shine through. It's during these times that we have the opportunity to dig deep within ourselves, tap into our inner well of determination, and push beyond our perceived limitations.

Striving for excellence despite adversity is about embracing the mindset of a warrior. It's about refusing to let circumstances define our potential or dictate our path. It's about taking that adversity and using it as fuel to ignite the fire of excellence within us.

You see, adversity has a way of revealing our true character. It's a test of our grit, determination, and steadfast belief in ourselves. When we face adversity head-on, we develop a resilience that can withstand the harshest storms.

Striving for excellence despite adversity isn't about being perfect or achieving some impossible standard. It's about giving our best, pushing our boundaries, and refusing to settle for mediocrity. It's about embracing the journey of growth and constantly seeking improvement, even when the odds seem stacked against us.

Remember, that adversity is not an endpoint. It's merely a chapter in our story—a chapter that we can use to shape our character and define our future. It's an opportunity to learn, adapt, and become better versions of ourselves.

—— DAY 120 ——

Health is true wealth

W HEN we think of wealth, we often think of financial prosperity—a large bank account, a luxurious lifestyle, and the ability to buy whatever we want. But in reality, true wealth goes far beyond financial assets. True wealth is about being healthy in body, mind, and spirit.

When we are healthy, we have the energy and vitality to pursue our goals and passions. We are able to enjoy the simple pleasures of life, like spending time with loved ones or going for a walk in nature. We are able to live life to the fullest and make the most of every moment.

But being healthy is not just about physical health. It also encompasses our mental and emotional well-being. When we have a positive mindset and a strong support system, we are able to navigate the ups and downs of life with greater ease and resilience. We are able to handle stress and adversity in healthy ways, rather than turning to unhealthy coping mechanisms.

Ultimately, health is true wealth because it allows us to live a life of purpose and meaning. When we are healthy, we are able to pursue our passions, connect with others, and make a positive impact on the world around us. We are able to contribute to society in meaningful ways and leave a legacy that will last long after we are gone.

Of course, achieving and maintaining good health is not always easy. It requires discipline, self-care, and a commitment to living a healthy lifestyle. This may mean eating a balanced diet, getting enough exercise, practicing stress management techniques like meditation or yoga, and seeking support when needed.

Some may argue that financial wealth is more important than health, while others may believe that health is a privilege and that not everyone has equal access to it. But the rewards of good health are well worth the effort. By prioritizing our health, we are able to live a life of true wealth, filled with joy, purpose, and fulfillment. Confucius said "A healthy man wants a thousand things, a sick man only wants one."

— DAY 121 —

Online presence masks real-life loneliness

I N today's hyperconnected world, the increase of social media platforms and digital communication tools has transformed the landscape of human interaction. With the touch of a button, we can connect with friends and strangers alike, sharing snippets of our lives and engaging in virtual conversations that span the globe. Yet, beneath the sparkling facade of our online presence, there lurks a dark reality that is all too often overlooked: real-life loneliness.

The paradox of our digital age lies in the fact that while we are more connected than ever before, we are also becoming increasingly isolated from the genuine, face-to-face interactions that nourish the human spirit. Our online personas, carefully curated and polished to perfection, can mask the profound loneliness that many of us experience in our daily lives. We can accumulate thousands of followers, receive countless "likes" and "shares," and still feel a deep sense of disconnection and isolation from those around us.

This phenomenon can be attributed, in part, to the superficial nature of many online interactions. Social media platforms encourage a culture of comparison, where we are constantly bombarded with images of others' seemingly perfect lives, fueling feelings of insufficiency and self-doubt. Moreover, the fleeting nature of digital communication often lacks the depth and substance that characterize genuine, in-person connections, leaving us craving for more authentic and meaningful relationships.

The irony of our online presence masking real-life loneliness serves as a touching reminder of the importance of cultivating genuine human connections in an increasingly digital world. While social media and digital communication tools can provide valuable opportunities for networking and staying in touch, they should not be a substitute for the deep, nourishing relationships that are forged through face-to-face interactions.

In essence, our online presence is a tool, a conduit, a digital meeting space, but it's in our offline world where life, in all its rawness and authenticity, truly happens. Recognizing and navigating this delicate balance might be one of our generation's greatest challenges, and perhaps, its most important triumph.

— DAY 122 —

The joy of giving is priceless

ISN'T it funny how we often think that the more we accumulate, the happier we'll be? We chase after wealth, power, and possessions, thinking they'll fill the void. However, there's a secret to genuine happiness that often lies unnoticed, like an unopened gift. It is the joy of giving, an act so profound and yet so simple that it can light up even the darkest corners of our existence with its inherent grace.

Let me tell you, giving is an experience like no other. There's something magical about reaching out of our own little worlds and connecting with someone else, not because we want something in return, but purely out of kindness. It's almost like we're proving to ourselves that we can be bigger, better, and more compassionate. And when you see the joy or relief on someone else's face—that's a reward money can't buy.

I'm not just talking about giving in terms of material things. Sure, presents and donations are great. But have you ever considered the value of giving your time, your empathy, or your experience? Sometimes, even a patient ear or a comforting silence can mean more than anything money can buy. There's a certain warmth that comes from knowing you've touched someone's life in a meaningful way—you've made their day brighter, their load lighter, and their path a little less lonely.

The beautiful thing is that giving isn't some grand event that we should reserve for special occasions. It's more like a lifestyle, an attitude. It's not about the size or value of what we give, but the love and sincerity behind it. A simple, genuine act of kindness can send ripples of positivity that reach farther than we could ever imagine.

So why not take a chance on giving? Try it out. Extend a helping hand, share a smile, lend your time, or offer your expertise. Witness how these acts of kindness light up someone else's world, and in the process, your own.

Giving is a joy that's truly priceless. It's like a mirror that reflects the best in us and the best in humanity. So let's embrace the art of giving and watch as it transforms not just the world around us, but also our very hearts and souls.

— DAY 123 —

Life is an unchosen game

HOW fascinating it is to consider life as an unchosen game, a complex dance of decision and consequence, choice, and outcome. None of us applied for our birth, for our existence, but here we are, partaking in the most complex, challenging, and fascinating game of all time.

Life, in its essence, seems to echo the structure of a game. Each of us is handed a set of cards—our genes, our environment, the historical and cultural context into which we're born—none of which we have chosen. And yet, like seasoned card players, we are expected to play our hand as best we can.

Our initial setup—the family we're born into, the town we grew up in, the color of our skin, and the socio-economic conditions of our upbringing—these are similar to the shuffled deck of cards distributed at the beginning of a game. We don't choose them, but they establish our starting position in this grand game of life.

However, the fascinating part about life is that despite its seeming randomness, it also offers us the ability to affect the trajectory of our game. Our ability to strategize, make choices, and decide how we react to our circumstances, grants us a certain level of power and control. We might not have chosen the game, or even the rules by which it's played, but we can choose how we engage with it.

That's where the real power lies. We can't choose the hand we're dealt, but we can choose how we play it. We can choose to fold, or we can choose to stay in the game, using our cleverness, determination, and passion to transform even the worst hand into a winning game.

Life's unchosen nature might seem overwhelming, even unfair at times. But there is something inherently beautiful and liberating in the realization that while we don't have control over everything, we can still influence the direction and quality of our lives through our choices, actions, and attitudes.

So, step back, see the board, understand your pieces, and learn the rules. Embrace the unchosen game of life. Play it with courage, wisdom, and a touch of daring. It's not just about winning or losing—it's about the journey.

— DAY 124 —

The universe has a way of restoring balance

LIFE often throws us off balance. We experience moments of triumph and moments of defeat, times of joy and times of sorrow. It is during these chaotic times that we question the fairness of it all. We wonder why some suffer while others succeed, why the world can seem so unbalanced. Yet, if we look closely, we can find solace in the realization that the universe has an inherent tendency to restore equilibrium.

Consider the planets, spinning on their axes, and hurtling around the sun in elliptical orbits. Their rotations and revolutions maintain a universal equilibrium that prevents catastrophic collisions. Gravity pulls them inward, while their orbital speed attempts to fling them outward, and yet, in this push and pull, the planets stay their course.

Now, let's bring it back home. Consider our Earth, with its carefully regulated ecosystems. Predators and prey, flora, and fauna, all contribute to maintaining an ecological balance. When one species expands, another counters it, keeping the ecosystem in check. Nature, in its silent wisdom, ensures the continuity of life by restoring balance when it's disturbed.

Take it even closer to home—your body, a complex system that constantly strives for balance. This internal equilibrium, known as homeostasis, regulates everything from your body temperature to your blood sugar levels, heart rate to hormone levels. The ceaseless work of millions of cells, performing a harmonious symphony, so that you may function optimally.

But the balance goes beyond the physical realm. It reaches into the realms of our mind and soul. Moments of joy are balanced by periods of sadness. Effort balances ease. Every surge of joy is balanced by a dip of reflection, the universal scales tipping back and forth, an eternal dance of duality.

The universe whispers a universal secret—it is all about balance. Everything we know, everything we are, and everything we experience is an endless quest for equilibrium. The universe itself is a giant balancing act, and we are but tiny dancers on its broad stage, falling and rising.

— DAY 125 —

Don't let others' poor decisions steal your peace

L IFE is filled with countless moments when people make choices that may not align with our values or expectations. It could be a friend who betrays our trust, a coworker who takes credit for our work, or a loved one who repeatedly makes harmful decisions. It's natural to feel disappointed or angry in such situations, but it's important not to let those emotions consume us.

The essence of the human experience is deeply interconnected with relationships. We interact, influence, and are in turn affected by others' choices. Now, when those choices are unwise, harmful, or downright detrimental, they act as ripples, disturbing our calm waters. However, let's take a step back and ask: Do they have to?

Here's where we delve into the realm of our minds. We can't control others' decisions. Just as the sun will rise and set, people will continue to make poor choices. This is an undeniable part of the human experience. What we can control, though, is our response to these decisions.

Our peace, my friend, is our sanctuary. It's a sacred space within us, a place of calm and resilience that allows us to navigate life's complexities with grace. When we allow others' poor decisions to penetrate this sanctuary, we surrender control of our emotional well-being. The key word here is "allow."

Imagine yourself as a mountain, strong and immovable. Let the poor decisions of others be like the winds that brush against you, but fail to shake your core. Maintaining this emotional steadfastness doesn't imply indifference or apathy.

The reality is, that there will always be storms, but remember, storms are temporary while the mountain endures. Like the mountain, we can weather any storm, remaining unshaken by the poor decisions of others. We can acknowledge and learn from them, but refuse to let them steal our peace.

To sum it up, don't give away your power. Hold on to your peace with tenacity. It's a precious entity, your shield in the chaotic battlefield of life. Stand tall like the mountain, let the winds of poor decisions blow, and watch as they eventually lose power, leaving your peace untouched.

— DAY 126 —

Life is a choice between comfort and growth

L IFE presents us with a fundamental choice: to remain in the cozy confines of our comfort zone or to embrace the thrilling path of growth. It is a choice that shapes our experiences, shapes our character, and determines the trajectory of our lives. Each day, we stand at the crossroads, faced with the decision to settle for what is familiar or to venture into the unknown. Life, it seems, is an everlasting dance between comfort and growth.

Life is kind of like being a comfy, snuggled-up caterpillar. There's a certain appeal to staying wrapped up in your leaf, munching away, watching the world pass by. But there's also that nagging whisper in the back of your mind, an inkling that there's more to life than your leaf.

I mean, sure, that leaf is safe. It's predictable. But it's also, dull. Because let's face it, staying in your comfort zone is a one-way ticket to stagnation. You're safe from the outside world, yeah, but you're also insulated from all the amazing things that could happen if you just took that leap of faith, if you just pushed beyond those comfortable boundaries.

That's where growth comes into play. Think back to that caterpillar. There comes a time when it just knows—it's gotta break out of its comfort zone. It's got to give up its leafy bed, wrap itself in a chrysalis, and undergo that painstaking transformation into a butterfly. Scary? Absolutely. But the reward is a life more colorful, more extraordinary than it could ever have imagined.

Now, let's snap back to us humans. Like that caterpillar, we too have our chrysalises. They're the challenges we face, the risks we take. It's in these trying moments that we stretch ourselves, that we discover what we're really made of. They're uncomfortable, yes, but they're also opportunities to grow, to transform into our own versions of a butterfly.

So there it is, my friend. Life is indeed a choice between comfort and growth. It's up to you to decide whether to stay wrapped in your leaf or to embrace the discomfort that comes with transforming into something beautiful. Remember, though, it's in the discomfort where the magic happens. After all, aren't we all just caterpillars waiting to become butterflies?

— DAY 127 —

Don't mock what others can't change

UPON the vast canvas of humanity, a breathtaking array of colors and patterns emerge, weaving a complex tapestry of individuality. We are all unique individuals, shaped by a multitude of factors that are beyond our control.

We live in a world where people are often ridiculed or bullied for things that are beyond their control. It could be their physical appearance, their ethnicity, their sexual orientation, their disabilities, or any other aspect of their being that makes them different from others. We must learn to celebrate differences and recognize the beauty in diversity.

Laughter and humor are undeniably captivating, but they can also be wielded as weapons of mockery and pain. When we target the unchangeable characteristics of others, we not only foster insecurity and isolation but also sustain a cycle of intolerance among non-participating observers.

When was the last time you or someone you know made fun of someone else's accent, height, or maybe a unique birthmark? Maybe it seemed harmless, just a passing joke, but have you ever considered the impact it might have on the person at the receiving end?

You see, when we mock what someone can't change, we're belittling a fundamental part of their identity. It's similar to trapping them in a cage, with their unique attribute becoming the bars. This cage obstructs their view, restricts their movement, and transforms their attribute from something unique to a source of embarrassment or insecurity. And that's a bitter pill to swallow.

Everyone carries a sense of pride in their identity. When we disrespect that, we're not just crossing a line; we're sabotaging a person's perception of self. They might start questioning their worth, doubting their abilities, and spiraling down the path of self-loathing.

On the other hand, imagine a world where instead of mockery, we embraced acceptance. Where every unique trait is celebrated, where our differences become the threads that weave the fabric of our society stronger, richer, and more vibrant. What an extraordinary life we would be part of.

— DAY 128 —

Talk or discard?

WITHIN the complex web of human communication, the decision to ask, talk, or discard holds profound influence, often serving as a spark for either growth or conflict. To comprehend this phenomenon's complexities, one must delve into the essence of human connection, examining the interplay between ego, empathy, and understanding that weaves our interactions together.

The core of every conversation lies in the inherent human need to articulate and grasp experiences, thoughts, and emotions. Nevertheless, it is within this realm that the threat of escalation arises, as individuals grapple with the delicate balance of self-preservation and openness. A misplaced word or silent emotion can shatter the facade of comprehension, spiraling the dialogue into a vortex of tension and strife. In this context, the choice to ask, talk, or discard emerges as a crucial factor, swaying between progress and discord.

The act of inquiring embodies an elemental vulnerability, a readiness to face the unknown and delve into the shadowy depths of another's mind. To ask is to open oneself to the possibilities of change, growth, and connection. Paradoxically, it also exposes one to the risk of misunderstanding, pain, and disconnection. The beauty and peril of inquiry lie in its transformative potential, capable of forging enduring bonds or permanently severing them.

Conversing, on the other hand, is an intricate dance of exposing and covering, a fluid interplay of viewpoints and emotions that simultaneously unites and divides. To engage in dialogue is to navigate the labyrinth of human experience, traversing the chasm between collective understanding and insurmountable differences.

Communication is a powerful force that can lead to either growth or conflict, depending on how we choose to navigate its complexities. The delicate balance between asking, talking, and discarding determines the outcome of our interactions. By being mindful of these choices and approaching them with empathy and understanding, we can avoid escalation and foster richer, more profound connections with those around us.

— DAY 129 —

Nonverbal cues define confidence

NONVERBAL cues are the unsung heroes of effective communication. They are the subtle signals that we transmit through our body language, facial expressions, and behavior. And when it comes to confidence, these cues play a pivotal role in shaping how others perceive us.

When we encounter someone who stands tall, with their shoulders back and head held high, we instinctively interpret them as confident. Their posture conveys a sense of confidence, even before they utter a single word. On the other hand, someone slouched, avoiding eye contact, and fidgeting betrays a lack of confidence.

But it doesn't stop there. Our facial expressions also speak volumes about our confidence. A genuine smile, accompanied by relaxed facial muscles, communicates a sense of ease and assurance. Conversely, a wrinkled forehead or tense jawline can give off an impression of anxiety or self-doubt.

The power of nonverbal cues goes beyond body language and facial expressions. It extends to the tone of our voice, the way we make eye contact, and even our hand gestures. Confident individuals often speak with clarity and conviction, using a tone that resonates with authority and certainty. They maintain steady eye contact, establishing a connection and displaying attentiveness. And their gestures are purposeful and controlled, emphasizing their points with finesse.

Let's be mindful of our body language, facial expressions, and the way we carry ourselves. Let's stand tall, maintain eye contact, and speak with conviction. As we align our nonverbal cues with confidence, we'll find that we not only influence how others perceive us but also how we perceive ourselves.

Confidence is a language that extends beyond words. It is conveyed through the unspoken messages we transmit to the world. So, let's harness the power of nonverbal cues and let our confidence shine. Remember, the way we carry ourselves speaks volumes, and by embracing our nonverbal cues, we can define and radiate true confidence in every aspect of our lives.

— DAY 130 —

True wealth lies in yourself

IN a world driven by consumerism and the pursuit of material gain, it's easy to get caught up in the belief that wealth is measured by the size of our bank accounts or the possessions we accumulate. But if we take a step back and reflect, we'll discover that the richest treasures are not found in our possessions, but in the depths of our being.

True wealth begins with self-discovery. It's about understanding who we are at our core—our values, passions, and dreams. It's about nurturing our mental, emotional, and spiritual well-being. When we invest in ourselves, we unlock a wealth that cannot be quantified by external standards.

Think about it: true wealth is having a sense of purpose—a deep knowing that our lives have meaning and that we are making a positive impact on the world. It's the fulfillment we feel when we align our actions with our values and contribute to something greater than ourselves.

True wealth is also about relationships—the connections we forge with others. It's the love and support we give and receive, the joy of shared experiences, and the comfort of knowing we have a community of people who genuinely care for us. It's the wealth of laughter, companionship, and emotional bonds that enrich our lives.

And let's not forget about personal growth. True wealth is the continuous journey of self-improvement, of expanding our knowledge, skills, and perspectives. It's about embracing challenges and embracing the discomfort of growth. It's the wealth that comes from constantly evolving, learning, and becoming the best version of ourselves.

When we focus solely on external wealth, we can easily fall into the trap of never feeling satisfied, always craving more. But when we shift our perspective and recognize that true wealth lies within, we find contentment and gratitude for what we already have. This perspective radically shifts the way we view wealth. It becomes less about accumulation and more about self-realization. When we understand that our true wealth lies within us, it's like discovering an unending source of abundance.

— DAY 131 —

Take ownership of your life and actions

L IFE is not a passive journey. It's not about waiting for things to happen or blaming external circumstances for our successes or failures. Life is an active, participatory experience, and it's up to each one of us to take ownership and responsibility for the choices we make and the actions we take.

Taking ownership means recognizing that you are the captain of your own ship. You hold the power to navigate the waters of life and chart your course. It's about embracing the idea that your life is your canvas, and you are the artist. Every brushstroke, every decision, and every action is an opportunity to create something extraordinary.

Consider your life as a novel, with you as its author. Each decision, each action is a sentence, contributing to the grand narrative that is your life. As the author, you can't control every circumstance, just as you can't control the weather in your story. Still, you can control your characters' responses, just as you control your own reactions and choices.

Ownership is about acknowledging this power and recognizing our decisions' consequences. Every action we take, every decision we make, weaves another thread into the tapestry of our existence. When we acknowledge this, we see our past not as a series of events that happened to us, but as an epic tale of our own making.

Furthermore, ownership brings accountability. It's easy to blame circumstances or others when things go wrong. But true growth blooms from the soil of personal responsibility. When we recognize that we played a part in our successes and failures, we unearth profound lessons that push us forward.

Owning our actions liberates us from the cycle of blame and empowers us to effect change. The script of your life doesn't lie in someone else's hands; it's held in yours. You're not a puppet in life's theatre but the puppeteer.

Seize your pen, my friend. Take ownership of your narrative. Ownership isn't a burden; it's a gift. It's the key to an autonomous, fulfilled life. Now, isn't that something worth striving for?

— DAY 132 —

Emotions are poor guides for decisions

HAVE you ever found yourself making decisions based solely on your emotions, only to regret them later? It's a common occurrence. While they are a crucial part of our human experience, relying solely on them can lead us off course.

Emotions are powerful forces that shape our perceptions and influence our actions. They can range from joy and love to anger and fear, and everything in between. When we make decisions based solely on our emotional state, we run the risk of clouding our judgment and overlooking important factors.

Here's why: emotions are fleeting and subjective. They can fluctuate based on various factors, such as our current circumstances, past experiences, or even our physical well-being. What we feel in a particular moment may not align with what is truly in our best interest in the long run.

Consider a situation where you're tempted to make an impulsive purchase because it brings you temporary excitement and happiness. In that moment, your emotions may be urging you to go for it. However, taking a step back and objectively evaluating the decision, considering factors like your financial situation, long-term goals, and whether the purchase aligns with your values, may reveal a different perspective.

Emotions can also be influenced by biases, prejudices, or limited information. They can lead us to make decisions based on preconceived notions or snap judgments, rather than taking the time to gather all the relevant facts and consider different perspectives. This can result in hasty or irrational choices that we may come to regret.

That's not to say that emotions should be ignored entirely. Emotions provide valuable insights into our values, desires, and intuition. They can serve as a compass, guiding us to what truly matters to us.

In a nutshell, it's all about balance. Let your emotions fuel your passion, but invite logic to the party when it's time to make decisions. That's how we navigate the complex journey of life without getting lost in the enchanting, but often misleading, forest of emotions.

— DAY 133 —

Unexpressed emotions will never die

IMAGINE walking through life carrying a backpack filled with stones. Each stone represents an emotion you've decided not to express. Love not confessed, grief not mourned, anger not acknowledged—they all find a place in your growing collection. Over time, this backpack becomes heavier, a constant burden you carry, not because you can't set it down, but because you've chosen to keep it zipped tight, convinced that ignoring it is the same as dealing with it.

Those emotions? They're alive. They breathe, they grow, they demand to be felt and acknowledged. Ignoring them doesn't make them disappear; it makes them stronger, louder, more insistent. They're like seeds planted in the fertile ground of your silence, waiting for the right moment to break through the surface and show themselves to the world.

This hidden emotional garden can become both a prison and a sanctuary. It's a place where unspoken words accumulate like debt, where the echoes of what could have been, should have been, or never was, stay like ghosts in the attic of your mind. They can haunt you, or they can teach you. The choice, as daunting as it may seem, is yours.

The beauty of this dilemma is that these emotions, when finally expressed, can transform. They can morph from heavy stones into birds, taking flight the moment you decide to open the backpack and let them out. This act of liberation isn't just about unburdening yourself; it's about honoring your feelings, giving them the space to exist outside the confines of your inner world.

Expressing these emotions doesn't mean they cease to exist. Rather, it means they evolve from silent shadows into articulated experiences, contributing to the mosaic of who you are. It's a process of turning inward, of listening to the whispers and roars within, and then turning outward to share your inner landscape with the world.

Consider this an invitation to unpack your emotional backpack, hold each stone in your hand, and decide which birds you're ready to set free. In doing so, you may just find that the weight you've been carrying has been the key to unlocking a more authentic, vibrant version of yourself all along.

— DAY 134 —

Money can amplify your impact and influence

T HIS simple phrase resonates deeply, encompassing a deep truth about the interplay of wealth, power, and effect. Money, that intangible entity, pursued by many, and possessed by few, serves not only as a means for survival but also as a tool that when wielded appropriately, can change the course of lives, communities, and even the world.

We exist in a society where our reach, our voice, and our very influence can be largely determined by our economic standing. Consider philanthropy, the act of giving back on a large scale. It is through financial means that individuals, foundations, and corporations can effect monumental change, whether by funding research that leads to lifesaving medical advances, supporting the arts and preserving our shared cultural heritage, or contributing to causes that protect our planet for future generations.

Yet, while the transformative power of wealth cannot be overlooked, it's crucial to acknowledge that money is not inherently good or evil. Instead, its impact is shaped by those who hold it. Like a loudspeaker, it amplifies the intentions of its possessor, be they compassionate or evil-minded.

Furthermore, it's important to recognize the difference between impact and influence. Impact is the tangible change one can effect in the world, the ripple effect of our actions. Influence, on the other hand, is the power to shape perspectives, to inspire thought and action in others. Money can certainly bolster both, but it is the individual at the helm who determines the direction.

Money is a tool, an amplifier that can exponentially increase our ability to make a difference and sway the course of events. However, it is not the sole determinant of impact and influence. These are also born from values, resilience, empathy, and the courageous belief that one can indeed ignite change. Money can amplify, but the tune it magnifies is composed by the heart and mind of its wielder.

So yes, money can amplify your impact and influence. But let's not forget the true source of the music. It's you, your actions, and your intentions. That's where the real magic happens.

— DAY 135 —

Cut ties with those who drain you

L ET'S talk about something we've all been through: relationships. I'm not just talking romance here; friendships, work relationships, you name it. It's a powerful concept that can bring about significant positive change in your life. When you have the courage to let go of toxic relationships, you create space for growth, happiness, and inner peace.

Imagine the tree having the power to choose, to deny the vine its stranglehold. This is exactly the kind of power we possess when it comes to relationships that diminish us, rather than uplift us. It's a power many of us are unaware of or hesitant to use—the power to cut ties with those who drain us.

Life is an extraordinary journey of self-discovery and growth. Along the way, we cross paths with a variety of individuals, some who light our path, while others cloud it. As we evolve, it becomes essential to surround ourselves with positivity, to be with people who fuel our ambitions, understand our flaws, and encourage our dreams. Yet, often we get entangled in relationships that offer no such support. These are the relationships that feel heavy, that leave us feeling smaller, sadder, or angrier.

Keeping tied to these draining entities is like volunteering to drown. It's like choosing to remain stuck in the same circle, preventing us from moving forward. It's detrimental not just to our mental health but also to our growth as individuals. We must recognize this pattern and find the courage to sever these ties.

Cutting ties doesn't mean you hold resentment or anger; it means you value your peace over the turbulent relationship.

It's essential to remember that like the tree, you too, have the right to thrive without the burden of draining relationships. You deserve to bask in the sun, to grow and spread your branches wide without the weight of a parasite. Cut ties with those who drain you. Choose growth over comfort, choose yourself over the exhausting need to please everyone else.

In the end, your life is about you, your journey, and your growth. Don't let it be overshadowed by those who drain you.

— DAY 136 —

The mind is like an iceberg

D IVE into the depths of human consciousness, and you'll find a world as mysterious and vast as the ocean itself. At the surface, our thoughts and actions might seem straightforward, but what lies beneath is a complex labyrinth of emotions, memories, and dreams, much like an iceberg floating in the sea. What we see above the water is only a fraction of its true mass; similarly, the conscious mind is just a small part of our psychological universe.

Consider the story of an accomplished musician. Onstage, her performance is flawless, each note played with precision and grace. Yet, the audience sees only the result of countless hours of practice and years of emotional struggles, failures, and triumphs that have shaped her artistry. The visible performance is just the tip of her vast, submerged world of dedication and passion.

Or think about an athlete whose physical prowess astonishes spectators. His abilities seem almost superhuman, but hidden beneath this visible excellence is a mental landscape filled with discipline, fear, ambition, and the psychological scars of past injuries and defeats. His achievements are not just a display of physical strength but a peak rising out of deep mental and emotional foundations.

In daily life, too, our interactions often skim the surface of a deeper reality. A simple smile might mask a whirlwind of anxiety, or a casual comment might stem from a deep-seated belief or experience. The mind, with its untold stories and hidden drives, operates beneath the waterline, steering the course of our lives in ways we might not even be aware of.

Understanding this, psychologists and therapists work like deep-sea divers, venturing into the depths to help bring some of that hidden world into the light. Through their work, we learn that by exploring our inner depths, we can begin to navigate our lives with greater awareness and purpose.

The challenge, then, is not to live as though we are only the tip of the iceberg but to acknowledge and explore the vastness beneath. In the vast, uncharted waters of the psyche, the journey of self-discovery awaits.

— DAY 137 —

Master money, or suffer from it later

J UST let that sink in for a moment. It paints a vivid picture, making you either the master or the victim of your financial decisions.

Money is a tool that allows us to fulfill our needs, pursue our dreams, and create a life rich in blessings. But here's the truth that often gets overlooked: money is a double-edged sword. If we fail to master it, we risk falling into a cycle of financial stress, missed opportunities, and unfulfilled aspirations.

Mastering money begins with understanding its value. It's about cultivating a healthy relationship with money and recognizing its role as a means to an end, rather than an end in itself. When we view money as a tool to support our goals and values, we gain a sense of empowerment and control over our financial lives.

But mastering money goes beyond earning and saving. It involves making informed decisions about spending, investing, and giving. It requires financial literacy, the ability to manage our resources effectively, and the willingness to prioritize our long-term financial well-being over short-term gratification.

When we master money, we create a solid foundation for our future. We are better equipped to weather financial storms, take advantage of opportunities, and pursue our passions. Financial security brings peace of mind and the freedom to make choices aligned with our values, rather than being driven solely by financial constraints.

On the other hand, neglecting to master money can lead to regret and a sense of missed opportunities. Living beyond our means, accumulating debt, or failing to plan for the future can limit our options and hinder our ability to live the life we desire. It's a hard lesson to learn when we realize that our financial choices have put us at a disadvantage.

This is your wake-up call. Take it seriously because, trust me, you don't want to find yourself on the other side of this coin, living a life of regret. Instead, arm yourself with knowledge, make wise decisions, and master your money. It's time to take control.

— DAY 138 —

Take risks and live without regret

L IFE, my dear friend, isn't designed to be a flat-line monotony. It's an intricate and thrilling rollercoaster, a series of highs and lows, twists and turns that make our hearts pound and minds spin. It's precisely the element of uncertainty, the taste of the unknown that gives it its flavor. As we navigate this incredible adventure, one thing becomes clear: taking risks and living without regret is the key to unlocking a life of true fulfillment.

Imagine a life without regrets, where you boldly pursue your dreams, seize opportunities, and push past the boundaries of what you thought was possible. This is the life that awaits those who are willing to take risks.

Taking risks is not about being reckless or impulsive. It's about acknowledging that growth, success, and fulfillment lie on the other side of fear. It's about mustering the courage to step into the unknown, challenge ourselves, and embrace the lessons that come with both success and failure.

When we take risks, we open ourselves up to new experiences, perspectives, and opportunities. We discover our true potential and the depth of our resilience. We learn that setbacks are not failures, but rather stepping stones on the path to success. And most importantly, we discover that regret stems not from the mistakes we make, but from the chances we didn't take.

Living without regret means embracing vulnerability and being open to the possibilities that come our way. It means pursuing our passions, even when they seem unconventional or uncertain. It means saying "Yes" to opportunities that excite us, even if they come with a dose of fear and uncertainty.

Regret often stems from the "what ifs" and the missed chances. It's a haunting feeling that reminds us of the dreams left unfulfilled and the untaken paths.

I say to you, embrace risks. See them not as fearsome monsters, but as powerful catalysts of growth and transformation. Venture forth boldly into the arena of life, armed with courage and lit with passion. You may stumble, you may fall, but you'll rise again, stronger and wiser. And when you look back, you'll have a life speckled with vivid memories, rich experiences, and zero regrets.

— DAY 139 —

Your speech patterns shape your credibility

EVERY time we engage in conversation, we are composing a rich narrative of words that reflects our character and competence. The way we express ourselves, the clarity of our thoughts, and the confidence with which we speak all contribute to our credibility. Our speech patterns hold the potential to either enhance or undermine our authority and influence.

Consider the difference between someone who stammers and struggles to find the right words and someone who speaks clearly and with precision. The latter instills confidence and commands attention, while the former may be perceived as uncertain or lacking in expertise. Our speech patterns, whether fluid or fragmented, carry profound implications for how we are perceived.

The insightful part is recognizing that our speech patterns are not fixed but can be improved with conscious effort. By paying attention to the way we communicate, we can refine our delivery, enhance our credibility, and elevate our ability to connect with others.

Speaking with clarity and confidence involves choosing our words carefully, using appropriate tone and body language, and adapting our style to suit different audiences. It's about conveying complex ideas in a manner that is accessible and engaging. It's about actively listening and responding thoughtfully, showing respect and empathy.

When we master our speech patterns, we cultivate trust and credibility. We project an image of competence and authority, drawing others to listen and engage with us. People are more likely to be influenced by someone who communicates effectively and confidently, as they feel a sense of trust and reliability in their words.

And then there's silence—the underrated star of our speech. Those pauses, those moments of silence give your audience the space to absorb, to connect with your words.

Isn't it amazing to think that as we fine-tune our speech, we're not just enhancing our communication but also carving our credibility? We're shaping how we are perceived, building trust and confidence with our listeners.

— DAY 140 —

Smile, the world's burdens aren't solely yours

I MAGINE a world where each person wears a genuine smile, radiating warmth and positivity. It may seem like a small act, but the impact is big. A smile has the power to uplift spirits, bridge divides, and remind us that we're all in this journey together.

When we smile, we acknowledge that the burdens of the world are not solely ours to bear. We create a ripple effect of positivity that touches the lives of those around us. A simple smile can brighten someone's day, offer comfort, and remind them that they are not alone in their struggles.

Smiling isn't just about bringing joy to others; it also benefits our own wellbeing. When we choose to smile, even in the face of adversity, we shift our perspective and embrace a more optimistic outlook. It becomes a reminder that we have the power to find beauty in the middle of chaos and strength amidst challenges.

A smile is a symbol of resilience, hope, and interconnectedness. It's a universal language that goes beyond barriers and fosters understanding. It bridges the gaps between strangers, brings people together, and reminds us of our shared humanity.

Give yourself permission to smile. Seek joy in the simplest of things—a brilliant sunrise, the smell of fresh coffee, a comforting chat with a friend. Remember, your smile is infectious. It might just inspire someone else to feel a bit lighter too.

The world's burdens aren't solely yours. Share, and let others share with you. And through it all, don't forget to smile. After all, we're all in this together, and a shared burden is a lightened burden.

— DAY 141 —

Mock others and face the echoed laughter

W E all know the power of laughter—it's contagious, uplifting, and brings joy to our lives. But what happens when laughter turns into mockery? When we use our words to belittle or ridicule others, we set off a chain reaction that can have far-reaching consequences.

Mocking others may seem harmless in the moment, a quick way to gain a few laughs or boost our ego. However, the echoes of that laughter have the potential to haunt us. They create a perception of who we are, shaping our reputation and influencing how others perceive us.

The enlightening aspect is understanding that our actions towards others have a way of coming back to us. The laughter that once echoed in our ears can turn into whispers of judgment, eroding our own sense of self-worth. When we mock others, we inadvertently invite mockery upon ourselves.

Furthermore, when we engage in mockery, we contribute to a culture of negativity and hurt. Our words have the power to inflict pain and damage relationships. What may seem like a momentary burst of amusement can leave lasting scars on the hearts of others.

This echo effect isn't confined to mockery. It's a profound principle of life, reflecting our actions back to us. The love you share today might comfort you tomorrow. The kindness you sow could grow into a tree of support when you most need it.

Consider how your words will bounce back. Consider how you'd feel on the receiving end. Could you smile at the echo of your words? Life's echo can teach us empathy, compassion, and maybe even a bit of foresight, if we're willing to listen. Now that's what I call an echo worth creating, don't you think?

— DAY 142 —

Tiny actions lead to grand results

IT'S fascinating how the tiniest pebble can create ripples that reach the farthest corners of a pond. In life, it's no different. Tiny actions, seemingly insignificant at first sight, have the power to shape our world in grand and aweinspiring ways.

Take a moment to think about the most monumental achievements in history. Behind each one of them lies a series of tiny steps, taken by individuals who believed in their power to make a difference. The grandeur of these accomplishments often overshadows the small beginnings that set them in motion.

Take the story of Rosa Parks, an ordinary woman who refused to give up her seat on a segregated bus. In that singular act of resistance, she ignited a fire that fueled the civil rights movement in the United States. Her small step towards equality paved the way for monumental changes, inspiring countless others to stand up against injustice.

Similarly, consider the work of scientists who make groundbreaking discoveries. These individuals set out on an endless journey of trial and error, conducting countless experiments in pursuit of knowledge. Each experiment may yield only a fraction of progress, but over time, these incremental steps lead to breakthroughs that reshape our understanding of the world.

In our own lives, we often underestimate the power of small actions. We dream of grand achievements and significant transformations, yet we fail to realize that it is through consistent, tiny efforts that we can bring about lasting change. It's the daily habits we cultivate, the small kindnesses we show to others, and the incremental improvements we make that accumulate over time and create a profound impact on our lives and the lives of those around us.

And so it is with life. Each decision we make, every step we take, no matter how tiny they may seem, carries a monumental potential. They are the small gears that drive the clockwork of our existence, the subtle brush strokes that create the masterpiece of our life's canvas. We must appreciate the potency of these tiny actions. For, as Lao Tzu once said, "The journey of a thousand miles begins with a single step."

— DAY 143 —

Wealth isn't just about money

OFTEN, in the whirlwind of life, we fall into the trap of equating wealth with financial abundance. We chase after big paychecks, luxury items, and bank balances with more zeroes than we can count. Yet, true wealth isn't just about money. It transcends tangible assets and ventures into territories that are, paradoxically, priceless.

So, what is wealth if not just money? Let's start by looking at knowledge. Knowledge, they say, is power, and rightfully so. The wealth of knowledge opens up a world of possibilities, instilling confidence, fostering creativity, and encouraging innovation. It is a treasure trove that never depletes, only grows with sharing, and its value cannot be measured in dollars and cents.

Next, consider health, the phrase "health is wealth" rings true. What good are the riches if we do not have the health to enjoy them? A strong body, a sound mind, and a peaceful spirit form the trinity of health and wealth. They are the bedrock upon which we build the edifice of our lives.

Then, there is the wealth of relationships. The bonds we forge, the love we share, the joy we find in each other—these are riches beyond compare. The heartwarming laughter of loved ones, the comfort of a friend's understanding nod, the soft, reassuring touch of a partner—these treasures are irreplaceable.

Let's not forget the wealth of time. Each moment, once gone, never returns. Time is an invaluable currency, a luxury even money can't buy. The wealth of time, therefore, is about making the most of each moment, creating memories, gaining experiences, and appreciating life's journey.

Wealth isn't just about money. It's about knowledge, health, relationships, time, and so much more. It's about the richness of our experiences, the depth of our learning, the quality of our relationships, and the wellness of our being. To acknowledge this is to realize that we are all wealthy in unique, immeasurable ways. And that, indeed, is mind-blowing.

True wealth lies in the richness of our lives, the depth of our experiences, and the love and wisdom we gain along the way. Because, at the end of the day, the most fulfilling wealth is the kind that money can't buy.

— DAY 144 —

Be your own light in the darkness

EVER feel like you're lost, wandering in some sort of existential darkness, just longing for a sliver of light? Yeah, me too. Sometimes life throws you such curveballs that you're knocked down, surrounded by shadows of despair and confusion. But here's a thought. What if, during these times, instead of searching for light outside, we ignite our own flame? How about we be our own light in the darkness?

I get it. We're so accustomed to seeking external sources of light, something, or someone to help us navigate the dark. But here's a bit of hard truth. While external guidance can help, the most brilliant, durable light is the one that we kindle within us. When we light that internal fire, we illuminate not just our path, but we radiate light that might guide others as well.

But, let's be honest. It's not an easy task to strike that internal match. It needs guts, strength, and a bucketful of acceptance. It's about looking your demons in the eye, admitting your mistakes, and embracing the mess-ups. It's about being bare, letting your raw, unfiltered self shine through, accepting the way you are, blemishes and all.

When you become your own light, there's a transformation that happens, and it's not just about seeing where you're going. It's about how you see. You start looking at obstacles not as stumbling blocks but as stepping stones. Failures? They're not dead-ends anymore; they're detours, or better yet, they become life's little tutorials. And the flaws, oh, those beautiful flaws become facets, unique, glittering aspects of your own, personal gem.

Next time you're stranded in the dark, instead of looking for a flashlight, try to find the spark within. Remember, you're not just a lost soul in the dark. You're a lighthouse under construction. Stand firm, let your light blaze, and see where it leads you. Don't just wander in the dark, illuminate it. Become your own light in the darkness, buddy. You might just end up finding your way home.

— DAY 145 —

Change actions to change outcomes

WE often find ourselves craving for different outcomes in life—whether it's achieving a goal, improving relationships, or finding happiness. Yet, we continue to do the same things, follow the same patterns, and expect things to miraculously change. But as Einstein famously said, "Insanity is doing the same thing over and over again and expecting different results."

To break free from this cycle, we must recognize the power of our actions. Our actions shape our reality. They are the building blocks that construct the outcomes we experience. If we desire different outcomes, we must be willing to change the way we act.

Consider this—when we take different actions, we introduce new variables into the equation. We disrupt the status quo, challenge our comfort zones, and open ourselves up to new possibilities. It's through these intentional shifts in behavior that we create the space for change and transformation.

Changing our actions requires self-awareness, courage, and a willingness to let go of old habits. It means examining our beliefs, values, and motivations. It means being open to new perspectives and embracing discomfort as a catalyst for growth. It's not always easy, but the rewards are profound.

Imagine the power of consciously choosing actions that align with your desired outcomes. Instead of waiting for circumstances to change, you take proactive steps to shape your reality. You become the author of your own story, crafting a narrative filled with intention, purpose, and fulfillment.

Change begins with small steps. It's not about making drastic, overnight transformations. It's about consistent, intentional actions that move you closer to your goals. It's about cultivating positive habits, embracing a growth mindset, and persisting even in the face of challenges.

Embrace the power of change, and the potential of new actions. Because the thrill of life lies not in the comfort of the known, but in the excitement of the new, the possibility of transformation. After all, life isn't about finding yourself; it's about creating yourself, one action, one changed outcome at a time.

— DAY 146 —

A supportive partner is more than looks

HAVE you ever felt drawn to a radiant face, an enchanting smile, or eyes that seem to hold galaxies within them? Of course you have. Physical attraction is an inherent part of our human experience. When it comes to choosing a life partner, a more significant determinant goes beyond the skin-deep. While looks might be the enticing cover of the book, it is what lies within the pages that will accompany us throughout our life journey.

Imagine you're building a house. Now, the facade is important, right? It's the first thing people see. But if the foundation isn't strong, if the rooms don't feel comfortable, and if the layout isn't practical, would the beautiful facade still be as appealing? Probably not. This is similar to relationships. Physical attractiveness, like a house's facade, might draw us in, but it's the underlying support, comfort, and practicality that sustain us in the long run.

Let's put some flesh on these bones. What's a supportive partner? It's someone who's there in the trenches with you, not just on the victory podium. It's the person who, after a tough day, offers a comforting embrace or a listening ear. It's that cheerleader who believes in your dreams, even when they seem impossible to others. It's the navigator who helps you find your way when you're lost. It's the teammate who rolls up their sleeves and jumps into problem-solving mode with you.

These traits go beyond physical appearance. They're about character, about emotional connectivity, about being a rock in a stormy sea. It's about walking together through life's ups and downs, growing together, learning from each other, and building a bond that goes beyond skin-deep attraction.

Words alone are not enough to define a supportive partner. Their actions speak louder. They show up consistently, offering acts of kindness, love, and support. They are your rock, a pillar of strength in the face of adversity.

In the grand scheme of life, a supportive partner isn't just a beautiful face that turns heads, but a pillar of strength, a light of support, and a catalyst of growth that turns life into a riveting journey of shared dreams, challenges, triumphs, and love.

— DAY 147 —

Mindset separates the rich and poor

I T'S fascinating how mindset can be the differentiating factor between the rich and the poor. We often associate wealth with financial abundance and material possessions, but the truth is, it goes much deeper than that. It's all about mindset—the lens through which we view the world and ourselves.

Imagine two individuals facing similar circumstances—let's call them Alex and Ben. Alex has a poverty mindset, constantly dwelling on limitations, scarcity, and the belief that success is elusive. On the other hand, Ben embodies a wealth mindset—a perspective rooted in abundance, possibilities, and the steadfast belief in their own potential.

The poverty mindset tends to breed a cycle of self-limiting beliefs. It traps individuals in a state of fear, focusing on what they lack rather than what they can achieve. It maintains the belief that resources are limited, opportunities are scarce, and success is reserved for a privileged few.

Conversely, the wealth mindset is a game-changer. It enables individuals to see opportunities where others see obstacles. It encourages a shift from scarcity to abundance thinking, where one recognizes the vast array of possibilities available and embraces them with open arms.

The rich and the poor may encounter similar challenges, but their mindset sets them on divergent paths. The rich see setbacks as temporary hurdles, learning experiences that propel them forward. They are willing to take calculated risks, driven by a deep belief in their ability to create wealth and manifest their dreams.

Shifting from a poverty mindset to a wealth mindset is a transformative journey. It begins with self-awareness—a conscious recognition of our thought patterns and beliefs. By challenging self-limiting beliefs and replacing them with empowering ones, we open ourselves to new possibilities and opportunities.

Mindset alone is not a magic formula for financial success. It is a critical factor, but it must be accompanied by action. A wealth mindset motivates individuals to take inspired action, seek knowledge, and persist in the face of challenges.

— DAY 148 —

Think before you speak

I T'S a simple phrase, but its signifiance's profound. In a world filled with rapid communication and impulsive reactions, taking a moment to pause and reflect before speaking can be a game-changer.

We live in an era where words hold tremendous power. With a single sentence, we can build bridges or burn them down. Our words can inspire, heal, and uplift, or they can wound, divide, and destroy. The choice is ours.

Consider the times when you've spoken without considering the impact of your words. How often have you regretted the things you've said in the heat of the moment? We've all been there. But when we take a moment to think before we speak, we give ourselves the opportunity to choose our words wisely and consider their potential consequences.

Reflect on the power of silence, too. Sometimes, the most profound statements are the ones left unsaid. In moments of conflict or misunderstanding, taking a breath and choosing not to react impulsively can be an act of great strength. It allows us to collect our thoughts, gain perspective, and respond with intention rather than emotion.

Thinking before speaking is not about suppressing our voices or censoring our thoughts. It's about cultivating mindfulness and empathy in our communication. It's about considering the impact our words may have on others and choosing to express ourselves in a way that fosters understanding, respect, and connection.

When we think before we speak, we also give ourselves the opportunity to communicate more effectively. We can articulate our thoughts with clarity, expressing ourselves in a way that resonates with others.

Let's not underestimate the power we wield with our words. Each conversation is an opportunity to plant seeds of positivity, encouragement, and love. So, let's embrace the pause, let's ponder our words, and let's create a garden that reflects the beauty of thoughtful communication. After all, as the saying goes, "The tongue has no bones, but is strong enough to break a heart. So be careful with your words."

— DAY 149 —

Don't let others' dislike destroy you

HAVE you ever been confronted with the disapproval of others? It can be a difficult pill to swallow, leaving us feeling wounded, rejected, and questioning our self-worth. You are stronger and more resilient than you realize.

In life, we encounter a multitude of personalities and perspectives. It's natural for people to have different opinions, preferences, and even prejudices. However, it's important to remember that their opinions do not define who they are. They are mere projections of their own insecurities, biases, and unmet expectations.

When faced with disapproval, it's crucial to develop a steadfast belief in your own worth and potential. Embrace the fact that you are unique, with a set of strengths, talents, and qualities that make you who you are. Recognize that you are a work in progress, constantly evolving and growing, and that not everyone will appreciate or understand your journey.

Don't allow the negativity of others to seep into your core and erode your self-esteem. Instead, use it as an opportunity for self-reflection and growth. Ask yourself if there is any truth in their criticisms that you can learn from, but don't let it define you. Choose to focus on the love and acceptance you have for yourself, rather than seeking external validation.

Surround yourself with people who genuinely support and uplift you. Seek out those who celebrate your uniqueness and encourage your personal growth. Surrounding yourself with positivity and encouragement will shield you from the destructive power of others' dislike.

Your happiness and self-worth should not be dependent on the opinions of others. Embrace the power of self-acceptance, self-love, and self-belief. When you stand firmly in your truth, rooted in your own values and aspirations, the disapproval of others will lose its power to harm you.

Don't let others' dislike destroy you. Rise above the negativity, knowing that you are on a journey of self-discovery and growth. The bottom line is, the most important opinion of you is your own. Because you are a masterpiece in the making, and no one else gets to decide that for you.

— DAY 150 —

Don't suffer imagined troubles

T HERE'S a funny thing about our brains. They're spectacularly good at conjuring up worlds that don't exist. You've done it, I've done it, we've all done it—lying awake at 3 am, thinking about the "what ifs" and the "could bes". We create imagined troubles out of thin air and suffer for it. We allow ourselves to be surrounded by the shadows of problems that aren't even here yet—and who knows, they might never even arrive.

Take a moment to consider this. How many times have you found yourself wound up in knots over a problem, only to have it never materialize? Or have the issue turned out to be nowhere near as catastrophic as you had pictured? The truth is, our imagination can often be our own worst enemy.

Now, don't get me wrong. I'm not saying we should never think about the future or potential challenges. A bit of forward-thinking and planning is necessary. But there's a difference, a vast one, between practical foresight and torturing ourselves over imagined troubles.

Let me paint a picture for you. Imagine spending an entire day at a beautiful beach. But instead of enjoying the sunshine, the soft sand, and the clear blue waters, you worry about a potential storm that might hit. You miss out on the joy of the present, awaiting a disaster that may never come. Doesn't make much sense, right? But that's exactly what we do when we let our minds fixate on imagined troubles.

Here's the thing—life will always have its share of real challenges. And that's okay. It's part of being human. But why add to the pile with imaginary ones? Why waste energy battling ghosts when there are actual dragons to slay?

The next time you find yourself slipping down the rabbit hole of "what ifs," take a step back. Ask yourself, "Is this a genuine problem, or is it an imagined trouble?" If it's the latter, let it go. Focus on the present, on the real, on the tangible. Trust me, your future self will thank you for it. Don't suffer imagined troubles. Not worth it. Enjoy the beach while you can, my friend. Who knows, you might even build a few sandcastles along the way!

— DAY 151 —

It's okay to not know

DO you ever feel the weight of expectation to have all the answers? In a world that often values certainty and expertise, it's easy to believe that not knowing is a sign of weakness or limitation. In fact, it can be a powerful catalyst for growth, discovery, and transformation.

We live in an era where information is at our fingertips, and the pressure to be knowledgeable about everything can be overwhelming. But, no one has all the answers. Even the most educated individuals continue to explore, question, and learn throughout their lives. Embracing the unknown is not a limitation; it's an invitation to set out on a journey of curiosity and lifelong learning.

When we accept that it's okay to not know, we free ourselves from the burden of perfection and the fear of judgment. We create space for curiosity, wonder, and the joy of discovery. Instead of striving for certainty, we become comfortable with ambiguity and open ourselves up to new possibilities.

Not knowing allows us to embrace humility and vulnerability. It's an acknowledgment that we are constantly evolving, and there is always room for growth. By letting go of the need for immediate answers, we become open to different perspectives and diverse ways of thinking.

The unknown holds immense potential for creativity and innovation. It's in those moments of uncertainty that breakthroughs occur and new paths emerge. When we let go of preconceived notions and the pressure to have all the answers, we tap into our innate creativity and problem-solving abilities.

Not knowing fosters a sense of curiosity and wonder that keeps life exciting and vibrant. It encourages us to ask questions, seek understanding, and explore the mysteries that surround us. It's through curiosity that we push boundaries, challenge the status quo, and make profound discoveries.

The next time you're faced with the unknown, don't recoil. Instead, remember: It's okay to not know. View it as a golden opportunity to learn, grow, and discover. In the dance with the unknown, you may just uncover something truly extraordinary.

— DAY 152 —

Time is your investment ally

TIME is the currency of life. Each passing moment is an opportunity—a chance to invest in yourself, your dreams, and the relationships that matter most. How we choose to allocate our time determines the returns we receive in various aspects of our lives.

Just like a wise investor carefully chooses where to invest their money, we must be intentional in how we invest our time. We have 24 hours in a day, and it's up to us to decide how we spend them.

Investing time in personal growth and self-care is an invaluable choice. It's about nurturing your mind, body, and spirit—engaging in activities that bring you joy, cultivating new skills, and pursuing your passions. By investing time in yourself, you lay the foundation for a fulfilling and meaningful life.

Time is also a powerful tool for building and nurturing relationships. Investing quality time in your loved ones, friends, and community strengthens bonds, fosters connection, and creates memories that last a lifetime. It's about being fully present, actively listening, and making an effort to show that you value their presence in your life.

Just like any investment, time requires careful consideration. We must be discerning about where we allocate our time and energy. It's about identifying activities and relationships that align with our values and goals, and letting go of those that drain our resources without providing meaningful returns.

The beauty of time as an investment ally lies in its potential for compounding returns. Small investments of time in consistent habits, personal growth, and building meaningful connections can yield exponential results over the long term. Every moment counts, and each investment of time, no matter how small, accumulates and contributes to your overall success and fulfillment.

Next time you feel impatient, remember, you have a powerful ally on your side—time. It's not just about investing money but also dreams, efforts, love, and growth. Trust in its power, be patient, and watch how time magnifies your investments, in every aspect of your life. Time is truly the architect of miracles.

— DAY 153 —

Create your own luck with hard work

LUCK, often regarded as a stroke of fortune or coincidence, is commonly seen as something beyond our control. But what if I told you that luck is not just a roll of the dice, but a result of our actions and mindset?

You know that person we all know—the one who always seems to be at the right place at the right time, catching all the lucky breaks? It's easy to attribute their success to pure luck, but have you considered what lies beneath that shiny surface? It's hard work, plain and simple.

We often perceive luck as something beyond our control—a roll of the cosmic dice that determines our fate. But what if I told you that luck is not just a random occurrence? It's a result of our actions, mindset, and the choices we make along the way.

Creating your own luck begins with embracing the power of hard work. It's about putting in the hours, pushing through obstacles, and persisting in the face of adversity. When you pour your energy and effort into your pursuits, you create a fertile ground for luck to thrive.

Luck is not an isolated event; it often disguises itself as an opportunity. By working consistently towards your goals, you position yourself to recognize and seize these opportunities when they arise. Hard work sharpens your skills, expands your knowledge, and hones your intuition, enabling you to make the most of fortuitous moments.

But creating your own luck is not just about sweat and toil—it's about developing a growth mindset. It's about viewing setbacks as stepping stones, failures as learning opportunities, and challenges as catalysts for growth. By adopting this mindset, you transform obstacles into chances to uncover hidden luck and emerge stronger than before.

Taking calculated risks is also key to creating your own luck. It's about stepping out of your comfort zone, embracing uncertainty, and venturing into uncharted territories. When you dare to explore new paths and embrace unfamiliar experiences, you increase your chances of stumbling upon fortunate circumstances.

— DAY 154 —

Life without difficulty is cheap

LIFE without difficulty is like a journey without purpose. It may seem appealing at first, but upon closer examination, we realize that it lacks depth, growth, and the true essence of what it means to be human. In fact, life without difficulty is cheap—it fails to capture the richness and transformative power that challenges bring.

Think about the times when you faced hardships, setbacks, or moments of uncertainty. In those moments, you were pushed beyond your comfort zone, forced to confront your limitations and seek solutions. It was in those difficult times that you discovered strength within you that you never knew existed. You found resilience, creativity, and determination.

Difficulties serve as catalysts for growth. They ignite a fire within us, compelling us to rise above our circumstances and become better versions of ourselves. Without challenges, we would stagnate, remaining confined within our comfort zones and never truly realizing our potential.

Consider the most awe-inspiring stories of human triumph. They are tales of individuals who faced seemingly unbeatable odds, yet found the courage to persevere. It is through their struggles that they transformed not only their own lives, but also inspired countless others.

Life without difficulty would lack contrast. We would not fully appreciate joy without experiencing sorrow, success without tasting failure, or light without knowing darkness. Difficulties provide us with a profound sense of gratitude and perspective, reminding us of the preciousness of life and the blessings we often take for granted.

It is through the challenges we encounter that we forge meaningful connections with others. Shared experiences of overcoming difficulties create bonds of empathy, support, and understanding. It is in our vulnerability and willingness to lend a helping hand that we truly connect with our fellow human beings.

After all, it's the storms that help us appreciate the stillness of calm seas. This profound realization indeed offers a radical and exciting perspective on life's adversities.

— DAY 155 —

Change is inevitable

NOTHING remains stagnant. The world around us is in an eternal state of flux. Seasons change, civilizations rise and fall, and technology evolves at an astonishing pace. Even our own bodies undergo continuous transformation, from the moment we are born until our last breath.

Change. It's a small word, but its implications are colossal. We see it everywhere, from the seasons cycling outside our windows to the ever-evolving skyline of our cities. Even on the smallest scale, our very cells are constantly renewing, keeping us alive. Life and change, are two sides of the same coin, eternally connected.

Now, imagine for a moment a world void of change. Monotony would shroud the magnificence of existence. A tree is forever a sapling, a child never growing old. Sounds almost dystopian, doesn't it?

Change, in its essence, is life's paintbrush, coloring our world with diversity and excitement. Change is more than just a physical phenomenon; it's a catalyst for personal growth. We stumble, we rise, we learn. We evolve, not despite, but because of the trials we face. Change paves the way for resilience and innovation, forging our character and feeding our souls.

Now, I know change can be scary. We are creatures of comfort, after all. But remember, a caterpillar has to endure change to become a butterfly. Aren't butterflies beautiful? Change, in essence, is the universe's way of saying, "Hey, there's room for something even better."

Here's another thought. You know those hard times when it feels like you're under a rock? Those moments are like a blacksmith's hammer, shaping and strengthening you. Without change, without these challenges, we wouldn't grow. We wouldn't learn resilience, wisdom, or grace. And we wouldn't be able to appreciate the good times quite as much, right?

With change as your ally, you become a river, constantly moving forward, sculpting your own grand landscape. Isn't that a breathtaking perspective? It's these thoughts that make life seem like an exciting adventure, forever unfolding, forever changing. Indeed, change isn't just inevitable; it's an incredible gift.

— DAY 156 —

Money eases life's struggles

MONEY, a fascinating concept that has the power to shape our lives in countless ways. It's often seen as a means to an end—a tool that eases life's struggles and grants us access to comfort, security, and opportunities. Money, in its basic essence, is a tool, a means to an end. It's like a ship that transports us from one shore to another, from desire to satisfaction. It offers the comfort of a warm home, the ability to eat nourishing meals, and access to education and healthcare. It's the key that unlocks the doors to these necessities, making our journey smoother. It's like a balm, easing the struggles that life often presents.

Imagine being able to pay your bills without worry, pursuing your dreams without financial constraints, and having the freedom to make choices that align with your desires. Money, in these instances, acts as a facilitator, smoothing the path and making life's journey a bit easier.

Money is not the ultimate solution to life's struggles. It is merely a tool—a means to an end. While it can ease certain challenges, it cannot address the deeper aspects of human existence.

Life's struggles encompass much more than financial burdens. They involve emotional, psychological, and spiritual dimensions. Money, however abundant, cannot heal a broken heart, provide inner peace, or fulfill our deepest longings.

True fulfillment and happiness come from within—from our relationships, personal growth, and connection to something greater than ourselves. It's about finding purpose, embracing gratitude, and nurturing our well-being.

In fact, the relentless pursuit of money can lead to a different kind of struggle—a never-ending chase that breeds dissatisfaction and disconnects us from the essence of life. It can create a false sense of security, overshadowing the importance of human connection and personal values.

Money is a tool that amplifies our choices, but it is up to us to make wise decisions. We must recognize that the real treasures in life—the love, joy, and meaning—are not tied to our financial worth. They are found in the moments we share, the experiences we cherish, and the impact we make on others.

— DAY 157 —

No shortcuts, put in the work

IMAGINE a world where success is just a quick fix away. A place where you could achieve your dreams without breaking a sweat, without putting in the time and effort required. It sounds tempting, doesn't it? However, there are no shortcuts to true success. To achieve greatness, you must be willing to put in the work.

Ever observed the finest sculpture, or a skyscraper touching the heavens, or even a top-notch athlete breaking records? Behind each of these marvels, there's a common thread, an invisible trail of painstaking labor. The sculptor chipping away for countless hours, the team of architects and builders methodically assembling the structure, the athlete waking before dawn for relentless training—no shortcuts, just pure, genuine hard work.

See, it's not just about reaching the summit, it's about the climb. It's about the bruises, the sweat, the self-doubt, and the determination to push past it. It's in this journey you discover your grit, your resilience. It's where you mold yourself, piece by piece, into the very essence of your aspirations.

There's no magic button to push or secret passage to take, and that's okay. In fact, it's better than okay. It's in the journey, the grind, where you unearth your potential. It's where you cross paths with failure, only to stand up and say, "not today."

Just picture it, every drop of sweat, every late-night struggle, every seemingly unbeatable challenge, it's all leading you to that moment of triumph. And when it arrives, it isn't just about the applause or the awards. It's about standing tall, looking back at the mountain you've conquered, and saying, "I did that. I put in the work."

No shortcuts, my friend. Embrace the grind, and cherish the journey. For it's the labor, the tenacity, that translates ordinary to extraordinary.

—— DAY 158 ——

Confident people make eye contact

I SN'T it amazing how a simple, effortless act like making eye contact can convey so much? It's in the way they hold themselves, the way they carry a conversation, and most importantly, it's in their eyes. Confident people make eye contact, and it's a powerful display of their self-assurance and presence.

Consider the last time you had a conversation with someone who maintained strong eye contact. It felt different, didn't it? There was a sense of trust, respect, and engagement. It was as if they were fully present, giving you their undivided attention. That's the power of eye contact.

Making eye contact is not just about staring into someone's eyes; it's about establishing a genuine connection, acknowledging the other person's presence, and showing them that you value their thoughts and feelings. It's a non-verbal language that conveys confidence, respect, and openness.

When we make eye contact, we invite others into our world. We let them know that we are not afraid to be seen, that we are comfortable in our own skin. It's a subtle yet profound way of communicating our self-assurance without saying a word.

Making eye contact requires vulnerability. It means being comfortable with who we are and embracing our imperfections. It means letting others see us as we truly are, without masks or pretense. It's a powerful statement that says, "I am here, I am present, and I am confident in my own skin."

Confidence isn't born overnight. It's a journey, a gradual accumulation of self-acceptance and growth, of understanding that it's okay to stumble, it's okay to be imperfect. And when this realization sets in, your eyes become a mirror to your soul, overflowing with confidence.

Now, isn't that something? A simple act like making eye contact, echoing volumes about your confidence! It's the small things, really, that can have the most significant impact. In your next conversation, lock your gaze, radiate your confidence, and remember—your eyes are your secret superpower! The subtle language of confidence. That's food for thought, eh?

— DAY 159 —

Habits define the future

I MAGINE waking up one day and realizing that your future has been shaped by the habits you cultivated along the way. The truth is, our habits have an immense impact on the trajectory of our lives. They are the building blocks that lay the foundation for our future.

Habits are the little actions we repeat day in and day out without even realizing their significance. They shape our behaviors, our thoughts, and ultimately, our outcomes. The choices we make today become the habits that define our future.

Every successful person you admire, every individual who has achieved greatness, didn't get there by chance. They cultivated habits that propelled them forward, habits that aligned with their goals and values.

Our habits are powerful forces that shape our character and determine the direction of our lives. They can either be our greatest allies or our biggest obstacles. It's up to us to choose which habits we want to embrace and which ones we need to let go of.

Let's say you've got this habit of working out a bit every day. It's tough, sure, but you stick to it. Fast forward a few years, and you're fitter, stronger, and healthier. The "everyday you" shapes the "future you." That's one stunning realization, isn't it?

But on the flip side, consider those habits that are not so constructive. Maybe you tend to put things off or love that extra helping of dessert every night. Fast forward a few years, and what's the picture? Unfinished projects, health issues—yep, it's a bit of ruin.

That's the thing about habits. They're not just these mindless things we do. They're the silent, tireless architects building our future, one brick at a time. It's a humbling thought. It tells us that the power to shape our future is right there—in the ordinary, the daily, the routine.

What kind of skyscraper are you building? Reflect on that the next time you're brushing your teeth or scrolling through your phone. After all, your future is in your hands—one habit at a time.

—— DAY 160 ——

Ever tried. Ever Failed. No Matter. Try again

W E live in a world that often associates failure with shame, disappointment, and regret. We fear it, avoid it, and let it define us. Take a moment to consider the great inventors, visionaries, and artists who have shaped our world. They didn't achieve greatness by avoiding failure; they embraced it.

Imagine the unsteady steps of a toddler learning to walk. The initial hesitations, the timid movement of small feet, the frequent tumbles. Every fall might seem like a failure, but they are, in fact, the fundamental blocks of success. Each time the child rises, they inch closer to mastering the art of walking.

Take this spirit and apply it to our lives. Somewhere along the line, the simplicity of this lesson gets lost in the labyrinth of adulthood, replaced by the fear of judgment, the shadow of failure hanging over. In the process, we begin to lose sight of the fundamental truth that failure, in its most raw form, is nothing more than a stepping-stone to success.

The archives of history are filled with tales of those who stumbled, fell, but rose again. They are the ones who shaped the world, created marvels, and inspired generations. Thomas Edison made a thousand unsuccessful attempts before he illuminated the world with his light bulb. J.K. Rowling was rejected multiple times before *Harry Potter* enchanted the globe. Each failure, each rejection, was a step forward on their path to success.

The key lies in the phrase "no matter." This powerful dismissal of failure is the pivot upon which the balance of our endeavors rests. Failure is not the end. Rather, it is a signal to reassess, to learn, and to come back stronger. The strength to say "no matter" when faced with failure, to get up and try again, is the essence of resilience.

We are all that child learning to walk. We will fall, we will stumble, but we have within us the strength to get back up. Failure, after all, is not the opposite of success. It's a part of it. Ever tried. Ever failed. No matter. Try again. This is the mantra we must carry in our hearts as we navigate the challenges of life.

— DAY 161 —

Every object was created by a human

T AKE a moment to look around you. Notice the objects that surround you—the chair you're sitting on, the computer or smartphone you're using to read this, and the artwork hanging on the wall. Have you ever stopped to think about the incredible fact that every single object you see was created by a human?

The journey of humanity has been one of continual creation. From the primitive tools shaped by our ancestors to the complex technologies of the modern era, every object is a tangible embodiment of an idea, a problem solved, a need fulfilled. They are proof of our ability to manipulate the world around us, to mold it to our will and our desires, and to improve upon the circumstances of our existence.

Consider, for instance, the evolution of the wheel. A circular object set in motion, a basic concept that revolutionized the way we live, travel, and interact with our world. From facilitating the movement of heavy loads to forming the foundation of vehicles that travel on earth and beyond, the wheel is a paradigm of human innovation.

Our man-made world extends beyond the tangible to the intangible. Systems of governance, economic models, languages, music, art—they are all constructs of the human mind. They shape our interactions, our perceptions, and our very understanding of reality. They are proof that our capacity for creation is not limited to the physical realm but extends to the abstract, the metaphysical.

It is a humbling thought that we, as humans, are the creators of our world, the authors of our collective narrative. Every object, every system, every concept that forms our reality was born out of a human mind.

In every object, in every creation, we see a reflection of ourselves—our triumphs and our mistakes, our learning and our unlearning, our ceaseless endeavor to adapt, to grow, to better our existence. We are not merely inhabitants of this world; we are its creators. And in that truth, lies our greatest power.

— DAY 162 —

Time will pass anyhow

TIME, as we know it, is a fascinating phenomenon. It slips through our fingers like sand, regardless of our awareness or acknowledgment. We often find ourselves caught in the whirlwind of life, wishing for more time, grieving its end, or desiring to somehow manipulate its flow.

Each day, each hour, and each minute ticks away with steadfast consistency. We cannot control its pace or direction. Time moves forward, steadfast in its progression, leaving us with a choice: to drift along with it or to harness its power and make the most of every precious moment.

Many of us live in the shadow of "one day." One day, I'll take that trip. One day, I'll write that book. One day, I'll have that difficult conversation. But the illusion of unlimited time tricks us into the belief that "one day" will always be just around the corner. However, days become weeks, weeks become years, and before we know it, the "one day" stays a shadow in our past.

Now, consider the alternative. Recognize that time will pass regardless of how we choose to spend it. This acknowledgment is not one of pessimism, but one of liberation. It's an invitation to seize the present, make every second count, to embrace our ambitions and passions without delay.

Time doesn't pause for our fears, hesitations, or uncertainties. It simply continues its relentless march forward. As such, our most significant decisions often boil down to how we will spend our time because it is the one thing we can never get back. Each moment we are given is a precious gem, holding within it the potential for joy, growth, and life-altering experiences.

In the grand scheme of things, our time here is but a blink of an eye, a mere heartbeat in the life of the universe. But in that heartbeat lies the potential for a symphony, a masterpiece of moments that we have the power to compose. Time will pass anyhow—a profound reminder to make every moment count, to not let our "one day" fade into yesterdays, but to seize them, here and now, and live our lives with purpose, passion, and verve.

— DAY 163 —

Life will one day screw you

AT some point, we all experience moments when life deals us a difficult hand. It could be a loss, a heartbreak, a setback, or an unexpected turn of events that leaves us feeling defeated and disheartened. It's in those moments that we come face-to-face with the harsh realities of life.

Life, this wild, wondrous journey we're all on, it's like a roller coaster ride. Ups, downs, loops, sharp turns, moments where you feel like you're flying and others when it feels like you're falling rapidly to the ground. And, yes, sometimes it's going to throw a curveball at you so fast and unexpected that you'll feel like you've been sucker-punched. That's the screwing part. No one is spared. It could be a heartbreak, a missed opportunity, a devastating loss. But hold on, there's more to this.

Now, I can hear you asking, "How can getting screwed over by life be a good thing?" Well, it's all about perspective and resilience. You see, those screw-ups, those hard times, they're not just pitfalls. They're stepping stones. They're the moments that push us out of our comfort zones, make us reassess our paths, and trigger growth. They shape us, mold us, and build our character.

Picture this, you're a master sailor, navigating through the stormy seas of life. When the storm hits, you don't abandon ship. Instead, you adapt, learn, and emerge stronger, and more capable. You cherish the calm because you've weathered the storm.

So yes, life will one day screw you. But when it does, remember that it's not a verdict, but a challenge. It's the dark cloud that precedes the rainbow, the cocoon before the butterfly, the sweat before the triumph. It's the very essence of what makes us human—the ability to rise, to adapt, and to evolve. Life's "screws" aren't mere setbacks, they are stepping stones toward becoming who we're truly meant to be.

—— DAY 164 ——

Simplicity unveils complexity's beauty

S IMPLICITY is often viewed as a lack of complexity, a way to streamline and simplify life's challenges. However, what if I told you that simplicity is actually the key to unlocking the beauty and wonder of complexity? That by stripping away the distractions and clutter, we are able to see the intricate and stunning patterns that lie beneath.

Consider for a moment the fundamental laws of physics. These laws, despite governing an extraordinarily complex universe, are remarkably simple. Newton's law of gravity, for instance, can be expressed in a single mathematical equation. Its simplicity belies the extensive dance of the cosmos it choreographs—from the falling of an apple to the orbits of planets.

This principle applies beyond the realm of physical sciences. In art, a simple line or shape can evoke profound emotional responses. Haiku, a form of Japanese poetry, captivates readers with its potent simplicity, using a mere seventeen syllables to capture the essence of a moment or a feeling. Even our daily interactions, stripped down to their most basic elements—a smile, a kind word, a gentle touch—often hold the most meaning.

Simplicity is not about dumbing down or reduction but rather about distilling, about getting to the heart of the matter. It is about cutting away the extraneous, the unnecessary, and the misleading to reveal the essence that lies beneath. It allows us to see the world more clearly, to understand it more deeply, and to appreciate it more fully.

In essence, simplicity unveils complexity's beauty by stripping away the noise and allowing us to focus on the signal. It reveals the patterns, principles, and laws that underpin the baffling complexity of the world. In doing so, it brings us closer to understanding the universe in its astonishing detail and majesty.

Let us seek simplicity in our understanding, our communication, and our way of life. As we peel back the layers of complexity, we will begin to see the world with new eyes. And in this newfound clarity, we will discover a richness and beauty beyond anything we had ever imagined.

— DAY 165 —

Life is fragile

ISN'T it funny how we move through life, making plans, ticking off items from our to-do lists, all the while forgetting this simple truth. You and I, my friend, we're not just flesh and bone, but fragile beings held together by a thread of borrowed time.

Consider a single leaf, fallen from the branch of a towering tree, with clear veins carved into its thin surface. Its delicate form is subject to the change of the wind, likely to rot and fall apart. Just like this leaf, our lives are just as delicate, constantly subject to the winds of change, fortune, and time.

The fabric of our lives is woven with threads of mortality, transient moments stitched together into a rich tapestry of experiences, a canvas filled with a melange of colors and shapes. Each stitch, a symbol of our laughter and tears, ´ our victories and losses, our hopes and fears, is equally valuable and vulnerable.

Life's fragility is a stark reminder of the temporariness of everything we hold dear. It breathes meaning into the transient beauty of a sunset, the fleeting joy of a shared laugh, the fleeting touch of a loved one's hand. It illuminates the paradox that though our bodies are fleeting, the impact of our actions and the imprint of our existence can ripple through eternity.

The inevitability of change and the prospect of an end can be terrifying. Yet, it is this very fragility that renders life so precious. It acts as a strong summon to treasure each tick of time, to celebrate the now, for it is all we truly have. It urges us to express our love, share our kindness, pursue our passions, and find our purpose, for time is fleeting.

The reminder that "life is fragile" is not to ignite fear, but to inspire respect for life. It is an invitation to dance with the temporariness, to sing in the face of the transitory, and to paint our dreams on the canvas of existence while we have the chance. It is an encouragement to nurture compassion, practice gratitude, and manifest love.

— DAY 166 —

Tell me, show me, involve me

WHEN we're learning something new, just hearing about it often isn't enough to really get it stuck in our heads. It's like when someone tells you how to do something, and you think you understand, but then when you try to do it yourself, you realize you don't really get it.

For example, think about trying to learn how to ride a bike. Someone can explain it to you all day long, but you're probably going to forget most of what they said once you actually get on the bike. However, if they show you how to do it, you'll remember a bit more because you've seen it in action. But the real learning happens when you get on the bike yourself and start pedaling. That's when you truly understand how to ride.

This idea also works with learning languages. You might forget the words you just heard, but if you see them being used in a conversation, they're easier to remember. And then, when you actually try to use these words in talking to someone, that's when you really start to understand the language.

Even in areas like teamwork and leadership, the same idea rings true. Hearing about effective communication is one thing, but it's quite another to see it in action during a group project or a team sport. Yet, it's when you take on a leadership role yourself, making decisions, resolving conflicts, and motivating others, that you truly grasp what it means to lead. Through involvement, theories about leadership transform into practical skills and insights.

Whether it's bicycling, learning a language, or leading a team, real understanding blossoms through doing. Engaging directly with tasks and challenges not only deepens our knowledge but also makes learning personal and meaningful, turning abstract ideas into skills and insights we can truly call our own.

— DAY 167 —

Throw away the past

THE past is a double-edged sword. It can be a source of wisdom, teaching us valuable lessons and guiding our decisions. It can also be a prison, holding us captive to old patterns of thought and behavior. We often find ourselves clinging to the past, unwilling to release our grip on what is familiar and known. We carry the scars of past traumas, the regrets of missed opportunities, and the fear of repeating past mistakes.

Now, I don't mean to say you should erase your past completely. No, no! Our past experiences, the good, the bad, the messy, all of them shape us. They help us grow, learn, and become who we are. But when the past becomes this huge anchor, holding you down, refusing to let you sail forward, that's when you've got to muster up the strength and throw it away.

Throwing away the past is not about forgetting, it's about accepting. It's about coming to terms with what's happened, letting it teach you its lessons, and then allowing yourself to move on. It's like clearing out an old, dusty attic, making space for new, exciting things to come.

But let me tell you, it isn't easy. It takes courage, resilience, and a whole lot of self-love. You need to allow yourself to feel, grieve, and forgive. Let go of the hurt, anger, and regret, and see how light you feel. Every sunrise gives us a chance to start anew.

Throwing away the past is like grabbing the steering wheel of your life. You're no longer a passive passenger, driven by past events. You are in control, in the driver's seat, with the power to decide where you want to go.

If you feel anchored to the past, remember, the key to the lock is in your hand. Release yourself from the burden, forgive, heal, and watch as your life unfolds beautifully. After all, life is meant to be lived forward, with the past as a teacher, not a jailer. In the grand play of life, let's remember the past is just the backdrop, the script is being written now, in the present, by you.

— DAY 168 —

Choose joy over age or career

I N our fast-paced, achievement-driven world, it can be easy to get caught up in the pursuit of success. We're told to strive for the best job, the most impressive career, and the most lucrative salary. And, as we age, we're often encouraged to measure our worth based on our accomplishments and milestones. But what if we were to prioritize joy above all else?

Let us take a moment to peel back the layers of this proposition. For centuries, societies across the globe have constructed timelines for human life, milestones established to be met at specific ages. Simultaneously, careers have become a yardstick of success, a symbol of identity. However, one might wonder, where does joy fit in this rigid frame?

Joy is an intangible, yet widespread element of human life. It is as fleeting as the moment that brings a smile to your face, and yet, as enduring as the memory of that warmth in your heart. It is not bound by age, not tethered to the corner office or the weight of your paycheck. It exists in the now, in the simple pleasure of a deep breath, in the laughter shared with a loved one, in the sense of accomplishment from a task well done, regardless of its perceived societal importance.

By choosing joy over age or career, we're not dismissing the value of ambitions or the significance of life's stages. Instead, we're redefining what these stages mean. We're challenging the linear narrative of life, allowing ourselves to seek joy in the present, to let that joy guide our steps towards our goals, rather than the other way around. We're learning to measure our lives not in years or career achievements but in moments of fulfillment, love, and joy.

So why should we make this unconventional choice? The answer is beautifully uncomplicated. Joy, unlike age or career, is timeless. It adds a richness to life that neither years nor professional achievements can offer.

In the end, the choice is ours to make. We can continue to chase the traditional milestones, allowing societal constructs to guide our path. Or, we can choose joy, turning our journey into a celebration of life in all its simplicity and complexity.

— DAY 169 —

Learning from failure never fails

LIFE can be a wild rollercoaster, full of twists and turns, thrilling highs, and, of course, those gut-wrenching drops. But as we navigate this thrilling journey, there's one thing that's inevitable: failure. Yeah, I know, it's a bit of a downer.

Imagine you're trying something new, and it doesn't go as planned. It's easy to feel defeated and want to give up, right? But instead of throwing in the towel, what if you took a moment to reflect on what went wrong? You see, failure is like a wise old teacher, always ready to offer valuable lessons if you're willing to listen. And when you embrace these teachings, you're giving yourself a chance to grow and come back stronger.

Now, I'm not saying it's a walk in the park. It takes courage to face our failures head-on, but the rewards are invaluable. By learning from our mistakes, we develop resilience, adaptability, and a deeper understanding of ourselves. And let's face it— who wouldn't want to be a more robust, wiser version of themselves?

But here's the coolest part: learning from failure is not just about personal growth. When we share our experiences with others, we create a ripple effect, empowering and inspiring those around us. Suddenly, our setbacks become a shared source of strength and wisdom, uniting us all in the pursuit of something greater. Talk about turning lemons into lemonade, right?

My friend, as we travel through this wild, unpredictable journey called life, let's remember that learning from failure never fails. Embrace the lessons, grow from the experience, and, most importantly, share your wisdom with others. Because when we face our failures together, we're unstoppable.

Failure is not a dead-end street. It's merely a detour on the road to success. And as long as we're willing to learn, adapt, and persevere, we'll continue to grow and thrive, no matter what obstacles come our way. After all, learning from failure never fails, and that is a lesson worth remembering.

— DAY 170 —

Your fear will be the source of your greatest regrets

F EAR is an unseen thread in our life, woven with joy, love, and grief. Fear has the uncanny ability to bind us, paralyze us, and throw a shadow over the radiant potential of our dreams. It is within this realm of fear that we risk falling victim to the siren call of inaction, a call that lures us into the depths of stagnation and despair.

As we navigate the shifting landscape of our existence, fear can manifest in countless forms, be it the fear of failure, rejection, or vulnerability. These fears, often rooted in the fragility of our ego, can constrain our growth and prevent us from embracing the fullness of our potential. In allowing fear to dictate the course of our lives, we accidentally sow the seeds of our deepest regrets, as we forsake the dreams and passions that define our essence.

To transcend the grip of fear, we must cultivate the courage to confront our anxieties, face the unknown, and delve into the uncharted territories that lie before us. It is within these moments of bravery that we uncover the true essence of our strength, as we embrace the boundless potential that resides within our hearts. By daring to challenge our fears, we embark upon a journey of growth and self-discovery, forging a new path marked by resilience, fortitude, and boundless possibility.

As we journey forth into the great unknown, we are reminded that the antidote to fear is not the absence of uncertainty, but rather the cultivation of courage, the unyielding resolve to face the challenges that lie before us. In casting aside the shackles of fear, we grant ourselves the freedom to forge our destiny, free from the constraints of doubt and apprehension. And in doing so, we open ourselves to the possibility of a life that is vibrant, expansive, and free from the weight of regret.

The recognition that fear will be the source of our greatest regrets serves as a strong call to action, an invitation to rise above the constraints of our anxieties and embrace the boundless potential of our dreams.

— DAY 171 —

Don't kill yourself for work

T HERE'S a saying that goes, "You can't take it with you." It's a reminder that no matter how much we accumulate in our lives, we can't take any of it with us when we leave this world. And yet, so many of us become obsessed with our careers, constantly chasing that next promotion, that next paycheck, that next big thing. But let's take a moment to think about what we're sacrificing in the process.

Now, I'm not saying we shouldn't work hard or strive for success. Of course not! But there's a fine line between being ambitious and being consumed by your job. When work becomes our entire world, we risk losing out on so much that life has to offer. Like spending time with loved ones, taking care of our physical and mental health, or simply enjoying the beauty of the world around us.

I mean, take a moment to reflect on this: when you look back on your life, do you want to remember the countless hours spent at the office, or would you rather cherish memories of laughter with friends, adventures with your family, and moments of personal growth and discovery? The choice seems pretty clear to me.

How can we strike that balance between career and personal well-being? It's all about setting boundaries and learning to prioritize what truly matters. Maybe it's leaving work on time so you can have dinner with your family, or taking a mental health day when you're feeling burned out. By taking control of our work-life balance, we can enjoy the best of both worlds—professional success and personal happiness.

As we journey through this crazy, unpredictable adventure we call life, let's remember not to kill ourselves for work. Because at the end of the day, our jobs are just one aspect of who we are, and there's so much more to life than just our careers. Let's strive for success, but not at the expense of our health, relationships, and happiness. Life is too short not to savor every moment and make the most of the precious time we have.

— DAY 172 —

Leaving your comfort zone is the root of greatness

HAVE you ever felt stuck in your life, like you're just going through the motions without really experiencing anything new or exciting? Well, I think I might have a solution for you, and it's all about leaving your comfort zone. I believe that stepping outside our safe little bubbles is the root of greatness. Let me explain why.

Our comfort zones are cozy, familiar places where we feel secure and in control. But, nothing ever really grows there. It's like a well-trodden path in the woods—everything around it is lush and vibrant, but the path itself is just dirt and dust. The real magic happens when we dare to venture off that path and explore the wild unknown.

When we leave our comfort zones, we open ourselves up to new experiences, new challenges, and new opportunities for growth. It's like a burst of fresh air that shakes up our lives and forces us to see the world from a different perspective. Sure, it can be scary and even a little uncomfortable, but that's where the magic happens.

Think about all the incredible people throughout history who have achieved greatness. What do they all have in common? They dared to step outside their comfort zones. They faced their fears, took risks, and pushed the boundaries of what they thought was possible. And in doing so, they changed the world.

I challenge you to leave your comfort zone. Try something new, whether it's taking up a new hobby, traveling to a foreign country, or even just striking up a conversation with a stranger. Embrace the unknown and see where it takes you.

Because, in the end, leaving our comfort zones is what enables us to grow, learn, and truly live our lives to the fullest. It's the root of greatness, the spark that ignites our potential, and the catalyst for the incredible adventures that await us just beyond the familiar. So, are you ready to take that leap? I know I am. Let's step outside our comfort zones and embrace the extraordinary lives we were always meant to live.

— DAY 173 —

Where expectations end, peace begins

Q UITE a punchy little statement, isn't it? It's got this poetic undertone that tugs at your heartstrings and makes you think, doesn't it? I'm sure we've all wrestled with expectations in one way or another, whether they're ones we've put on ourselves or ones that others have placed on us.

Expectations, in essence, are the blueprints we draw up in our minds of the future yet to unfold. They piece together a rich story of aspirations, dreams, and desires, knitting together a reality we wish for. Yet, these anticipated realities often become the benchmark against which we measure our lives, continuously gauging the distance between where we stand and the mirage of our expectations.

This continuous assessment, more often than not, births dissatisfaction and unrest, turning our lives into an endless chase. We start to view our present through a lens of lack, blinded by what's missing rather than appreciating what exists. Thus, by anchoring our happiness to the fulfillment of expectations, we unintentionally construct barriers to the very peace we seek.

Now, let's imagine for a moment, an existence where expectations cease to persist. A life where the invisible finish lines we have drawn are erased, where we no longer await the future to validate our present. This is the space where peace resides.

With the dissolution of expectations, we free ourselves from the constraints of anticipated outcomes. Our lives are no longer a complex algebra equation to solve, but a fluid dance to embrace. As we shift from a future-focused to a present-oriented perspective, we create room for peace. The present moment, untouched by the shadows of what should be, unfolds in its purest, most authentic form. We learn to adapt and flow with life, rather than control or direct it.

In this realm of existence, acceptance takes the place of expectation. We begin to appreciate life as it is, in all its imperfect glory. Each moment, whether it aligns with our initial desires or not, is recognized as a vital part of our unique journey.

— DAY 174 —

Don't sacrifice dreams for an ideal child image

THERE'S this crazy thing about the society where we're all expected to fit into a certain framework, especially when it comes to our kids. It's like there's this unspoken rule that our children have to be perfect, well-rounded little angels, excelling in everything from academics to sports to socializing. This whole "ideal child" concept is totally unrealistic and actually harmful to our kids and their dreams.

Every child is unique. They each have their own interests, talents, and dreams just waiting to be discovered. But when we push them to fit into that "ideal child" image, we're basically telling them that who they are isn't good enough. And the more we do that, the more we squash their individuality and the dreams they've been nurturing inside.

Instead of trying to make our kids into these cookie-cutter versions of perfection, we should be encouraging them to explore their own interests and figure out who they really are. Let them try new things, make mistakes, and learn from their experiences. In doing so, we're helping them build resilience and determination, which are crucial skills they'll need throughout their lives.

And you know what else? When we create a culture of acceptance and understanding, we're teaching our kids that their worth doesn't come from the awards they win or the milestones they hit. It comes from their ability to empathize, to show kindness, and to love others. These qualities might not seem as important as straight A's or a spot on the A team, but they're the foundation of a more compassionate and inclusive world.

Stop trying to force our kids into this unrealistic "ideal child" box. Instead, let's celebrate their uniqueness and encourage them to chase their dreams. In doing so, we'll not only help them grow into their authentic selves, but we'll also create a world that's more diverse, vibrant, and full of possibility. Recognize the importance of balancing your children's well-being with your own, and work towards finding joy and fulfillment in both. Pursue your passions and goals, and inspire your children to do the same.

— DAY 175 —

Better single than unhappy marriage

HAVE you ever heard the saying "Better to be single and happy, than in a relationship and unhappy?" The truth is, marriage isn't some magical potion that guarantees a life full of companionship and happiness. In fact, being stuck in an unhappy marriage can actually be way lonelier than being single.

When you're single, you have the freedom to spend your time with whoever you want and to do whatever you want. You can hang out with friends, join clubs, take up new hobbies, or just enjoy your own company. And in doing all these things, you have the chance to meet new people and form new connections. Sure, you might have moments when you feel lonely, but that's just part of the human experience.

On the other hand, when you're in an unhappy marriage, loneliness can feel like a heavy weight that never leaves your side. You might be living with someone, but if you can't connect with them on a deep, emotional level, it's like you're sharing your life with a stranger. And that kind of loneliness—the kind where you're physically close to someone but emotionally miles apart—can be absolutely soul-crushing.

What's more, when you're in a miserable marriage, it can be really hard to maintain other relationships or pursue your own interests. You might find yourself pulling away from friends and family, or giving up on things that used to bring you joy. And that just leaves you feeling even more isolated and alone.

Instead of buying into the idea that marriage is the ultimate solution to loneliness, let's start recognizing the value of being single. Let's celebrate the freedom it gives us to explore our interests, develop our sense of self, and build meaningful connections with others. Because at the end of the day, it's way better to be single and surrounded by people who genuinely care about you than to be trapped in an unhappy marriage, feeling lonelier than ever. Attract healthy, fulfilling relationships into your life, and form deeper, more meaningful connections with those around you.

— DAY 176 —

Your thoughts are like a boomerang

EVER wondered how our thoughts work? It's kind of fascinating. The more I think about it, the more I realize that our thoughts are a lot like a boomerang. You know, those curved, flat wooden sticks that come back to you when you throw them right? Well, let me explain why I think our thoughts work just like that.

First off, when you throw a boomerang, it goes out into the world and then comes back to you. Similarly, when you think something, it doesn't just stay in your head. Instead, it affects your emotions and your actions, and eventually comes back to impact your life. So, if you're constantly dwelling on negative thoughts, you might find that negative things keep happening to you. But if you focus on positive thoughts, you're more likely to see positive changes in your life.

And it's not just about the things that happen to you, either. Our thoughts also affect how we perceive the world. When we're in a bad mood or feeling negative, everything around us can seem dark and grim. But when we're feeling good and thinking positively, suddenly the world appears brighter and more inviting. It's like our thoughts are a pair of glasses we wear, and the lenses change depending on what we're thinking.

Our thoughts don't just affect us, they also affect the people around us. Have you ever noticed how your mood can change when you're around someone who's really happy or really sad? It's because our thoughts and emotions are contagious. So when we fill our minds with positive thoughts, we're not just helping ourselves, we're also making the world a better place for everyone around us.

In the end, realizing that our thoughts are like a boomerang means understanding that we have the power to shape our lives and our world. If we want to create a life full of love, happiness, and success, all we have to do is start by changing our thoughts. So go ahead and give it a try. Throw out some positive thoughts and watch as they come back to you, just like a boomerang.

— DAY 177 —

There are two sides to every experience

L IFE is a series of ups and downs. But what if I told you that every positive experience you have is actually linked to a negative experience? And, believe it or not, the opposite is also true. Let me explain.

Consider the last time you felt really happy. Maybe it was after getting a promotion, going on an amazing vacation, or falling in love. Those moments feel incredible, but they wouldn't be as special if you hadn't experienced some kind of struggle or pain before. It's like the negative experiences set the stage for the positive ones to really shine.

Now, let's flip it around. Remember the last time you felt down or sad? It's not as fun to think about, I know. But, in a weird way, those negative moments can actually make the positive ones even better. Like, when you finally get over a tough breakup and find love again, it's that much sweeter because you know what it's like to be heartbroken. The negative experiences can teach us to appreciate the good times even more.

But it's not just about appreciating the good times. The balance between positive and negative experiences also helps us grow as people. When we face challenges and hardships, we're forced to dig deep and find the strength we never knew we had. And then, when we come out on the other side, we're stronger and better equipped to handle whatever life throws our way.

So, what can we take away from this? Well, for starters, maybe we should stop trying to avoid all the negative stuff in life. I'm not saying we should go out and seek pain or misery, but if we can learn to see the value in our struggles, we might just find that they're not so bad after all.

In the end, life is all about balance. We need the good and the bad, the ups and the downs, to make our lives complete. Next time you're riding high or feeling low, just remember: every positive experience has an opposing negative experience, and vice versa. And that's what makes life so beautifully complex and wonderfully unpredictable. Build resilience in the face of adversity, and inspire others to do the same.

— DAY 178 —

Retire TO something rather than FROM something

T HE very essence of life is progress and growth, an endless journey of discovery and self-improvement. Yet, there comes a time when the fast pace of life slows down, and we find ourselves at the edge of retirement. Retirement often signifies a transition, a move away from a career, or a lifestyle that has defined us for years. However, it is crucial to approach this phase of life not as an end but as a beginning, a chance to retire TO something rather than merely retiring FROM something.

Imagine waking up each morning, the sun gently peeking through your curtains, with no goal or purpose to fuel your day. Life may seem empty, stripped of meaning, as the absence of a driving force casts a shadow over your existence. This is the reality for many who retire without considering the importance of having a goal or passion to pursue in their newfound free time.

Retirement is a golden opportunity to rediscover one's self, explore interests that were once buried under the weight of responsibilities, and ignite passions that have been idle for a long time. It's a time to cultivate hobbies, engage with the community, or perhaps embark on a new journey of learning and personal growth. The key is to find a purpose that energizes and excites you, something that makes you leap out of bed each morning with enthusiasm and anticipation.

One way to ensure that you retire to something fulfilling is to plan ahead. Before leaving your job or career, take the time to reflect on what truly matters to you. What have you always wanted to do but never had the time or resources for? What passions have you neglected in the pursuit of professional success? Answering these questions can help you craft a vision for your retirement that will bring meaning and joy to your life.

By consciously choosing to retire TO something rather than FROM something, you can transform this stage of life into a period of growth, exploration, and profound personal fulfillment. Let your retirement be a celebration of all that you have achieved and a stepping stone to the rich and meaningful experiences that await you.

— DAY 179 —

"No" is a complete sentence

I N this crazy society we're often taught to say "Yes" to everything that comes our way. Whether it's for work, friends, or family, we're expected to accommodate and please others. But the truth is, saying "No" is an act of self-preservation.

Believe it or not, "No" is a complete sentence. And I know what you're thinking, "How can such a small word have so much power?" Well, it's simple. Saying "No" allows us to set boundaries and protect our own mental and emotional health. It's not just about being stubborn or inflexible; it's about knowing our limits and making sure we don't stretch ourselves too thin.

How many times have you said "Yes" when you really wanted to say "No"? How many times have you found yourself swamped with tasks, barely keeping your head above water, all because you couldn't bring yourself to say that one little word? I know I've been there—and it's not a fun place to be.

Now, don't get me wrong. Saying "No" isn't always easy. It takes guts, especially when we're so used to putting others' needs before our own. But the more we practice saying "No," the easier it becomes.

When we learn to say "No" with certainty, we start to prioritize our own well-being. We're able to focus on the things that really matter to us—our passions, our goals, and our relationships. And that is the key to a happier, more fulfilling life.

If you find yourself on the brink of saying "Yes" when you really want to say "No," remember: "No" is a complete sentence. It doesn't need an explanation, and it doesn't need to be wrapped up in a pretty bow. It's a powerful statement that tells the world you value yourself and your boundaries. Recognize the importance of saying "No" when you don't want to do something, and work towards prioritizing your own well-being. Say "Yes" to what serves you, and build a life that's fulfilling and meaningful. Inspire others to do the same.

— DAY 180 —

Always empty your cup

IMAGINE you are holding a teacup, filled to the top with tea. Now, imagine someone tries to pour more tea into it. What happens? The tea overflows, making a mess. The same holds true in life—if our minds are already filled with preestablished assumptions and fixed ideas, there is no room for new knowledge, growth, or change. The key, then, is to always empty your cup.

This concept is rooted in Zen philosophy, emphasizing the importance of approaching life with an open mind and an empty cup. It is through the conscious act of "emptying our cup" that we transform from passive vessels to active participants in our intellectual journey. It pushes us to question, reevaluate, and adapt our understanding, catalyzing intellectual evolution. For the knowledge that once served us well, may not always be conducive to the ever-evolving realities we encounter.

Emptiness, though often viewed through the lens of lack or deficiency, is in this context, a state of openness, a space overflow with potentiality. It is the fertile soil, ready to nurture the seeds of wisdom we sow consciously. By maintaining an "empty cup," we remain adaptable and agile, navigating the dynamic currents of life with grace and equanimity.

To "empty your cup" is also to practice humility. It is an acknowledgment that no matter how far we've journeyed in the pursuit of knowledge, there remains a universe yet unexplored. This humility encourages empathy, patience, and understanding, weaving a social fabric of mutual respect and collective growth.

In conclusion, "always empty your cup" is not a call to forgetfulness or ignorance, but rather an exhortation to lifelong learning. It is an invitation to create room for the new, the strange, the challenging. It is about cultivating a mindset that isn't just open, but is also eager and ready for the endless opportunities that life throws our way. It reminds us that the process of learning is an unending adventure, one that requires an empty cup, an open mind, and a resilient spirit.

— DAY 181 —

Lesson repeats until learned

L IFE has a funny way of teaching us the lessons we need to learn. It often presents us with similar situations and challenges, hoping that we will finally grasp the underlying wisdom. Think back to the times when you found yourself facing the same obstacles, making the same mistakes, or encountering similar patterns in your relationships or career. It may have felt frustrating and repetitive, like being stuck in a never-ending loop. But what if these repetitions were not mere coincidences or bad luck?

Ever feel like you're running into the same problems over and over again? Like you're spinning your wheels in the mud, facing the same kinds of toxic relationships, or making the same old mistakes? Yeah, me too. It's not by accident. Nope. It's life, throwing you a rerun of the same episode until you understand the plot.

Imagine it like you're stuck on a game level, fighting the same boss battle until you figure out the strategy to beat it. Annoying, right? But oh-so-satisfying once you've cracked the code. It's the same thing with life lessons. They keep popping up, dressing in different clothes, wearing different masks, but at their core, they're the same.

What's beautiful about this repetition is that it's life's way of saying it believes in you. It's shouting, "Hey, I know you can figure this out! So I'm going to keep throwing this at you until you do." It's not punishment, but the universe's unique, if a bit annoying, form of faith in our capacity to grow.

So, the next time you're feeling stuck in a pattern, take a step back, and look at the bigger picture. What lesson is life trying to teach you? Unravel that mystery, and you won't just break the cycle, you'll level up.

Of course, learning a lesson is not always easy. It requires us to be honest with ourselves, to acknowledge our flaws and weaknesses, and to make changes in our thoughts, behaviors, and attitudes. But the rewards that come with this kind of growth and self-improvement are immeasurable.

— DAY 182 —

The first try at anything is rarely successful

T HINK back to your own experiences. Can you recall a time when you tried something for the first time and succeeded immediately? Probably not. The reality is that mastery and accomplishment require dedication, perseverance, and a willingness to embrace failure as an essential part of the process.

Imagine a toddler teetering on chubby legs, toppling over only to rise again. Each topple, a brush with failure, yet simultaneously, a stepping stone to the desired goal of walking. This is the essence of the human experience, an intrinsic rhythm of trials, errors, and perseverance.

Our earliest attempts at anything new are full of mishaps and missteps. Whether it's baking your first cake, painting a landscape, or crafting a poem, initial attempts often result in a mess of half-baked dough, distorted perspectives, or shocking verses.

The first tries are where we find the edges of our current abilities. They are our forays into the unknown, riddled with stumbles, and fraught with frustration. But they also provide the blueprints for our growth. They help us identify gaps in our knowledge, and unravel our strengths and weaknesses.

Rarely being successful on the first try might seem like a harsh reality. But it's this very reality that gives us space to learn, explore, and grow. It humbles us, reminding us of the universal truth that success isn't an event, but a process. It underscores the importance of patience, resilience, and above all, the power of persistence.

Imagine a world where we succeed in everything at the first attempt. It might seem appealing initially, but soon the monotony would settle in. Without the struggle, the victory would lose its flavor. Without the journey, the destination would lose its worth.

The "first try" isn't about success or failure. It's about stepping into the arena of uncertainty, embracing the discomfort of learning, and persisting in the face of setbacks. It's about celebrating the effort, the courage to try, and the will to keep trying. For, as they say, the road to success is always under construction, and every failed first attempt is a brick in that road.

— DAY 183 —

Don't dwell in the middle

IN a world that often values conformity and familiarity, it is all too easy to find ourselves trapped in the middle ground—a place where we feel secure and unchallenged, but where true growth and self-discovery remain difficult to find. The middle ground represents the status quo, a place where we adhere to societal expectations, and where we are satisfied to let life pass us by.

The middle is safe and secure, free from the danger of failure and the fear of the unknown. It's predictable and comfortable, where we adhere to the status quo and avoid ruffling feathers. But it's also stagnant, devoid of innovation and creativity. The middle lacks the exciting views that lie beyond the edges, the possibilities that exist outside the box.

Life in the middle may provide comfort, but it's often at the cost of personal growth and fulfillment. Living in the middle means adhering to the norms and not challenging them, following paths laid down by others instead of carving your own. It's the realm of the follower, not the leader; the copier, not the creator.

However, when we step out of the middle, we step into the realm of possibility. We ignite the spark of creativity, embrace the thrill of uncertainty, and become the architects of our own destiny. We don't just follow trends; we set them. We don't just adapt to change; we drive it. We move from being spectators in the game of life to being active participants, influencing outcomes and leaving our unique imprint on the world.

Don't dwell in the middle; dare to go beyond. Venture into the unknown, brave the storm, scale the peaks, and plunge into the depths. Embrace the discomfort that comes with challenging norms, for it's in this discomfort that growth happens. It's when we push the boundaries, defy the odds, and test our limits that we truly come into our own.

Life is too short, and too precious to be lived in the shadows of the ordinary. Let us step out of the middle, into the extraordinary, and embrace the magic that lies in the pursuit of greatness. For, in the words of George Bernard Shaw, "Life isn't about finding yourself. Life is about creating yourself."

— DAY 184 —

You don't have to have an opinion

WE live in an age of information overload, where news, social media, and conversations bombard us with a constant stream of opinions. It's easy to feel the pressure to form an opinion on every topic, to align ourselves with one side or the other. But in this pursuit of having an opinion, we often lose sight of the deeper truth—that sometimes, it's okay not to know.

Consider the social media platform, a battleground of competing viewpoints, where every user is expected to take a stand, pick a side, and voice an opinion. The like, share, and comment dynamics create a compulsive need to express, often leading to the premature formation of half-baked, uninformed opinions. But pause for a moment and contemplate—isn't it perfectly alright to abstain, to withhold judgment, to simply soak in the views of others without feeling compelled to react?

Silence, in the face of a flood of information, can be a sign of strength, an indication of a mind that prefers depth over breadth, contemplation over impulsivity. There's a special kind of wisdom in knowing that we don't have to fill every silence with our thoughts, that we can be comfortable with the emptiness and savor the beauty of nonjudgmental existence.

Moreover, not having an opinion doesn't equate to ignorance or indifference; it often is a representation of open-mindedness, a willingness to learn and understand before making a judgment. It's an acceptance of one's lack of knowledge and an invitation to acquire more. It's a humble submission to the vast expanse of wisdom the world has to offer, a recognition that we are eternal students of life.

It is also crucial to remember that our views are never static, but dynamic entities that evolve with time and exposure to new information. Not having an opinion now doesn't mean never having one; it could merely signify the maturation period of a more informed, well-rounded perspective

— DAY 185 —

Your company reflects your character

T HE people we surround ourselves with have a significant impact on our lives. They shape our beliefs, attitudes, and values, and influence the way we see ourselves and the world around us. It suggests that our interpersonal relationships serve as a reflection of our inner selves, highlighting the interconnectedness of our individual journeys and the collective human experience.

The idea that we are mirrors of those we spend the most time with underscores the subtle yet powerful influence our social environment applies to our psyche. As social beings, we are inherently vulnerable to the attitudes, values, and behaviors of those around us. Through a process of osmosis, we absorb the perspectives and emotional states of our companions, gradually integrating their qualities into our own identity. This phenomenon, often referred to as *Social Contagion*, has the potential to shape our worldview, aspirations, and sense of self in profound ways, ultimately influencing the trajectory of our lives.

In light of this understanding, the statement becomes a call to action, urging us to be intentional in our choice of companions and to prioritize relationships that inspire, challenge, and elevate us. It is a reminder that our personal growth and well-being are relentlessly linked to the company we keep and that the pursuit of self-discovery and personal development is, in many ways, a collective endeavor.

Of course, this is easier said than done. It's not always easy to let go of relationships that no longer serve us, especially if they have been a part of our lives for a long time. But if we want to create the life we truly desire, we need to be willing to make the hard choices and surround ourselves with people who align with our vision and values.

When we do this, we become a direct reflection of the people we surround ourselves with. We start to embody the positive attitudes, behaviors, and qualities that we admire in them, and we become more confident and self-assured as a result.

Take a look at the people you spend the most time with. Are they uplifting and supportive, or do they bring you down?

— DAY 186 —

The best apology is changed behavior

IN a world quick to say "sorry," the true measure of regret is not found in words, but in the actions that follow. An apology, no matter how sincere, becomes empty if the behavior that caused the hurt remains unchanged. It's in the transformation, the effort to do better, that we find the essence of a genuine apology.

Consider the journey of a public figure caught in the web of scandal. Public apologies flood the media, yet it's not the expressive speeches that restore their reputation, but the tangible steps they take to rectify their wrongs. It's the philanthropist, once criticized for being out of touch, who rolls up their sleeves and gets involved in grassroots projects, learning from those they aim to help. Their shift from detachment to engagement speaks volumes, offering a model of how true repentance leads to transformation.

Or reflect on the personal growth of an athlete known more for their temper than their talent. The world watches as they stumble, their apologies becoming as predictable as their outbursts. Yet, over time, something shifts. The athlete begins to channel their passion into discipline, both on and off the field. This change, hard-won and deeply personal, becomes their true apology, turning former critics into their most passionate supporters.

These stories resonate because they reflect a universal truth: a real apology is an ongoing process, not a one-time event. It's about recognizing the impact of our actions, taking responsibility, and then working to make things right. This journey isn't easy. It requires humility, patience, and a commitment to personal growth that goes beyond mere words.

In our own lives, we face countless opportunities to choose between empty apologies and meaningful change. Whether it's repairing a strained relationship, correcting a mistake at work, or addressing our own biases, the path to redemption is built with actions that speak louder than words. By embracing this ethos, we not only heal the wounds we've caused but also embark on a journey of selfimprovement, proving that the best way to say "I'm sorry" is to show it through our actions every day.

— DAY 187 —

Work hard, play hard

I N the quest for success and fulfillment, we often find ourselves caught in the split of work and play. We are told that to achieve our goals, we must work hard and dedicate ourselves to our pursuits. Yet, in the pursuit of our ambitions, we must not forget to gratify the pleasures of life. This delicate balance between work and play holds the key to a life well-lived.

Let's start with the first half: "Work hard." The importance of hard work is as old as civilization itself. We labor to earn our keep, to satisfy our basic needs, and to turn the wheels of progress. But it goes beyond mere survival. When we engage in our work, especially work we're passionate about, we experience a sense of purpose, a fulfillment that only comes from watching the fruits of our labor come to life.

In a society that celebrates achievement, it's easy to lose oneself in the rhythm of labor. We often mistake busyness for productivity, glorifying the grind while ignoring the importance of rest. However, continuous exertion, without an equal measure of relaxation, can lead to burnout. And here's where the second half of the phrase comes in: "Play hard."

Playing hard isn't about mindlessly indulging in hedonistic pursuits. Instead, it's about creating balance. It's about investing as much energy toward restoring ourselves as we do into our work. This could mean engaging in a hobby, connecting with loved ones, or simply basking in solitude. Play recharges us, providing an essential counterweight to our work, a sweet release from our duties.

In a society that is often divided between work and play, setting one against the other, we must recognize that these two entities are not mutually exclusive but exist in a symbiotic relationship. They provide a counterbalance, a rhythm that, when maintained, leads to a fuller, more meaningful life.

This is not just a catchy phrase, it's a philosophy of balance. A reminder that our life should oscillate between periods of focused work and periods of mindful play. Each one feeds into the other, creating a beautifully balanced existence, that overflows with purpose, fulfillment, and joy.

— DAY 188 —

Kindness is a language understood by all hearts

K INDNESS has the power to transform lives, mend broken spirits, and bridge the gaps that divide us. It is a universal language that can heal wounds, restore faith, and bring hope to even the darkest of times. The beauty of kindness lies in its simplicity. It requires no special skills, no grand gestures, and no material wealth. It is the act of extending a helping hand, offering a smile, or speaking words of encouragement.

From the bustling metropolis of New York to the tranquil silence of a Himalayan hamlet, the understanding of kindness remains constant. It's a language that doesn't need a dictionary or a translation app. It's universal, like laughter or tears, transcending the barriers of language, culture, and creed.

In this grand theater of life, we all play different roles, with different scripts, but the resonance of kindness touches us all. The glimmer of joy in someone's eyes when you help them unexpectedly; the bond that forms when you lend a hand to a stranger; or the weight that lifts off a friend's shoulder when you stand by them in their hour of need. These are moments that don't require words, yet they speak volumes.

Let's take it a step further. Take a moment to think about the last time you were kind to yourself. It's harder than it sounds, isn't it? We've become so accustomed to being our own harshest critics, that we often forget to show ourselves the kindness we readily extend to others. But once you do, you'll understand the healing power of self-love, and that, my friend, is a game-changer.

This doesn't mean that kindness is always easy. In fact, it can be hard. It requires courage to step out of our comfort zone, and an open heart that's willing to risk hurt. Yet, its rewards are limitless. For every drop of kindness you pour into the world, you make it a little softer, a little warmer, and a lot more beautiful.

Whether it's a gentle word, a warm smile, or a helping hand, remember that kindness is a language that every heart understands. It's a simple, yet profound way to say, "I see you. I understand you. I care for you." And in a world that's often dominated by differences, isn't that a language worth speaking?

— DAY 189 —

Zero to hero is a choice

LIFE is not a lottery where some hit the jackpot while others are left holding onto mere scraps, my friend. No, life is a journey, a series of choices leading us from zero to hero, or unfortunately, vice versa. But it's not where you start that determines your worth, it's the courage to choose, to strive, and to evolve that does.

"Zero to hero"—we've heard it, we've seen it. It's the stuff of folklore, of cinema, of biographies that keep us up all night. A script as old as time itself, yet it never ceases to inspire. But have you ever wondered why? Because it reminds us of the incredible power of choice and how it can alter the course of our lives.

Choosing to become a hero from a zero isn't about putting on a cape and saving the world. It's about embracing the zero within us. The shortcomings, the failures, the times we fell flat on our faces, and the world seemed too heavy to carry on. Recognizing our zero is the first step toward the hero's journey.

Once we acknowledge our zero, we must choose to rise. Every single day, we must decide to grow, to learn, to work on the pieces of us that make up our zero. Some days it's easy; some days it feels like scaling Everest barefoot. But the choice to keep climbing, that's what separates heroes from the rest.

Remember, no hero is devoid of failures. The phoenix first turns to ash before it rises again. Similarly, heroes are formed in the cauldron of failures, mistakes, and heartbreaks. It's their resolve to stand up each time they fall that makes them extraordinary.

And lastly, the choice to become a hero is not a one-time act. It's a daily commitment to better oneself, to turn yesterday's impossible into today's "I'm possible." It's about stretching the boundaries of your potential until zero fades into the horizon, and all that's left is the hero you've become.

Life is indeed a series of choices, my friend. Whether you stay a zero or become a hero, in the end, it's entirely up to you. So, what do you choose?

— DAY 190 —

Respect diverse perspectives

E ACH individual carries within them a unique set of experiences, beliefs, and values that shape their worldview. These perspectives are formed by cultural backgrounds, personal histories, and the multitude of influences that have shaped us as individuals. By respecting diverse perspectives, we open ourselves up to a world of knowledge, growth, and understanding.

Perspectives are the lenses through which we view the world. Each one is shaped by a unique combination of experiences, beliefs, culture, and individual personality. Just like no two snowflakes are alike, no two perspectives are the same. They are the unique fingerprints of our mind, the distinct echoes of our thoughts.

Respecting diverse perspectives is about acknowledging this richness of thought, and the multitude of ideas. It's about celebrating the multiplicity of voices that make up the symphony of human existence. Because a single tune can never create a melody as enchanting as a harmonious orchestra.

But why should we respect diverse perspectives? Simple, because they help us grow. They challenge our prior assumptions, question our biases, and push us to see beyond the confines of our understanding. They show us the world through a prism we may never have considered, and in doing so, they expand our mental horizons.

Respect for diverse perspectives also fosters empathy, a virtue so rare yet so essential. It urges us to step into another's shoes, see the world through their eyes, and feel their joys and sorrows as our own. It is the birthplace of understanding, compassion, and ultimately, unity.

Furthermore, diverse perspectives are the lifeblood of innovation. The greatest breakthroughs, be it in science, technology, art, or any other field, have emerged from the confluence of diverse thoughts, ideas, and perspectives. They are the seeds that sprout into the tree of progress.

So, let's respect diverse perspectives, not just because it's the right thing to do, but because they enrich us, broaden our worldview, and construct the dynamic pattern of human existence.

— DAY 191 —

Life is the product of your decisions

L IFE is not a random montage of chaotic events. It's a compelling story with a plot twisted and turned by an incredible writer—you! Yes, indeed, life is largely the product of our decisions. Every choice, big or small, shapes our path and determines the course of our journey.

We are all born into situations that we didn't choose. Some of us get a head start, while others have to sprint to catch up. But the real game, the race of life, isn't just about where we start, but how we navigate the course, and that's where our decisions strut onto the stage.

Imagine life as a maze, an extensive labyrinth of paths. Each path at each moment is a decision we make. One path might lead to a dead-end, another to a stunning vista. But remember, there's beauty in the dead-ends too. Each wrong turn, each stumbling block, is a lesson learned, a step closer to the right path. So, in essence, our wrong decisions are not our failings, but our teachers.

And here's some food for thought. Even our decision not to decide, is, in itself, a decision! When we shy away from making choices, we're making a conscious decision to let life's current carry us instead of swimming toward our chosen destination. And that can make all the difference between living life and merely existing.

Now, I'm not saying that every decision we make will lead us to an enchanted castle. Sometimes, it might lead us into a dragon's den. But hey, wouldn't slaying that dragon make a far more exciting tale?

Decisions give us control over our destiny. Every choice is a brush stroke on the canvas of our life, slowly but surely creating a masterpiece that's uniquely ours. In essence, our lives aren't merely happening to us, we are happening to our lives.

Life is the product of our decisions. We have the power to shape our future through the choices we make. Let us embrace this power, and make decisions that align with our values and priorities.

— DAY 192 —

Tidy space, tidy mind

FROM the moment we open our eyes each morning, we're greeted by our environment. The sight that first meets our gaze can set the tone for the rest of our day. Imagine waking up to a room that's a total mess, with clothes everywhere, books all over the place, and an untidy desk. Now, tell me, wouldn't this sight instantly generate a wave of disorder within you?

Pause for a moment and consider the sanctuary of a Zen monk—minimalist, orderly, calm. Every item has a place, and every place has a purpose. This is not an aesthetic notion, but a profound acknowledgment of the human psyche's innate desire for order, its wishing for harmony. And this isn't just philosophical, science backs it up too!

Numerous studies confirm a significant correlation between our physical environment and our mental state. An organized, decluttered space can lead to clearer thought processes, heightened creativity, and increased productivity.3 If your surroundings are a tempest, it's likely that your thoughts will mirror this storm.

Let's take another plunge into this thought ocean. Have you noticed how cleaning your space can often feel like therapy? As we clear the physical clutter, we somehow manage to sort through the cobwebs of our minds. The process of organizing our external world brings an incredible sense of calm and clarity. It's as though each discarded item is a dismissed worry, each organized drawer a sorted thought.

Maintaining a tidy space is not just about cleanliness, it's about mindfulness. It's a continuous, conscious choice to respect and value the objects we own and the space we inhabit. It's a daily act of gratitude towards our environment.

I'm not urging you to become a minimalist overnight or develop an obsession for cleanliness. The idea here is to appreciate the influence our environment has on us and to use it to our advantage. After all, isn't life more enjoyable when we have the headspace to savor it?

— DAY 193 —

Success needs a present mindset

TAKE a moment and think about success. What does it look like to you? A luxurious mansion, a fast car, a top-level job, maybe a happy family? But here's the real question. Where is this success? In the future, right? See, that's where most of us get caught. We're always chasing this elusive future, hustling, running, panting, and yet, it seems to always be a step ahead.

Let me tell you a secret, my friend. Success isn't a destination, it's a journey. It's not a pot of gold waiting at the end of the rainbow, it's the rainbow itself. It's not about the towering peak, it's about the climb. It's not about "then", it's about "now". Alright, let's dig a bit deeper.

Imagine you're an actor preparing for a big role. You've got your script, you know your lines, and you're all geared up. Now, when you're on stage delivering your dialogues, are you thinking about the applause at the end? No. You're living the character, feeling each emotion, focusing on each word. That's what a present mindset is all about. It's about living in the moment, being completely engaged in the current task, rather than worrying about the future applause.

"But what about goals? Don't we need to focus on our future success?" you may ask. Yes, goals are important. But consider this—what's the point of a goal if you're not taking steps in the present to achieve it? The present moment is all we have, all we control. Success then is not about reaching a distant future goal, it's about taking purposeful, mindful actions now, in this very moment.

So, next time you find yourself getting lost in dreams of future success, stop. Take a deep breath. Bring yourself back to the present. Engage fully with the task at hand. The key to success lies not in the distant future, but right here, right now. Every moment we dedicate to learning, every risk we undertake, every failure we bounce back from— these are victories in their own right. The future will arrive in its own time. Until then, let's enjoy the journey, because my friend, success needs a present mindset.

— DAY 194 —

We cannot achieve all of our objectives

IN a world that emphasizes success and achievement, it can be easy to fall into the trap of thinking that we must accomplish every goal we set for ourselves. We are taught to believe that with enough determination and effort, anything is possible. While it is true that we can achieve great things, it is also important to recognize that we cannot achieve all of our objectives.

It's easy to get caught up in the whirlwind of desires, goals, and objectives. The modern world applauds the "do-it-all" mentality. Yet, in the middle of this vortex of aspirations, we often neglect the central character of this drama—our finite selves. We have limited resources—time, energy, and attention—but a limitless set of objectives. Mathematics alone tells us the impossibility of this equation.

Understanding the impossibility of attaining all objectives is not an invitation to abandon ambition, but a call to focus on what is truly important. It is a journey of understanding the essential from the desirable. This implies that while some objectives may remain unrealized, the ones that truly align with our inner values and life's purpose get our undivided attention and resources.

Embracing this truth liberates us from the shackles of continuous dissatisfaction. It allows us to celebrate our achievements without the lingering shadow of unmet objectives. We begin to appreciate the journey as much as the destination, finding joy and fulfillment in the process, rather than the outcome.

Perhaps the most enlightening aspect of accepting this truth is the shift in our understanding of failure. Unmet objectives are no longer seen as personal failures but as natural consequences of life's vast array of possibilities. This reframing transforms our perception of failure from a personal deficiency to an integral part of our shared human experience.

The belief that we can achieve all our objectives is not just an unrealistic expectation but a harm to our holistic well-being. The acceptance that we cannot achieve all our objectives paradoxically refines our focus, fosters peace, and enlightens our perception of failure.

— DAY 195 —

Procrastination kills success

THE subtle art of procrastination is an unruly beast, often hiding behind lies of "later," "not now," or "tomorrow." Its insidious effect spreads throughout the fabric of our dreams and desires, throwing a shadow of stagnation that paralyzes our drive for success.

We've all been there, my friend. It starts innocently enough—a small delay here, a minor distraction there. But before you know it, time slips through your fingers like sand, and you're left wondering where it all went wrong. Procrastination preys on our vulnerabilities, whispering sweet lies that sound oh-so-tempting. "You have plenty of time, you can do it later" it says.

But the truth is, later never comes. It's just an illusion, a mirage in the desert of our excuses. And while we find joy in the comfort of our procrastination, success slips further and further away.

But why do we procrastinate? Fear is often the underlying reason. Fear of failure, fear of the unknown, fear of stepping out of our comfort zones. We create these mental barriers that keep us trapped in the realm of procrastination. We convince ourselves that we're not ready, that we don't have what it takes. But let me tell you a little secret: None of us are ever truly ready. Success doesn't wait for perfection; it demands progress.

So how do we break free from this cycle? It starts with a shift in mindset. We must recognize that time is our most valuable resource, and every moment wasted in procrastination is a moment lost forever. We must cultivate discipline, self-awareness, and a deep sense of purpose. It's about finding the fire within us, the burning desire to make our dreams a reality.

Sure, it won't be easy. Procrastination has a way of luring us back in with its siren song of comfort and familiarity. But we must resist its call. We must create a roadmap, set clear goals, and hold ourselves accountable.

The choice is ours. We can continue to dance with procrastination, watching success slip through our fingers like smoke. Or we can rise above it, seize the day, and carve our own path. The power is within us—it always has been.

— DAY 196 —

Networking triumphs Ivy League education

Y OU'VE heard it before, "It's not what you know, it's who you know." But have you really reflected on that? In the labyrinth of success, multiple paths promise to guide us to our destination. The path of formal education, particularly one bordered by the hallowed halls of Ivy League institutions, is frequently praised as the royal road to achievement. But, while the value of a high-quality education is undeniable, there's another route that possesses an equally potent, yet often underestimated, capacity to shape our journeys.

Don't get me wrong—higher education has its merits. Institutions like the Ivy League offer unmatched scholarly intensity, top-notch professors, and a reputation that can pave the way. However, in a landscape where knowledge is readily available at our fingertips, it is the connections we forge that can set us apart.

Networking goes beyond swapping business cards or collecting LinkedIn connections. It's about nurturing genuine relationships founded on trust, shared interests, and mutual respect. By cultivating a diverse network, we gain access to a wealth of knowledge and experiences that cannot be found within the confines of a classroom.

Through networking, we connect with like-minded individuals who inspire and challenge us. Mentors and industry leaders become our guides, sharing invaluable insights gained from real-world experiences. We expand our horizons, gaining perspectives from a range of fields and industries that may have otherwise eluded us.

The power of networking lies in its ability to uncover hidden opportunities. It is through personal connections that we stumble upon unadvertised job openings, exciting projects, or career-defining moments. Recommendations and referrals hold more weight than a precisely crafted resume. By tapping into our network, we gain access to a world of possibilities. Education is undeniably important, but it is networking that brings knowledge to life.

— DAY 197 —

Love yourself first to love others

LOVE is a powerful force that has the ability to transform lives, heal wounds, and create deep connections. We often think of love as something we give to others, pouring out our affection, care, and support. But within the chaos of loving others, we sometimes forget the essential truth: to truly love others, we must first love ourselves.

Loving oneself might seem like a detour to narcissism, or at worst, a form of selfishness. But is that truly the case? No, far from it. Self-love isn't about ignoring others' needs or being self-centered. Instead, it's about nurturing an authentic relationship with oneself, about understanding, appreciating, and accepting who we are.

To love others genuinely and unconditionally, we must first know how to give that same kind of love to ourselves. We must know what it feels like to be gentle with our mistakes, value our worth, and celebrate our strengths. And how could we possibly do this for others if we haven't first done it for ourselves? It's like trying to fill other's cups from our own that is empty.

Interestingly, this self-love journey also illuminates our understanding of others. As we grow kinder to our own shortcomings, our empathy for others' imperfections increases. We become more patient, more understanding, and less judgmental. Love becomes less of an exchange and more of a natural overflow from our own fulfilled hearts.

When we love ourselves first, we set a benchmark for how we expect others to treat us. We communicate to the world that we deserve respect, kindness, and love, indirectly inviting others to do the same. This boundary-setting is a vital aspect of healthy relationships and a byproduct of self-love.

Loving yourself first isn't a self-serving act, but the foundational layer to love others effectively. It's about filling your cup first, not to be fuller than others but to let your love overflow into them. It's about understanding the light and dark corners of your soul, to illuminate empathy and patience for others. It's about setting the tone for how you should be treated, raising the bar of love higher for all.

— DAY 198 —

Reading unlocks life's mysteries

IMAGINE holding a key that has the power to open doorways into different worlds, different times, even different minds. This key isn't forged of metal but of ink and paper, imagination and intellect. We're talking about books, of course, and the divine act of reading.

Reading is an act of mental time travel, a voyage through the cosmos of knowledge. It's like diving into a treasure chest stuffed with what people have learned, a real Pandora's box, but instead of curses, it's packed with eye-opening insights and wisdom. Every book, every word, every thought carefully inked on paper is a star in this vast galaxy, offering light to navigate the expanse of life's mysteries.

And what are these mysteries that reading can unlock? They span the spectrum from the realms of quantum physics to the intricacies of human emotions, from the patterns of ancient civilizations to the complexities of modern societies. Reading, as a tool, allows us to follow the threads that weave the human experience into a single, interconnected tapestry.

Each book we encounter is a conversation, a dialogue between the reader and the author. Through this communication, ideas spark and thoughts converge, igniting the flame of comprehension. Herein lies the profound beauty of reading; it is not a mere spectator sport but an active engagement, an opportunity for readers to question, reflect, and decode the complex puzzle that exists.

Through reading, we become active participants in the collective wisdom of humanity. We inherit the lessons of generations past, and we contribute to the ongoing dialogue that shapes our future. Each word we read, each idea we absorb, is a stepping stone on our personal quest for knowledge, understanding, and growth.

My fellow adventurer, let us never underestimate the power of a book. Let us embrace the opportunity to unlock life's mysteries through the written word. As we turn each page, let us remember that reading is not a passive act but a transformative experience—one that has the potential to shape our lives and illuminate the path to our own greatness.

— DAY 199 —

Reduce stress for a better life

YOU'RE standing in the middle of a bustling city, surrounded by the chaos of noise, traffic, and hurried footsteps. Your mind feels like a whirlwind of responsibilities, deadlines, and expectations. You long for a moment of peace, a respite from the stress that seems to consume your every waking moment.

Stress, although typically viewed as the villain in our life story, is a tool, a signal from our brain that something requires our attention. The trick isn't to entirely eliminate stress, for that would be similar to removing an important instrument from our orchestra. Instead, we should aim to tune this instrument so that it plays in harmony with the rest of our symphony.

The journey to reducing stress starts with self-awareness. It requires us to pause, take a deep breath, and examine the factors that contribute to our stress levels. Is it the demands of work, the pressure to meet societal expectations, or the weight of our perfectionism?

One of the most powerful tools in our arsenal against stress is mindfulness. The practice of mindfulness invites us to be fully present in the here and now, to observe our thoughts and emotions without judgment.

Another essential ingredient in reducing stress is self-care. We often neglect our own needs in the pursuit of productivity and success. But true success is not measured by the number of hours worked or the achievements amassed; it is measured by our ability to prioritize our well-being. Engage in activities that bring you joy, whether it's reading a book, taking a walk in nature, or spending quality time with loved ones. Nurture your body, mind, and soul.

In our modern, hyperconnected world, it's crucial to disconnect and create boundaries. Establish designated times for rest, free from the incessant demands of technology. Permit yourself to unplug, to be present with yourself and those around you.

Finally, seek support from others. We are not meant to navigate life's challenges alone. Reach out to friends, family, or professionals who can provide guidance and a listening ear. Surround yourself with a supportive network that uplifts and encourages you.

— DAY 200 —

Agree to disagree

H AVE you ever found yourself engaged in a passionate debate, firmly convinced that your perspective is the only valid one? It's a common occurrence in our diverse and opinionated world. It is a skill that many struggle to master. We live in an era of polarization, where people are quick to condemn those who hold opposing beliefs. But what if we shifted our approach and embraced the idea that disagreement is not a barrier, but an opportunity?

It's not the disagreement itself that holds the power, it's the agreement part. It's the conscious choice to accept and respect a difference of opinion without letting it break the bonds that unite us. It's a mutual understanding that our diversity in thought is not a chasm to be feared but a spectrum to be celebrated.

The idea is simple: we're all different. Different backgrounds, different experiences, different views. And that's beautiful. It's what makes life vibrant. Imagine a world where we all thought the same, felt the same, believed the same. Sounds lifeless, doesn't it?

But here's where the challenge lies, and where "agree to disagree" becomes more than just a phrase. You see, it's one thing to tolerate differences when they're minor, like preferring apples over oranges. But what about when the differences are deep, touching on the very core of our beliefs? It's a tougher pill to swallow, isn't it?

And that's exactly when the magic happens. By choosing to agree to disagree, we're practicing empathy and understanding. We're signaling that we value the relationship more than the argument, that we respect the other person's right to their perspective, even if it diverges from ours.

But don't mistake this for weakness or an admission of defeat. On the contrary, it's a testament to strength, maturity, and wisdom.

Remember, it's not always easy. It takes courage, patience, and a whole lot of empathy. But next time you find yourself on the opposite side of a heated debate, take a step back. Breathe. And then, agree to disagree. Because at the end of the day, our relationships and our shared humanity are worth more than winning an argument, don't you think?

— DAY 201 —

Boredom breeds creativity

PICTURE this: you're sitting on your couch, stuck in the quiet monotony of a lazy Sunday afternoon. You're bored. Now, hold that thought. What if I told you that this boredom, this seemingly dull moment, is a secret doorway to a world of untapped creativity?

First off, let's get friendly with boredom. It's not the enemy; it's just misunderstood. In the whirlwind of our fast-paced lives, we're constantly bombarded with information, tasks, and entertainment. When we suddenly hit the brakes, our minds, unaccustomed to the quiet, perceive it as boredom.

Here's the cool part. When left to its own devices, our mind begins to wander, freeing itself from the chains of structure and routine. It's like a bird released from its cage, soaring through the vast skies of imagination, free to explore and discover. In these calm, unhurried moments, the magic of creativity often sparks.

Boredom encourages us to daydream, to question, to invent. It's like being an explorer, adventuring into the uncharted wilderness of our minds, picking up abstract ideas, and weaving them into something new and exciting. Whether it's a groundbreaking solution to a tricky problem, a melody that makes your heart dance, or a storyline for a captivating novel—these are the treasures unearthed from the mine of boredom-induced creativity.

Plus, let's not forget the introspection that comes with boredom. It's an opportunity to reflect, to connect with our inner selves, which can lead to incredible self-discoveries and personal growth. Talk about a win-win!

Boredom isn't an empty space; it's a creative greenhouse. It's not a gray, dull void, but a canvas awaiting the strokes of our imaginative prowess. When boredom comes knocking next time, make sure it's not an unexciting visitor, but a hidden ally. Embrace it, allow your mind to wander, and who knows what incredible ideas you'll stumble upon?

Boredom becomes a gateway to novel ideas, fresh perspectives, and innovative solutions. It's in boredom that we unlock our creative potential and embark on a journey of limitless possibilities.

— DAY 202 —

Big risks yield big rewards

I T'S a captivating concept, isn't it? The idea that venturing outside our comfort zones, embracing uncertainty, and taking bold risks can lead to extraordinary rewards. It's a belief held by visionaries, pioneers, and those who have dared to dream beyond the confines of the ordinary.

Big risks are inherently intimidating. They challenge our sense of security and push us to confront our fears. But within that discomfort lies the potential for incredible growth and transformation. When we take big risks, we step into uncharted territories, unafraid to challenge the status quo and explore new horizons.

Consider the remarkable individuals throughout history who have achieved great things by taking monumental risks. Think of explorers like Christopher Columbus, who set sail into uncharted waters, or inventors like Thomas Edison, who relentlessly pursued their ideas despite countless failures. These individuals understood that the biggest rewards come from daring to go where no one else has gone before.

Taking big risks requires a belief in ourselves and a steadfast faith that we are capable of achieving the extraordinary. It demands a willingness to embrace failure and setbacks as stepping stones on the path to success. It's about seeing obstacles as opportunities for growth, and rejection as redirection towards something better.

But let's not forget that big risks also come with the potential for big rewards. They offer us the chance to uncover hidden talents, discover new passions, and experience moments of triumph that forever shape our lives.

However, it's important to approach big risks with thoughtful consideration and a calculated strategy. Blind leaps into the unknown rarely yield the desired outcomes. It's about weighing the potential risks against the potential rewards, assessing the situation, and making informed decisions.

Remember, the comfort zone might be safe, but it's in the realm of risk where life's greatest rewards often reside. It's where you'll discover not just what you're capable of achieving, but who you're capable of becoming.

— DAY 203 —

Pedal or stay behind in life

A LBERT Einstein said it perfectly; "Life is like riding a bicycle. To keep your balance, you must keep moving." The phrase holds a deeper wisdom than you might think. Let's take a moment to reflect on this potent idea.

Consider each turn of the pedal as your effort to move forward, your decision to embrace change, your determination to navigate life's twists and turns. It's you saying, "I'm the pilot of my life, and I'm not just along for the ride." Every push, every rotation, is a testament to your resilience, your ability to challenge yourself, and your refusal to be stuck in the rut of stagnation.

Of course, pedaling isn't always a breeze. It requires strength, endurance, and sometimes, pure grit. There are steep hills to climb, sharp turns to navigate, and unexpected potholes to avoid. Yet, it's these very challenges that offer opportunities for growth, learning, and self-discovery. It's during these times that we truly push our limits and discover what we're made of.

But what happens if we choose not to pedal? We stay put, don't we? Life carries on, the world continues to spin, and we are left behind, rooted in comfort yet devoid of progress. Life, like a river, is in a state of constant flow, and to resist this motion is to miss out on the exciting opportunities that lie downstream.

The choice is yours. Will you embrace the adventure and pedal with determination, passion, and purpose? Or will you let fear and comfort keep you stagnant? Life is a journey meant to be experienced, savored, and lived to the fullest.

Each pedal stroke is an opportunity to grow, discover your true potential, and leave a lasting mark on the world. Pedal with all your might, embrace the challenges, and seize the opportunities that come your way. Step out of the shadows, feel the wind in your hair, and experience the exciting ride that awaits you. It's time to pedal forward and create a life that surpasses your wildest dreams.

— DAY 204 —

The banks have raped society

I MAGINE you're at a high-stakes poker game. There's one player, let's call him The Bank, who plays with a devil-may-care attitude, taking wild, reckless risks. He wins big, pocketing the profits for himself. But when he loses, it's everyone else at the table who has to chip in to cover his losses.

When banks gamble with complex financial instruments, there's the potential for monumental profits. These gains, however, are often enjoyed exclusively by the banks themselves and their shareholders. When the bets pay off, it's a private party of wealth accumulation. Yet, this is only half the story.

Turning our attention to the financial crisis of 2008. Banks, engrossed in their high-stakes game, took excessive risks, resulting in losses so enormous they threatened to sink the whole financial system. Now, remember our poker table? Just like the other players having to cover The Bank's losses, it was the taxpayers who were called upon to bail out the banks. Society bore the brunt of these losses, not through choice, but out of necessity to keep the financial system afloat.

In essence, the banks privatized the wins but socialized the losses. This reckless behavior not only jeopardized the global economy but also deeply eroded public trust in the banking sector. The disappointment stems from this stark contrast between the banks' prosperity in good times and their reliance on public funds during crises. It's the perception of an unfair system, where the banks can't lose, and society can't win.

The banks' actions reveal a deeper flaw in our societal structure, exposing inherent inequities and the importance of questioning accepted norms. We need to cultivate critical thinking, so we don't merely accept such practices as business as usual. It's not just the banks; our system itself fosters disparity, where certain entities are protected, while others bear the consequences.

Let it be clear, this is not an angry rant but a ringing call to awareness. The discontent we feel is a summons to question and to engage. If our trusted banks can privatize their wins and socialize their losses, what other imbalances might we be overlooking in this chaotic world?

— DAY 205 —

Time is life's currency

TAKE a moment and imagine you're walking into life's marketplace, where time is the currency. It's not dollars or euros, bitcoins or gold, but the seconds, minutes, and hours that make up your life. It is, without a doubt, life's currency. A currency that is limited, non-renewable, and incredibly precious.

We spend our days, our years, and our entire lives in the exchange of time. Every decision we make and every action we take, involves a transaction of this valuable currency. We invest it in relationships, careers, hobbies, and pursuits. Unlike any other currency, time cannot be earned, saved, or multiplied. Once spent, it is gone forever.

Time is a relentless reminder of our mortality—a constant ticking of the clock, urging us to make the most of each passing moment. It compels us to reflect on how we choose to spend this precious currency. Do we waste it on trivial matters, allowing it to slip through our fingers like sand? Or do we invest it wisely, nurturing meaningful connections, pursuing our passions, and leaving a lasting impact?

The true power lies in recognizing the value of every passing second and embracing the profound potential that lies within it. Time is not meant to be hoarded or wasted; it is meant to be cherished and utilized to create a life of purpose and significance.

Just like with any currency, we must be mindful of how we spend it. Are we caught up in the frenzy of busyness, sacrificing moments of connection and self-care?

We must also acknowledge that time is not infinite. Its scarcity makes it all the more valuable, urging us to seize the day and make the most of the opportunities presented to us. Each passing moment is an invitation—a chance to grow, learn, love, and create memories that will endure long after our time on this earth has ended.

It's a compelling reminder. It's urging us to spend wisely, to choose experiences over possessions, and to value our time as we do our money. Because at the end of the day, isn't life all about how well we've spent our time?

— DAY 206 —

Always ask

C URIOSITY is the driving force behind human progress. It is the spark that ignites innovation, fuels exploration, and propels us forward on the journey of knowledge. And at the core of curiosity lies a simple yet powerful action: asking questions.

Every moment, every interaction, every experience is brimming with potential knowledge. Yet, often, we stand at the cliff of understanding, afraid to take the plunge. But what holds us back? Is it the fear of appearing ignorant? Or the discomfort of venturing into the unknown? Whatever it may be, remember, every question is a step forward, a key unlocking doors to endless possibilities.

Take a walk down memory lane. Remember the childlike wonder with which you approached the world, the relentless curiosity that propelled you to question everything around you? "Why is the sky blue?", "What makes the flowers bloom?", "Why do stars twinkle?". Each question was a journey, an adventure, a story that unfolded the mysteries of the world, shaping your understanding and perception.

As we grow older, we somehow lose this natural curiosity. We settle into our comfortable bubbles of perceived knowledge, seldom questioning what lies beyond. But, isn't it a bit contradictory? As our spectrum of knowledge expands, shouldn't our questions also multiply? After all, every answered question gives birth to new ones, doesn't it?

Now imagine harnessing this power of inquiry in every aspect of your life. In your relationships, ask not just what you can receive, but what you can give. In your personal growth, ask not just where you are, but where you want to be. In your work, ask not just what is required of you, but what more can you do.

Let's break free from our inhibitions, and self-constructed barriers. Let's rekindle our lost curiosity. Let's not be afraid to admit our lack of knowledge. Let's ask, because only then can we learn, grow, and understand.

After all, we are all sailors in this vast ocean of life. Let our questions be our sails, the wind that propels us forward in this incredible journey. Always ask my friend, always ask.

— DAY 207 —

Have a rainy day fund

L ET'S talk about something that might sound a bit mundane at first, but trust me, it's a game-changer. Imagine a world where the sun always shines, where the skies are always blue, and the rain never falls. It sounds idyllic, doesn't it? But within the beauty of eternal sunshine lies a profound truth—life is unpredictable, and storms are inevitable. That's why it's crucial to have a rainy day fund, a safety net to weather life's unexpected challenges.

Having a rainy day fund is more than just financial preparedness—it's a mindset, a way of approaching life with resilience and foresight. It's about acknowledging the uncertainty that exists and proactively planning for the unexpected.

Just as raindrops fall from the sky, life throws us curveballs—job loss, medical emergencies, or unforeseen expenses. These storms can catch us off guard, leaving us vulnerable and scrambling for cover. But with a rainy day fund, we have the means to protect ourselves and navigate through the downpour.

A rainy day fund provides us with a sense of security and peace of mind. It's like an umbrella that shields us from the chaos and uncertainty. Knowing that we have a financial cushion allows us to face challenging times with confidence, knowing that we have the resources to withstand the storm.

But let's not forget that a rainy day fund is not just about money—it's about building a foundation of resilience in all aspects of life. It's about having emotional support, nurturing relationships, and building a network of people who have your back when the storm hits.

Life is full of surprises, but by building a safety net, we can navigate through the storms with grace. It's time to be proactive, protect ourselves, and embrace the peace of mind that comes from knowing we're prepared for whatever comes our way.

— DAY 208 —

Life's fairness is an illusion

L IFE'S fairness is an illusion. It's a hard pill to swallow, but it's the truth. We all grow up hearing phrases like "life isn't fair," but we don't really understand the full extent of it until we're faced with our own struggles and hardships.

We like to believe that if we work hard and do everything "right," we will be rewarded accordingly. But that's not always the case. Sometimes, bad things happen to good people, and good things happen to those who don't deserve them. It's easy to feel bitter and resentful when we see others who seem to have it all, while we struggle to make ends meet. But the truth is, life doesn't owe us anything.

As we delve deeper into the labyrinth of life's fairness, we are confronted with the notion of serendipity—the unpredictable and lucky events that have the power to alter the trajectory of our lives. It is tempting to believe that these chance encounters are guided by some cosmic hand, meting out justice and ensuring that life's scales remain balanced. Yet, as we navigate the ebb and flow of fortune, we must confront the unsettling reality that unexpected luck may simply be a product of chaos and chance, with no regard for the perceived fairness of its distribution.

In our contemplation of life's fairness, we must also grapple with the role of personal responsibility. The belief in our agency and the power to shape our destiny is a cornerstone of human existence. However, this belief can be shaken when we witness the seemingly unpredictable nature of life, where the virtuous suffer while the wicked prosper. It is in these moments that we must confront the possibility that life's fairness is not a universal truth, but rather a construct that we cling to make sense of an unpredictable and often unforgiving world.

As we emerge from the shadows of our exploration, we are left with the realization that life's fairness may indeed be an illusion. However, in the face of this disquieting revelation, we are presented with an opportunity—a chance to redefine our understanding of fairness and to find meaning in the chaos.

— DAY 209 —

Every day is a new opportunity

EVERY morning, as the sun rises and casts its warm glow upon the world, we are presented with a remarkable gift: a new day, brimming with endless possibilities. It's a chance to start afresh, embrace the unknown, and seize every moment with a sense of purpose and wonder.

The beauty lies in the realization that each day is unique and irreplaceable. The past is behind us, and the future has yet to unfold. We stand at the threshold of possibility, with the power to shape our destiny. It's a humbling and aweinspiring concept that should ignite a fire within us.

Every day is an opportunity for growth and transformation. It's a chance to learn from past experiences, refine our understanding, and expand our horizons. The mistakes and setbacks of yesterday need not define us. Instead, they serve as stepping stones toward a brighter future.

It's a celebration of potential, a recognition of the infinite possibilities that each new day brings. Whether it's an opportunity to learn something new, fix an old mistake, forge a new relationship, or take a step toward our dreams, each day is brimming with potential if we only dare to seize it.

Here comes the twist. This philosophy is not just about doing, but also about becoming. Each day is an opportunity to evolve, to become a slightly better version of ourselves. It's about self-improvement, personal growth, and continuous learning. It's about knowing that every sunrise brings us one step closer to being the person we aspire to be.

This isn't just an inspirational quote. It's a call to live in the now, to grab life by the horns, to be the architects of our own destiny. It is an invitation to embrace change, strive for growth, and remain optimistic, knowing that no matter what, another opportunity is always on the horizon. Doesn't that perspective give you an adrenaline rush, making life seem like an exciting adventure rather than a monotonous routine? That is the magic hidden in this simple phrase, my friend.

— DAY 210 —

Live like you will die tomorrow

I N our fast-paced and ever-changing world, it's easy to get caught up in the worries of tomorrow or the regrets of yesterday. I mean, let's think about it. This statement is not asking us to plunge into despair about the end of life. Far from it! It's more of an invitation, a daring challenge, to experience life in its fullness, to seize every moment like it's a golden ticket. Life is an unpredictable, wild ride, with all its ups and downs, victories and defeats, joys and sorrows.

Now, don't get me wrong. Living as if you're going to die tomorrow doesn't mean becoming reckless or impulsive. It's more about embracing a heightened sense of life's fleeting beauty and using it to steer our actions, our relationships, and our choices. It's about putting our fears aside, saying those words we've been holding back, chasing those dreams we've been neglecting, reaching out to those people we've been avoiding.

Take a moment to imagine this; if you knew tomorrow was your last, wouldn't you want to make beautiful memories with the people you care about? Would minor misunderstandings or petty issues still matter? Or would you rather gaze at the world with fresh eyes, admiring and appreciating every little detail?

The very fact that life is temporary makes each moment more beautiful. It helps us to enjoy the small things, like the soothing rhythm of rain, the cool breeze on a summer's day, or the twinkling of distant stars. It encourages us to inject love into every interaction, infuse every thought with gratitude, and pour our passion into every venture.

Living like you will die tomorrow invites a sense of urgency. It awakens us from the slumber of self-satisfaction and pushes us to take action. It encourages us to embrace new opportunities, step out of our comfort zones, and live with intention.

Despite life's fleeting nature, let's celebrate. Let's vow to live our lives with a sense of urgency, an insatiable hunger to love more deeply, explore more bravely, learn more voraciously, and feel more intensely. Because life's too short for anything less.

— DAY 211 —

No time is perfect

HOW often do we find ourselves waiting for the "perfect" time to act? To start a new project, to make a lifestyle change, or to pursue a lifelong dream? This illusion of perfection often becomes an invisible barrier, holding us back from achieving our potential.

We all love the idea of a "perfect" moment. It's comfortable, it's safe. It's like this shiny, well-lit stage where we can't possibly mess up. But here's the catch—life isn't a well-rehearsed play. It's messy, unpredictable, and a whole lot of fun if we learn to roll with it.

Why do we chase this elusive "perfect" moment? Maybe it's because we're scared of tripping up, of not getting it right the first time. But consider this. Did Edison invent the light bulb in a "perfect" moment? Or the Wright Brothers—did they wait for the perfect time to give flight to their dreams? No. They just dived in, faced the chaos head-on, and came out on top.

It's a shift in perspective. It's about realizing that the magic doesn't happen in some far-off, flawless moment. It happens here and now, amidst the beautiful chaos of the present.

And there's another thing. When we're so focused on finding that perfect moment, we end up missing the amazing things happening right now. We miss the joy, the lessons, the unexpected opportunities that make life such a wild ride.

No time is perfect, but every moment is an opportunity for growth, connection, and transformation. By releasing the need for perfection, we free ourselves from the constraints that hold us back. We allow ourselves to take risks, to learn from failures, and to embrace the beauty of the present moment.

Let go of the illusion of perfection. Embrace the messiness of life and recognize that there is no "perfect" time to start. The time is now. Seize the opportunities that come your way, even if they are accompanied by uncertainty. Embrace the journey of growth and discovery, and watch as the imperfect moments unfold into something truly extraordinary.

— DAY 212 —

Wealth unveils one's true character

WEALTH, with all its appeal and power, has an unusual way of revealing the true essence of individuals. It serves as a magnifying glass, exposing the depths of character that lie beneath the surface. For some, wealth becomes a catalyst for generosity, compassion, and noble pursuits. For others, it amplifies greed, arrogance, and a disconnect from the realities of the world. In the journey of acquiring and managing wealth, one's true character is unveiled, and the choices made along the way shape the legacy they leave behind.

Wealth isn't just about the bank balance, it's a mirror. A really big, flashy mirror that reflects who we are, what we are made of, and what's tucked away inside us. It's like that one friend who never sugarcoats anything. It shows us raw, unedited versions of ourselves.

Picture this. You hit the jackpot. Millions pouring into your account. How would you behave? Would you go on an extravagant shopping spree, or maybe set up a charity foundation? Would you hoard it, or share it? See, that's where the core of the matter lies. The moment wealth steps in, our true selves step up.

Those who remain humble, kind, and selfless in the middle of an avalanche of money, they've got it figured out. They're the ones who understand that wealth doesn't make them superior, it simply underscores their existing goodness. But then there are those who let wealth change them into something unrecognizable, letting their inner demons dance in the spotlight.

Here's the thing we need to remember—wealth, in itself, is neutral. It's like a paintbrush in the hands of an artist. The final picture isn't about the brush, it's about who's holding it. Wealth simply hands us a bunch of options and steps back, waiting to see what we do next.

So, if one day, you're sitting atop a mountain of gold, don't let it change you. Use it to be a better version of yourself. The real measure of wealth isn't your bank balance, it's the richness of your character. When you've got that, my friend, you're truly wealthy. Because, in the theatre of life, wealth is just a prop, you're the star.

— DAY 213 —

Today's actions shape tomorrow's life

YOU know what's interesting? The fact that today's actions have the power to shape our entire future. It's easy to overlook amid our hectic lives, but every single thing we do, every choice we make, has a ripple effect that reaches far beyond the present moment.

Think about it. When you make a conscious decision to take action today, you're essentially laying the groundwork for the life you want to create tomorrow. It's like planting seeds and nurturing them, knowing that they'll grow into something beautiful and fulfilling.

Let's take an example. Say you have a dream of becoming a successful entrepreneur. You can't just sit around daydreaming about it and expect it to magically happen. No, you need to take action. Start by researching your market, developing your skills, and connecting with like-minded individuals. Each step you take today brings you closer to building that thriving business tomorrow.

It's not just the big, obvious actions that matter. Even the seemingly insignificant choices you make daily can shape your future. Take a moment to reflect upon the person who consistently chooses to practice gratitude and embrace a positive mindset. By doing so, they cultivate resilience, attract opportunities, and create a life filled with joy and abundance.

On the flip side, there's the individual who constantly dwells in negativity and self-doubt. Their actions today, or rather their lack of action, hold them back from reaching their full potential. They become trapped in a cycle of selfsabotage, unable to break free and create the life they truly desire.

Life is unpredictable. It throws curveballs, challenges, and surprises our way. How we respond to those curveballs, how we adapt and persevere, that's what truly shapes our tomorrow. It's in those moments of adversity that our character is tested and our true potential is revealed.

Today's actions are the building blocks of your future. They pave the way for the life you want to live.

— DAY 214 —

Your pace, your path

HAVE you ever watched a marathon? Not those Olympic sprints, but the long-distance ones. Notice how every runner has their own rhythm? It's not all about who's fastest, it's about who can keep their stride, and endure till the end. That is a perfect metaphor for life, my friend.

Society has a way of pressuring us to follow a predetermined path, to "keep up with the Joneses" and meet certain milestones at specific ages. But let me tell you a secret: life is not a race, and there is no one-size-fits-all formula for success and fulfillment.

From the moment we're born, it's like we're pushed onto this track, expected to sprint towards a finish line crowded with societal norms. But what if we flip that concept on its head? What if life isn't a race against others, but a personal marathon?

Take a moment and consider it—your life, your journey. It's unique, isn't it? Your path isn't my path. Your dreams, challenges, and triumphs are entirely yours. You might be trekking through a dense forest while someone else is climbing a steep mountain. That's the beauty of life. It's not a one-size-fits-all highway, but a winding, branching pathway that adapts to your steps.

Consider your pace. Some folks are natural sprinters, rushing through life at lightning speed. Others prefer to jog, taking in the sights, the experiences. Heck, some even like to walk, soaking up every moment, every sensation. And guess what? It's all okay. Your pace doesn't have to match anyone else's.

This perspective is truly liberating, isn't it? It frees us from that exhausting sprint, that constant pressure to "keep up with the Joneses." It encourages us to embrace our path and to run at our pace. It allows us to ditch the stopwatch and put on dancing shoes, because life isn't a timed race—it's a dance.

Remember, your pace, your path. Walk it with intention, with curiosity, and with the steadfast belief that you have the power to create a life that is uniquely yours. And when you look back on your journey, you'll realize that it was in honoring your own rhythm that you found true fulfillment and joy.

— DAY 215 —

Money is the language of this planet

TO view money as a language is to acknowledge its role as a medium of communication and an instrument of negotiation in our society. Money communicates our values and priorities, reflecting what we choose to invest in and what we neglect. It is a dialogue we have with ourselves about what we find essential and the trade-offs we're willing to make.

Consider the charitable donations we make. The cash we give is more than mere currency; it's a testament to our compassion and our commitment to social change. It tells a story about who we are and what we care about. And it's through this language that we engage in a global conversation about poverty, education, or health care.

Or take investments, for instance. When we invest in a company, we're not just buying stocks; we're endorsing their practices, products, and ethos. Our money becomes a vote of confidence and a signal of belief in their potential.

But, like any language, money can be misused. It can become a tool for exploitation and inequality. When wealth becomes concentrated in the hands of a few, the dialogue turns into a monologue, and the language loses its power to communicate universally.

It's essential, then, to become fluent in this language. To understand how to earn, save, invest, and donate responsibly and effectively. To use it not just to amass wealth, but to express our values, advance our principles, and impact our world positively.

Money may be the language of our planet, but it's up to us to determine the dialogue. Let's ensure that our words are filled with generosity, empathy, and purpose. Let's redefine the meaning of wealth and cultivate a society where everyone has the opportunity to thrive.

Money, in this context, is more than just a necessity or a resource. It's a lexicon we use to interact with the world, shaping it, and being shaped by it in return. So next time you think about money, remember you're engaging in a global dialogue—one transaction at a time.

— DAY 216 —

Measure yourself by your impact

W HEN we think about success, we often focus on personal achievements such as wealth, power, or status. However, true success should be measured by the impact that we have on others and on the world around us. The mark we leave on the world is a legacy that lasts long after we are gone, and it is this impact that truly defines our success.

The concept of impact transcends the boundaries of material success and external validation, delving into the very essence of what it means to be a contributing member of the human community. Our impact is not merely a reflection of our accomplishments, titles, or awards, but rather the ripple effect that our actions, decisions, and presence have on the lives of others and the world at large. Measuring ourselves by our impact shifts our focus from the pursuit of individual glory to the cultivation of a collective legacy, rooted in the principles of empathy, compassion, and shared responsibility.

The recognition that our influence will always play a factor in our lives serves as both an inspiration and a challenge. It inspires us to harness the power of our actions and choices to create positive change, whether by uplifting those around us, advocating for justice, or leaving a lasting mark on our environment. At the same time, it challenges us to confront the potential consequences of our actions, holding ourselves accountable for the ways in which our influence may contribute to suffering or discord.

Our influence will always play a factor, we are compelled to consider not only the pursuits that bring us joy and satisfaction but also the ways in which these pursuits intersect with the greater good. This holistic approach to selfassessment fosters a sense of purpose and fulfillment that transcends the confines of individual achievement, allowing us to recognize and celebrate the profound impact that our lives can have on the world around us.

Measuring ourselves by our impact is a powerful way to define our success. It means shifting our focus away from personal achievements and towards the positive change that we can create in the world.

— DAY 217 —

Don't wait for permission to start something new

ENVISION a world where Thomas Edison waited for permission to experiment with electricity, or where Amelia Earhart sought approval before soaring into the sky. These pioneers didn't stop when it came to doing things the usual way, waiting for a nod of approval. We all have that dream or that idea that keeps us up at night, that we're just buzzing to get started on, but we just, well, don't. What stops us? Why are we stuck in this eternal state of waiting? We often find ourselves caught up in this mindset that we need someone else's approval, someone else's go-ahead to start something new.

This potent phrase urges us to adopt the same daring spirit, challenging us to step beyond the confines of permission and the fear of the unknown. It reminds us that permission, more often than not, is a phantom gatekeeper. Its authority lies not in its own power, but in the power we ascribe to it.

Consider the example of the Wright Brothers, who didn't wait for permission when they decided to make human flight a reality. They dared to dream, to innovate, to face ridicule and failure, and the world, as a result, has never been the same since. Their courage is a testament to the fact that permission is not a prerequisite for greatness.

And let's get real—who are you waiting for permission from anyway? Is it your family, your friends, or society? Or is it that little voice inside your head saying, "What if I fail?"

Most of the time, the truly revolutionary stuff—the ideas that flip the script, that change the game—they're not exactly welcomed with open arms. The internet? People thought it was a fad. Electric cars? Too impractical. Yet, look where we are now.

This is your golden ticket. It's urging you to shake off those shackles of doubt, to step out of your comfort zone. It's about taking a leap, even if you're not entirely sure where you'll land.

Next time you have an idea or a dream, don't stand around waiting for someone to give you a nod. Dive in. Start creating. Who knows, you might end up changing the world.

— DAY 218 —

Social media masks poverty

D O you ever stop to think about how social media can be a mask that hides poverty behind a façade of riches? It's a concerning truth that often goes unnoticed among the glittering images and glamorous lifestyles portrayed online. We scroll through our feeds, bombarded with images of luxury, riches, and seemingly boundless wealth. But what if I told you that behind those pictureperfect posts lie stories of struggle, deprivation, and hidden poverty?

In our digital age, social media has become a powerful tool for shaping perceptions and projecting idealized versions of ourselves. We carefully curate our online presence, choosing the perfect angle, lighting, and filters to present a glamorous life. We showcase the latest fashion, exotic vacations, and mouthwatering meals, creating an illusion of abundance and prosperity. It's easy to get caught up in the appeal and start comparing our own lives to these seemingly perfect portrayals.

Social media can be false and misleading. It masks the realities of poverty that exist behind closed doors. People might be grappling with financial hardships, struggling to make ends meet, and yet their digital persona portrays a life of luxury. The gap between appearance and reality is a stark reminder of the dangers of comparison and the pressure to keep up with an unattainable standard.

But it's not just about raising awareness; it's about fostering empathy and inspiring action. We must look beyond the glossy surface and acknowledge the underlying issues that perpetuate poverty. It requires us to question our own assumptions, challenge the narratives, and engage in meaningful conversations.

Instead of being passive consumers of social media, we can actively choose to be catalysts for change. We can use our platforms to uplift and support those facing poverty, to share stories that go beyond the façade, and to advocate for systemic changes that address the root causes of poverty.

As you scroll through your social media feeds, remember that what you see is not always the whole truth. Don't fall into the comparison trap or be swayed by the illusion of wealth.

— DAY 219 —

You are not average

AT times, we may feel like we're just an ordinary part of the crowd, like we're nothing special. Have you ever caught yourself thinking, "I'm just an average person doing average things?" We've all been there. It's so easy to lose ourselves in this vast world teeming with extraordinary talents. But the truth is, we're not average.

You see, "average" is just an idea that we've been taught. It's a gray line smack in the middle of the color spectrum of life. But the beautiful truth is, life doesn't come on average. It comes in different sizes, shapes, colors, and flavors. And so do you.

Take a moment to reflect on this—the cosmic lottery that had to be won for you to be here, right now, reading this. All the precise, complex series of events leading back to the *Big Bang,* happening in just the right way for you to exist. You're a marvel made by the universe. Now, tell me, what's average about that?

And it doesn't stop there. The color of your eyes, the tone of your laugh, the way your mind weaves thoughts—there's a distinctness in these, a uniqueness that is thoroughly, wonderfully you. You're a blend of genetic traits and experiences that have never existed before and will never exist again. In the dictionary of life, you are your own definition.

Now, let's take a trip inside your mind. That little world you've created, filled with dreams, stories, jokes, and thoughts—it's a universe that's solely yours. It's shaped by your experiences, your knowledge, your imagination, and it's different from anyone else's universe.

Average is too small a word to define you. It's too... average. You are an anthology of thoughts, a carnival of colors, a symphony of emotions, an art of stardust.

There's nothing wrong with being mediocre, but if you're ever feeling like you're just "average," remember this: You're a stardust miracle, a one-of-a-kind person, with a story that's unique to you. There's nothing average about that. In reality, you're pretty amazing!

— DAY 220 —

Freedom lies in clearing your debts

PAUSE for a moment and let that sink in. It's a powerful statement, one that holds the key to unlocking a life of true financial independence and peace of mind. Debt is a burden that shackles us, limiting our choices and weighing us down. Whether it's financial debt, emotional baggage, or unfulfilled obligations, the weight of these debts can hold us back from experiencing true freedom.

Debt has become a societal norm, an accepted part of modern life. We accumulate credit card debt, student loans, mortgages, and more, often without fully grasping the long-term consequences. We find ourselves trapped in a cycle of payments, living paycheck to paycheck, and sacrificing our dreams for the sake of meeting financial obligations.

But what if we challenged this norm? What if we saw debt as a barrier to freedom rather than a necessary evil? Clearing your debts is not just about financial gain; it's about regaining control of your life and making choices based on your desires rather than your financial obligations.

Imagine a life free from the shackles of debt. A life where every dollar earned is not claimed by creditors, but rather directed towards building a future of abundance and fulfillment. With the weight of debt lifted, you can breathe easier, sleep soundly, and set out on a path of financial well-being.

Clearing your debts is an act of empowerment, a declaration that you refuse to be bound by the chains of financial burden. It requires discipline, determination, and a commitment to making sacrifices in the short term for long-term gain.

The journey to debt freedom is transformative. It requires facing your financial reality, developing a plan, and taking deliberate action. It may involve downsizing, cutting back on expenses, and making tough choices.

Financial freedom means having the ability to live life on your terms. It means having the flexibility to pursue your passions, travel, invest in experiences, and build a secure future for yourself and your loved ones. It means no longer being held captive by debt, but rather being the master of your destiny.

— DAY 221 —

Don't let age limit your potential

AGE is just a number, they say. But do we truly believe it? Age is often seen as a defining factor in our lives. We are categorized, labeled, and sometimes even limited by the number of years we have lived. Society tells us that certain accomplishments are only for the young, that dreams must be realized before a certain age, and that we should resign ourselves to the idea that our best years are behind us.

When we are young, life seems to be an expansive canvas, swarming with limitless opportunities. This feeling of potential and possibility during youth often leads to the mistaken belief that our best years are those of our youth. But does potential truly diminish with age? Or is it our mindset, shaped by societal expectations and self-imposed boundaries, that leads us to think so?

Imagine an autumnal tree. Its leaves may be weathered and its branches may lack the vibrant bloom of spring, but does it lack potential? Quite the opposite. The tree welcomes the change, shedding old leaves to make room for new growth. Like that tree, we too are capable of continual growth and transformation regardless of our age.

The later years of our life bring us wisdom, resilience, and a deeper perspective. Our collected experiences, the many victories and defeats, help to expand our understanding and enrich our worldview. From this position, we can identify opportunities and solutions that may have eluded our younger selves.

Take, for example, Colonel Sanders. He was 65 years old when he started *Kentucky Fried Chicken (KFC)*. His story proves that potential isn't a finite resource that diminishes with age. Instead, it's an inherent, eternal quality that evolves and expresses itself in different ways throughout our lives. Whether it's learning a new skill, switching careers, or reigniting a long-lost passion, age doesn't have to be a hurdle. The limitation lies not in our chronological age but in our minds.

Let's reshape our understanding of age. Let's replace "too old" with "why not now?" Let's aim to emulate the autumnal tree, embracing each life season with grace and determination.

— DAY 222 —

Accept rejection for happiness

I T'S a concept that may seem counterintuitive at first, but bear with me, and you'll discover just how transformative it can be. Rejection is something we all experience at some point in our lives. Whether it's a job opportunity, a romantic relationship, or a creative project, rejection can leave us feeling disheartened and defeated. But here's the insightful truth: by accepting rejection and embracing it as a part of life, we pave the way for true happiness.

Rejection is not a reflection of our worth or abilities. It's simply a redirection—a sign that there's something different, something better waiting for us. It's an opportunity for growth, self-reflection, and a chance to realign our path toward greater fulfillment.

When we resist rejection and let it define us, we hold ourselves back from the happiness that lies beyond. We become trapped in a cycle of self-doubt and fear, hesitant to take risks or pursue our dreams. But by accepting rejection, we free ourselves from its grip and open ourselves up to new possibilities.

Accepting rejection means acknowledging that not everything will go according to plan. It means releasing the need for external validation and finding validation within ourselves. It's about recognizing that rejection is not a reflection of our worth but rather a stepping stone toward personal growth and self-discovery.

When we embrace rejection, we cultivate resilience and develop a deeper understanding of ourselves. We learn to navigate uncertainty and setbacks with grace and determination. We discover hidden strengths and talents that may have remained dormant otherwise.

Rejection can lead us down unexpected paths, opening doors to opportunities we never would have considered. It pushes us out of our comfort zones and forces us to explore new territories. In these moments of trial, our true selves emerge, along with an understanding of what joy truly means to us. We're invited to view rejection not as a setback but as a guide, pointing us to the veiled chances for growth it carries with it.

— DAY 223 —

Never rely on one income source

IN a rapidly changing and uncertain world, relying on a single income source can be a risky proposition. This statement challenges the traditional thinking that one consistent income source, often a full-time job, is the key to financial security.

We often grow up with the idea that having a stable job and relying solely on a monthly paycheck is the norm. However, this traditional approach leaves us vulnerable to economic fluctuations, job insecurity, and limited financial growth. By relying on one income source, we place all our eggs in one basket, and if that basket were to falter, our entire financial stability would be at risk.

Firstly, understand this, the economy is like a vast ocean, ever-changing, with high tides and low tides. Complete reliance upon one income stream is similar to building a castle on the beach; it might hold against the gentle lapping of waves during economic calm, but a sudden financial storm could erode its foundations. Multiple income streams, however, are like a robust fortress, resilient and resistant to economic oscillations.

Secondly, multiple income sources foster financial independence. You're no longer solely dependent on the monthly paycheck from your day job; you have the freedom to explore, create, and grow without the nagging worry of monetary constraints. With financial independence comes the luxury of choice. You can choose to pursue a hobby, learn a new skill, or even take a career break.

Take the example of a famous American talk show host, Oprah Winfrey, who despite achieving significant success with her talk show, didn't stop there. She diversified into acting, started a magazine, co-founded a TV network, and also launched her own radio channel. By doing so, she not only amplified her income but also reduced her dependence on a single source.

Lastly, by cultivating multiple income sources, you stimulate creativity and growth. It's a call to action, a nudge to explore uncharted territories, learn new skills, and step outside the comfort zone.

— DAY 224 —

Express love before it's late

A life filled with love, joy, and deep connections. We all long for it, but often, we take it for granted. We assume that love will always be there, waiting for us to express it when we're ready. We must embrace the urgency of the present moment and express love before it's too late.

Love is a powerful force that has the ability to transform lives and bring immense happiness. Yet, in our busy lives, we often let time slip away, assuming there will always be another opportunity to show our love and appreciation. But life is unpredictable, and we can't take for granted that there will always be a tomorrow.

The insightful realization is that expressing love is not something to be saved for a special occasion or a future moment. It's something to be embraced and shared in the here and now. It's about taking action, speaking our hearts, and showing those we care about how much they mean to us.

Consider the elderly couple who spent a lifetime together, but never fully expressed their love for one another. They assumed the other person knew, but the words were left unspoken. Then, one day, it's too late. That opportunity to express their deep affection and gratitude is gone, and all that remains is regret.

Don't wait for the perfect moment or the right circumstances to express love. Every moment is an opportunity to show love and appreciation to the people who matter most to us. It can be as simple as a kind word, a heartfelt gesture, or a moment of undivided attention. It's about making the people we love feel seen, valued, and cherished.

We often prioritize other things in our lives—work, responsibilities, and distractions—while neglecting to express the love that resides within us. But love is not something that can be stored away for later. It's meant to be shared, nurtured, and expressed freely.

Express love before it's too late. It's not just a quote—it's a wake-up call. It's about seizing the moment and making sure our love isn't just felt, but known.

— DAY 225 —

Buying ≠ affording; know the difference

T HE modern world is dominated by consumer culture, where the phrase "I want, therefore I get" is the governing principle. This makes it easy to fall into the tricky trap where buying is often mistaken for affording. The distinction between the two is crucial and fascinating, transforming how we perceive our relationship with money and material possessions.

The capacity to buy is merely a function of having money at a given moment. It's the instant gratification, the thrill of acquisition, the fleeting happiness of owning something new. We swipe our credit cards, we exchange currency, and voila! We've bought something. But does that imply we can afford it?

Affording, on the other hand, is a much deeper concept. It transcends the immediate financial transaction and delves into our long-term financial health and well-being. Can we sustain this purchase in the long run without negatively impacting our financial stability? Can we maintain this product, fuel it, repair it, and ultimately replace it without destabilizing our budget? Can we enjoy this without sacrificing something more essential or compromising on our savings?

Consider the classic example of buying a car. One might have the money or credit to purchase the vehicle—but can they afford the insurance, maintenance, fuel costs, and potential repairs? Not always. Therefore, the real cost is not just the price tag, but the cumulative sum of all these ensuing expenses.

The distinction between buying and affording is not just about finance; it also ties into our perception of value and self-worth. The societal pressure of "keep up with the Joneses" often pushes us into equating our self-worth with our purchasing power. This misleading idea can lead to financial stress and an endless cycle of unnecessary consumption.

Understanding the difference between buying and affording is crucial in achieving financial stability and personal satisfaction. It helps us differentiate between momentary pleasure and long-term comfort. More than a financial lesson, it's a philosophical one. It guides us to value experiences over material possessions.

— DAY 226 —

Value tiny moments in life

L IFE is a strange creature. It's vast and complex, yet it's in the smallest, seemingly mundane moments where we find its true beauty. Let me share a little secret with you: those tiny moments? They're everything. Yes, the tiny stuff! The smile of a stranger, the smell of your morning coffee, or the feel of your favorite book in your hands. They're the magic hidden in plain sight.

I get it. We live in a world that cherishes the grand and spectacular. Everyone is seeking that "big break," the life-changing event. And hey, there's nothing wrong with that. But what if I told you the real magic is woven into the fabric of your day-to-day life? Would you believe me?

Take a second to think about it. Remember the relief when you slide into your bed after a long day? The quiet joy of watching the sunset? The warmth that spreads through you when your favorite song plays on the radio? These moments, they're the real deal. They're what makes life worthwhile.

What's beautiful about these moments is how personal they are. Your tiny moments are yours and yours alone. They're like secret treasures, hidden in the vast sea of life, waiting to be discovered, appreciated, savored.

So here's my advice: start looking out for these moments. No, you don't need a telescope or a map. Just an open heart and a keen eye. Slow down, look around, and breathe. Recognize these moments for what they are: little gifts from life itself.

Start valuing these moments, and you'll see a shift. Your life will transform from a race to a journey, a beautiful adventure filled with joys tucked into the most unexpected places. It's amazing how much magic we can find when we take the time to appreciate the tiny moments. They're waiting for you, you know. You just need to notice them.

In the grand theatre of life, it is the tiny moments that paint the most vibrant and meaningful strokes. Slow down, take a deep breath, and bask in the magic of the present. Value the tiny moments, for they hold within them the essence of life's greatest joys.

— DAY 227 —

Graduation is not end

OUR lives are a collection of chapters, each marked by significant events, milestones, and achievements. In this anthology of life, graduation is often seen as a major turning point, a pinnacle of success; a grand finale of sorts. But what if we view it differently? What if graduation is not the end, but rather a beginning?

Graduation is an ending only in the most superficial sense. Yes, it signifies the conclusion of a structured educational journey, the culmination of years of studying, learning, and growing. But in the grand scheme of life, it's more of a comma than a full stop. Graduation is less about ending and more about transition. It's the bridge that connects who we were with who we might become.

Think of graduation as a launching pad. The knowledge you've gathered, the experiences you've accumulated, the character you've shaped during these years are the fuel propelling you into the vast cosmos of opportunities. Graduation is not a sunset, but a sunrise; the start of a new day, the beginning of a journey filled with possibilities.

Take a moment to reflect on this: If graduation were the end, then all that we have learned, all the skills we have acquired, would serve no purpose beyond the academic sphere. But that's not the case, is it? The real learning, the practical application of our knowledge, and the exploration of our full potential, all of these begin after graduation.

Embrace graduation not as a close, but as an open door, a portal into a world where you have the power to apply what you've learned, to make a difference, to shape your destiny. The diploma you receive isn't a ticket to self-satisfaction but a license to venture into the expansive universe of life.

As you toss your cap into the air, remember that graduation is not the end. It is a starting line, a launching point, the dawn of a new phase of learning, growth, and discovery. Celebrate it as the beginning of everything that lies ahead. In the vast narrative of life, the most exciting chapters are yet to be written.

— DAY 228 —

Eat the frog first

MARK Twain once said, "If it's your job to eat a frog, it's best to do it first thing in the morning. And if it's your job to eat two frogs, it's best to eat the biggest one first." No, this is not a call to develop a taste for frogs. This nugget of wisdom offers a profound lesson about procrastination and productivity.

"Eating the frog" is a metaphor for tackling the most challenging, most daunting task of your day first. It's about eating that "ugly frog"—the task you're dreading—before anything else. Why? It's simple. Your energy and willpower are highest in the morning, and completing the hardest task first creates a sense of accomplishment that fuels productivity for the rest of the day.

You see, the "frog" represents the tasks we tend to put off, the ones we dread and postpone until it's absolutely unavoidable. We like to distract ourselves with smaller, easier tasks, tricking our minds into believing we're productive. But deep down, we know we're just avoiding that big, ugly frog.

But imagine the relief, the triumphant joy of having swallowed that frog first thing in the morning. The rest of your day is freed up, unburdened by the lingering dread of the task you've been putting off. Everything else you accomplish feels like a bonus, boosting your mood and productivity even further.

"Eating the frog first" is a lesson in courage, discipline, and resilience. It's about embracing discomfort, tackling challenges head-on, and harnessing the power of accomplishment to fuel your day.

The magic of eating the frog first is that it's not just about getting things done, it's about empowering yourself. It's about claiming your day before the sun's barely up, and the adrenaline rush that follows, it's addictive.

The next time you're faced with that frog, keep this in mind: Eat the frog first. Once you swallow that frog, the rest of your day is dessert.

— DAY 229 —

Learn something new every day

I T'S a phrase you've likely heard before, an encouragement flung around as though it's as easy as tying a shoe. But let's unpack it. The concept is much more than a simple platitude. It's a philosophy, a compass directing us toward personal growth and an invigorating existence.

Learning is not confined to classrooms or textbooks. It's a mindset, a way of engaging with the world around us. By adopting the practice of daily learning, we open ourselves to a world of endless possibilities and transform each day into an opportunity for growth and enrichment.

Imagine waking up each morning with a thirst for knowledge, a curiosity that propels you forward. It's like setting out on a treasure hunt, where every day holds the promise of discovering something new and exciting. Whether it's a fascinating fact, a new skill, or a fresh perspective, there is always something waiting to be learned.

Learning is not just about acquiring information; it's about transformation. When we learn something new, we expand our minds, broaden our horizons, and become more adaptable and resilient individuals. We develop a deeper understanding of ourselves and the world, challenging our beliefs and embracing new possibilities.

Learning something new every day is not limited to grand gestures or monumental achievements. It's about finding beauty and value in the small moments—the snippets of knowledge, the tiny revelations that pepper our lives. It's noticing the intricacies of a flower, learning a new word, or trying a new recipe. Each day holds opportunities for growth and discovery, if we're open to them.

Moreover, learning is a lifelong journey. It knows no age or boundaries. It's about constantly seeking growth and embracing the unknown. When we make learning a daily practice, we tap into our innate curiosity and cultivate a growth mindset—a mindset that enables us to adapt, evolve, and thrive in an ever-changing world.

— DAY 230 —

Focus on ONE thing

IN a world of endless distractions and competing priorities, the concept of focusing on one thing may seem counterintuitive. We are constantly bombarded with messages telling us to multitask, juggle multiple responsibilities, and be masters of all trades. However, amid this chaos, there is great power in focusing on ONE thing.

Consider your smartphone. Isn't it fascinating how it can do a million things? It's a camera, a phone, a television, a music player, and a thousand things more. But while it can do everything, it excels at nothing. The pictures are often "okay," and the sound quality is "passable." A DSLR would snap better pictures, and a dedicated music system would play sweeter melodies.

Life is much like that of a smartphone. The more tasks we juggle, the more we dilute our effectiveness. Each new undertaking, each new ambition, they're all like apps running in the background, draining our energy, our focus, and our time.

Imagine, instead, pouring all that energy, all that focus into one single task. To truly master it, to excel at it. Wouldn't that be something? It's not that we shouldn't dream big or multitask, but when we scatter our attention, we often end up shortchanging ourselves. We lose the joy of deep focus, the satisfaction of immersion, and the thrill of mastery.

As Steve Jobs rightly said, "People think focus means saying YES to the thing you've got to focus on. But that's not what it means at all. It means saying NO to the hundred other good ideas that there are." The next time you're juggling tasks, stop for a moment, take a breath, and ask yourself, "What's my ONE thing right now?" You'll be surprised how this small shift in perspective can change the game for you.

Remember the old proverb: "If you chase two rabbits, you will not catch either one." It's not about doing less, it's about getting more. More understanding, more connection, more depth.

— DAY 231 —

You're mortal on a small planet

ISN'T it fascinating, in an existentially humbling sort of way, how we're all just specks of stardust, living out our brief lives on a small planet in an infinite universe? It's the ultimate reality check. You're not just mortal, my friend, you're mortal on a pretty small stage.

Not to sound eerie, but it's kind of liberating. The universe doesn't care if you had a bad hair day or bombed that presentation at work. In the grand universe, our daily troubles diminish into insignificance. This realization is our ticket out of self-created dramas and into the theater of life's grand spectacle.

Our lives are fleeting, like the fleeting colors of a sunset. Each sunrise, each turning tide, and each season's change is a testament to the transience of our existence. We are mere observers, visitors, privileged enough to witness the grand spectacle of the universe unfolding.

Our smallness and mortality can foster humility. It can teach us that we are not the masters of the universe but part of its beautiful experience. It can also awaken in us a sense of responsibility to care for our planet and each other, aware that our actions have an impact, however tiny it might seem on the cosmic scale.

Moreover, being mortal on this small planet should prompt us to cherish our brief time in the sun. To seize each moment and make it count. To appreciate the wonderful beauty around us, from the grandeur of a mountain range to the simple elegance of a leaf's design.

Finally, it brings home the lesson of unity. In the cosmos' expanse, boundaries and divisions fade away, and we see ourselves as one species sharing a home. Our trials, struggles, joys, and sorrows are shared experiences, tiny threads that weave together to form the rich experience of human life on Earth.

Dear reader, remember that while you may be mortal on a small planet, your potential for growth, kindness, and love is as boundless as the universe itself. Celebrate this incredible journey we're on, respect the natural world, and let's make our brief time here a beautiful testament to our capacity for greatness.

— DAY 232 —

Simplify to amplify

I N an era characterized by digital noise and nonstop distractions, the complexity of our lives can often be overwhelming. We are constantly told to do more, be more, and achieve more. But have you ever stopped to consider the power of doing less? Yes, I'm advocating for simplicity, a philosophy that whispers: "To amplify, first simplify."

"Simplify to Amplify" is a call to return to the essentials, to cut away the extraneous, and to give importance to what truly matters. It's about understanding that the most potent signal does not arise from amplifying the volume, but from reducing the noise. In life, we often chase complexity, thinking it holds the key to growth and success. But in reality, it's simplicity that often brings the most profound results.

Consider the timeless beauty of a single flower, standing alone in its elegance, commanding our attention and appreciation in a way a field of flowers seldom does. It's the very simplicity of this singular blossom that amplifies its beauty, forcing us to notice its colors, textures, and scent. The same principle applies to our lives. When we simplify, when we reduce the number of our pursuits, commitments, and possessions, what remains gains a significance it didn't have before.

Think of Leonardo da Vinci's famous quote, "Simplicity is the ultimate sophistication." It reflects a deep understanding that the path to true wisdom and effectiveness is not through adding more, but through removing what's not needed.

In our daily lives, simplifying might mean decluttering our physical spaces, cutting back on commitments, or narrowing down our goals to what's truly meaningful. As we simplify, we clear the fog of chaos and distraction, allowing our core values and goals to shine brightly. We can hear our inner voice more clearly, and our actions align more closely with our true selves.

We should strive to simplify, filter out the unnecessary, and concentrate our energy and attention. In doing so, we will realize that the real power lies not in complication and excess, but in simplicity and moderation.

— DAY 233 —

Life problems teach unique resilience

L ET me tell you, life isn't all rainbows and butterflies. It's a rocky mountain route filled with pitfalls, wrong turns, and uphill battles. You get winded, worn out, and sometimes, you might even consider turning back. But you know what? It's those very hardships, those problems that life throws at us, that teach us a remarkable thing: unique resilience.

Problems are the gritty sand that irritates the oyster, leading to the creation of a lustrous pearl. Each problem we face is not a sign of life's cruelty but an invitation to rise, adapt, and learn. It's a call to develop a unique resilience that's as individual as our fingerprints.

Consider an iron forged into a sword. It endures the searing heat, the hammer's ruthless beat, and the quenching coolness. Sounds harsh? But without this process, it would never transform into an elegant, resilient, and effective weapon. Similarly, our problems and challenges forge our character, revealing our inner strength and tenacity.

In the face of adversity, we discover the depths of our courage, the breadth of our empathy, and the height of our potential. Problems push us out of our comfort zones, shattering the illusion of safety, but revealing a vibrant world of growth and learning. Each hurdle surmounted builds our resilience muscles, enhancing our capacity to handle future challenges.

Resilience is not just about bouncing back. It's about growing through the struggle, absorbing the lesson, and transforming it into a springboard for life. It's about understanding that the storm is not a punishing force but a cleansing, renewing, and strengthening agent.

Life's problems are the things that sculpt our resilience, carving out who we are and turning us into people who can deal with life's rough storms.

— DAY 234 —

Practice empathy

EVER wonder what it's like to walk a mile in someone else's shoes? This is the essence of empathy—the profound ability to immerse ourselves in the emotions, thoughts, and experiences of others. Far from a mere sympathetic nod, empathy requires us to shed our self-centered perspectives and delve into the universe of "the other."

Think about it. When we engage empathetically, we abandon our island of self-interest and set sail for the vast, often stormy ocean of human emotion. This voyage allows us to witness the world from vantage points different from our own, making us realize how intricately diverse, yet strikingly similar, our journeys are. This ability, my friends, is no less than a superpower—one that turns perceived differences into shared experiences.

But empathy isn't just about understanding; it's also about connection. The empathetic process facilitates profound bonds that transcend the ordinary, sparking transformative conversations and collaborations. You see, when we allow ourselves to truly feel what another person feels, we build bridges over vast canyons of misunderstanding, fostering a sense of unity that is rare and precious.

As the world accelerates into an era of technology and virtual connection, the need for empathy becomes even more crucial. With screens separating us, the human touch risks becoming lost in translation. Empathy can act as a powerful antidote, ensuring that the undercurrent of human connection remains strong amidst waves of digital distraction.

The practice of empathy, therefore, isn't just a personal endeavor; it's a collective necessity. It is what fuels compassion, drives generosity, and ultimately, shapes societies. Practice empathy, let's cultivate it like a precious garden, nourishing it with understanding and care. For in this garden of empathy, we will find our shared humanity, blooming in vibrant colors of love, kindness, and mutual respect.

— DAY 235 —

You'll never be prepared to see your parents die

L ET'S sit down for a chat, and let's talk about something we're all pretty good at avoiding—the inevitable departure of our parents. It's a bitter pill to swallow, and let's be honest, no one ever really feels ready to talk about it, much less experience it.

Isn't it curious how we spend years preparing for the most diverse range of life's ups and downs? We're pretty good at bracing for the big things like our first job, falling in love, and maybe even our retirement. But when it comes to our parents leaving us, well, we're like deer in the headlights.

You see, our parents, they're our first love and our first heroes. They're like that old tree in your childhood backyard, always there, providing shade, shelter, and a sturdy branch to lean on. Their existence is a constant in the whirlwind of our lives, a lighthouse guiding us home.

So when that light dims, when that old tree falls, it's like the rug is pulled from under our feet. The universe seems to tilt off its axis, and we're propelled into an unfamiliar world without a compass. Even if we saw it coming, even if we thought we were bracing for it, the blow hits harder than we could ever anticipate. Suddenly, we're walking through life without our safety net, our guiding star.

But here's the flip side, my friend. Through the heartache, through the loss, there's also a strange sense of awakening. You begin to grasp the fragility, the fleeting beauty of life, and it makes you love deeper, and live bolder. You realize that even in their absence, our parents continue to shape and guide us.

In the end, we may not be ready for our parents' departure, but that's okay. Their teachings, their love, and their values continue to live within us, shaping the way we navigate the world. We start to understand that while their physical presence may fade, the impact they've made, remains, burning brightly in our hearts and lives.

— DAY 236 —

Work smart, not hard

W E live in a world where busyness is glorified, and long hours of labor are seen as markers of success. But what if I told you that there's a better way? What if I said that working smart, not hard, is the key to unlocking productivity, efficiency, and a fulfilling life?

Working smart means shifting our focus from the quantity of work to the quality of work. It's about being intentional with our time and resources, maximizing our efforts, and achieving better results with less exertion. It's a paradigm shift that challenges the notion that success is directly proportional to the number of hours we put in.

Let's go on a journey. Imagine a man hammering away at a huge boulder, sweat trickling down his furrowed brow, muscles straining with each powerful blow. Now, that's what we call hard work. But, regardless of his efforts, the boulder only crumbles a little at a time. Now picture another man, looking at the same boulder, but instead of picking up the hammer, he walks around it, observes it, and studies it. He's looking for weak spots, for cracks. Then, he takes a chisel and a small hammer and with calculated taps, manages to split the boulder in half. That is smart work.

Our society often admires the "hustle" and "grind," to the point where exhaustion is a badge of honor and burnout is seen as a milestone. But it's high time we change this narrative, don't you think? The "work smart" philosophy isn't about reducing effort but about maximizing impact.

Look at successful people. More often than not, it isn't just about endless hours of toil. It's about strategic thinking, wise decisions, leveraging resources, and finding innovative solutions. It's about working effectively rather than exhaustively.

Take a moment, put down your hammer, and look at your boulder. Can you find a better, more effective way to crack it?

Life isn't a sprint, it's a marathon. It's not just about getting to the finish line but also about enjoying the journey. Why not make that journey a bit smarter, a bit smoother? Work smart, not hard. Now, that's a mantra worth living by.

— DAY 237 —

Discipline prevents self-sabotage

THE dance of life is often a delicate balance between freedom and discipline. Freedom, that thrilling feeling of boundless possibilities, can, if unchecked, spiral into chaotic self-destruction. Discipline, on the other hand, with its rhythms and routines, could become a prison stifling our creativity. Yet, it's discipline, which, when embraced with wisdom and understanding, becomes the guiding force that keeps self-sabotage at bay.

Self-sabotage is the shadowy villain that lurks in the background of our lives, secretly undermining our efforts and ambitions. It whispers sweet excuses in our ears, tempting us with instant gratification, and distracting us from our long-term goals. It's the alluring sirens' song luring us away from the path of success onto the rocks of failure.

Discipline is the bright light of hope that keeps this villain at bay. It's the precise compass that keeps us on course even in the dense fog of temptations and distractions. It's the steady hand on the wheel of our life, preventing it from heading into a complete disaster.

Discipline isn't about a strict life absent of joy and spontaneity. It's about setting clear boundaries for our behavior, drawing a line between what's beneficial and what's detrimental. It's about making a pact with ourselves, a pact of respect, of love, of care, where we commit to only what nurtures us, strengthens us, and elevates us.

This commitment to self prevents self-sabotage. It calms down our wild side, reins in our crazy ideas, and checks the thoughtless actions that could get us into trouble. It ensures that we don't become our own worst enemy but remain our best ally.

In the grand dance of life, discipline is the choreographer that orchestrates our steps, our moves, and our twirls, ensuring we don't trip over our own feet. It's the gentle but firm hand that guides us toward the grand finale of our success, ensuring that we don't sabotage ourselves along the way. Remember, discipline isn't a chain that binds you, but a ladder that helps you ascend to your highest potential.

— DAY 238 —

Humor eases hard times

L IFE is a wild rollercoaster ride, filled with thrilling highs and daunting lows. During those challenging moments, when we feel like the weight of the world is on our shoulders, there is one powerful tool that can lighten the load and bring solace: humor. Yes, my friend, humor is the secret ingredient that can transform even the darkest of times into moments of joy and resilience.

Isn't it amazing how a dash of humor can turn even the grayest clouds into a vibrant rainbow? A simple chuckle can unfold the tightly clenched fist of life's hardships, making them appear less daunting, less threatening. It's like a little spark that can ignite the dark and gloomy tunnels of despair, revealing a hidden realm of joy and laughter.

Humor is that magic potion, that secret ingredient, that breathes life into the lifeless, brings light into the darkness, and eases the discomfort of the hard times. It has the power to flip the most grim circumstances, making them less threatening and more manageable.

Think of humor as a mental judo move, using the weight of the hard times against itself, toppling it with a hearty laugh. It transforms the weight of the world into helium-filled balloons that lift your spirits, making you rise above your problems.

Humor is a perspective, a different lens to look at life, a lens that doesn't focus on the hardships, but finds the unique, the funny, the amusing within them. It tickles your mind, stirring a laugh, a smile, a chuckle, which soon reverberates through your entire being, lightening the load of the hard times.

Remember that humor isn't just about laughing out loud at jokes, it's about an attitude, a mindset, a way of living that embraces the absurdity, the silliness, the ridiculous side of life. It's about finding joy in the journey, no matter how rugged the road, how steep the climb, or how heavy the load is.

So next time life gives you lemons, don't just make lemonade, try juggling with them, make a funny face, or even a lemon hat. Let humor be your guiding light in the gloomy tunnels of hard times, leading you to the sunny meadows of joy and laughter. A life seasoned with humor is a life well-lived.

— DAY 239 —

Write to clarify your life

YOU'RE walking through a dense forest, thick with ideas, emotions, and experiences. Each tree, a thought; each leaf, a fleeting emotion; every bird song, an echo of an experience. It's beautiful, but it's also overwhelming. How can you make sense of this leafy chaos? The answer is simple and elegant—write.

Writing isn't just about creating stories or sharing information; it's about bringing order to the chaos of our minds. It's the act of translating the abstract contours of our thoughts into tangible lines of ink and paper. It's about giving form to the formless, making the nebulous concrete, and the vague, precise.

Consider your mind as a cloudy sky, full of swirling thoughts and feelings. Writing is the process of catching these clouds, squeezing them, and watching as the pure rain of understanding falls onto the parched ground of confusion. It's through this rain that the seeds of clarity germinate and grow.

Each word you write, each sentence you form, acts like a gentle hand, separating the tangled threads of your thoughts and laying them out straight and clear. You begin to see patterns, understand connections, and discern the shapes hidden within the fog of your subconscious. The act of writing becomes a voyage of discovery, a journey into the depths of your psyche.

In writing, we uncover truths about ourselves that we were previously unaware of. The page becomes a mirror, reflecting our hopes, fears, dreams, and doubts. And as we read our own words, we begin to understand ourselves better. Our values become clear, our passions more evident, and our paths in life more distinct.

So, take a pen, find a quiet place, and start writing. Let the words flow, let the thoughts tumble out, and watch as the chaos of your mind transforms into the order of understanding. Write to clarify your life, because, in the end, writing is less about impressing others and more about understanding oneself.

— DAY 240 —

Focus by filtering distractions

L ISTEN up, my friend! In a world lit up by countless screens and riddled with relentless notifications, focusing has become as rare as it is precious. It's like trying to catch a butterfly in a hurricane. But here's the secret sauce—the key is not just focusing, but mastering the art of filtering distractions.

The first step towards cultivating focused attention lies in understanding the nature of distractions. They come in various forms, masquerading as urgent tasks, addictive social media feeds, or even mundane thoughts that sneakily invade our minds. Distractions thrive on our vulnerability to instant gratification, enticing us with quick hits of dopamine that leave us craving for more.

To combat this onslaught, we must build filters that shield our attention from unnecessary diversions. This starts with setting clear intentions and prioritizing our objectives. By defining what truly matters to us, we can create a mental roadmap that guides our attention toward meaningful pursuits. This conscious decision-making process acts as a filter, sieving out distractions that do not align with our goals.

Furthermore, we must curate our digital environments to minimize temptation. Unsubscribe from irrelevant email lists, mute nonessential notifications, and declutter social media feeds by unfollowing accounts that do not add value to our lives. By intentionally reducing the noise, we create space for deep work and sustained focus.

Equally important is the cultivation of mindfulness. In a world that thrives on multitasking, we must relearn the art of single-tasking. By immersing ourselves fully in one activity at a time, we develop the ability to concentrate deeply and engage with the present moment. Mindfulness acts as a shield against distractions, allowing us to become aware of their appeal and consciously choose to let them pass.

However, it is essential to recognize that distractions will always exist, no matter how diligently we filter them. In a world where attention is a precious commodity, the ability to filter distractions and maintain focus is a superpower.

— DAY 241 —

Commit, be consistent, persevere

WHEN you're hustling to reach your dreams, three magic words become your best buddies: Commit, be consistent, persevere. It's as if life's grand recipe has these as its main ingredients.

Commitment is the first note in our power trio. It is the passionate promise to oneself, and the dedicated resolve that propels us forward. It is a determined "Yes" to a cause, a goal, a dream, setting the stage for the act that follows. In a world that distracts us with the discord of options and noise, commitment is that single, clear note that cuts through, providing direction and focus.

However, a solitary note, no matter how strong, cannot create a symphony. It is here that consistency, the second note of our power trio, makes its mark. Consistency is commitment in action, it's the discipline of repeatedly playing our note, despite the dissonance of doubt and fear. It is the daily ritual that compounds over time, turning a single, committed action into a powerful melody that shapes our lives.

But what if our melody encounters resistance, or our notes falter in the face of setbacks? Here, perseverance, the final note in our trio, comes to the rescue. Perseverance is commitment's strength and consistency's resilience, enabling us to keep playing our melody, even when our strings threaten to break. It is the tenacious resolve that turns setbacks into comebacks, discord into harmony, and trials into triumphs.

When these three notes—commitment, consistency, and perseverance—play in harmony, they create a force that transforms dreams into realities, goals into achievements, and aspirations into fulfilled destinies. This power trio does not promise a journey devoid of obstacles or challenges, but it does ensure that we remain persistent, our resolve steadfast, and our symphony ultimately triumphant. It's the harmonious blend of these three elements that sets the stage for a life that truly sings.

— DAY 242 —

Meditate for focus in the tech age

I N our technologically surcharged era, we are continuously swept by an endless tide of stimuli. Our minds are ceaselessly assailed by the chatter of social media, the incessant hum of notifications, and the pressure to remain continually connected. Amid this chaos, meditation emerges as a powerful tool to regain control, find clarity, and cultivate steadfast focus.

Meditation, a practice steeped in millennia of tradition, serves as a counterweight to the pressures of modern life. It's a refuge from digital overload. Imagine it like pressing the refresh button on your overloaded browser, closing those extra tabs, and leaving open only what is truly necessary.

The fundamental goal of meditation is to foster a deep, calm focus. It's a kind of mental decluttering, a process of gently putting aside the non-essential to embrace the essential, the present moment. It's like closing your eyes and diving into a serene ocean, away from the relentless wave of digital disruptions.

Consider the impact of this heightened focus on your life. You become more present, more mindful, and, most importantly, more peaceful. Tasks that once seemed daunting now become manageable. Complex problems find simpler solutions. Relationships deepen. Creativity flourishes.

By engaging in meditation, you are training your mind, much like how a runner trains their body. You're learning to unplug from the ceaseless technological barrage and reconnect with yourself. You're building a mental firewall, a buffer against the digital noise.

Meditation enhances empathy, compassion, and understanding, traits increasingly important in our globalized, interconnected world. As tech continues to evolve, it tends to focus on the "I," the individual. Meditation, on the other hand, nurtures the "we," reminding us of our shared human experience.

— DAY 243 —

Joy's source is often sorrow's well

ISN'T it funny how life works sometimes? We're told to seek joy, right? But what if I told you that to truly understand and appreciate joy, you'd have to experience sorrow first? It's as if they are secret allies. It's an uncanny paradox that life often presents us with—that our deepest sorrows can change into our greatest joys, and that our most profound losses can lead to our most meaningful gains.

To understand this, consider the transformative power of sorrow. It's during our darkest hours that we most starkly confront ourselves, our beliefs, and the world around us. These moments of pain and despair strip away the superficialities, revealing the raw, unfiltered essence of our being. They push us, willingly or not, into the melting pot of change and growth. It's in this furnace that sorrow starts to forge into something unexpected—joy.

But how does sorrow pave the way for joy? It's through the process of healing, acceptance, and personal evolution that the answer unfolds. We learn from our sorrows, not despite them. The loss, the heartbreak, the disappointment—these experiences equip us with resilience and empathy. They teach us to appreciate the fleeting, fragile beauty of our existence. They make us understand what truly matters. Through these lessons, sorrow becomes a wellspring of joy.

This isn't to say that joy is exclusively the domain of those who have experienced great sorrow. Rather, it's an invitation to view sorrow differently, not as an enemy, but as a guide. It's about understanding that joy and sorrow aren't opposites on life's spectrum, but companions, each illuminating the other.

Think about the joy of a hard-won achievement, the sweetness magnified by the struggle it took to reach it. Consider the depth of love and compassion born out of shared grief. Reflect on the profound gratitude for life's simple pleasures discovered in the wake of loss. Each of these joys finds its source in a well of sorrow.

— DAY 244 —

Control what you can change

IN the journey of life, many things seem beyond our control. We find ourselves grappling with circumstances, events, and people that we wish we could change. It's easy to become overwhelmed and disheartened by the seemingly invincible challenges that life throws our way.

Life, in its beautiful yet baffling complexity, is a blend of constants and variables, the known and the unknown, the controllable and the uncontrollable. This contrast, intrinsic to our existence, often muddles our understanding and ability to act effectively. The key to unraveling this entanglement lies in the realization of a simple, potent truth—we can exert control only over what we can change.

Indeed, our lives pivot around our actions, emotions, choices, and attitudes—the elements within our control. By controlling these variables, we shape our destiny. Consider this: we cannot control the weather, but we can control our response to it. If it rains, we can either mourn the downpour or savor the rhythm of falling drops. The choice is ours.

Furthermore, recognizing what lies beyond our control—the fluctuations of the stock market, the passage of time, and the actions of others—frees us from unneeded stress and unsuccessful attempts to govern the ungovernable. This liberates immense energy that can be harnessed to manage our spectrum of influence effectively.

This philosophy doesn't advocate passivity but rather mindful activity. It empowers us to focus our efforts where they bear fruit and conserve energy where they don't.

It's about focusing on the steering wheel, accelerator, and brakes of your life. The stuff you can actually affect. Your thoughts. Your reactions. Your attitude. When you take control of these, you take control of your happiness and peace of mind. Life still throws traffic and bad weather your way, but you're navigating calmly, maybe even humming along.

Remind ourselves every day: Control what you can change. The rest? Let it go.

— DAY 245 —

An open mind is life's best teacher

IMAGINE your mind like a parachute. You've probably heard the saying, it works best when it's open, right? With an open mind, we have the chance to turn every twist and turn in life, every new encounter, and every unexpected situation into a learning experience.

Take a moment to imagine the parachute. A closed parachute is just a pack on your back, but once it's open, it's a life-saving, transformational tool. The same goes for our minds. A closed mind can't learn or grow; it's just an echo chamber of already-known facts and opinions. But, when we open our minds, we essentially open the parachute. We can soar, explore, and experience things beyond our initial beliefs and boundaries.

You may ask, why is it the best teacher? That's where things get really interesting. An open mind doesn't restrict learning to classrooms or textbooks. It sees every moment of life as a lesson. When we spill coffee, it's not just a mess; it's a gentle reminder to slow down. When we get stuck in traffic, it's not a waste of time; it's a chance to cultivate patience.

Beyond personal lessons, an open mind fosters empathy. By being willing to understand differing perspectives, we become more accepting of others, and through that, we learn compassion, kindness, and tolerance—values that textbooks can often only theoretically explain. Take Nelson Mandela, for instance. His open mind allowed him to learn from his prison experience, rather than let it embitter him, and look at the difference he made.

Opening our minds is not a one-time act; it's a conscious decision we must make every day. And yes, it's challenging. We have to confront our biases, question our beliefs, and be willing to change our views when presented with new evidence. It's through this process that we can truly learn and grow.

— DAY 246 —

Procrastination is laziness's ally

PROCRASTINATION, the silent enemy that lurks within us all. It's a tempting ally of laziness, a deceptive companion that disguises itself as a harmless delay.

Procrastination, the art of delaying action, has long been known as the silent killer of dreams. It whispers sweet promises of future endeavors while gently rocking us into the lullaby of inaction. You'll write that book... tomorrow. You'll start the diet... next week. The garage can be cleaned... later. There's always a later. And suddenly, the days turn into weeks, the weeks into months, and those months into years.

On the other side of this duo is laziness, a state of inertia, characterized by a lack of effort or energy. Laziness doesn't whisper; it sleeps soundly, nestled comfortably in the cozy bed of status quo. It prefers the familiar, the routine, and the effortless. While procrastination dreams of tomorrow, laziness thrives in the indifferent comfort of today.

Together, procrastination and laziness make a formidable team, arm in arm, skipping happily down the path of inaction. They are the main enemy of progress, the foes of productivity, and the adversaries of accomplishment.

So, how can we break this alliance? The key lies in understanding their tactics and confronting them with action. Recognize procrastination as the crafty illusionist it is. The "perfect moment" it promises rarely comes. And laziness? Well, challenge it with the thrill of new experiences, small steps that gradually move us out of our inertia.

As we consciously decide to act now, breaking tasks into manageable pieces, and valuing progress over perfection, we weaken the alliance of procrastination and laziness. And as we consistently move, one step at a time, we transform ourselves. We are no longer victims of the alliance but warriors of our own will.

But every alliance has its weakness, and in this battle of will, action is our greatest weapon. Armed with this knowledge, we are more than capable of overcoming this alliance and stepping into a realm of productivity and progress.

— DAY 247 —

Shift view for growth mindset

I MAGINE a world where you have the power to shape your destiny, where challenges become opportunities, and growth knows no bounds. This is the world of a growth mindset, a transformative concept that holds the key to unlocking your full potential.

A growth mindset, a term coined by psychologist Carol Dweck, is the belief that abilities and intelligence can be developed through dedication and hard work.[4] It champions the idea that potential is not fixed, but expandable. The key lies in the shift of view, the pivot from seeing challenges as unbeatable obstacles to viewing them as opportunities for learning and growth.

A shift in view signifies planting new seeds in this field. It means deliberately choosing to replace the familiar crops with unknown seeds, banking on their potential to grow into something more fulfilling, more enriching. It's about fostering a mindset that embraces change, cherishes learning, and sees challenges as opportunities rather than obstacles.

Consider the story of Thomas Edison. His shift in perspective led him to view failure not as a setback but as a stepping-stone toward success. Each unsuccessful attempt to invent the electric light bulb was, in his eyes, a successful discovery of a way that didn't work. This shift in view, this growth mindset, allowed him to persist until he achieved his goal.

Companies like Netflix and Amazon embraced the shift in view to disrupt their industries. They chose to see changes in technology not as threats but as opportunities to redefine entertainment and shopping, respectively. Their growth mindset has set new standards, revolutionizing the way we live.

Shifting the view for a growth mindset is not just about embracing change; it's about being the change. It's about realizing that the most formidable barriers to growth often exist in our minds. Once we make the conscious choice to view the world differently, we expose ourselves to limitless possibilities.

— DAY 248 —

Death is what gives life its value

LET'S face it, we all know that death is a part of life. It's the one thing every single one of us has in common. Yet, we spend most of our lives trying not to think about it. I mean, who wants to focus on the end when there's so much living to do? But here's food for thought: what if acknowledging death, and embracing its inevitability, could actually make our lives richer?

If you've ever stayed up to watch a meteor shower, you know the most breathtaking moments are those shooting stars, those bright flashes that are gone in an instant. Or maybe you've tasted a limited-edition dessert that you know you might never have again. Didn't that make every bite just a bit more delicious?

That's what death brings to life. It's the ultimate deadline, the final call. It's the thing that makes every moment we have here on earth precious. Every laugh, every tear, every hug, every argument—each one is priceless because there's a limit to how many we get.

And when we realize that, really internalize it, something amazing happens. We start to live more authentically. We let go of the small stuff, because who has time for that? We chase our dreams, open up to love, and take those risks, because we understand that we've only got this one shot. Instead of fearing death, let it be our guide—a reminder to make the most of each moment. Let's live with intention, purpose, and authenticity. Let's cherish every breath and create a life that reflects our deepest desires and aspirations.

Death is what gives life its value, my friend. Let's make each breath count and leave a lasting impact on the world. The choice is ours, and the time is now. Let's embark on this extraordinary adventure together and celebrate the beauty and significance of our existence. Let's make it count.

— DAY 249 —

Even a broken clock is right twice a day

S OUNDS a bit odd, doesn't it? Like one of those old-timey sayings your grandpa might have said. But let me tell you, there's a whole world of wisdom wrapped up in those few words. Despite its apparent failure, this simple timepiece carries a powerful message: even in our moments of imperfection and vulnerability, there is still a glimmer of truth and insight to be found.

Let's imagine a clock for a moment. You know, the one that ticks away, counting the seconds, minutes, and hours. But what if the clock breaks? The hands freeze, and time seems to stand still. The funny thing though, is that clock, as broken as it may be, hits the nail right on the head twice each day. It might be stuck, but it sure has its moments of perfect accuracy. Amazing, right?

This is more than an interesting aspect of how we monitor time; it's a metaphor for life. Don't we all have moments when we feel "broken," yet somehow, against the odds, we find ourselves exactly where we need to be? In those instances, we're that clock, imperfect, yet perfectly aligning with life's grand symphony.

Picture this. An artist struggling to make ends meet, but then, out of nowhere, she paints a masterpiece that rockets her to fame. Or a writer, almost ready to throw in the towel, but then his manuscript gets picked up by a big publisher. We often say, "Wow, they got lucky!"

But isn't it more than that? It's life's way of proving that, no matter how "broken" we might feel, we can still have our moment in the sun. But this old saying has a flip side, too. It reminds us that nobody, and I mean nobody, is perfect all the time. Even the smartest people make mistakes. The most successful folks trip up. And even the most loving souls can utter words they regret. We all mess up; we all miss the mark. But just like that broken clock, those off moments don't define us.

So, the next time you feel broken, remember the clock. Recall that it too stands still, its purpose seemingly lost. But also remember that even in its stillness, it finds moments of accuracy, and so will you. No matter how broken we are, we all have our moments of glory, and that's a fact worth remembering.

— DAY 250 —

You can't repay sleep debt

I N the stillness of the night, as the clock ticks closer to the dawn, countless individuals lie awake, burning the midnight oil or tossing and turning restlessly. Sleep, an elusive yet essential aspect of our lives, often takes a backseat to the hustle and bustle of modern living. The belief that one can repay sleep debt—a cumulative result of chronic sleep deprivation—by simply "catching up" on sleep during weekends or holidays is a pervasive, dangerous misconception that deserves to be debunked.

Sleep is a complex biological phenomenon that transcends the boundaries of consciousness, delving deep into the realms of our physiology, cognition, and emotional well-being. The truth is that sleep is an indispensable element of our existence, and its demands cannot be met by simply catching up on lost hours.

The idea of sleep debt is rooted in the human body's innate need for a specific amount of sleep to function optimally. When we consistently fall short of meeting this requirement, our bodies accumulate sleep debt, which can take a toll on our cognitive abilities, mood, and physical health. Many people, driven by the notion that lost sleep can be "repaid" by simply sleeping longer during weekends or holidays, unwittingly exacerbate the problem. This belief, upon closer examination, is fundamentally flawed.

Scientific research has demonstrated that catching up on sleep is not an effective strategy for reversing the adverse effects of chronic sleep loss. A study conducted by the *National Institutes of Health* revealed that weekend recovery sleep does not counteract the damage caused by sleep deprivation during the week.[5] On the contrary, this inconsistent sleep pattern may disrupt our circadian rhythm, further impairing our bodies' ability to function at their best.

Perhaps the most poignant aspect of our inability to repay sleep debt lies in the fact that it serves as a stark reminder of our limitations as human beings. We live in a world that encourages us to push past our boundaries in the pursuit of success, often at the expense of our well-being.

— DAY 251 —

Listen to understand, not to reply

IN a world consumed by noise and chatter, the art of listening has become a lost skill. We find ourselves engaged in conversations where our minds are already formulating responses, eager to share our own thoughts and opinions. To truly understand, we must listen not to reply, but to understand.

Imagine a world where each conversation is not just an exchange of words, but a transfer of understanding, empathy, and respect. Sounds beautiful, doesn't it? But let's be real, we've all been guilty of merely waiting for our turn to talk, strategizing our next retort, or constructing our defense, while the other person is still speaking. We are often so caught up in the need to express ourselves that we forget the essence of communication is not speaking, but understanding.

Consider an example from nature. Reflect on the roots of a tree. The strength of a tree lies not in its branches that reach out for the sun, but in its roots, which silently listen to the earth, understand its nutrients, water levels, and even the presence of nearby trees. This deep, silent understanding is what nourishes the tree and enables it to flourish.

In the same vein, truly effective communication requires us to be like the tree's roots. We must silence our inner noise and open ourselves to the other person's perspective. It's about receiving their thoughts, experiences, and feelings, about understanding their joys and their sorrows, their fears and their dreams.

This approach has the power to transform our relationships. When we listen to understand, we acknowledge the other person's value and worth, building a foundation of trust and respect. Suddenly, conflicts don't seem insurmountable, because we're no longer adversaries but partners, united in our quest to understand each other better.

At this point, you might wonder, "But what about expressing my perspective?" Here's the beautiful part: When we create a space of understanding, we also create an environment where our own thoughts can be expressed and truly heard.

After all, when we shift our aim from replying to understanding, we don't just change the conversation, we change the world.

— DAY 252 —

Education and intelligence are not the same

TYPICALLY, we intertwine the two, assuming one means the other like a predictable linear equation. However, dare to flip this coin, and you'll realize a whole new dimension, a paradigm-shattering concept: they are separate entities, each valuable and potent in their unique ways.

Education, as we traditionally know, is a system, a structured journey that navigates through the landscape of knowledge, gathering information, collecting skills, and amassing degrees. It equips us with a standard toolkit, a survival guide for the intellectual jungle. It's like a train ride, charted on the tracks of curriculum, taking us from point A to B. But that's not all there is, is it?

Enter intelligence. This one is a wild horse. Unrestrained, independent, and fiercely unique. It's not bound by the rails of curriculum or the stations of examinations. It's about an innate curiosity, a knack for problem-solving, a flair for innovative thinking, and an intuitive understanding of the world. It's the capacity to question, analyze, synthesize, and create. An intelligent mind is like an eagle soaring high, unrestricted, charting its unique path.

Consider this: all the pioneers, inventors, and revolutionaries, had something in common. Yes, most of them had an education, but it was their intelligence, their ability to think outside the box, to challenge norms, to innovate and adapt, that made them truly extraordinary.

Let's redefine our understanding. Education is a journey, a process, an important one, indeed. But intelligence, it's the spark, the magic ingredient, the wild card that brings life's experiences into sharp, insightful focus.

They are not the same, no. But when these two forces collide, when education fuels intelligence and intelligence shapes education, well, that's when the real magic happens, and ordinary lives become extraordinary.

— DAY 253 —

Productivity isn't measured by exhaustion

I N today's fast-paced and competitive world, it is all too common for individuals to equate productivity with exhaustion, measuring their worth by the extent of their physical and mental fatigue. This flawed perception, which often manifests in a relentless pursuit of success at the expense of personal well-being, serves as a barrier to achieving genuine fulfillment and satisfaction in life.

The idea that productivity is inextricably linked to exhaustion is a misconception that undermines the potential for genuine growth and self-discovery. Contrary to popular belief, true productivity is not measured by the number of hours we spend laboring away at our desks or the extent of our sleep deprivation; rather, it is characterized by the intentional pursuit of goals that align with our values, passions, and aspirations. This form of productivity fosters a sense of accomplishment and purpose, allowing us to live more fulfilling and balanced lives.

At the heart of this reimagined concept of productivity lies the recognition that our minds and bodies are not inexhaustible resources. Just as a well-tuned machine requires regular maintenance and care, so too do we require periods of rest, reflection, and rejuvenation to function at our highest capacity. By honoring our innate need for balance, we can cultivate a more sustainable and compassionate approach to productivity, one that is rooted in self-awareness and respect for our limitations.

This shift in perspective invites us to reevaluate our priorities and redefine our understanding of success. No longer confined to the narrow confines of exhaustion and burnout, productivity becomes an expansive and holistic concept that encompasses personal growth, emotional well-being, and the pursuit of a meaningful life. It is in this space that we can experience the "Aha" moment of realizing that our worth is not determined by the extent of our fatigue, but rather by our ability to live with intention, cultivate self-awareness, and engage in activities that align with our deepest values.

— DAY 254 —

Value your time more than your possessions

W E live in a world driven by consumerism, where our value is often associated with what we own. We are bombarded with messages telling us that our possessions define us and bring us happiness. But in this pursuit of material wealth, we often sacrifice the one thing we can never get back: time.

Now, I know what you're thinking—"Time is money, and money buys possessions. So why not value possessions?" Let's flip that narrative around. You can always make more money, but can you create more time? Time, once spent, never comes back.

Our life, essentially, is a tapestry woven with the threads of time. Each moment we live, each experience we have, adds another unique thread to this fabric. Our possessions, on the other hand, are like the decorations on this tapestry. While they may make our tapestry appear richer and more beautiful, they do not constitute the fabric itself.

The most memorable and meaningful moments of our lives are seldom centered around possessions. The joyous laughter of a family dinner, the quiet satisfaction of a job well done, the warm fuzziness of a loved one's hug—these are the moments that truly enrich our lives, and none of them can be bought or sold.

So, what happens when we value possessions more than time? We end up trading away precious threads of our life's tapestry for mere decorations. We sell our time for money, then use that money to buy possessions that we hope will make us happy. But can a house filled with gold and diamonds ever be a home without the laughter, love, and memories?

On the other hand, when we value our time more than our possessions, we focus on creating a rich, vibrant tapestry that's filled with joyous experiences, meaningful relationships, and personal growth. We stop chasing after possessions and start living our lives fully and authentically.

Dear reader, ask yourself—are you spending your time wisely, or are you simply spending it? Remember, time is the most precious treasure you have. Value it, cherish it, and most importantly, spend it on what truly matters.

— DAY 255 —

Birds of the same feathers flock together

HAVE you ever felt that urge to "keep up with the Joneses," to match their shiny new car, their latest smartphone, or their swanky holiday pictures? We've all been there, haven't we? But let's pause for a second and ponder over something.

We live in a world hooked on instant gratification, where the "likes" on our social media posts often determine our happiness quotient. We spend money we may not have, on things we may not need, to impress people we may not even care about. It's like we're spinning in a hamster wheel, constantly chasing, never reaching.

Consider the shimmering feathers of a peacock, so eye-catching and magnificent. Their vibrant display is nature's way of attracting a mate. Similarly, we sometimes get caught up in the temptation of materialism, buying the latest gadgets and expensive designer clothes, all to catch the eyes of those around us. But amid this quest for external validation, are we neglecting our inner worth? Are we overlooking the importance of our values, passions, and relationships?

Let's face it, the admiration we seek is as fleeting as a shooting star. One moment it's there, lighting up our world, the next moment, it's gone. Today's must-have gadget is tomorrow's old news. Yesterday's trending outfit is today's charity shop donation.

This is a wake-up call. It's urging us to step off that hamster wheel, to ask ourselves, is this fleeting applause really worth it? It's encouraging us to invest in ourselves—our skills, dreams, and well-being—not just our wardrobes or gadget collections.

Please, resist the appeal of "keeping up with the Joneses." Don't go broke trying to impress others. Instead, focus on your own financial well-being and the pursuit of a meaningful life. Surround yourself with people who appreciate you for who you are, not for what you have.

In the end, the only person you need to impress is yourself. Don't let the pursuit of impressing others leave you broke and unfulfilled. Choose a life of authenticity and create your own definition of success.

— DAY 256 —

You are not entitled

PICTURE this: you're born into a family where success is the status quo, your neighborhood is beautiful, your parents are pillars of society, your skin is deemed "perfect" by societal standards, and even nature seems to have dealt you a good hand in the beauty department. You'd feel pretty lucky, right? Now imagine feeling like all these factors entitle you to a smooth ride through life. But here's where it gets interesting because life doesn't quite work like that.

Imagine the universe for a moment. Infinite. Vast. Majestic. Astonishingly fair. It doesn't care if you were born in a mansion or a shack, if your parents are tycoons or teachers, or if you're considered attractive or not. The universe treats us all the same: we live, and eventually, we die.

Look, your circumstances, however fortunate, don't automatically stamp your passport to the land of easy success. Yes, they might provide opportunities, a nudge in the right direction, but they don't guarantee achievement. Success isn't about where you start. It's about the journey you undertake, the hurdles you leap over, and the growth you experience along the way.

Physical attractiveness, too, should not be a basis for entitlement. Beauty is subjective, and our worth should not be determined by our appearance. True value lies in our actions, our character, and the positive impact we have on others. It's the content of our hearts and minds that truly defines us, not our external features.

Remember, we're all just inhabitants of a tiny blue dot, spinning in a galaxy that's just one of billions. The universe couldn't care less about our social status or looks; it only acknowledges our deeds, our endeavors, and our humanity.

In a nutshell, no one is entitled to anything. Success is earned, not inherited. Worth is realized, not given. Each of us, no matter our origin story or skin color, must pave our own path, earn our own keep, and make our own mark. Because, in the grand scheme of things, it's not about where you're from or how you look. It's about who you are and who you become. Now that's a conversation worth having, don't you think?

— DAY 257 —

Worthwhile goals require patience and time

W E'RE living in a time where everything is immediate. Fast food, instant messaging, next-day delivery, you name it. But when it comes to life's goals, the most meaningful ones? Well, they're more like a slow-cooked meal that's been brewing for a while, soaking up all the flavors. And trust me, the result is worth every second.

Consider this, imagine you're planting a tree. You can't just toss a seed on the ground, pour a bucket of water on it, and expect a fully grown tree the next day, right? It takes time for the roots to reach down into the earth, for the stem to break through the soil, and for the branches to reach out to the sky. It's a slow dance with nature, a test of patience, but when you finally sit under the shade of that tree, it's pure satisfaction.

This tree-growing business, it's pretty much the same deal as your goals. Consider the best things in life, the most rewarding ones, they're not a mad dash to the finish line. They're more similar to an expedition, a journey. There are going to be flat plains, steep climbs, and maybe a few unexpected detours. But that's part of the fun, isn't it?

We're so often sold these stories of overnight success, but let's be real. Behind every "sudden" success story, there's a lot of unseen work, years of perseverance, countless moments of self-doubt, and plenty of patience.

In a world that values instant gratification, patience becomes a radical act of rebellion. It allows us to savor the journey, appreciate the small victories, and cultivate a sense of resilience that propels us forward.

Here's the deal. When it comes to your goals and your dreams, don't be afraid to play the long game. Embrace the journey, and enjoy the ride. Like a fine wine, it's going to take time to mature. But, when you finally get to uncork that bottle and take a sip, it's going to taste so, so sweet. Patience and time, my friend, that's the secret sauce to cooking up some worthwhile goals.

— DAY 258 —

Luck favors persistence and hard work

LUCK—a concept that often triggers feelings of mystique and uncertainty. Some believe it to be a random force, an unpredictable stroke of fortune that favors the few. However, upon closer examination, we come to realize that luck is not an arbitrary phenomenon. In fact, luck has a profound attraction for those who embody two key qualities: persistence and hard work.

Imagine you're an explorer, seeking a hidden treasure. You are equipped with a map, but the exact location of the treasure is a mystery. Luck, in this context, might be stumbling upon the treasure at your first dig. But how often does that happen? Instead, you will likely have to dig multiple times, in multiple places, sometimes hitting a rock, other times finding irrelevant artifacts. Your hands might get bruised, and your spirit might get disheartened, but you continue.

Persistence, in this journey, means you keep digging, regardless of the disappointments and failures. It's a stubborn refusal to give up, a tenacity that pushes you to try one more time. Hard work is what fuels this persistence. It's the sweat on your brow and the strength in your arms as you wield the shovel time and again.

Now, when you finally uncover the treasure, is it luck? Or is it the result of your persistence and hard work? One could argue that it's a combination of both. However, without persistence and hard work, the chance of unearthing the treasure reduces significantly.

Take Thomas Edison's invention of the light bulb for instance. He made 1,000 unsuccessful attempts before he could make it work. Was the successful attempt luck? Perhaps. But that "luck" was brought about by persistence and hard work. If he had given up after the first, second, or even the 999th try, we wouldn't be illuminating our world as we do today.

So, does luck favor persistence and hard work? Absolutely. The more you work and the more persistent you are, the higher the chances you'll be in the right place at the right time, ready to seize the opportunities, or the "luck," that comes your way.

— DAY 259 —

Nothing is good or bad, but thinking makes it so

S HAKESPEARE elegantly captured this idea in his play Hamlet when he wrote, "Nothing is either good or bad, but thinking makes it so." In this seemingly simple statement lies a transformative realization—that our thoughts hold the power to shape our experiences and determine the meaning we assign to them.

Imagine waking up to a thunderstorm when you had plans for a beach day. Your initial reaction might be one of disappointment, maybe even frustration. The rain, in this case, seems like a bad thing. But what if you're a farmer, desperate for water after weeks of dry heat threatening your crops? For you, that very same rain is a blessing, a relief, the difference between a failed crop and food on the table. The rain itself hasn't changed, only our perception of it.

It's the same with our lives, isn't it? We label events, people, and things as "good" or "bad" based on our beliefs, values, and current situation. These labels are not inherent qualities, rather, they are the product of our minds, of our thinking.

Here's where it gets interesting: if our thinking has the power to determine whether something is good or bad, then it also has the power to reframe our perception. Yes, it's a bold idea. But isn't it liberating to think that we have the power to shape our reality, to define our experiences?

Take a failed business venture, for instance. Many would label it a "bad" event, a setback. But what if we choose to view it as a learning experience, an opportunity to identify our mistakes, improve, and come back stronger? Suddenly, the failure isn't so "bad" anymore, is it?

This way of thinking does not mean denying the harsh realities of life or glossing over pain and suffering. It simply means understanding that our perception plays a major role in shaping our experience and that we have the power to choose a more empowering perspective. It's all a matter of perspective, and it all starts with our thinking.

— DAY 260 —

Dream big, live small

T HE starlit night sky above, vast and infinite, is a reminder of life's boundless potential. As we look up at the starry sky, we are urged to dream big, to reach for the stars, to touch the edge of the universe with our aspirations. Yet, in the middle of these colossal dreams and grand visions, we must find our grounding, our contentment in the modest and humble. This is the paradox of life—to dream big, yet live small.

Dreaming big is to imagine a world beyond your immediate surroundings. It is to perceive life beyond the constraints of the now and to envision the reality you wish to shape. It invites courage, optimism, and inventiveness. Our dreams give us purpose, direction, and a sense of meaning. They ignite the boldness in our hearts, compelling us to reach beyond the perceived limits of our abilities. Yet, dreams are only one part of the equation. How we choose to live our lives in pursuit of these dreams is equally crucial.

Living small, contrary to popular belief, does not imply a life bound by limitations or a lack of ambition. Rather, it signifies a life embraced with humility and grounded in simplicity. It is to appreciate the beauty in the everyday, to cherish the fleeting moments of joy that are often overshadowed by our relentless pursuit of bigger, better, and more. Living small is to foster a sense of gratitude for what we have, even as we reach for what we aspire to have.

In dreaming big, we push the boundaries of our potential, reaching for heights unseen and unimagined. Yet, in living small, we keep ourselves anchored, preserving our sense of humility, gratitude, and contentment. This contrast serves as a counterbalance, keeping us from being lost in the vast expanse of our dreams or getting comfortable in the familiarity of our comfort zones.

Therefore, dream big, for dreams fuel the fire of ambition and carve the path to progress. But live small, cherishing the journey, relishing the moments of joy and learning that the pursuit of dreams offers. It is in this delicate balance of dreaming big and living small that we truly embrace the beauty of life, living a life rich in purpose, yet grounded in gratitude and simplicity

— DAY 261 —

Time with loved ones is limited

I T'S funny how we often get caught up in the hustle and bustle of life, focusing on our careers, our to-do lists, and everything in between. But have you ever stopped to reflect upon the fact that our time with our loved ones is limited? I mean, really thought about it? It's a sobering thought, but one that's incredibly important to acknowledge.

Our lives are like a ticking clock, with each second bringing us closer to the moment when we have to say goodbye to those we care about most. We can't stop it, and we can't slow it down. That's why it's so crucial to make the most of every moment we have with our loved ones. Because, in the grand scheme of things, those moments are what truly matter.

I've found that when you embrace this realization, it changes the way you approach life. You start to prioritize the people who mean the most to you, making an effort to spend quality time with them and create lasting memories. You become more present, savoring the simple moments that might have once gone unnoticed. And, in a way, it makes your relationships even more special, because you're fully appreciating the time you have together.

This awareness of time's limitations can also help us navigate the inevitable losses we'll face in our lives. It's never easy to say goodbye to a loved one, but knowing that you made the most of the time you had together can provide a sense of comfort and peace. It's a reminder that, while their physical presence may be gone, the memories and love you shared will live on forever.

Let's make a promise to ourselves and each other. Let's cherish the time we have with our loved ones, because we know all too well that it's limited. Let's be present, create memories, and celebrate the connections that make our lives so incredibly rich. Because, in the end, it's not the material possessions or the awards that we'll remember—it's the love we shared with those who mattered most.

— DAY 262 —

If you don't let go, it will hold you back

L IFE is a constant cycle of beginnings and endings. We encounter people, experiences, and circumstances that shape our journey. But what happens when we hold on tightly to something that has already served its purpose? The truth is, if you don't let go, it will hold you back.

Imagine carrying a heavy backpack filled with memories, attachments, and regrets. The weight of the past can be overwhelming, making it difficult to move forward. Whether it's a toxic relationship, a failed venture, or a past mistake, holding on prevents us from embracing new opportunities and growth.

Letting go is not a sign of weakness; it's an act of courage and self-preservation. It's about releasing what no longer serves us, creating space for new possibilities to emerge. Just as a tree sheds its leaves in autumn to make way for new growth, we must learn to let go to move forward.

When we cling to the past, we imprison ourselves in a cycle of stagnation. We remain stuck in familiar patterns, unable to break free and embrace the unknown. Letting go allows us to break those chains, freeing ourselves from the limitations of the past and opening ourselves up to new adventures.

It's important to acknowledge that letting go is not always easy. It requires self-reflection, acceptance, and forgiveness. It's a process of releasing attachments, expectations, and regrets. It's about finding the strength to say goodbye and trusting in the possibilities that lie ahead.

The past has its place. It can serve as a wellspring of wisdom, guiding us as we navigate life's labyrinth. But it's essential to remember that the past is a place of reference, not residence. We must cherish the lessons it provides without allowing them to shadow our present.

So, let's resolve to let go, to unburden ourselves from the weight of our past. Like a river, let us flow forward, adapting and evolving. In the end, we'll realize it's not about forgetting our past but about accepting it, learning from it, and daring to move forward, free and unencumbered. Because life waits for no one, and neither should we.

— DAY 263 —

Calm seas don't breed skilled sailors

WHEN we face difficult challenges in life, it can be tempting to wish for calm seas and smooth sailing. But the truth is, it is only through facing adversity and navigating rough waters that we can truly grow and become skilled sailors in the journey of life.

We all sail on the vast ocean of life, where calm waters often represent our comfort zones—routines, predictability, and familiar surroundings. Although these calm seas provide a sense of safety and stability, they rarely offer opportunities for growth or self-improvement. It's in the uncharted waters, the rolling waves, and stormy seas where we are pushed to our limits, allowing us to discover our true potential.

In calm waters, sailors aren't tested. They glide effortlessly, navigating with ease. However, it's the storm that brings out their true colors. The high winds demand courage, and the monstrous waves demand perseverance. When the sailors fight against these elements, they sharpen their skills, broaden their knowledge, and deepen their wisdom. Similarly, in life, it is through the storm of trials and tribulations that we acquire resilience, adaptability, and strength.

A life devoid of challenges may seem appealing, a peaceful sea with no storms in sight. But such calm rarely propels us forward. Instead, it breeds selfsatisfaction, luring us into a state of passive acceptance where personal growth becomes stagnant. In contrast, it is in the midst of our battles—whether personal, professional, or emotional—that we truly evolve. These life storms are not here to break us, but to make us, to refine us into our strongest selves.

So, when you find yourself in rough seas, remember the words of the great Stoic philosopher Seneca, "A gem cannot be polished without friction, nor a man perfected without trials." Embrace the storm, for it is an opportunity disguised as a challenge. Each wave that hits, each gust of wind that blows, molds you into a skilled sailor in life's turbulent ocean.

— DAY 264 —

Focus determines your current and future life

I T is not just a catchy phrase but a deep truth that has the power to shape the direction of our lives.

In the grand scheme of life, where countless threads of experiences, decisions, and actions interweave, it's our focus that pulls particular threads into prominence, defining our current realities and future possibilities. When we focus on something, we give it power, we give it a distinct shape and texture in our life's narrative.

Our focus can be our North Star guiding us through the night, or it can be the fog that clouds our path. A focused mind, driven by purpose, passion, and persistence, can turn the wildest dreams into reality. Conversely, a lack of focus can lead us off track, casting us adrift on the seas of life, vulnerable to the whims of external forces.

Consider successful individuals across all domains. Inventors, artists, entrepreneurs, athletes—regardless of their field, their focus is their common denominator. Ludwig van Beethoven's profound focus on his compositions, even in the face of worsening deafness, led to some of the most influential music in the Western classical tradition. Serena Williams' steadfast focus crafted her into a tennis titan.

Conversely, think about times when a lack of focus derailed your intentions. Maybe you tried to juggle too many tasks at once and ended up accomplishing none. Perhaps you let distractions divert you from your goals, leading to halfhearted results.

However, the beauty of focus is that it's adaptable and trainable. Like a muscle, it strengthens with practice. The more we flex it, the more control we gain over our lives. We can shift our focus, adjust its intensity, and refine its clarity, making it an active participant in shaping our lives, not just a bystander.

To summarize, our focus is not just an observer of our lives—it's an architect. It builds bridges to our dreams and digs tunnels through our obstacles. So, hold your pebbles carefully, aim well, and remember, where they land today will ripple through the waters of your life tomorrow.

— DAY 265 —

Regret is painful at 65

REGRET—the haunting specter that lingers in the depths of our consciousness, a reminder of roads not taken and opportunities missed. It is a profound and often painful emotion that can consume us as we reflect upon our lives. Regret, when left unaddressed, can be particularly painful at the age of 65, when the weight of time brings clarity and perspective.

Picture yourself at 65, sitting comfortably in an old armchair, flipping through the pages of your life. This book isn't filled with words but with memories, moments, and choices. Each page, whether filled with joy or engraved with sorrow, is a part of who you have become. But what about those blank pages, the missed opportunities, the path not taken? Those gaps in your narrative are the breeding ground of regret.

Regret is a strange emotion. In youth, it can propel us forward, urging us to correct our mistakes, learn, grow, and become better. But at 65, it's not as easy to correct course. Time has solidified our paths, the cement of life has hardened, and altering the design can feel impossible. It's this realization that adds a sting to regret in our later years.

The narratives of our lives are ours to write. Each decision, each action or inaction, is a line in our story. The trick is to ensure that our narrative is not one of regret but one of satisfaction. Satisfaction doesn't mean a life devoid of mistakes, but rather a life where mistakes are understood as a part of the process, as stepping stones, not stumbling blocks.

This isn't a dark prediction. Instead, it's a wake-up call, an encouragement to live fully and boldly now. It's a reminder that at the end of the day, it's not the years in your life, but the life in your years that count. So, let's fill our pages, one conscious choice at a time, and craft a story that resonates with fulfillment, not regret.

— DAY 266 —

Remind the body who is in charge

L ET me tell you a story about the body and the mind. It's an age-old tale of rebellion and power, but also of understanding and harmony. Picture this: your body is a wild horse, untamed and free, while your mind, it's the seasoned rider, holding the reins, guiding and leading.

Isn't it funny how the body sometimes seems to have a mind of its own? Like when you're on that healthy diet, and yet, as if on autopilot, your hand reaches out for that extra slice of pizza. Or when you've planned an early morning workout, but your body sticks to the bed like a stubborn magnet. Sounds familiar, doesn't it?

Consider those moments, not as losing a battle but as a dance. A dance where sometimes the body leads, but it's the mind that sets the rhythm.

It's all about having a conversation with your body, a bit like negotiating with a stubborn but lovable kid. You explain, persuade, sweet-talk, and sometimes even beg. Because let's face it, the body is just like that kid, craving the sweet, the easy, the comfortable. But you, with the wisdom of the mind, understand the bigger picture.

Remember, it's not about going into battle with your body; that's neither productive nor healthy. It's about teaching the body to listen to the wisdom of the mind. It's about creating harmony and balance. It's like being a loving parent or a considerate boss, guiding gently, understanding the tantrums but never losing sight of what's essential.

You have the power to shape your physical reality. Remind the body who is in charge and watch as it responds with increased energy, vitality, and resilience. Embrace the incredible connection between your mind and body, and let it guide you on the path to optimal well-being.

The next time your body seems to go rogue, chuckle a bit, shake your head, and remind it lovingly—"Hey, I am in charge here." Trust me, your body, just like that wild horse, can be tamed, not with force but with love, respect, and a bit of firm talking. And that's one incredible dance to master!

— DAY 267 —

Life without adventure is lifeless

C ONSIDER for a moment, the thrill of stepping onto a plane destined for a far-off land you've never visited. The jolt of adrenaline as you race down a white-water river, or the soul-stirring sensation as you gaze upon an aweinspiring sunset from the pinnacle of a mountain you've just conquered. Now, let's imagine a life devoid of such experiences—a life without adventure. It's like a book with blank pages, a song with no melody, a painting absent of colors. Simply put, it's lifeless.

Adventure breathes life into our existence, adding color, texture, and depth. It's the spice that flavors our life's soup, preventing it from turning into a bland, uninspiring soup. Adventure is not about seeking danger or thrill for the sake of it, it's about pushing boundaries, stepping out of comfort zones, and truly discovering who we are. It's about opening our hearts and minds to the unknown, allowing the world to sculpt us into better, more enlightened versions of ourselves.

An adventure can be a solo backpacking trip around the globe, but it can also be as simple as trying a new cuisine or picking up a challenging hobby. It's about embracing uncertainty and viewing it as an opportunity for growth, not as a source of fear. It's about understanding that the most breathtaking views come after the hardest climbs and realizing that those climbs, challenging though they may be, make us resilient, adaptable, and full of life.

In a life filled with adventure, we collect stories that ignite our souls and nourish our spirits. We build connections with people, cultures, and places that broaden our perspectives and enrich our lives. We learn to embrace uncertainty, savor the present moment, and cherish the beauty of the journey itself.

Let's not treat our lives like an endless cycle of predictable routines. Let's seek adventures—big and small, far and near. Let's imbue every moment with excitement, curiosity, and the anticipation of something novel. After all, life is not measured by the number of breaths we take, but by the moments that take our breath away. Let us remember that life, without adventure, is merely existence—flat, monotonous, and truly lifeless.

— DAY 268 —

Goodbyes hurt when a value exists

E VER wondered why saying "goodbye" feels like a punch in the gut sometimes? It's an interesting phenomenon, don't you think? Some farewells are just a casual wave of the hand, while others feel like extracting a part of your soul. How come? It's simple yet profound: goodbyes hurt when the entity you're parting with holds significant value in your life.

Think about your favorite coffee mug. The one with the chipped edge and faded design, the one you've used every morning for years. Imagine you accidentally drop it one day, and it shatters. That tiny crack in your heart? That's the sting of a valuable goodbye.

Now magnify that a hundred times, a thousand times. Think about bidding farewell to a close friend who's moving continents, or leaving behind the house you grew up in, full of precious memories. It's like someone turned off the music in the middle of your favorite song, isn't it? The pang you feel, that's the cost of value. The deeper the bond, the harder the goodbye.

That pain you feel, it's not just about loss. It's a testament to the strength of your feelings and the depth of your connections. It's proof that you had something or someone in your life that made it richer, more colorful.

Yes, goodbyes may leave an ache in our hearts, but they also remind us of the richness of our experiences and the people who have touched our lives. They teach us about the fragility and temporariness of life, prompting us to seize the present moment and treasure the connections we have before they slip away.

Honor the goodbyes, my friend. Embrace the mix of emotions they bring, for they are a testament to a life well-lived, a heart fully engaged, and a soul that has embraced the beauty of connections. Goodbyes may sting, but they also remind us of the profound impact we can have on each other's lives.

— DAY 269 —

Life skills have no gender

I N the grand symphony of existence, there are chords that, when played right, create a harmony that transcends all barriers, borders, and binaries. Life skills are those chords, my friends. What's remarkable about them is that they know no gender, no race, no religion. They are universally applicable, equally essential, and fundamentally human.

Imagine a world where we no longer assume who should cook dinner or who should change the car tire based on outdated stereotypes. Picture a reality where everyone knows how to sew a button, pay their taxes, do the laundry, or perform a basic health check—not because of their gender, but because these are skills required to lead an independent life.

Gendering life skills is a relic of a past society that was deeply entrenched in rigid roles. In today's world, this idea seems not just outdated, but counterproductive. When we prescribe skills based on someone's gender, we limit their potential and cripple their independence.

In fact, when we embrace the idea that life skills have no gender, we unlock a world of potential and empower individuals to explore their full range of capabilities. We create a more inclusive society where everyone is free to pursue their passions, contribute their unique talents, and lead fulfilling lives.

Imagine a world where individuals are not confined by gender norms but are encouraged to cultivate skills and qualities that resonate with their true selves. Imagine a society that values empathy, communication, problem-solving, and resilience, regardless of gender identity.

Together, let us create a world where the potential of every individual knows no bounds, where skills are celebrated regardless of gender. Let us break free from the limitations imposed by societal norms and embrace the limitless possibilities that await us when we recognize that life skills are truly universal.

— DAY 270 —

Your only competition is your past self

L IFE has a funny way of convincing us that it's one giant race where we're all competitors, hustling for success. But here's food for thought. What if the only real rival you're racing against isn't your neighbor, your co-worker, or that person whose life seems picture-perfect on Instagram? What if, in this grand marathon of life, your only real competition is, in fact, your past self?

You're standing at the starting line in a stadium, crowds cheering, your heart pounding. As the gun fires, you're not sprinting against a lineup of opponents, but rather against a ghost—the ghost of who you were yesterday, last week, last year. Engaging, isn't it?

Let's dissect this idea. In this race, the finish line isn't some elusive "success" point that keeps shifting with every societal trend. Nah, success here is a better you. The aim? To outperform, outlast, and outgrow your former self. It's about recognizing past mistakes as life lessons, using past victories as stepping stones, and continuously blooming.

Shifting the focus from external competition to internal evolution, now that's liberating! It frees us from comparison traps and boosts our resilience. This race is not against the world, but within ourselves. That's the power move, my friend.

Isn't it wild to realize that you are both your biggest rival and cheerleader? The secret is that winning this race doesn't mean outrunning everyone else. No, it's about outgrowing, out-learning, out-loving your past self.

Every day is a new lap in this infinite race of self-improvement. And the trophy? It's the profound satisfaction that comes from knowing you're evolving, you're growing, you're stepping into a better version of yourself. Isn't that a race worth running? Let's keep moving, keep growing, because in this race, every step forward is a win!

— DAY 271 —

Sex and love aren't synonymous

IN a world that often interconnects the concepts of sex and love, it is essential to recognize that they are not synonymous. These two powerful experiences, powerful and captivating in their ways, are often perceived as two sides of the same coin, merged, tangled, indistinguishable. But, upon closer introspection, one recognizes their distinct identities and roles in human life.

Sex, a physical act of intimacy, is a natural and primal expression of human desire. It is a powerful force that can ignite passion and pleasure, leaving us excited and fulfilled. However, sex alone does not encompass the depth and complexity of love. It is a transient experience, subject to the ebb and flow of desire, chemistry, and physical gratification.

Love, on the other hand, transcends the physical realm. It is a profound and often mysterious emotion that encompasses care, understanding, and a genuine connection with another soul. Love goes beyond the confines of our bodies, touching the depths of our hearts and souls.

This isn't to undermine the power of sexual intimacy in a loving relationship. Sex, when infused with love, can become a powerful expression of deep emotional connection. It can create a sense of closeness and vulnerability that strengthens the bond of love. However, equating sex with love can lead to misguided expectations and misunderstandings. Physical attraction can be mistaken for love, and the absence of sexual desire can be misinterpreted as a lack of love.

Recognizing the distinction between sex and love is crucial for nurturing healthy relationships. It allows us to appreciate the complexity of our emotions and physical desires, and negotiate them in ways that contribute to our wellbeing and happiness. It fosters more profound connections based on mutual respect and understanding, rather than mere physical attraction.

It is vital, then, to acknowledge and respect the distinct identities of sex and love. To realize that the absence of one doesn't invalidate the presence of the other. In understanding this, we open our minds to a broader perspective on human relationships and the manifold ways in which they manifest.

— DAY 272 —

Self-evaluation leads to growth

T HE journey of self-improvement is a voyage of endless revelations, fascinating discoveries, and profound transformations. The compass guiding this expedition is self-evaluation—a process that invites introspection, encourages change, and ultimately, facilitates growth.

To begin, imagine yourself as a seed nestled within the womb of the earth. Much like this seed, each one of us carries the potential to grow, sprout, and flourish. However, for the seed to transform into a towering tree, it needs the right nourishment. Similarly, our growth requires nourishment, and this nourishment comes in the form of self-evaluation.

Self-evaluation is the conscious effort to analyze our thoughts, emotions, actions, and their consequences. It's about pausing in our tireless race against time, looking inwards, and genuinely asking ourselves, "How am I doing?" It's about acknowledging our strengths and accomplishments, identifying our weaknesses and mistakes, and most importantly, learning from them.

When we indulge in regular self-evaluation, we gift ourselves the opportunity to understand who we truly are, independent of external validation. We uncover truths about ourselves that we may have previously overlooked or deliberately ignored. We discover patterns in our behavior that either help or hinder our progress. Most importantly, we perceive the values, passions, and purposes that drive our actions and decisions.

The beauty of self-evaluation lies in its ability to ignite change. When we identify aspects of ourselves that require improvement, we can consciously make efforts to modify them. We become proactive participants in our journey of growth, rather than passive spectators. We adapt, we evolve, and we inch closer to becoming the best versions of ourselves.

Self-evaluation fosters resilience. As we become comfortable acknowledging our failures and weaknesses, we learn to view them not as setbacks, but as stepping stones towards growth. We develop the courage to face challenges head-on and the tenacity to persist in the face of adversity.

— DAY 273 —

We suffer more in imagination than in reality

W ITHIN the realm of our minds, a powerful force often takes hold—the force of imagination. It is through this incredible faculty that we can create vivid worlds, explore endless possibilities, and conjure up the deepest fears and anxieties.

The human mind, a magnificent product of evolution, has the uncanny ability to time travel. With remarkable ease, it can delve into the depths of the past, or catapult into the future. However, this ability, when unchecked, often transforms into a source of distress. Our minds, wandering through the labyrinth of "what was" and "what could be," fabricate scenarios filled with regrets, fears, and anxieties, overshadowing the peace of the present.

The silent suffering of imagination is profoundly rooted in our fears. Picture this: You're about to deliver a public speech. Before stepping onto the stage, your mind spirals into a whirlpool of worst-case scenarios—stumbling over words, forgetting lines, and audiences laughing. In this imaginative scenario, you've endured the anguish of failure multiple times before the event has even occurred.

Consider another instance—your loved one is late coming home. Immediately, your mind creates an illusion of disastrous situations—an accident, a mugging, a sudden illness. In reality, they've just been caught in a mundane traffic jam. In both instances, the reality is far less distressing than the imaginative scenarios.

Regret, like fear, is another potent facilitator of imaginative suffering. We replay past mistakes in our minds, concocting alternative scenarios where we acted differently, achieving more desirable outcomes. This retrospective reimagining traps us in a cycle of remorse and distress, even though the reality is that the past is immutable.

How do we break free from this cycle of imaginary suffering? The key lies in mindfulness, the practice of being fully present and engaged in the current moment. When we anchor ourselves in the now, we resist the mind's tendency to wander.

— DAY 274 —

The soul is not bound by time or place

THE idea that the soul is not bound by time or place invites us to ponder the mysteries of our existence. It encourages us to explore the depths of our being and the interconnectedness of all things. It suggests that our experiences and connections extend beyond the constraints of our earthly lives, reaching into realms we cannot fully comprehend.

To begin, consider the concept of time. We, humans, have anchored ourselves so rigidly to the notion of time that our lives are dictated by the ticking hands of a clock. Yet, the soul remains detached from this rapid pace. The soul is timeless, free of the past's specter or the future's appeal. It dwells in a sphere of durability, an everlasting present, immune to the unending flow of time that governs the physical world.

Next, let's contemplate the idea of place. Our physical presence is confined to geographic locations, bound by the laws of space. However, the soul, in its magnificent solitude, transcends these spatial boundaries. It isn't limited to a specific point on the globe or a particular spot in the universe. Instead, it fills all spaces, from the vast, star-studded expanses of the cosmos to the tiny specks within the realm of atoms.

The existence of the soul beyond time and space raises fascinating possibilities. It suggests that our essence is unconfined by physical death, that we are part of an expansive, interconnected cosmos, and that our capacity for knowledge, wisdom, and experience far surpasses our earthly existence. The effects are liberating, filling us with a sense of wonder, fascination, and a wish for understanding.

This realization cultivates a deep sense of unity. As we acknowledge the soul's boundless nature, we realize our deep interconnection with all that exists. The divisions constructed by time and space dissolve, replaced by a sense of oneness, a recognition of a shared journey in this expansive cosmos.

— DAY 275 —

Stopping is worse than moving slowly

I N life's grand marathon, we often find ourselves captivated by the appeal of speed, measuring success by the swiftness of our stride. Yet, amidst this fascination with velocity, we overlook a fundamental truth—that stopping is worse than moving slowly. This notion may seem counterintuitive, but delve deeper and you'll uncover the profound wisdom embedded within.

Imagine you're driving a car on a foggy night, the visibility near zero. Would you stop the car in the middle of the highway just because you can't see far ahead? No. You would slow down, turn on the fog lights, and continue cautiously. Similarly, in life, the road often gets foggy, the path unclear. The best thing you can do is slow down, turn on the "lights" of wisdom, and move ahead, carefully but surely. Isn't it refreshing to think that your journey need not stop, just because things aren't ideal?

Consider a river that faces a massive rock in its course. Does it stop flowing? No, it meanders, it slows down, but it keeps moving until it finds a way around the obstruction. In the end, the consistent flow of water can even wear down the rock. Such is the power of slow, yet consistent motion.

Consider once more the example of Thomas Edison, who, even after encountering failure a thousand times, continued steadfastly and gradually advanced toward his objective of inventing the light bulb. If he had stopped, our nights would still be lit by candles and lanterns. His story is a living testament to the fact that stopping halts progress while moving slowly eventually leads to success.

In reality, moving slowly often gets a bad rap, perceived as a lack of progress. But remember, even the slowest pace is lapping everyone who's sitting on the couch. Slow progress is better than no progress. Stopping is resigning, it's a full stop. But moving slowly? That's a comma, a pause. And after a pause, the sentence always continues, right?

Whether it's a foggy road, a big rock, or a failed experiment, don't stop. Understand that progress doesn't always come quickly but with patience and persistence. Just keep moving!

— DAY 276 —

Prioritize health to age well

HOW often do we hear the phrase "health is wealth" and nod in agreement, but continue to prioritize everything else in our lives above our own health? Here's a thought that might stop you in your tracks: prioritizing health is the secret sauce to aging well. Let's unbox this idea.

The journey of life is a beautiful marathon, not a chaotic sprint. Each passing year is a collection of experiences, joys, and challenges. As we age, the goal isn't just to add years to life but, more importantly, life to years. And the key to that? You guessed it, a robust foundation of health.

Prioritizing health isn't about merely avoiding illness. It's about cultivating a vibrant state of well-being that saturates the mind, body, and spirit. It's about fueling your body with nutritious food, engaging in regular physical activity, nurturing positive relationships, and fostering a healthy mindset. This holistic approach becomes your armor, defending against the adversities of aging and enhancing the quality of life.

As you prioritize health, the impacts aren't just confined to the physical realm. It echoes into mental, emotional, and spiritual dimensions. It sharpens the mind, cultivates emotional resilience, and nurtures spiritual growth. With health as your ally, you're not just surviving with age, you're thriving!

Moreover, it's never too late to make health a priority. The power to age well isn't just in the hands of time, it's in your hands too. Every day presents a new opportunity to make healthier choices, commit to wellness, to rewrite your future narrative.

A life where each added year is a celebration of vitality, resilience, and fulfillment. Picture yourself embracing the golden years with vigor, grace, and a spirit that refuses to age. That's the magic of prioritizing health. It's the unwritten chapter in the manual of aging well, the secret ingredient in the recipe for a fruitful life. Not merely a cliche, "health is wealth" becomes a powerful mantra for a remarkable journey of aging.

— DAY 277 —

Life's perception is subjective

F ROM the moment we are born, we embark on a personal journey shaped by our environment, upbringing, and interactions with the world. Our experiences become the filters through which we make sense of the world, coloring our perceptions and influencing our understanding of reality. What one person perceives as joy, another may interpret as sorrow. What one finds beautiful, another may find mundane.

Let's begin our exploration with a simple sunset. Some might look at it and see an ending, the close of another day, or perhaps even a form of loss. But to another set of eyes, the same sunset could symbolize beauty, tranquility, or the promise of rest. The same natural phenomenon, yet there are countless interpretations. Isn't that a testament to the ever-changing subjectivity of our perspectives?

Every one of us is a unique mix of experiences, memories, beliefs, and aspirations, which together form our perceptions. We're like different musical instruments in an orchestra, each playing our distinct notes, yet contributing to the symphony of life. Think about it. Isn't it fascinating that the world is not just one thing but a collection of billions of perceptions?

Now, let's step into the art gallery of life. Two people stand in front of the same painting. One sees chaos and disarray; the other identifies patterns and beauty. The painting remains the same, but the viewers, through their unique lenses of perception, create their own version of reality. Makes you wonder—are we experiencing the world as it is, or as we are?

Remember the tale of the blind men and the elephant? Each one touched a different part of the beast and formed disparate perceptions of what an elephant "is." Yet, were any of them entirely wrong? No, because their perception was based on their limited experience. It illustrates how our slice of experience colors our perception of the entirety.

Perception, at its core, is personal, a dialogue between the world and our mind. It's our mind's paintbrush, coloring our experiences. We need to appreciate that my "blue" might be your "green," and that's perfectly okay.

— DAY 278 —

Don't watch the news

NOW that's a headline you won't see in the paper, but let's take a moment and consider it. Quite a thought, isn't it? We've grown up considering the news as our reliable lookout, our lens into the world's happenings. But what if, in our quest for information, we've forgotten to question the nature and quality of that information?

We live in an era of hyper-connectivity, where we're ceaselessly barraged with information. The news, especially, presents us with a real-time encyclopedia of global happenings. It is a vortex of data that we find ourselves entrapped in. Yet, paradoxically, our awareness of the world doesn't necessarily make us better informed. It often leaves us feeling overwhelmed, anxious, and helpless in the face of events we can't control.

This isn't a call to ignorance. It's about understanding the difference between being informed and being overwhelmed. News is essential, but the constant bombardment of information can distort our perspective, making us focus more on the chaos than the calm, more on the tragic than the joyful.

Consider the time we devote to absorbing news. We often do it reflexively, not realizing how these minutes add up and nibble away our time. That time could be better invested in pursuits that enrich us—learning a new skill, engaging in meaningful conversations, and even appreciating the beauty of silence. When we unshackle ourselves from the obsessive need to "stay updated," we free up mental space to learn, create, and grow.

Not watching the news doesn't mean disconnection from the world. It implies a shift in focus, from the transient to the enduring, from the sensational to the substantial. Reading books, watching documentaries, and engaging in community work—these are potent sources of information and wisdom, providing a more nuanced understanding of our world.

This writing is not a call to blindness but a call to see more clearly. It's asking us to step away from all the negative noise and the surface-level stuff that comes at us non-stop. It's a powerful reminder that in an age of information overload, the choice of what to ignore is as crucial as what to focus on.

— DAY 279 —

It goes on

L IFE, with all its ups and downs, triumphs and tribulations, continues its relentless march forward. It is a reminder that in the middle of chaos and uncertainty, there is an underlying current of resilience and perseverance that carries us through.

Take a moment and recall any hardship you've encountered. Painful breakups, loss of a loved one, career setbacks, life-altering illnesses. During these trials, it may have felt as though life had come to an end. But it didn't. The sun still rose. The world kept turning. You kept breathing. This is the reality "it goes on" professes. Despite our challenges, life persists, moving at its relentless pace, pulling us along in its enduring rhythm.

Imagine you're stargazing on a clear night. You see the universe in its infinite expanse, with countless celestial bodies in motion. The cosmos embodies this principle. It has been expanding for billions of years, enduring through unimaginable cataclysms and rebirths. It teaches us that everything we face is fleeting, a speck in the cosmic time scale. Our setbacks, no matter how colossal, are temporary. "it goes on" encapsulates this cosmic truth, reminding us that life's trajectory is one of continued evolution and transformation.

Yet, this phrase isn't just a testament to life's resilience. It's also a challenge to us, a call to action. It asks us to carry on, even when the path is treacherous. It urges us to adapt, learn, and grow from our experiences. To become the captains of our destiny and steer our ship through life's tumultuous seas, even when the storm rages on.

Let this phrase be a light of hope when you're enmeshed in sorrow. A reassurance during your moments of doubt. An anthem of your strength and resilience. Because, ultimately, life is a symphony of change. And just as the day turns into night and the seasons change, life continues its dance of evolution.

— DAY 280 —

Independence lies in essential skills

INDEPENDENCE is often associated with external factors like wealth, status, or autonomy. But true independence goes beyond surface-level measures. It resides in the mastery of essential skills that enable us to navigate the complexities of life and shape our own destinies.

Think of the skills we master, like cooking a meal, managing our finances, or navigating a new city. These aren't merely tasks ticked off a list. No, they're stepping stones to independence, the keys that unlock the door to self-reliance. As we add more skills to our repertoire, our experience grows richer, and our independence stronger.

Each skill is a spark of empowerment, igniting the flame of independence. But it's not just about the tangible skills; it's also about the intangible ones; resilience, empathy, adaptability.

Imagine for a moment you're out in the wilderness. The sun's setting, you're all alone, and you need to make a shelter. The ability to make a fire, to build a shelter, to find food—those are essential skills, right? In that moment, those skills are your ticket to independence.

But let's bring it back to everyday life. Can you cook a meal from scratch? Can you budget your expenses? Can you navigate the public transportation system? Each one of these skills gives you a certain degree of independence, a freedom to rely less on others and more on yourself.

But hang on, it's not just about the practical stuff. What about skills like resilience? That's the ability to bounce back when life knocks you down. Or adaptability? That's the knack for rolling with the punches when things change unexpectedly. And let's not forget empathy, the capacity to understand and share the feelings of others. These might not be "tangible" skills, but they're just as essential when it comes to leading an independent life.

When you boil it down, independence isn't about being alone or doing everything yourself. No, it's about having the right skills, the essential skills, to navigate life on your own terms. It's about the freedom to make your own choices and take responsibility for them.

— DAY 281 —

First impressions matter every day

S URE, it seems pretty straightforward. You meet someone for the first time, and bam, that's the impression that sticks. But I'm here to tell you that there's a twist. First impressions aren't just for first-time encounters; they matter every day.

Let's start by looking at our day-to-day lives. Every morning, we're gifted with a new day, a fresh start. It's like the universe saying, "Hey, here's another chance. Make it count!" The way we perceive the start of each day sets the tone for everything that follows. Have you ever noticed that if you wake up grumpy, the whole day just feels off? That's your morning making its first impression on you. It's crucial to meet it with positivity, gratitude, and even anticipation, to set the stage for a good day.

But the plot thickens. These daily first impressions aren't just about the sunrise or the taste of your morning coffee. It extends to the people we interact with daily. Take a moment to reflect on this. You have a work colleague, right? You see them every day. But you know what? They're not the same person every day. Like us, they're evolving, changing. Every interaction with them is a "first" in its own way.

This isn't just some philosophical reflection. There's a real, tangible impact here. If we start treating each interaction as a chance to form a new first impression, imagine how much more open and understanding we'd become. We'd appreciate the uniqueness of each day, each person, and each moment.

So, what's the big takeaway here? It's an invitation. An invitation to experience the newness in every day, in every interaction. It's a chance to redefine relationships, to see the world with fresh eyes, and most importantly, to make every day count.

Next time you wake up, remember: today is a new day, and it's all about first impressions. You get to decide what kind of impression you want it to make on you, and vice versa.

— DAY 282 —

Knowledge without action is useless

T HE world today is awash with knowledge. Information is at our fingertips, readily accessible, waiting to be absorbed. Yet, this vast ocean of knowledge means little if it remains stagnant within us. For knowledge to truly matter and to have a tangible impact, it needs to be coupled with action. Knowledge is like a seed—its true potential is realized only when it is sown and allowed to grow.

How many times have you acquired knowledge, whether through reading, research, or personal experience, only to let it sit idle, unused? We convince ourselves that by simply acquiring knowledge, we are somehow better off. But knowledge, in and of itself, is just potential. It's through action that knowledge becomes transformative.

Knowledge without action is like having a map but never embarking on the journey. You may have all the information, and all the directions, but if you never take that first step, the map is worthless. It's the same with knowledge. We can accumulate facts, theories, and insights, but if we don't put that knowledge into practice, it remains confined to the realm of intellectual exercise.

The true value of knowledge lies in its application. It's through action that we bring knowledge to life, transforming it into wisdom and tangible results. It's through action that we make a difference in our own lives and the lives of others.

The same applies to our personal lives. We can accumulate knowledge about self-improvement, relationships, and personal growth, but if we don't put that knowledge into action, it remains superficial and meaningless. It's through action that we embody the principles and values we've learned.

Challenge yourself to bridge the gap between knowledge and action. Start small, but start now. Take the lessons you've learned, the insights you've gained, and put them into practice. Embody the principles that resonate with you, take risks, and embrace the possibility of failure, knowing that it's through action that true growth and transformation occur.

— DAY 283 —

Music and nature heal

C LOSE your eyes for a moment and let's explore the deep connection between music and nature—a bond that has the power to heal, inspire, and transport us to a realm beyond words.

Nature and music, so different yet remarkably alike, have a profound ability to heal. Their power is not just anecdotal; scientific studies attest to their therapeutic effects. Listening to natural sounds and engaging with music can lower stress, improve mental well-being, and even assist physical recovery. But let's explore it a step further.

In the whisper of the wind, the roar of the sea, the chatter of a flowing river, nature sings a song of life, endurance, and transformation. It's a song that reminds us of the cycles of life—that after every storm, the sun will shine again, and after every winter, spring will return. In this harmony of life, we find comfort, resilience, and an invigorating sense of peace.

Similarly, music, with its intricate melodies and resonant harmonies, tells stories that words often can't. It's a universal language that transcends borders and cultural barriers. Whether it's a sad song that expresses our sorrow or an uplifting tune that echoes our joy, music mirrors our emotional landscapes, providing emotional release and evoking empathy.

Both music and nature function as healing balms for our souls. They invite us to pause, listen, and connect with our deepest selves and the world around us. They remind us that amidst chaos and change, there exists a sanctuary of peace and harmony, accessible through the simple act of attentive listening. Next time you're feeling overwhelmed, why not take a walk in the woods with your favorite playlist? After all, in the symphony of life, music, and nature are the most healing of melodies.

— DAY 284 —

Life is a long lesson in humility

FROM the moment we take our first breath, life sets out on a relentless journey to teach us humility. It humbles us through the countless trials and tribulations we encounter along the way. The failures and setbacks we face, like painful scars etched upon our souls, remind us that we are imperfect beings in an ever-changing universe. In these moments of defeat, we come face to face with our limitations and vulnerabilities, prompting us to reevaluate our perspectives and strive for personal growth.

Humility whispers in our ears during moments of success and triumph, reminding us that our achievements are not solely our own. It reminds us of the countless hands that have supported us, the mentors who guided us, and the circumstances that aligned in our favor.

Through humility, we gain the capacity for empathy and compassion. It teaches us to view others as equals, to recognize their struggles, and triumphs as reflections of our own. It encourages us to set aside our egos and embrace the interconnectedness of all life forms. In this interconnectedness, we find the seeds of unity and understanding, transcending the boundaries that divide us.

Yet, humility is not a virtue easily attained or maintained. It requires a constant willingness to unlearn, to shed the layers of pride and arrogance that cloak our true selves. It calls for a surrender of our preconceived notions, inviting us to embrace uncertainty and acknowledge that wisdom lies not in absolute certainty but in the endless pursuit of knowledge and self-improvement.

Ultimately, life's long lesson in humility leads us to a profound realization: that the greatest wisdom lies in acknowledging our ignorance. As we stand humbly before the vast expanse of the unknown, we open ourselves to the wonders and mysteries that lie beyond our comprehension.

In this never-ending classroom called life, humility is the greatest lesson of all. It is the catalyst for personal evolution, the bridge between our individual selves and the collective consciousness of humanity. As we navigate the winding path of existence, let us walk hand in hand with humility, for it is through its teachings that we find our true purpose and fulfill our highest potential.

— DAY 285 —

True friendship is beyond money's influence

A statement as old as time, yet as fresh as the morning dew. The shapes of friendship are shaped not by the clinking coins of affluence but by the delicate threads of shared emotions and mutual respect.

Human relationships are diverse, but friendship, in its purest form, is an alchemy of souls. It is an unrestricted symphony of love, trust, and empathy that dances to the rhythm of the heart, untouched by the discordant notes of materialistic concerns. The essence of true friendship transcends the influence of wealth or the lack thereof; it is a realm where authenticity triumphs over artifice, where shared laughter and tears outweigh shared economic interests.

Friendship is not a marketplace for trading favors, nor a bank for hoarding emotional debts, but a sanctuary where the human spirit finds solace and resonance. The transactions in the market of true friendship are not of gold or silver, but of kindness and understanding. Material possessions may add comfort to life, but they faint in comparison to the invaluable treasure of a friend's comforting presence in times of despair or joy.

A true friend is a steadfast lighthouse, brightening our path during the darkest storms, their worth immeasurable in any currency. They aren't swayed by fluctuations in our financial standing, for their loyalty is anchored not in our wallets, but in our hearts. They are the companions who journey with us across the shifting sands of time, rejoicing in our prosperity, yet not shying away from our poverty.

What makes this bond special, invincible even, is its stubborn challenge against the superficiality of wealth. The beauty of friendship lies in its democratic spirit; it knows no boundaries, be it social, racial, or economic. It embraces all with open arms, revealing a world where emotional wealth is the true marker of richness.

The next time you sit across from a friend, remember, it's not your financial prowess that has brought you together, but the intangible thread of shared experiences, mutual respect, and unconditional love.

— DAY 286 —

Problems lead to new perspectives

W E all have problems. Big, small, mundane, or monumental, they're part of life. But have you ever noticed how problems have this remarkable skill of shaking things up? One minute you think you've got everything figured out, the next—bam!—a problem rolls in and you're suddenly viewing life through a whole new lens.

When everything's smooth sailing, we tend to coast, right? We stick to our safe paths, our tried-and-true routines. But the moment a problem comes knocking, we're jolted out of our comfort zones. We're forced to think, adapt, and look for solutions in places we've never ventured before. And that's where the magic happens.

You see, problems are like personal trainers for our minds. They flex our mental muscles, pushing us to stretch, grow, and exceed our limits. They force us to innovate, invent, and discover. And in the process, we often stumble upon new ideas, new paths, and yes, new perspectives.

Take a moment to reflect on history. From the most significant scientific breakthroughs to the awe-inspiring works of art, problems have always been at the heart of human progress. It was a problem that propelled Newton to ponder the laws of gravity. It was a problem that drove Einstein to revolutionize our understanding of space and time. And it was a problem that fueled the creative genius of artists like Picasso and Van Gogh.

But problems don't just lead to new perspectives on a grand scale. They also shape our personal growth and transformation. When we encounter difficulties in our relationships, our careers, or our internal battles, we are faced with the opportunity to examine our beliefs, values, and behaviors. We are given the chance to redefine who we are and what we stand for.

In those moments of frustration and despair, it may seem like the world is crumbling around us. But it is precisely in those moments that we are invited to shed old patterns, embrace change, and discover a depth of resilience and strength we never knew we possessed.

— DAY 287 —

Whoever is happy will make others happy too

HAPPINESS is a contagious force that radiates from the depths of our being, permeating the world around us. It is a deep truth that whoever is happy will make others happy too. This simple yet profound statement holds the key to unlocking the transformative power of our emotions and the ripple effects they create.

Think about a time when you encountered a truly joyful person. Perhaps it was a friend, a family member, or even a stranger whose infectious smile lit up the room. How did their happiness make you feel? It likely sparked a warmth within your own heart, evoking a sense of joy and positivity. This is the essence of the human connection— our emotions have the remarkable ability to transcend barriers and touch the lives of those around us.

When we are genuinely happy, our energy shifts. We become hopes of light, spreading joy like wildfire. Our interactions with others become infused with kindness, compassion, and a genuine desire to uplift those we encounter. It is in these moments that we realize the true power of our emotions—they have the capacity to shape the world in profound ways.

But let us not confuse happiness with mere fleeting moments of pleasure or the pursuit of external validation. True happiness, my friend, is an inner state of being—a deep satisfaction that arises from within. It is the result of aligning our actions with our values, nurturing meaningful relationships, and cultivating a sense of gratitude for the present moment.

We have witnessed this phenomenon throughout history. From the wisdom of ancient philosophers to the teachings of spiritual leaders, the message remains consistent: our inner state of being has the power to influence the world around us. Whether it is the laughter of a child, the selfless acts of a humanitarian, or the transformative impact of a leader, happiness has the power to transcend boundaries and inspire others to follow suit.

For it is through our own happiness that we have the power to make others happy too, and in doing so, we create a ripple effect that can change the course of the world.

— DAY 288 —

We are dying every day

EVERY breath we exhale, every second that ticks by, every moment we live, we are inching closer to the end of our present self, shedding old skin, and becoming someone new. Life is not static, but a continuity of births and deaths, beginnings and endings, experiences collected, and lessons learned.

Life, in its infinite complexity, is often likened to a cosmic dance. We are born into this world, and from that moment, a countdown begins, each day subtly chipping away at the time we are allocated. We're like sand trickling through the hourglass of time, continuously transitioning toward the inevitable end.

In the hustle and bustle of modern life, we often forget this truth. We put things off for tomorrow, hold grudges, or refuse to let go of past failures and regrets. We behave as though we have an endless expanse of time stretching ahead of us, but in reality, none of us are immune to the relentless march of time.

What happens when we internalize that we are dying every day? It breeds a severe awareness of life's temporariness, leading us to live in the present, to appreciate fully the ordinary moments that make up our everyday existence. It teaches us to embrace life's fluidity and be adaptable. We become more forgiving, releasing old resentments knowing that our time is too precious to be wasted on such burdens.

It fosters courage in us to take risks, to step outside our comfort zones, for we understand that our time is limited, and every moment spent not chasing our dreams is a moment lost. We become more open-hearted and generous, knowing that our wealth, status, and material possessions will not follow us beyond the grave.

Understanding that we are dying every day also encourages us to cherish our relationships. We begin to express our love and gratitude freely, hold our loved ones a little closer, and forgive a little faster, knowing that these moments of connection and love are what truly enrich our lives.

— DAY 289 —

Distinguish between existing and living

EXISTENCE and living are two sides of the same coin, yet they represent vastly different ways of experiencing life. It's easy to confuse the two.

Existing is easy. We breathe, we eat, we sleep, and we go through the motions of the day—work, entertainment, and rest in repeated cycles. Existing is like floating on the surface of the ocean, bobbing with the waves, carried along by the currents of societal norms and expectations. It's routine, it's predictable, it's safe. It is our biological state, but it lacks the vitality and richness of living.

Living, on the other hand, is an art form. It's plunging beneath the surface, immersing ourselves in the depths of life's ocean, exploring the dazzling corals and mysterious caverns of experiences, emotions, and relationships. It's about making conscious choices, seeking growth, fostering connections, and pursuing passions.

Living is embracing the joy and the pain, the victories and the defeats, the love and the loss, that define the human experience. It is about curiosity and courage, about asking questions and seeking answers, about falling and rising, about making mistakes and learning.

Living is a state of active engagement with the world. It's about kindling the flame of our potential, illuminating our path, and casting light on those of others. It's about making a difference, however small, in the experience of life.

The distinction between existing and living is vast yet subtle. One can spend an entire lifetime existing without truly living. The transformation from existence to life demands a shift in perspective, a conscious decision to not just be a spectator, but a participant in the grand spectacle of life.

Distinguishing between existing and living is an invitation. It is an invitation to engage with the world, to connect deeply with ourselves and others, and to leave a legacy that resonates long after we are gone.

Ask yourself, am I just existing or am I really living? Because life isn't just about being a passenger, it's about getting in the driver's seat and steering your own journey. It's about not just existing, but truly living.

— DAY 290 —

Prioritize your mental wellness

M Y friend, in the middle of our fast-paced and demanding world, it's all too easy to neglect the most essential aspect of our well-being: our mental health. That's why I encourage you to prioritize your mental wellness, for in doing so, you unlock a world of personal growth, resilience, and inner peace.

Our mental well-being is the foundation upon which our entire lives are built. It shapes our perceptions, influences our emotions, and impacts our relationships. Yet, it often takes a backseat to the demands of work, social obligations, and external pressures. It's time to shift the paradigm, my friend, and place mental wellness at the forefront of our priorities.

Imagine your life is like a shiny, high-tech car. The body, that's the exterior, the engine, the wheels—everything that people can see. But your mental wellness, that's like the software that runs the car. It's not visible, but without it, the car is pretty much a decorative piece. And just like you'd update that software regularly, your mental wellness needs constant care and attention.

Now, prioritizing your mental wellness doesn't mean you have to become a Zen master or spend hours meditating. It's about tuning into your emotions, acknowledging your feelings, and not just brushing them under the carpet. It's about setting healthy boundaries, taking breaks when needed, and not feeling guilty about it.

Think of it this way. When you're physically unwell, you rest, right? Similarly, when you're feeling mentally overwhelmed, it's okay to step back, take a breather, to do something that rejuvenates you. And it's not just about handling the tough times; it's also about savoring the good ones. It's about being present, fully enjoying the moments that make you smile, and holding onto that positive energy.

A healthy mind isn't just about combating mental illnesses, it's about fostering a state of well-being that allows you to thrive in every aspect of your life. It's about turning that shiny, high-tech car into a powerful, smooth-sailing vehicle that's ready for any journey, no matter how rough or long.

— DAY 291 —

Anger steals happiness

A NGER is a powerful and primal emotion that resides within each of us. It can surge like a raging storm, clouding our judgment and engulfing our hearts. A phrase that instantly stirs our deepest emotions, urging us to reflect on the subtle but profound influence of anger on our lives. Three simple words, yet they pack quite a punch.

When anger takes hold, it consumes us. It robs us of our peace, our joy, and our ability to see the beauty that surrounds us. We become prisoners to its grip, trapped in a vicious cycle of resentment, hostility, and negative energy.

Anger is like a thief in the night. It sneaks in, stealing away our happiness and leaving behind a void of bitterness. It blocks our capacity for forgiveness, compassion, and understanding. It erects walls between us and the world, isolating us from the very connections that bring us fulfillment and joy.

Anger is a choice. We have the power to choose how we respond to life's challenges and provocations. We can choose to let anger reign, allowing it to steal our happiness, or we can choose a different path—a path of peace, empathy, and emotional freedom.

When we let go of anger, we open ourselves to a world of possibilities. We free ourselves from the chains of resentment and bitterness, and we allow happiness to reclaim its rightful place in our lives. We regain control over our emotions, choosing love, forgiveness, and understanding instead.

Anger steals our happiness, but it also steals our ability to truly connect with others. It erects barriers, creating divisions and conflicts that hinder our relationships. But when we release anger's grip, we create space for genuine connections—deep, meaningful bonds that bring joy, support, and a sense of belonging.

By learning to master our anger, we reclaim the happiness it tends to steal. We restore the harmony of our life's painting, each emotion in its rightful place, contributing to a beautiful, balanced masterpiece. That is the beauty of this insight—it doesn't merely expose a problem, but it illuminates a path towards a more peaceful, happier existence.

— DAY 292 —

Real wisdom is accepting ignorance

IN our quest for wisdom, we often seek knowledge, answers, and certainty. We believe that the more we know, the wiser we become. In a world that idolizes expertise and certainty, the acknowledgment of what we do not know can be both humbling and liberating.

Wisdom is more than an accumulation of facts or mastery of skills. It transcends the realm of knowing, reaching into the deeper, less tangible aspects of understanding and perception. It is a perception that allows us to navigate the complex labyrinth of life with grace, humility, and an openness to continual growth.

Recognizing our ignorance, and our limitations in knowledge and understanding, forms a crucial aspect of wisdom. It is not about embracing ignorance in the sense of celebrating a lack of knowledge or rejecting learning. Rather, it means acknowledging that no matter how much we know, there is always more to learn, more perspectives to understand, and more depths to explore.

Accepting ignorance does not mean reveling in it but using it as a springboard for curiosity and discovery. When we admit, "I don't know," we create space for new knowledge to enter, for growth and expansion. It is in this unknowing that we become receptive to the infinite wisdom of the universe.

To illustrate, consider one of the greatest scientists Albert Einstein. Despite his significant contributions to science, he once claimed, "I am neither especially clever nor especially gifted. I am only very, very curious." This curiosity, stemming from an acceptance of his ignorance, fueled Einstein's lifelong pursuit of knowledge, establishing his legacy as a beacon of wisdom.

Embrace that moment. Be excited about the opportunity to learn something new. Because admitting you don't know is the first step to gaining knowledge. And transforming that knowledge into wisdom? Well, that's the real prize.

— DAY 293 —

Self-destruction is still addiction's reward

THINK about what attracts people to addiction in the first place. The appeal of escape, the promise of instant gratification, or even the thrill of the forbidden—that's what draws us in. It's like a shiny, irresistible prize dangling in front of us. But here's where it gets interesting—that prize? It's not what it seems.

Let's be real here. The "reward" of addiction isn't some long-lasting joy or fulfillment. No, it's a temporary high, a fleeting rush that leaves as quickly as it comes. And what's left in its wake? An uncontrollable craving for more and an ever-deepening spiral of self-destruction. It's a tricky, dangerous cycle.

The harsh truth is that addiction's reward is not the euphoria it first promises but rather self-destruction. Yet, this seems counterintuitive, doesn't it? Why would anyone seek a reward that ultimately leads to their downfall? The answer lies in understanding the intricate maze of addiction.

Addiction lures us with instant gratification, blinding us to long-term consequences. It appeals to our innate desire for reward, creating a seemingly unbreakable loop—the more we succumb to addiction, the more we crave its false reward, and the deeper we descend into self-destruction. It's similar to a moth drawn to the deadly flames, entranced by its glowing lure.

This is a wake-up call. It's a challenge to confront our addictions, to question the very nature of the "reward" we seek. It's a sobering reminder that the path to true reward—be it peace, joy, or fulfillment—does not lie in selfdestruction but in self-construction, in nurturing ourselves, not tearing ourselves down.

But there's a silver lining here. Recognizing this harsh truth is the first step towards breaking free from addiction's chains. It's about understanding that true rewards don't come at the cost of our well-being. True rewards lie in the pursuit of self-care, resilience, and a life lived authentically.

— DAY 294 —

Optimism turns obstacles into opportunities

WE are all familiar with obstacles. They come in different forms—personal losses, career setbacks, failed relationships, and more. They appear like unachievable mountains, blocking our path, and imposing a sense of despair. But suppose we adjust our lens and gaze at these obstacles not as dead ends but as detours to something greater?

Optimism is not blind positivity or denial of the hardships we face. It's a resilience of spirit, a resolve to look beyond the immediate problem and envision the growth potential it carries. It's about perceiving obstacles not as impassable blockades, but as stepping stones leading us to unseen paths and unexplored opportunities.

Think of Michael Jordan, whose journey was marked by setbacks and rejections that did not lead him to defeat, but to the path of greatness. When reflecting on his challenges, he famously said, "I've missed more than 9,000 shots in my career. I've lost almost 300 games. Twenty-six times, I've been trusted to take the game-winning shot and missed. I've failed over and over and over again in my life. And that is why I succeed." His unwavering perseverance turned obstacles into stepping stones, culminating in a career that redefined basketball.

For better clarity, let's turn to the profound wisdom of Ryan Holiday in his book *The Obstacle is the Way*.

Holiday elegantly captures the essence of the phrase in his observation, "Where one person sees a crisis, another can see opportunity." This is the core of optimism: recognizing that each setback is a fork in the road leading to new paths. In the face of adversity, the optimist doesn't crumble; they adapt, innovate, and create.

Consider Holiday's inspiring call to action: "The impediment to action advances action. What stands in the way becomes the way." Here, optimism is not blind positivity; it's a compass guiding us through the storm, urging us to face our challenges head-on, not as hurdles but as catalysts for growth. Every blockage, every setback, can be the spark that lights the way to untapped opportunities.

— DAY 295 —

Courage leads to new horizons

A phrase that might sound cryptic, but let's break it down. So, what exactly is courage? Well, it's not about being fearless. In fact, it's all about taking that leap even when your knees are shaking, it's about saying, "Yes, I'm scared, but I'm going to do it anyway."

Courage, as a virtue, is often misunderstood. Many mistake it for a fearless stance in the face of danger, but courage is not the absence of fear. Rather, it is the determination to act in spite of it. It is that leap of faith, that daunting first step into the unknown, that fiery resolve that propels us forward despite the tremors of fear echoing in our hearts.

A horizon represents the future, the infinite, the yet-to-be-discovered. It is the separation of the known and the unknown, the familiar and the unfamiliar. When courage becomes our compass, we find ourselves embarking on journeys to these new horizons, journeys we would never have dreamt of.

Take for instance, the courageous move of a person quitting a comfortable yet unfulfilling job to pursue their passion. The future may be filled with uncertainties and doubts. However, the courage to embrace these uncertainties uncovers new horizons— maybe a successful startup, perhaps a fulfilling career, or even a significant contribution to society.

Or consider the poignant example of a woman standing up against injustice in her society. The courage she displays, despite the backlash she might face, opens up new horizons, not only for her but for many who suffer in silence.

Life's beauty lies in its unpredictability. Yet, many of us remain chained to our comfort zones, entranced by the safety they offer. It is here that courage plays its role, breaking these chains and pushing us toward the unexplored. Each courageous act, no matter how small, expands our world, introducing us to new experiences, people, ideas, and even aspects of our own selves.

— DAY 296 —

Hydrate beyond thirst

W ATER is the essence of life itself. Thirst is our body's way of signaling a need for hydration. It's a physiological response that tells us we're running low on fluids. But what if I told you that relying solely on thirst is limiting our potential for optimal health?

Imagine you're on a long, demanding hike. Sure, you drink when you're thirsty, but what happens when you only drink when that dry feeling kicks in? That's right, you're on the fast track to dehydration. The same principle applies to life. We can't wait for crisis moments to start taking care of ourselves; that's like waiting till you're dizzy from dehydration before taking a sip.

Hydrating beyond thirst means going beyond simply satisfying our body's basic needs. It means recognizing that water is not only essential for survival, but also a key component of vibrant health and vitality.

Water is a miraculous substance, my friend. It nourishes our cells, supports digestion, regulates body temperature, and aids in detoxification. It is the elixir that keeps our bodies functioning optimally.

When we hydrate beyond thirst, we give our bodies the hydration they truly need. We drink water not just when we feel dry, but as a regular practice to support our overall well-being. We make it a priority to replenish our cells, nourish our organs, and maintain optimal hydration levels.

Consider your relationships. We cannot wait until bonds are strained to invest time and affection in them. Or think about your mental health. It isn't wise to wait until stress escalates into anxiety before we practice mindfulness or seek help. It's about hydrating beyond thirst—tending to our life's various facets before the signs of neglect become apparent.

Raise a glass, my friend. Here's to hydrating beyond thirst, to living a life of proactive care and relentless growth. Cheers!

— DAY 297 —

Forget credit. Do the work

I N our society, where instant gratification is the norm, the idea of laboring without immediate reward may seem counterintuitive. We often seek credit, validation, or praise as a measure of our work's value. The applause, the awards, the admiration— these become the motivators, the indicators of success. But let's stop for a moment and think, does the value of our work diminish if left unrecognized? Do the mountains lose their majesty if no one is there to admire them?

The beauty of work lies in its transformative power. Like a sculptor chipping away at a block of marble, the process of work chips away at us, revealing our potential, refining our skills, and shaping us into versions of ourselves we could never have imagined. Work is the furnace wherein raw talent is forged into proficiency and, with time, perhaps even mastery.

Anonymity, often viewed as a disadvantage, can be a surprising ally in our journey of work. Free from the burden of others' expectations, unencumbered by the limelight, we find the liberty to stumble, falter, and get up again. In the privacy of our workspace, our failures serve as secret milestones, marking our path toward growth and mastery.

The act of prioritizing work over credit also realigns our focus from the extrinsic to the intrinsic. A job well done becomes its own reward, and our motivation is fueled by the satisfaction derived from each task, each project, and each creation. The love of the craft outshines the lure of applause.

Let us consider legendary artists such as Vincent van Gogh or writers like Edgar Allan Poe, both of whom received recognition only after death. Was their work any less because it wasn't celebrated in their lifetime? Or does their belated fame underscore the fact that the work stood on its own, irrespective of the credit accorded?

Forget credit. Do the work. As we embody this mantra, we find ourselves in a space where work is not a means to an end, but the end itself. We stop working for the applause and start working for the joy of creating, the thrill of learning, and the fulfillment derived from a task well accomplished.

— DAY 298 —

Learn to love your worst enemy

OUR worst enemy is often a mirror reflecting the aspects of ourselves that we struggle to accept or understand. They embody the qualities we find most challenging, the traits we judge and reject within ourselves. This idea aligns with Carl Jung's belief that the characteristics in others that bother us are reflections of the parts of ourselves that we deny.

Consider for a moment that your worst enemy isn't a person, but a part of you. It is your fear, your self-doubt, your guilt, or any other negative emotion that undermines your potential and happiness. These feelings, these internal enemies, often have a more significant impact on our lives than any external foe could ever exert.

To love your worst enemy then suggests not a surrender to these negative emotions but an acceptance of their presence. It means acknowledging these feelings, understanding why they exist, and using them as tools for self-growth. It is about embracing the shadows within ourselves, to illuminate our path towards self-improvement.

For instance, fear, one of our most primal enemies, isn't inherently bad. It alerts us to danger, prepares us to face challenges, and can motivate us to exceed our limitations. By accepting and understanding our fear, we can harness its power to drive us forward rather than hold us back.

Similarly, self-doubt, while weakening in large doses, keeps us grounded and reminds us of our humanity. It is a reminder that we can always learn, improve, and evolve. By loving our self-doubt, we transform it into a springboard for continuous self-improvement and lifelong learning.

And then there's guilt, an internal enemy that weighs heavy on our hearts. But even guilt can be a moral compass, guiding us towards better decisions and actions. When we learn to love our guilt, it becomes an opportunity to learn from our past and foster empathy and kindness towards ourselves and others.

To love your worst enemy, then, is a journey of acceptance and transformation. It encourages us to treat our internal enemies not as obstacles, but as instruments of self-understanding and growth.

— DAY 299 —

Unhealthy habits come with costs

THIS sentence, brief and straightforward as it might appear, conveys a profound truth about our life's trajectory. We often think of the cost in monetary terms. However, when it comes to habits, the true cost extends far beyond the wallet, seeping into our health, time, relationships, and ultimately, the quality of our life.

Consider the common habit of unhealthy eating. Its immediate cost is monetary, purchasing fast food or processed snacks. But it's the hidden, long-term cost that we should truly fear. Poor nutrition can lead to obesity, heart disease, and diabetes—conditions that cost not only financially but also physically, as our bodies suffer under the strain of ill health. The expense isn't just measured in medical bills, but in the decreased capacity to enjoy life fully, to play with our children, to hike a beautiful trail, or to simply move without pain.

Similarly, the habit of procrastination comes with a hefty price tag. On the surface, we might seem to gain time by postponing tasks. But as deadlines emerge and tasks pile up, the true cost reveals itself. It comes in the form of stress, reduced sleep, and a constant sense of impending doom. It robs us of peace of mind and the satisfaction of accomplishment.

Or consider smoking, a habit with a twofold cost. The financial impact of buying cigarettes is immediate and recurrent. But there's also the health cost—the increased risk of cancer, heart disease, and stroke. And beyond health, there's the social cost: isolation from loved ones who detest the habit, the stigma attached to being a smoker, and the impact on the beauty of one's skin and the freshness of one's breath.

Each of these examples underlines the same truth: unhealthy habits come with far-reaching costs, affecting every facet of our lives. These habits rob us not only of our wealth but also our health, our time, our happiness, and our relationships. Recognizing these costs, we're empowered to make a change. Replacing unhealthy habits with healthier ones is an investment in ourselves, paying dividends in improved health, increased time, enriched relationships, and ultimately, a life of better quality.

— DAY 300 —

Solve problems to become wealthy

WEALTH is not simply a matter of luck or inherited privilege; it's the result of solving problems that people are willing to pay for. Whether it's a product or a service, a business that solves a problem and provides value to its customers has the potential to become wealthy. However, it's important to note that solving problems is not just about making money. It's also about making a positive impact on the world.

The concept of wealth is intrinsically tied to value. What is value? Value is what someone is willing to exchange something else for—typically time, effort, or resources. If a product or service provides a solution to a problem, it holds value for the person facing that problem.

Consider Bill Gates, the co-founder of *Microsoft*. He saw a problem: the world was advancing technologically, but personal computing was still largely inaccessible to the masses. Gates helped solve this issue by developing software that made personal computing simpler, more affordable, and more accessible. The result? *Microsoft's* value skyrocketed, and Gates became one of the wealthiest individuals in the world.

Or consider Jeff Bezos and *Amazon*. Bezos identified a problem: shopping was time-consuming and sometimes inconvenient. His solution was to create a platform where people could purchase virtually anything they wanted and have it delivered directly to their doorstep. *Amazon* became a colossal marketplace, generating immense wealth for Bezos.

Now, you might be thinking, "Well, that's all well and good for them, but what about me? I'm not a tech genius or an innovative businessperson." Here's where the real beauty of this statement lies: problems are everywhere.

You don't need to invent the next *Microsoft* or *Amazon* to generate wealth. All you need is to identify a problem that you're uniquely suited to solve. If it solves a problem, money will be thrown at it. If it's a million-dollar problem, the solution will make you millions. If it's a billion-dollar problem, the solution will make you billions. Think about all the problems *Amazon* has solved.

— DAY 301 —

If you don't risk anything, you risk even more

THIS statement may seem counterintuitive, but it's a powerful reminder of the importance of taking risks in life. It's easy to fall into the trap of playing it safe, avoiding risks, and staying within our comfort zones. But in doing so, we risk missing out on opportunities for growth, learning, and success.

You see, life is this amazing, ever-changing adventure, filled with twists and turns at every corner. It's within this unpredictable and uncertain landscape that we stumble upon opportunities to push ourselves, to journey beyond the borders of our comfort zones, and to embrace the unknown with open hearts.

Now, imagine if you decided to avoid all risks. You might think you're playing it safe, shielding yourself from potential heartache or loss. But in reality, you'd be closing the door to countless opportunities. You risk more by not taking chances, by not daring to dream, to try, to fail, and ultimately, to grow.

Consider the case of a student scared of pursuing a challenging major, worrying they might fail. By not taking that risk, they might miss out on their true passion and settle for a career that's safe but unfulfilling.

Reflect on the most successful people you know. How did they get where they are today? Was it by playing it safe, or was it by taking calculated risks, stumbling, picking themselves back up, learning, and daring to continue?

This truth doesn't just apply to significant life-altering decisions but also to our daily lives. It's about the risks we take to stand up for our values, voice our opinions, learn something new, make a new friend, and open our hearts to love and kindness.

Yes, risk-taking can be scary, it can lead to temporary failures, but those who dare to step into the unknown often find that what awaits on the other side is worth every moment of fear and uncertainty. Because by not risking anything, we risk living a life that's far less than the one we're capable of living. In the end, the greatest risk is not in daring to live but in choosing not to.

— DAY 302 —

If you're going through hell, keep going

T HESE firm words, linked to Winston Churchill's steadfast spirit, convey deep wisdom that spans beyond adversity and success. Life, with its inevitable ups and downs, is a journey through diverse landscapes, and when faced with the fires of hell, the only way forward is to persevere.

Every one of us has our own version of "hell." It could be the loss of a loved one, a struggle with mental health, a harsh professional setback, or an existential crisis. These are the times when life feels unbearable, akin to being in a continuous, burning furnace.

But let's consider for a moment what "hell" represents. It is a place of suffering, yes, but it is also a process, a journey. The very phrase "going through" implies movement and progress. Hell is not a destination, but rather a difficult passage on our life's path.

What happens if you stop in the middle of this fiery path? You remain stuck in the heat, engulfed by suffering, and trapped in despair.

But, what if, in the face of blistering adversity, you decide to keep going? The suffering persists, yes, but with every step forward, you are actively combating despair. You move closer to the end of the furnace, inching towards the possibility of relief and a brighter tomorrow.

Remember the story of Walt Disney, who was fired from a newspaper for "lacking imagination" and faced multiple business failures before creating Disneyland and the empire that bears his name? Or J.K. Rowling, who faced numerous rejections and personal setbacks before *Harry Potter* took the world by storm? They, and countless others, endured their own versions of hell, but they kept going.

In the end, "If you're going through hell, keep going" is an anthem for the human spirit. It serves as a reminder that resilience and perseverance, in the face of great adversity, are our greatest allies. It encourages us to endure, to push through the pain, and to continue the fight, because it is through the flames of our struggles that we truly find our strength and pave the path toward hope, healing, and growth.

— DAY 303 —

Indecision costs more than wrong decisions

THERE is an insidious enemy that often goes unnoticed in our lives, silently sabotaging our dreams and aspirations. It's not failure or adversity. Instead, it's something far more subtle: indecision.

To make this clearer, consider a situation where you have an opportunity to invest in a business. You're not sure if it's the right move. Days turn into weeks, then months, and you're still on the fence. Finally, you decide to take the plunge, but it's too late.

The cost of your indecision? A missed opportunity to increase your wealth, learn from the experience, and grow as an investor. Even if you had made a decision earlier and it turned out to be the wrong one, you still would have gained valuable insights that could guide your future endeavors.

What does a wrong decision cost you? Often, it's a temporary discomfort, a momentary setback, or a bruise to your ego. But these costs come with a hidden dividend—the invaluable learning from our mistakes. Every failed venture and every incorrect choice leads us to better understanding and growth.

In contrast, indecision leaves you stagnant. It's a paralysis of potential, an inertia that keeps you from progressing. While you're caught in the throes of indecision, life moves forward, and opportunities slip by unnoticed. The cost is the loss of what could have been—the experiences untasted, the lessons unlearned, and the growth unattained.

Consider the story of *Blockbuster*, once a giant in the movie rental industry. They had the opportunity to buy *Netflix*, a fledgling DVD mail-order service at that time, for a mere $50 million. Unable to foresee the potential and caught in indecision, *Blockbuster* declined. Today, *Netflix* is worth billions and *Blockbuster* is a relic of the past. Their indecision cost more than any wrong decision could have.

In life, we are defined not just by the decisions we make, but also by the ones we fail to make. So, dare to decide. Dare to be wrong. Remember, it's through our wrong decisions we find the right path, but through indecision, we may never find a path at all.

— DAY 304 —

Habit outlasts inspiration

AS the sun sets on the horizon of human endeavor, the glowing embers of inspiration often shimmer with the promise of greatness. But as the dark veil of reality obscures these shimmering sparks, we find ourselves navigating through the inky void, guided only by the steadfast beacon of habit.

It is indeed a fascinating spectacle to observe the birth of an inspiration. The spark of a new idea can ignite a wildfire of enthusiasm, propelling us with an electrifying energy. Whether it's a sudden interest in learning a new instrument, or a groundbreaking business idea, inspiration can be powerful. However, its flame, as bright as it might burn initially, is subject to the volatile winds of our fleeting attention and diminishing enthusiasm.

Inspiration is, without a doubt, a terrific starting point. But alone, it cannot sustain the long, often difficult journey towards accomplishment. The truth is, there are days when inspiration decreases, when the initial spark flickers and threatens to die out. It's in these times that habit becomes our true ally.

Habit is the disciplined soldier, marching steadfastly despite the storm or the sweltering heat. It's not subject to our moods or circumstances, and it does not rely on the sporadic gusts of inspiration. Instead, it's built on routine, consistency, and small daily actions that accumulate over time.

Consider any accomplished individual—a renowned author, an Olympic athlete, or a successful entrepreneur. Behind their achievements, more often than not, you'll find an unsexy but reliable framework of habits. The author writes daily, regardless of whether inspiration strikes. The athlete trains consistently, irrespective of mood. The entrepreneur analyzes markets and strategizes, even when the initial fervor of a groundbreaking idea has faded.

The most beautiful symphony, the most successful venture, or the greatest masterpiece wasn't created in a single burst of inspiration. Instead, they were sculpted, note by note, decision by decision, brushstroke by brushstroke, in the routine, in the mundane, and in the power of habit.

— DAY 305 —

Society judges by appearance

I N an era where images are constantly thrust upon us, where social media presides over our daily lives, and where the visual, more often than not, override the textual, it is unsurprising that society's judgments are primarily founded on appearance. This superficial examination creates a painted reality, a facade that reveals little about the essence of individuals or circumstances. Yet, despite its limiting view, this reliance on appearance holds a firm grip on our collective mindset, shaping how we see and interact with the world around us.

Think about the role of aesthetics in our daily interactions. In the few seconds, it takes to form a first impression, we unknowingly assign values based on physical appearances, extrapolating qualities that may not exist while missing those that do. The tall, well-dressed stranger at a party is assumed successful; the ragged individual on the street is branded as lazy. These judgments, made in a flash, are as effortless as they are unfair.

Similarly, in the world of goods and services, we are hypnotized by shiny packaging and slick marketing. A product's value is often blended with its outward appearance, leading us to overlook functionality or necessity in favor of aesthetics.

And yet, reality often challenges these superficial judgments. The stranger at the party might be drowning in debt, and the individual on the street might have been dealt an unfair hand in life. The shiny item could be of poor quality, while an unassuming one might be of superior quality.

This brings us to a crucial point. While it is natural to lean on visual cues, it is critical to question these immediate judgments, to dig deeper, and to allow for understanding and empathy. Only then can we break away from the confining lens of appearance-based assessments and appreciate the mix of experiences, values, and capabilities that lie beneath the surface.

In essence, we must remind ourselves that appearance is merely the outer shell, often providing a distorted perspective. While society might insist on judging a book by its cover, it falls upon us as individuals to read the pages within.

— DAY 306 —

Hold on tight when life gets tough

IT sounds like something you'd find on a motivational poster, right? Life, in all its beauty and wonder, often serves as a curious blend of sunshine and storms. It is in these moments of turbulence, when the strong winds blow fierce, that the phrase echoes with a profound resonance.

Consider for a moment a tiny sapling weathering a tempest. It bows to the wind, bends almost to breaking, but never snaps. It clings to the earth with tenacious roots, resilient, and steadfast. This is the essence of perseverance, the very heartbeat of survival. Just as the sapling clings to its nurturing earth, so too must we hold tight amidst life's tempests.

These challenging moments, though turbulent, are rich with transformative potential. Like the churning of rough seas forming radiant pearls within oysters, our trials can forge in us an inner strength, an unseen pearl of resilience. Holding on tight in these times is not about remaining static or resisting change; instead, it is about embracing adversity as a catalyst for growth, using it to cultivate an inner resilience that shines through even the most daunting storms.

Like the ship anchored steadfastly against the raging storm, we discover our ability to weather any tempest life may unleash. This realization, this unyielding spirit, fuels us to persevere and to maintain our course even when waves threaten to overwhelm us. It is a testament to our innate resilience, our profound strength, and our unyielding courage.

In a world that often glorifies the idea of letting go, holding on tight becomes an act of defiance—a statement of our steadfast spirit and determination. It's a reminder that we are not alone in our struggles and that we possess the strength to overcome whatever obstacles come our way.

Hold on tight when life gets tough, my friend, for within the depths of struggle lies the potential for transformation and the seeds of a brighter tomorrow. Trust in your own strength, lean on the support of others, and keep moving forward with steadfast determination. After all, it is in the face of adversity that our true character shines brightest.

— DAY 307 —

Deep work fuels productivity

I N our modern and constantly connected world, it can be difficult to find the time and focus to get deep work done. Deep work refers to the kind of work that requires intense focus and concentration, such as writing, coding, or analyzing data. But despite the challenges, deep work is essential for productivity, creativity, and achieving our goals.

When we engage in deep work, we are able to tap into our creativity and problem-solving abilities in ways that are not possible when we are constantly distracted or multitasking. By focusing our attention on a single task, we can enter a state of flow, where we are completely absorbed in our work, and time seems to fly by.

Deep work also allows us to produce higher-quality work in a shorter amount of time. When we can focus our attention on a single task, we can achieve a level of mastery that is not possible when we are constantly switching between tasks or checking our email. This, in turn, allows us to produce better work in less time, which is essential for productivity and achieving our goals.

But deep work is not easy to achieve. It requires discipline and the ability to resist the constant distractions and interruptions that are a part of modern life. It may mean turning off our phone, closing our email, and setting aside a specific time each day for deep work.

However, the rewards of deep work are well worth the effort. By engaging in deep work, we can tap into our full potential and achieve our goals with greater ease and efficiency. We are able to produce higher-quality work, tap into our creativity and problem-solving abilities, and feel a sense of accomplishment and fulfillment that is hard to achieve when we are constantly distracted or multitasking.

Deep work is essential for productivity, creativity, and achieving our goals. While it may be challenging to achieve in today's fast-paced world, the rewards are well worth the effort.

— DAY 308 —

Life's inequality demands adaptive resilience

ADAPTIVE resilience is the capacity to navigate the uneven terrain of life, to withstand the challenges that inequality presents, and to transcend the limitations created by external circumstances. It is the recognition that life's inequality demands not just endurance, but a proactive and adaptable approach to finding balance and creating opportunities for growth.

Life is a lot like a game of cards. We're all dealt a hand, and let's be honest, the cards are not always evenly distributed. Some folks get aces and kings, while others draw a bunch of twos and threes. That's the inequality part. It's not necessarily fair, but it's part of the game.

So, where does adaptive resilience come in? It's the ability to bounce back, to keep going despite the setbacks and challenges. It's not just about gritting your teeth and plowing through. It's about adapting, learning, and growing from experiences, much like a tree bending with the wind instead of snapping.

Think of it this way: you've got a tough hand, but you're still in the game. Can you change the cards? No. But you can change how you play them. Maybe you bluff. Maybe you fold this round and wait for the next. That's adaptive resilience—making the best of what you've got, adapting your strategy based on the situation.

The beautiful thing about resilience is, it's like a muscle. The more you use it, the stronger it gets. And sometimes, it's the two and three-card hands that end up teaching us the most valuable lessons. They shape and form us into more resilient players, ready for the next round, whatever it might bring.

And this, perhaps, is the true beauty of life's inequality. It's not a bug in the system, but a feature. It's a call to action, a demand that we become better, stronger, and more resilient. It's a reminder that our path isn't set in stone and that we have the power to adapt, to overcome, to turn adversity into advantage.

Life's inequality demands adaptive resilience, and this is a call we can answer. We are all capable of resilience, adaptability, and growth. And when we embrace these qualities when we meet life's inequalities with courage and determination, we are not just surviving—we are thriving.

— DAY 309 —

Let go of relationships that don't serve you

W E are social beings, wired for connection and belonging. It's natural to form relationships and invest our time and energy into them. However, not all relationships are meant to last forever. As we evolve and grow, our needs, values, and aspirations may change, and some relationships may no longer align with who we are becoming.

Letting go of relationships that no longer serve us is not an easy task. It requires courage, self-reflection, and a willingness to embrace the unknown. But in doing so, we open ourselves up to the possibility of forming healthier, more fulfilling connections.

Consider the relationships in your life—both personal and professional. Do they uplift and support you, or do they drain your energy and hinder your growth? Do they align with your values and aspirations, or do they hold you back?

When we let go of relationships that don't serve us, we create space for personal growth, self-discovery, and authentic connections. We liberate ourselves from toxic dynamics, negative influences, and emotional baggage. We give ourselves permission to prioritize our own well-being and pursue relationships that align with our values and aspirations.

Letting go does not mean dismissing or devaluing the experiences shared with someone. It means recognizing that people come into our lives for various reasons and seasons, and sometimes, their role in our journey may reach its natural conclusion.

As we journey through life, we must continually evaluate the relationships that shape our world. Are they lifting us or holding us back? Are they adding value or causing distress? Are they helping us grow or pulling us down?

You are the artist, and your relationships are the colors with which you paint your world. Choose your colors wisely, and never be afraid to discard the ones that dull your masterpiece. After all, your canvas deserves nothing but the most vibrant and uplifting colors.

— DAY 310 —

Your best effort is more important than comparison

W E dwell in a world that thrives on comparison, where success is often measured by ranking against others rather than personal development. However, this pursuit of external validation can divert us from our unique journeys and potential. Comparison can shroud our vision, obstructing the view of our accomplishments and shadowing them with others' perceived success.

In contrast, anchoring our aspirations on personal effort shines a beacon of light onto our paths, illuminating a way toward authentic growth. It encourages us to strive, not against others, but against our own past selves. When we focus on honing our skills, mastering our craft, and persisting through challenges, we unlock doors to improvement and self-enhancement. It is this spirit of effort that propels us forward, fueling our growth.

Every individual has a unique array of talents, experiences, and potential. Thus, comparing our journeys to others is like comparing the radiance of the sun to the tranquility of the moon—both magnificent, yet inherently different. Focusing on our best effort enables us to appreciate our unique brilliance, acknowledging that our journey's worth is not measured by comparison but by the strength of our determination and the magnitude of our growth.

Every one of us is on a unique journey. There's no sense in comparing your Chapter 1 to someone else's Chapter 20. It's apples and oranges, my friend. Instead, put that energy into giving your best, into learning and growing, and becoming a better version of yourself.

So, let's break free from the chains of comparison and focus on what truly matters— our efforts, our journey, our growth. It's all about being the best "you" you can be, not better than someone else.

Comparison is the thief of joy. Embrace your own journey, give your best, and celebrate the progress you make along the way. The true measure of success lies not in outperforming others but in the growth and self-improvement you achieve through your best effort.

— DAY 311 —

Sync your body clock for a healthy rhythm

YOUR body operates on a natural time-keeping system known as the circadian rhythm, or the body clock. This rhythm is a 24-hour internal clock that cycles between sleepiness and alertness at regular intervals. It's also known as your sleep/wake cycle. A disruption to this cycle can lead to feelings of jet lag, difficulty sleeping, and other health issues.

What's fascinating is that this clock can be influenced and reset. Our body clocks are primarily regulated by light and darkness in an environment. Exposure to natural light during the day helps keep our rhythms healthy and can improve mood and energy. On the flip side, limiting exposure to artificial light, especially closer to bedtime, can help ensure a good night's sleep.

In today's fast-paced world, it's easy to get out of sync with our natural rhythms. Late nights in front of screens, irregular eating patterns, and constant exposure to artificial light can disrupt our internal harmony. We become like a chaotic ensemble, producing discord rather than harmony.

However, the good news is that we have the power to regain control and sync our body clock for a healthy rhythm. It starts with creating a consistent sleep schedule. By going to bed and waking up at the same time every day, we allow our body clock to regulate our sleep patterns effectively. It's like giving the conductor a clear baton to direct the orchestra.

Another vital aspect is exposure to natural light. Our body clock relies on sunlight to set its rhythm. By getting outside and basking in the sun's rays, especially in the morning, we signal to our body clock that it's time to be alert and active. This not only improves our mood and energy levels but also enhances our overall well-being.

Aligning our body clock is not rocket science. It just requires simple yet significant lifestyle changes. Regular sleep and wake times, exposure to sunlight during the day, reduced screen time at night, regular physical activity, and balanced nutrition—these are the composition of our body's symphony.

— DAY 312 —

Don't spend your life in regret; learn from it

REGRET. That haunting feeling that creeps into our minds when we look back at certain moments in our lives. We all have them, those instances where we wish we had acted differently, made better choices or taken a chance on something we now realize we missed out on. But here's the thing: regret doesn't have to be a life sentence. In fact, it can be a powerful teacher if we're willing to listen.

Consider this. Regret is like a mirror that reflects the choices we made, the paths we took, and the consequences that followed. It shows us the gap between who we were then and who we are now, and that awareness is a gift. It's an opportunity to grow, evolve, and become better versions of ourselves.

Sure, it's easy to get lost in the "what ifs" and "should haves." We torture ourselves with imagined scenarios, wondering how things might have turned out if only we had chosen differently. But dwelling on the past is like driving with our eyes fixed on the rearview mirror. We'll never move forward, and worse yet, we might crash into the same mistakes again.

Instead, let's shift our perspective. Let's see regret as a valuable source of wisdom. Each regret holds a lesson, a nugget of insight that can shape our future choices. We can choose to embrace these lessons, learn from them, and integrate them into our lives. It's like an upgrade, a chance to level up our decision-making skills.

Imagine if we took the time to reflect on our regrets, not as sources of pain, but as opportunities for growth. What if we used them as stepping stones to a more fulfilling life? We could use the knowledge gained from our missteps to make wiser choices, take calculated risks, and seize the moments that come our way.

Life is too short to be consumed by regret. Instead, let's view it as a teacher, a guide, and an ally. Embrace the lessons, cherish the growth, and remember that the only real regret lies in not learning from our mistakes. My friend, let's leave the regrets behind and step boldly into the future, armed with newfound wisdom and an unshakeable determination to make each day count.

— DAY 313 —

The art of life is living unattached

LIVING unattached—the phrase carries an air of mystique and intrigue. On one hand, it suggests a sense of detachment, a liberation from material possessions, relationships, and circumstances. On the other, it hints at a deeper understanding of life itself, an existential art of being.

The concept of unattachment isn't about isolating oneself or embracing indifference. Rather, it's a profound recognition of life's transient nature and the conscious choice to avoid being ensnared by fleeting realities. To live unattached is to engage fully with the world, cherishing every moment and interaction, yet maintaining an internal equilibrium, unperturbed by external influences.

Imagine a leaf floating on a stream. The leaf is fully in contact with the water, moving along its course, but it isn't tethered to any part of the stream. It basks in the sunlight, dances in the wind, and savors every ripple and turn, yet, its essence remains unchanged. This is the art of living unattached—to navigate life's ebbs and flows, yet remain true to one's core, unswayed by the constant flux around.

Possessions, relationships, achievements—they can enrich our lives, but they can also confine us if we allow them to define our identity or happiness. True freedom lies not in having or not having, but in being—being content, being at peace, and being oneself irrespective of external conditions.

Living unattached doesn't mean forsaking love or connection. It means experiencing them in their purest forms, free from conditions, expectations, or fear of loss. It's to love deeply, yet freely, to connect authentically, yet openly.

The art of living unattached is an invitation to embrace the world, yet remain inwardly free. It's about nurturing an inner sanctuary of peace that the waves of change cannot disturb. It's the embodiment of the saying, "You can't stop the waves, but you can learn to surf."

— DAY 314 —

Self-improvement benefits all

S OCIETY often romanticizes the idea of self-improvement, picturing it as a relentless pursuit of perfection, an infinite climbing of the ladder. But the essence of self-improvement, in its purest form, transcends personal accomplishments. It interweaves with a tapestry of collective betterment that extends its reach beyond the individual, subtly but surely benefiting all.

When we water a plant, it doesn't just flourish on its own. It contributes to the ecosystem by providing food, shelter, and contributing to the balance of oxygen and carbon dioxide. Similarly, our personal growth isn't just about us. It has ripple effects, shaping the world around us in unforeseen ways.

Our personal growth expands our capacities, skills, knowledge, and perspective, enabling us to make valuable contributions to the world. The entrepreneur who hones her leadership skills can build a thriving enterprise that creates jobs. The teacher who commits to being a lifelong learner can inspire generations of students. The parent who cultivates patience and understanding can foster a nurturing home environment, shaping the future of his children.

Self-improvement doesn't operate in isolation. It influences the environment we create, the relationships we nurture, and the culture we foster. Our attitudes and actions, shaped by our personal growth, can uplift, inspire, and positively influence others. When we strive to be kinder, more understanding, and more informed, it's not just us who change. We implicitly encourage those around us to do the same.

However, let's not forget that self-improvement isn't a quest for an elusive state of perfection. It's about progress, about being a little better than we were yesterday. It's about expanding our understanding, fostering our empathy, sharpening our skills, and, in the process, making the world a slightly better place.

The journey of self-improvement benefits all, transforming the self, and subtly weaving a web of collective growth. It truly encapsulates the essence of the phrase, "Be the change you wish to see in the world."

— DAY 315 —

Discomfort fosters growth and development

NAVIGATING the rough terrain of discomfort isn't a route many would willingly choose. Human nature intuitively seeks comfort and stability; we're hardwired to find respite in the familiar, the calm, the predictable. Yet, this journey towards a comfortable life often bypasses a profound truth: discomfort is the melting pot for growth and development.

Picture the caterpillar, suspended in its cocoon, anticipating the moment of metamorphosis. The cocoon, however warm and secure, is not its destiny. The caterpillar endures a phase of disquiet, ultimately emerging as a resplendent butterfly.

This biological metaphor holds deep wisdom. As humans, our personal and professional development isn't typically the product of comfort and selfsatisfaction. Instead, it's the offshoot of challenges faced, the fruit of discomforts weathered. Every hardship, every pang of discomfort, every moment of doubt, it all matters. It all contributes to a grand, yet subtle, shift within us.

Consider moments in your life when true growth occurred. Were you relaxing in the lap of luxury, or were you grappling with challenges, striving against the odds? Chances are, the latter rings truer. Perhaps it was the disquiet of a failed venture that propelled you to acquire new skills, or the discomfort of a lost relationship that nurtured resilience and self-awareness. It's through discomfort that we shed the old, inviting the potential for new strengths, insights, and perspectives.

We should not misinterpret this promotion of discomfort as a condemnation of comfort. Comfort is essential, providing much-needed respite, a sanctuary where our spirits find rejuvenation. Yet, it's the oscillation between comfort and discomfort that creates the rhythm of growth.

Thus, let's see discomfort for what it truly is—not a menace, but a mentor. A silent guide nudging us toward our most potent potential. Embrace it, allow it to mold you, challenge you, and most importantly, transform you. Because, at the heart of it all, discomfort doesn't just breed growth, it is the essence of growth.

— DAY 316 —

New perspective, new world

HAVE you ever looked at the world through someone else's eyes? It can be a transformative experience, one that opens us up to new perspectives and ways of thinking. When we see the world through a new lens, we can break out of our own limitations and biases and see the world in a new light. This is the power of a new perspective, and it has the ability to change the world.

We've all heard the story about the half-full or half-empty glass. The glass is the same, but the way you see it can determine whether you're an optimist or a pessimist. Your perspective isn't just about how you see things. It's about how you live, how you react, and, ultimately, who you are.

Imagine you're stuck in traffic, a situation most of us despise. But what if you changed your perspective? Instead of viewing it as lost time, what if you saw it as an opportunity to listen to an audiobook, learn a new language, or simply appreciate the world around you? Suddenly, traffic doesn't seem so bad, does it?

Or consider your problems. We all have them, and they seem huge, unbeatable. But what if we shift our perspective and see them not as obstacles but as opportunities? As lessons that help us grow? As tests that make us stronger? Doesn't that make them less daunting?

The magic of a new perspective is that it transforms the world without changing anything in it. The traffic remains the same, the problems persist, but they don't affect us the way they used to. They don't bring us down. Instead, they fuel us, they empower us, and they add a dash of excitement to our lives.

Changing our perspective is like rewriting the code of our life. It's the same game, but we're playing it differently, we're playing it better. It's like discovering a whole new world within the world we already live in.

The journey to adopt a new perspective is an exciting adventure that holds the key to unlocking a whole new world.

— DAY 317 —

Discipline is key to freedom

WHEN we think of discipline, we often associate it with rigidity, sacrifice, and limitations. It's a word that can evoke feelings of resistance and constraint. We often think of discipline as a sort of prison. A world of strict rules, rigid routines, and seemingly endless hard work. Sounds more like a life sentence than a ticket to freedom, right? But what if I told you that discipline is actually the key to freedom? Yeah, I know it sounds weird. But hear me out.

When we think of discipline, the mind often conjures images of strict teachers, stringent rules, and grueling training schedules. It carries associations with imprisonment, control, and rigidity. And in the face of such severity, freedom seems like a far cry, a dream wilted under discipline's iron grip. But what if we've misunderstood the essence of discipline?

Discipline is not about oppression; it's about direction. It's not about forfeiting spontaneity; it's about fostering focus. Consider discipline as a riverbed, guiding the ceaseless flow of water toward the vast ocean. The riverbed does not confine the water but directs it, enabling it to journey toward its ultimate freedom. Similarly, discipline guides our energies, ambitions, and dreams toward our defined goals—our oceans of freedom.

Then arises the question, freedom from what? And this is where discipline shines. Discipline grants us freedom from chaos, procrastination, and ineffectiveness. It frees us from the clutches of waywardness and empowers us with a sense of purpose, direction, and clarity. It brings freedom from the whirlpool of distractions and offers us the gift of focus.

Take a disciplined musician, for instance. Hours, days, and years of structured practice may seem restrictive, yet it's this very discipline that eventually allows the musician to move freely across the scales, creating melodies that stir souls. Similarly, an athlete's disciplined training brings freedom to perform at their peak, surpassing boundaries and setting records.

Therefore, it's through discipline that we attain mastery, and in mastery, we find freedom. Freedom to express, to innovate, to transcend ordinary limits. It's the freedom to dance with grace, sing with soul, and live with purpose.

— DAY 318 —

Our greatest weakness lies in giving up

L IFE, with its complex accumulation of experiences, often threads us through the needle's eye of adversity. Whether it's a personal goal, a professional milestone, or a shared aspiration, the road is rarely smooth. We encounter roadblocks, detours, and dead ends. It's in these moments of hardship that the temptation to give up becomes the greatest.

You see, when we face challenges, we naturally gauge the situation based on our current abilities. And the scarier part? We often underestimate our potential to learn, adapt, and grow. We see a mountain and think, "Well, I've never climbed a mountain before, so I probably can't do it." But is that the absolute truth?

Let's think about this another way. Have you ever seen a baby learning to walk? Do they give up after falling down for the umpteenth time? No. They fall, they rise, they stumble again, and yet, they persist. And eventually, they conquer the art of walking.

Then why, as adults, do we allow failure to deter us? Why do we abandon our dreams at the first sign of hardship? This surrender, this defeatist attitude, is our most significant weakness. More often than not, the difference between success and failure isn't talent or intelligence, but grit and perseverance.

Consider the paths of Kathryn Johnson, a pioneering mathematician who overcame racial and gender barriers to play a crucial role in the U.S. space program, and Stephen King, whose early writing was frequently rejected. Johnson's precision and King's perseverance through rejection exemplify how resilience, rather than avoidance of failure, is the true hallmark of strength.

And you know what's even more intriguing? This power of persistence is available to all of us. It's not exclusive to the geniuses of the world. Every single one of us has the potential to transform our greatest weakness into our most substantial strength.

In the face of adversity, let's remember that our power lies not in never falling, but in rising every time we fall. Let's strive to turn our weakness of giving up into the strength of persevering.

— DAY 319 —

The best revenge is not to be like your enemy

IN our lives, we often face situations where people might treat us unfairly or unkindly. It's a natural reaction to want to respond in the same way, to give them a taste of their own medicine. However, there's a much more powerful and positive way to deal with such challenges, a way that involves being the better person, not stooping to their level.

Consider the story of Nelson Mandela. Mandela was imprisoned for nearly three decades because of his fight against apartheid, a system that segregated people based on race. When he was finally released, he had every reason to be angry and seek revenge against those who wronged him. Instead, Mandela chose a path of peace and reconciliation. He worked with his former enemies to heal his country and bring people together, proving that forgiveness is more powerful than revenge.

Another remarkable example is Malala Yousafzai, a young Pakistani activist who stood up for her right to education in the face of extreme danger. After surviving an attack meant to silence her, Malala didn't respond with hatred. Instead, she continued to advocate for education, showing incredible courage and resilience.

These stories are not just about not being like those who may wish us harm; they're about transforming our struggles into opportunities for growth and positive change. They teach us that our actions can lead to healing, not just for ourselves but for our communities and even the world.

This approach to conflict, characterized by a refusal to adopt the tactics of those who do us harm, is deeply healing. It asserts that true power lies not in conquest or revenge, but in the ability to remain true to oneself, to elevate one's principles unbiased. In doing so, individuals like Mandela and Malala become more than just victors in their battles; they emerge as architects of a new reality, one where light counters darkness, and integrity triumphs over adversity.

— DAY 320 —

Start from where you are

M ANY of us spend our lives trapped in the snare of "when and then" thinking. When I have more time, then I will start my passion project. When I save more money, then I'll invest. When I feel ready, then I'll make that life-changing decision. The problem is that "when" seldom comes, and "then" remains an elusive promise. Life unfolds in the present, and if we fail to act in the here and now, we risk being spectators of our destiny. We get caught up in comparing ourselves to others, setting unrealistic expectations, and feeling overwhelmed by the gap between where we are and where we want to be.

Starting from where you are means accepting your present circumstances, your strengths, your weaknesses, and your unique journey. It's about honoring your starting point as the foundation upon which you build your dreams and aspirations. It's about recognizing that every great journey begins with a single step. But here's the coolest part—when you choose to start from where you are, you're not only choosing action over inaction, you're also embracing yourself. You're saying, "Yes, this is me, this is where I am, and I'm okay with that."

Starting from where you are eliminates the scope for procrastination and cuts through the haze of overwhelm. It implores us to take stock of our current reality, however imperfect, and initiate steps toward change. It reminds us that the most remarkable journeys begin with a single, humble step.

But the beauty of this proposition goes deeper still. Implicit in these words is a lesson in self-acceptance. It nudges us to acknowledge our current abilities, our limitations, and our unique circumstances. It is a call to embrace our imperfections and still take decisive action toward our goals.

Starting from where you are is a potent distillation of wisdom that nudges us to take charge of our destiny. It champions the power of now, endorses selfacceptance, and underscores the importance of taking action. Whether it's a new project, a healthier lifestyle, or a dream long postponed, the message is clear. The perfect time will never come. The perfect place doesn't exist.

— DAY 321 —

Marry for love, not gain

I N an era where strategic alliances and the pursuit of wealth and power seem to dictate many a decision, the notion of marrying for love might seem a tad idealistic. However, the wisdom embodied in this phrase isn't a mere fairy-tale concept; it holds a profound truth that is universally relevant.

In a world that often prioritizes wealth, status, and material possessions, it's easy to lose sight of the true essence of a fulfilling and meaningful partnership.

Love, in its purest form, is a combination of respect, trust, and a deep sense of belonging. It's about looking at the other person and seeing a companion, a confidant, someone with whom you can navigate the winding roads of life.

When you marry for love, you invest in the deep connection between two souls. This creates a resilience that can weather the stormiest of times, for love gives us strength even in our weakest moments. When marriage is viewed as a transaction or a stepping stone for gain—be it social, financial, or otherwise—the foundation of the relationship becomes shaky. It becomes a bargain, a contract of mutual benefit, where love and genuine companionship might be compromised. In such situations, when the tides turn and challenges surface, the superficial bonds are often not strong enough to hold the relationship together.

Let love guide your heart. Seek a partner who aligns with your values, who accepts you for who you are, and who brings out the best in you. Look beyond external factors and focus on the qualities that truly matter—kindness, laughter, the shared dreams.

Life is an unpredictable journey filled with twists and turns. Marrying for gain may offer momentary triumphs, but they are fleeting. On the other hand, love, the kind that allows you to be your authentic self, that celebrates your individuality while nurturing a shared growth, is enduring.

Marry for love, for the deep, raw, pure love that transcends materialistic gains and societal definitions of success. Because in the end, it's the warmth of love, not the cold glitter of gold, that truly enriches our lives.

— DAY 322 —

Stay humble, stay strong

I N a world that often glorifies ego and power, staying humble is a revolutionary act. It's about recognizing our place in the grand theatre of life, acknowledging our strengths and weaknesses, and remaining grounded in the face of success or adversity. It's a reminder that true strength comes not from arrogance or dominance but from a deep sense of self-awareness and humility.

You see, life's a funny thing. One minute, we're on top of the world, basking in success. The next, we're tumbling down a rabbit hole of uncertainty and challenge. That's the thing about life. It's full of ups and downs, like a rollercoaster ride that never quite ends. And how do we ride this rollercoaster with grace and dignity?

Let's break it down, starting with strength. When I say, "stay strong," I'm not just talking about physical strength. Sure, that's important, but there's a different kind of strength that really matters. It's the kind that comes from deep within, a tenacious spirit that refuses to bow down in the face of adversity. It's the strength to keep going when every fiber of your being wants to give up, to dare to dream when the world seems shrouded in darkness, and to continue loving when your heart is heavy with hurt. That's the real strength.

But strength alone isn't enough. We need humility to balance it out. Why, you ask? Picture this. You're climbing a mountain, pushing your limits, inching closer to the summit. You finally make it to the top, euphoric and triumphant. Now, you have two choices. You could either look down at the world below, a sense of superiority swelling in your chest. Or you could remember the mountain's mighty expanse, the countless others who've scaled the same peaks, and feel humbled. The latter choice, that's the essence of humility.

Humility reminds us that no matter how high we climb, we're just tiny specks in a grand, sprawling universe. When humility and strength walk hand in hand, they create a formidable duo. Humility keeps us grounded, reminding us of our roots, while strength propels us forward, instilling in us the courage to reach for the stars.

— DAY 323 —

Mortality reminds us to live

M ORTALITY. Now that's a word that makes most people break into a cold sweat. It's like the houseguest that's overstayed their welcome, always lurking in the back of our minds, ready to crash our party at any moment. But have you ever considered that our friend Mortality might not be the grim reaper we all fear, but instead, a life coach in a dark cloak?

Mortality may seem like a chilling specter, a grim reaper, eager to snuff out the flame of our existence. Yet, in a mind-bending paradox, it is also the reason why our lives blaze with so much intensity. Each tick of the clock, each fleeting moment, is a stark reminder that our time here is limited, urging us to seize the day and live our lives to the fullest.

What would you do if you knew that tomorrow was your last day? The instinctive answer, for most, would be to do everything they've ever dreamed of, to live as if there was no tomorrow. It is this urgency, this desperation to make each moment count, that mortality inspires.

Life, when viewed through the lens of mortality, is no longer a meandering journey but a race against time. Each moment becomes precious, every interaction meaningful, every dream worth pursuing. It forces us to reassess our priorities, to focus on what truly matters. It compels us to love deeply, dream passionately, and live authentically.

To embrace our mortality is to accept the inevitability of our existence. It's to understand that we are mere passengers on the voyage of life, not the voyage itself. And in that acceptance, we find a profound freedom—the freedom to live without fear, without regret.

Let mortality not be a source of fear, but a catalyst for life. Let it be the nudge that pushes us out of our comfort zones, the force that propels us toward our passions. Let it remind us not of our impending end, but of our vibrant, pulsating existence. Let mortality be the reminder that every day is a gift, every moment a chance to live. After all, we're not just here to exist—we're here to live.

— DAY 324 —

One positive thought can change everything

I N the whirlwind of life, it's easy to get caught up in negativity, doubts, and worries. One single thought can change everything! It might seem exaggerated or oversimplified to assert that one positive thought can change everything. Yet, in the intricacy of our human mind and the complex puzzle that is our life, it's a singular, glimmering piece of optimism that has the power to reshape the entire picture.

Our thoughts shape our reality. They have the ability to influence our emotions, our actions, and the energy we radiate out into the world. When we choose to embrace a positive thought, even just one, we set in motion a powerful chain reaction of positivity that can ripple through every aspect of our lives.

Consider a day when everything seemed to go wrong. Your alarm didn't go off, you spilled coffee on your favorite shirt, and the traffic was unbearable. It's easy to give in to negativity and let it taint your entire day. But what if you were to block this chain of thought with one positive reflection? Perhaps you take a moment to appreciate the beautiful sunrise, the warmth of your coffee, or your favorite song playing on the radio.

One positive thought can create a domino effect, pushing out negativity, shifting your mood, and subtly influencing your decisions and actions. It's like a pebble thrown into a pond, creating ripples that expand far beyond the point of impact.

The power of positivity has been endorsed by science too. Studies reveal that positive thinking can boost your problem-solving abilities, enhance your well-being, and even improve your physical health.[6] Now, isn't that mindblowing?

In a world where negativity often holds sway, one positive thought can be revolutionary. It has the power to transform your perspective, enrich your experiences, and indeed, change everything. So why not give it a try? Remember, your reality is a reflection of your thoughts. Make it a positive one, and watch as your world transforms. One positive thought can indeed change everything; it's a small investment with an infinite return.

— DAY 325 —

Know why you do what you do

DURING the hustle and bustle of life, it's easy to get caught up in the daily grind without questioning the underlying purpose behind our actions. We go through the motions, doing what needs to be done, but often fail to pause and reflect on why we're doing it.

In the grand theater of life, actions form the visible part of our identity, the scenes we allow the world to witness. Yet behind these actions, the invisible director guiding the play is our "why." It's the driving force, the fuel that propels us forward, the rationale underpinning every step we take.

Life isn't just a random sequence of actions, but a carefully curated dance between intent and response, thought and action, aspiration and achievement. But in the whirlwind of life, we often find ourselves merely going through the motions, losing sight of the "why" behind the "what." Our actions become reactions, our lives, a series of tasks ticked off a checklist. Let's pause for a moment. Picture an archer with a bow and arrow. The arrow represents our actions, the bow, our potential, and the target, our goals. But what gives direction and momentum to the arrow? It's the tension in the bow, our "why." Without it, the arrow falters, losing its path and purpose.

Understanding our "why" fosters alignment between our actions and values, which is crucial to living a fulfilling life. It helps us cut through the clutter, focus our energies, and steer our lives with a sense of purpose. It lends resilience in times of adversity, clarity amid confusion, and courage in the face of fear.

Remember, our "why" isn't set in stone. As we evolve, so do our motivations, interests, and aspirations. So, it's crucial to continually reevaluate and understand our "why," ensuring it remains a true reflection of who we are.

In the words of Friedrich Nietzsche, "He who has a why to live can bear almost any how." Let's go for a ride on the journey to uncover our "why," to sculpt our lives with conscious intent, to ensure our actions aren't just empty echoes, but resonant melodies strummed from the strings of our soul's deepest desires. Because when we know why we do what we do, we no longer merely exist—we truly live.

— DAY 326 —

Philosophy is the roadmap, not the destination

HAVE you ever tried to assemble a piece of *IKEA* furniture without the instruction manual? Pretty tricky, right? But when you have the manual, even if it's not perfect, you can figure it out. That, my friend, is the power of philosophy. It may not give us the exact answers, but it helps us navigate through the complexities of life. It's like a roadmap guiding us through the twists and turns of existence.

We embark on our philosophical journey, our hands running over the scroll of ideas and theories, searching for the right path. It may not be well-lit or well-trodden, but it's ours. We examine existential questions, ethical dilemmas, metaphysical mysteries, and logical mysteries. We explore and learn from the wisdom of great thinkers, taking detours through Socrates' musings, Kant's imperatives, Nietzsche's critiques, or de Beauvoir's feminist existentialism.

Our philosophical explorations illuminate the world in a different light, teasing apart complexities, and revealing hidden dimensions of reality. As we traverse the expanse of human knowledge and thought, we acquire tools to navigate life's journey. We learn to question assumptions, discern truths from misconceptions, foster empathy, and appreciate diverse perspectives. Our philosophically honed mind becomes a compass, always seeking, always questioning.

In our contemporary world obsessed with certainty and immediate gratification, philosophy urges us to appreciate ambiguity, paradox, and the long road of discovery. It cautions us against intellectual self-satisfaction, against the illusion of having arrived. It continuously points towards the horizon, whispering, "keep going."

The measure of a life well-lived is not in the arrival but in the journey. It is in the quality of our questions, the depth of our understanding, the breadth of our empathy, and the courage of our convictions. Philosophy may not be the destination, but it is a profound, energizing, and enlightening roadmap. It shapes our journey, and in doing so, it shapes us. It encourages us to keep seeking, to keep learning, and to relish the ongoing voyage of life.

— DAY 327 —

New thinking solves old problems

W E all encounter those familiar problems that seem to haunt us, recurring like an endless loop. We scratch our heads, trying the same old solutions, hoping for a breakthrough. Although Albert Einstein warned us about this in his own words, "Insanity is doing the same thing over and over and expecting different results."

Let's delve into the realm of medicine, for instance. For centuries, diseases like smallpox and polio were the harbingers of death and despair. However, it wasn't until we altered our perspective, shifting from treatment to prevention, that we developed vaccines. This shift in thought not only eliminated these once-deadly diseases but revolutionized our approach to medical science.

Reflect upon the groundbreaking shift from a geocentric to a heliocentric model of our solar system. The paradigm-shattering work of Copernicus, Galileo, and Kepler altered our understanding of our place in the universe and ushered in the era of modern astronomy.

In our everyday lives too, we grapple with problems, some longstanding, some more immediate. Often, these problems persist not due to their inherent insolubility but due to our reluctance to change our approach. It's easy to fall into the trap of doing things the way they've always been done. But when we dare to step out of the box, to question the status quo, to view the problem through a different lens, we often find a solution within our reach.

Innovation, after all, is not just the invention of new things but the reinvention of old ones. It's about viewing the old from a new vantage point, exploring it with a new curiosity, and understanding it with a new wisdom.

Embrace this philosophy. Allow it to fill your life. Dare to question, dare to explore, dare to evolve. Remember, new thinking does not just solve old problems; it transforms them into stepping stones toward a brighter future. It's not merely a tool for problem-solving but an ethos that fosters growth, progress, and evolution. And it all starts with a simple decision to think anew.

— DAY 328 —

Prioritize future over temporary emotions

ISN'T it wild how a brief flash of emotion can influence us to act against our best interests? We've all been there—experiencing the rollercoaster of regret after letting a transient feeling call the shots.

First, let's acknowledge the power of emotions. They paint our world in vivid colors, shaping every experience, every moment. We feel happiness, sorrow, anger, and love, and these sensations give life its depth. However, problems arise when we let these emotions control our actions, steering us away from our long-term goals, and from the future we desire.

Consider a young artist full of talent but sensitive to criticism. A harsh review might cause a temporary surge of hopelessness, and she may be tempted to abandon her canvas forever. In this fleeting emotional whirlwind, she risks sacrificing a future brimming with potential masterpieces.

Or imagine a situation where a professional receives a more lucrative job offer from a rival firm. Excitement and greed might spur him to grab the opportunity, ignoring potential ethical dilemmas or long-term career implications. The immediate emotion, if allowed to decide, could jeopardize his future professional standing.

So, how do we counteract this emotional impulsivity? Well, the first step is to recognize the transience of our emotions. They are, by nature, fleeting. They rise, they peak, and then they fade, replaced by another in the endless cycle of human experience. Remembering this can help us avoid making impulsive decisions that might impact our long-term objectives.

Secondly, we must cultivate the skill of emotional detachment when making significant decisions. This doesn't mean ignoring our emotions. Instead, it's about acknowledging them and then making a conscious decision to act in a way that best serves our long-term interests.

So the next time you feel a strong emotion nudging you towards a hasty decision, take a pause. Remember that this feeling is temporary, and it's your future at stake. Prioritize wisely. After all, it's not just about surviving the storms, but learning to sail your ship to your chosen horizon.

— DAY 329 —

Take advantage of other people's work

A T first glance, the idea of taking advantage of someone else's work may raise eyebrows and evoke thoughts of exploitation.

Imagine you're tasked with building a car from scratch. Not just any car, but a technologically advanced electric vehicle. Now, how would you go about it? Would you start by discovering how to make rubber for the tires, or mine and refine metals for the body? That would take you years, maybe even decades! Here's the thing. You don't have to do that, because that knowledge already exists thanks to the tireless work of others.

This concept is true not only for physical creation but also for intellectual and creative work. Consider writing a novel. Would you begin by inventing a new language? Of course not. You'd use the language that others have developed and refined over centuries, infusing it with your unique voice to create something new.

Let's step into the world of science. Every ground-breaking research paper builds upon the work of previous scientists. Even Sir Isaac Newton, one of the greatest minds of our species, famously said, "If I have seen further, it is by standing on the shoulders of giants." Here, "giants" are the intellectual predecessors whose work paved the way for his discoveries.

This perspective isn't about stealing or exploitation, it's about leveraging the cumulative progress of humanity. It's about standing on the shoulders of those who came before us and pushing the boundaries even further. It's about acknowledging and appreciating the collective wisdom, hard work, and creativity of those who paved the path we're walking on today.

You don't need to start from scratch. Look to the work of others—not to copy, but to inspire, to challenge, to spark the flame of your own unique idea. It's about recognizing that we are all links in the grand chain of knowledge, each building upon the last, propelling humanity forward one idea at a time.

— DAY 330 —

The root of procrastination is a fear of success

N ORMALLY we'd align procrastination with laziness, lack of time management, or just plain disinterest. However, a more profound, unexplored cause lurks beneath the surface, an idea that may seem paradoxical at first glance—the fear of success.

Let's entertain this thought. Imagine you're sitting on a brilliant idea for a novel, and you're more than capable of writing it. But you find yourself constantly deferring the task, inventing excuses, and letting days turn into months. You're procrastinating, sure, but why? Is it just laziness or is there something deeper lurking in the shadows of your subconscious?

Success, on the face of it, looks enticing with its promise of recognition, satisfaction, and sometimes even wealth. But with success also comes change, and that's where the fear creeps in. We are creatures of habit, hardwired to resist change. Even if it's positive, change can be scary. And that's because it takes us into the unknown.

Imagine, if your novel becomes a bestseller, your life would change. You might face public attention, demands on your time and privacy, and expectations for your next piece. Could it be that, subconsciously, you're stalling to avoid this potential shift in your reality? Then there's the fear of failing after succeeding. Once you've tasted success, the fall feels much harder and steeper. What if your second novel isn't as successful? What if people think you're a one-hit-wonder? The fear of not maintaining success can be paralyzing, triggering procrastination before you've even begun.

And finally, there's the fear of outshining others. It's called the *Tall Poppy Syndrome*. Some of us worry that by achieving success, we'll attract resentment or make others feel inferior, so, we hold ourselves back.

Could our procrastination be a defense mechanism, a subconscious attempt to protect ourselves from the dangers that we believe success could bring? It's a radical idea, but it holds water. The next time you find yourself procrastinating, instead of scolding yourself for being lazy or undisciplined, dig a little deeper.

— DAY 331 —

Work hard, leave your mark

I T'S a phrase that resonates with a call to action, echoing with the primal urge to carve out our path and leave a legacy that speaks our name long after we are gone. We live in an era of instant gratification and fleeting attention spans, yet there is something undeniably timeless and enduring about the idea of working hard and leaving our mark.

Consider the work we do. Not just our jobs, but every act, every decision, every relationship we cultivate. It is a testament to our existence. It is our sculpture, our painting, our lyric poem in the vast gallery of life. But to make that mark, we must first understand the value of hard work, for it is the chisel that shapes our legacy.

The glamour often associated with success overshadows the hard work it necessitates. The countless hours, relentless dedication, and resilience in the face of failures—all these create the foundation on which success is built. But it's not just about achieving success. It's about the journey, the process, and the grit it takes to keep going when the going gets tough.

The paradox here is that while hard work often goes unseen, it leaves the most lasting mark. Consider the Pyramids of Egypt or the Great Wall of China, colossal achievements of human endurance and dedication. They stand the test of time, symbols of the incredible power of hard work.

In a more personal sense, think of the impression left by a dedicated teacher, a committed parent, or a passionate artist. Their hard work might not be visible in the everyday, but the mark they leave is profound. It shapes lives, alters trajectories, and even redefines what's possible.

The reality, however, is that our society often mistakes noise for significance and confuses visibility for value. The loudest voice in the room is not necessarily the most influential. The most flashy character is not always the most memorable. It's the work that we do, the dedication we show, and the legacy we leave that truly counts. Leaving your mark is not about carving your name on a trophy or a plaque.

— DAY 332 —

Allow time to heal your wounds

A T one point or another, each of us has experienced wounds—deep, painful ones, the kind that threatens to tear us apart. These wounds may be physical, but more often than not, they are emotional or psychological, inflicted by traumas, heartbreaks, losses, or disappointments. In the aftermath of such pain, it might seem that life has lost its color, its vibrancy. Yet, as a timeless healer, time, steps in to repair our broken hearts and spirits.

Time, they say, heals all wounds. It is a cliche we have heard so often that ´ it might seem banal, even hollow, especially in the depths of our suffering. Yet, there is an undeniably profound truth encapsulated in these words—a truth as old as life itself. Time is not simply the ticking of a clock or the turning of a calendar page. It is a complex, ceaseless process of transformation and renewal.

In the realm of the physical, time orchestrates a symphony of cellular repair and regeneration, healing cuts and fractures. Emotionally, it works on a subtler, deeper level. It does not erase the pain—some wounds are too deep for oblivion—but it softens the edges of our hurt, weakens our grief, and slowly changes the hue of our heartbreak from a piercing, stark red to a softer, manageable shade.

The healing power of time is not a passive process. It does not simply happen to us. It requires our active participation. It demands that we bravely confront our pain, that we embrace and understand it instead of denying or repressing it. It requires patience, acceptance, and the courage to let go, to move on.

As we journey through the labyrinth of our grief, time provides us with the tools to rebuild ourselves. It offers us perspective, allowing us to see our wounds as part of our journey rather than our destination. It grants us resilience, helping us realize that we are stronger and more capable than we thought possible.

Wounds are inevitable. They leave scars, unforgettable marks that map our journeys and growth. Time, with its gentle, unstoppable rhythm, mends these wounds, transforming them into badges of survival, resilience, and wisdom.

— DAY 333 —

Social media is a comfort zone

I T'S an odd thought. We think of comfort zones as our favorite cozy corners in our homes or the warm familiarity of routines. At its core, isn't comfort about the ease and familiarity that something brings?

Let's travel back in time, to when we had only landlines, letters, and faceto-face meet-ups. Connection, in its rawest form, demanded effort, patience, and courage. Striking up a conversation with a stranger or maintaining a longdistance relationship was no small accomplishment.

Fast forward to the era of social media, and everything has changed. You can now communicate with someone halfway across the globe with a single tap. Strangers become "friends" at a click. But, what price do we pay for this convenience?

Social media, with its charm and convenience, can subtly turn into a comfort zone. It soothes us into the illusion of connection and interaction while buffering us from the authenticity of in-person experiences. It's easy to curate a life, put up a facade, and interact behind the safety of a screen.

Just as we favor our comfort zones, we favor social media. It's our go-to space for news, entertainment, and socializing. It's where we celebrate wins, share sorrows, and voice opinions. Yet, it's also where reality gets blurred with the reel, where genuine interactions get replaced with emoji reactions.

Getting out of our comfort zone is scary, right? It means stepping into the unknown, opening up to potential rejection, failure, or embarrassment. The same goes for stepping out of the comfort of social media.

Growth, innovation, and genuine relationships—they all lie outside the comfort zone. The same can be said for social media. Outside of it lies raw, unfiltered, personal experiences. It's where authentic relationships are forged, where critical thinking thrives, and where we truly live.

In a nutshell, social media, like anything else, has its ups and downs. Let's remember to disconnect to connect, step into the real world, and dare to step out of our digital comfort zones. Because that's where life happens, right outside of our comfort zone.

— DAY 334 —

Fail forward with enthusiasm

FAILURE. It's a word that often brings up feelings of disappointment, shame, and fear. We're conditioned to avoid failure at all costs, to strive for perfection and success without any setbacks. But what if I told you that failure is not the end, but a launchpad towards greatness?

The way I see it, life is a bit like a game of pinball. We launch ourselves into the game with high energy and bright-eyed hope, aiming for the highest score. We hit a few targets, score some points, but inevitably, we also hit bumpers, flippers, and sometimes we end up right down in the drain. Each hit, each stumble, it's akin to a failure in life. But the beautiful part? Each failure propels us forward, back into the game, with a new opportunity to score.

You see, we've got failure all wrong. Our society paints it as this ghastly ghost, haunting our dreams and aspirations. But what if we chose to see failure not as a stop sign but as a detour or a reroute, leading us down a path we hadn't initially considered? Each failure, then, becomes a stepping-stone, a catapult, launching us further toward our goals and our true potential.

Now, let's talk about that second part—with enthusiasm. Picture this: you're playing that game of pinball, you've just taken a hit, and you're flying back into the game. You have two choices. You can either face this next round with dread and fear of another hit, or you can embrace it with enthusiasm, seeing it as another shot at hitting your targets.

Is it easy? Enthusiasm is like a magic potion here. It allows us to find joy in the journey, not just the destination. It helps us develop a "growth mindset," an understanding that ability and success can be achieved through dedication and hard work. Failure, then, is no longer our foe but our tutor, teaching us resilience, patience, and the power of perseverance.

Let's not fear it, dread it, or avoid it. Let's fail forward and let's do it with unrelenting enthusiasm. Because in the end, it's not the failure that defines us, but how we rise from it.

— DAY 335 —

Short parental disapproval or long-term misery?

A S individuals, we often find ourselves torn between societal expectations and our desires. We desire the approval and acceptance of our parents, wanting to make them proud. But what if I told you that sacrificing our own happiness for the sake of parental approval can lead to long-term misery?

On one side, there's the sacredness of the bond we share with our parents, the deep-rooted respect, and the unspoken agreement to honor their hopes and expectations. You know, it's funny how we, as children, are innately wired to seek approval from our parents. It's almost like our happiness is somehow interconnected with their smiles, their nods of agreement, their pats of appreciation. And the thought of disrupting that harmony with our divergent choices often sends chills down our spines

On the other side, there's the appeal of authenticity, the freedom to express, explore, to become who you truly are. Isn't it equally important, or dare I say, even more critical? After all, this is your life, your journey. Shouldn't you be the one holding the reins, deciding the path, making the choices?

Choosing your path doesn't necessarily mean disregarding your parents or their wishes. It doesn't mean stepping on their dreams as you chase yours. No. It means having an open, honest conversation with them, helping them understand your perspective, your passion, and your vision for your own life.

Will it be easy? Probably not. Change rarely is. But would you rather face that challenging, perhaps even painful, conversation now or live a lifetime of regret and dissatisfaction, wondering "what if?"

The truth is, short parental disapproval is far better than long-term misery. It's not a pleasant choice, but it's a necessary one. It requires courage, openness, and sometimes, a willingness to stand alone. But, at the end of the day, your life is your story. And you should be the one writing it, even if the pen trembles in your hand as you do.

— DAY 336 —

Life is essentially an endless series of problems

FROM the moment we enter this world, we are confronted with challenges, big and small. It starts with learning how to walk, then evolves into solving complex equations, navigating relationships, and facing existential dilemmas. Problems are an inseparable part of our existence.

We're problem solvers by nature, you and I. It's one of the things that makes us human. From the moment we open our eyes in the morning to the moment we close them at night, we're solving problems. It's part of the very fabric of our existence. From "What am I going to wear today?" to "How can I secure a future for myself and my loved ones?" it's all problem-solving, all the time.

Some individuals may perceive this as overwhelming. It's essential to remember that feelings are transient, and any sense of being overwhelmed will eventually shift. Each obstacle or challenge presented by life provides an opportunity for growth, education, and self-improvement.

Problems, in this light, become less about the struggle and more about the victory that lies beyond them. They become less about the fear of failure and more about the joy of accomplishment. They become less about the roadblock and more about the journey.

And the endless series of problems life throws at us? It's the world's toughest training program, designed to bring out the best in us, to shape us into capable, resilient, extraordinary beings.

Life progresses through a sequence of problems, with each solution naturally leading to new challenges. This cycle signifies ongoing growth and learning, as each solution paves the way for new, more sophisticated issues to tackle.

Next time you find yourself standing in front of a locked door, a problem that seems invincible, remember this: You are a problem solver. You are built for this. And with every problem you overcome, you become a little bit stronger, a little bit wiser, and a whole lot more capable. After all, life is an endless series of problems.

— DAY 337 —

Do not restrict yourself

T HESE four words have a profound depth of meaning. As human beings, we often find ourselves confined within the limitations we place on ourselves. We create mental barriers, believing that we are incapable, undeserving, or unworthy of reaching our fullest potential.

Imagine for a moment an invisible thread connecting all human endeavors—art, science, philosophy, exploration, and everything in between. What keeps this thread tight is not conformity or adherence to rules, but the limitless potential of the human spirit. Think of the masters in any field. Picasso did not restrict himself to traditional techniques or forms, Einstein did not limit his thought experiments to the realm of the observable, and Amelia Earhart did not confine herself to a "woman's place." They all dared to color outside the lines.

At the heart of this concept is a deep-rooted trust in our capacities. So often, we limit ourselves due to the fear of failure, the fear of judgment, and the fear of standing out from the crowd. Yet, the seeds of greatness are sown in the soil of self-belief. Without the courage to make mistakes, to risk appearing foolish, to be the lone voice in a wilderness of conformity, how can we ever truly realize our potential?

Yes, each of us is born into a world of physical laws and societal norms. We cannot fly unaided, nor should we seek to disrupt social harmony without cause. But we must distinguish these fundamental restrictions from the psychological barricades we erect within our minds. These are not unbreakable walls but insubstantial curtains, and they part at the slightest touch of determined selfbelief.

Please, do not restrict yourself. The universe is wide and full of wonders, and you are a creature of infinite potential. Let your thoughts be free, let your heart be open, let your actions be bold. Dance to the beat of your own drum. Embrace the glorious mess that you are. Only by doing so can we uncover our true selves, and leave a meaningful imprint on this wondrous experience we call life.

— DAY 338 —

Fault and responsibility are not the same

W HEN something goes wrong, it's natural for us to look for someone to blame. We want to assign fault, to pinpoint the cause of the problem. We tend to view fault and responsibility through the same lens, perceiving them as synonymous. But, when dissected and analyzed, these two concepts provide a profound insight into the human psyche, and the role we play in our own lives.

Consider fault. It's a word that brings to mind blame, guilt, and wrongdoing. We assign fault when something goes wrong, or when an action has led to a negative outcome. The person at fault is perceived as the cause of the problem. But herein lies the subtlety—being at fault is usually related to a specific past action or event. It's historical, often singular, and unchangeable.

Now, shift your focus to responsibility. It's not about blame, but rather about ownership and accountability. Unlike fault, responsibility isn't confined to the past. It stretches forward into the present and future. Responsibility is about taking charge, deciding to make things right, and looking for solutions. It's not about dwelling on past mistakes, but about learning from them and making efforts to correct the course.

To illustrate, imagine you're walking on a sidewalk and trip over an uneven pavement. Is it your fault? No, the fault lies with whoever was in charge of maintaining the pavement. But who's responsible for your response to the fall, and your subsequent actions? You are. You have the choice to dwell in self-pity, complain about the uneven pavement, or get up, dust yourself off, and perhaps even report the hazard so others don't trip.

That's the core of the distinction—fault is about the cause, and responsibility is about the response. This understanding can have transformative implications for our lives. You may not be at fault for the circumstances life has dealt you, but you are responsible for how you deal with them. You are responsible for your actions, your emotions, and your future.

Understanding the difference between fault and responsibility empowers us. It takes us away from a mindset of blame and victimhood, and places us firmly in a position of control and agency over our own lives.

— DAY 339 —

If you want to change the world, start with yourself

IT'S natural for us to look at the world and wish for change. We desire a better future, for a world filled with compassion, equality, and harmony. We often imagine changing the world as a Herculean task, reserved for the likes of presidents, philanthropists, and pioneering scientists. But the truth is that we hold the power of change within us. The world is not just an entity that exists out there; it is an interconnected network of human experiences and actions, in which we all participate. Our actions, no matter how insignificant they seem, contribute to the world's story.

Every great movement, every remarkable transformation throughout history has begun with individuals who chose to cultivate change within themselves. Mahatma Gandhi once said, "Be the change you wish to see in the world." These words resonate with the profound truth that true change starts from within.

We must not underestimate the power we wield when we decide to make a change in ourselves. Think of the energy we put into the world when we decide to be more compassionate, to listen more, to judge less. Consider how our habits can shape the environment around us. Choosing to reduce, reuse, and recycle can create a substantial impact on our planet. When we begin with ourselves, we set in motion a wave of change that can cascade and influence others.

Changing ourselves is not about striving for unattainable perfection, but about striving to be better, to do better. It's about becoming aware of our actions and our impact on others and the world around us. It's about aligning our actions with our values and making decisions that reflect who we want to be and the world we want to live in.

A simple act of kindness, an honest word of encouragement, a stand against injustice—all these are seeds of change, sown in the fertile soil of our everyday lives. If we all start with ourselves, imagine the forest of change we could grow. It's often said that a journey of a thousand miles begins with a single step. Well, changing the world starts with changing yourself.

— DAY 340 —

Live below your means

L IVING below your means is a concept that may seem counterintuitive in a society that constantly encourages us to seek more, to accumulate wealth, and to give into extravagant lifestyles. In our world that thrives on wealth, the statement may seem like a piece of advice from a forgotten era. Yet, if you peel away its surface of simplicity, it unveils profound wisdom that holds the key to financial freedom and genuine contentment.

The principle's magic lies not in the scarcity it implies but in the abundance it ultimately creates. It's not about denying yourself all of life's pleasures. Instead, it's about giving yourself the greatest pleasure of all—peace of mind. In an age of consumerism where advertisements shout at us to buy more, to own more, to be more, choosing to live below your means is an act of quiet rebellion. It's about unshackling yourself from the chains of unnecessary debt and the anxiety of living paycheck to paycheck.

Living below your means opens up a world of possibilities. It allows you to save and invest, laying the foundation for financial independence and stability. It opens the door to experiences you may have thought were beyond your reach—starting a business, going back to school, taking a break, or even retiring early.

It's not about frugality for frugality's sake. It's about realizing that life's quality is not measured in the accumulation of things but in the richness of experiences, the strength of relationships, and the fulfillment of purpose. It's about distinguishing between what we want and what we need, and finding joy and satisfaction in the things that truly matter.

Choosing to live below your means shows you've got grit. It takes discipline, resilience, and the guts to say "No" in a world pressuring you to constantly say "Yes." It plants the seeds for a life of financial security, freeing you to live your life, your way.

The concept might seem radical, but once you've tasted the liberation that comes with living below your means, you'll realize it's not about limiting life. It's about living life limitless.

— DAY 341 —

Self-deception is the ultimate betrayal

WHEN we think of betrayal, we often imagine someone else deceiving us, breaking our trust, and causing us pain. But what if I told you that the ultimate betrayal lies within ourselves? Self-deception is a silent betrayer that can have a deep impact on our lives and relationships.

Betrayal—it's an uncomfortable word. It reminds us of backstabbing, dishonesty, and a treacherous stab in the heart. And yet, the subtle art of selfdeception, deceiving the person you should know the best—yourself—well, isn't that the symbol of betrayal?

Self-deception, my friend, is an enticing mirage in the desert of self-knowledge. It's a seductive song luring us away from the path of authenticity and clarity. It may seem comfortable to dodge the painful truth, to hide behind lies, to weave complex narratives to escape the discomfort of confronting our imperfections. But this comfort is a facade, an illusion that slowly gnaws at our very essence.

Let me tell you something: self-deception doesn't solve problems; it simply delays the explosion. It's akin to plugging your ears to drown out the ticking bomb in the room. The truth, even if it's uncomfortable, even if it hurts, is still the truth. Burying it doesn't make it any less true. It merely weakens the ground beneath our feet, waiting for the moment to give away.

Lying to oneself isn't just lying. It's a denial of our human experience. It's a refusal to acknowledge our flaws and our growth potential. It robs us of the chance to learn, to adapt, to become a better version of ourselves.

The path out of self-deception is a journey of courage. It's about embracing vulnerability and opening our hearts to our own weaknesses. It's about understanding that we are, at the end of the day, humans—beautifully flawed, infinitely complex, and wonderfully unique.

In the battle between truth and comfort, it's crucial to choose truth. Not just for the sake of honesty, but for the sake of our growth, our authenticity, and our self-respect. Remember, no deception can be as heartbreaking, as crushing, or as shattering as the deception that comes from within.

— DAY 342 —

You'll hurt someone eventually

F IRST things first, it's important to acknowledge that as human beings, we are imperfect creatures. No matter how well-intentioned or kind-hearted we may be, we are bound to hurt someone at some point in our lives. It's a natural part of the human experience, for we are all vulnerable to making mistakes, being thoughtless, or inadvertently crossing boundaries.

Everyone, no matter how moral or compassionate, will inevitably cause hurt to someone else in their journey. This pain may take the form of sharp words spoken in the heat of an argument, broken promises due to unforeseen circumstances, or perhaps the simple yet profound hurt that comes from not being there when needed. This is not a judgment of character, nor a damning prediction, but a reality of our imperfect human nature.

At our core, we are beings of emotion, and these emotions, as beautiful as they can be, also have the capacity to wound deeply. But let's flip the narrative a little. Consider this: Isn't it the very possibility of causing hurt that also allows us to cherish, love, and respect others?

The very same emotional complexity that enables us to cause pain also grants us the power to heal, comfort, and uplift. The possibility of hurt is not a villain to be feared, but rather, a strange ally that underscores the importance of empathy, kindness, and respect in our interactions.

Life, in its simplest form, is a series of connections. These connections are not always smooth; they are filled with missteps, misunderstandings, and, yes, hurt. However, they are also filled with moments of understanding, connection, and love. The understanding that we can cause pain should not paralyze us, but rather, motivate us to strive for greater empathy, to pause before we act, to consider our words, and to seek to heal when we have caused hurt.

Knowing that we can inflict pain shouldn't freeze us in our tracks, but rather encourage us to pause before we react, think before we speak, and always try to repair the hurt we've caused. We are bound to hurt someone eventually, just as we're bound to feel hurt. But it's how we deal with this inevitable truth that reveals our character

— DAY 343 —

In the book of life, the answers aren't at the back

I N our journey of life, we often find ourselves grappling with deep questions about purpose, meaning, love, loss, success, and failure. We might search tirelessly for definitive answers, like a student thumbing through the back of a textbook for solutions.

Life, unlike a well-structured book or carefully designed experiment, does not provide us with neat, one-size-fits-all answers. It is an intricate, multilayered narrative woven with threads of experiences, emotions, and interactions, filled with unexpected twists, unpredictable turns, and moments of exhilaration and despair. It's a journey, not a math problem to be solved.

The questions life poses are not meant to be answered quickly or definitively. Instead, they are prompts, invitations for us to embark on journeys of exploration and discovery, to navigate the labyrinthine corridors of the human experience, to peel back layers of reality, and to uncover the countless complexities beneath.

We must understand that life's questions are not a test or a puzzle to be solved. They are an integral part of our narrative, shaping our worldview, fueling our growth, and enriching our human experience. They encourage us to probe, ponder, and reflect.

Rather than flipping to the back of the book in search of ready-made answers, we must learn to relish the process of exploration and discovery, to cherish the questions themselves. The German poet Rainer Maria Rilke once advised a young talent to "live the questions now," suggesting that we might gradually, without even noticing it, "live along some distant day into the answer."

In the grand narrative of life, each chapter, each page turn, brings us closer to understanding, to wisdom, to our unique truths. The answers we seek may not be neatly spelled out at the back of the book, but they are there, hidden in plain sight, inscribed in the very fabric of our experiences. It's not about finding answers, but living the questions.

— DAY 344 —

Clean up your mess

L IFE can be messy. We navigate through a labyrinth of challenges, setbacks, and mistakes, leaving behind a trail of chaos. It's easy to become overwhelmed, to let the mess pile up until it feels insurmountable. We all make mistakes.

We stumble, we fall, and sometimes we even crash and burn. It's a natural part of the human experience. But what sets us apart is how we handle those moments of messiness. Do we let them define us, or do we rise above them and take responsibility for our actions?

Cleaning up our mess begins with self-awareness. It's about facing our shortcomings, acknowledging our mistakes, and taking ownership of the chaos we've created. It requires humility, honesty, and the willingness to confront the uncomfortable truths about ourselves. It's not an easy task, but it's a necessary one if we want to grow and evolve.

Cleaning up our mess also involves forgiveness—both of ourselves and others. We must learn to let go of the guilt, the shame, and the resentment that can weigh us down. By forgiving ourselves, we create space for healing and growth. By forgiving others, we break free from the chains of bitterness and open ourselves up to new possibilities.

But cleaning up our mess goes beyond the personal realm. It extends to our relationships, our communities, and our planet. We live in a world that is in dire need of cleaning up. It's a world plagued by inequality, injustice, and environmental degradation.

Cleaning up this collective mess requires collective action. It demands that we confront the uncomfortable truths about systemic issues, challenge the status quo, and work towards a more equitable and sustainable future. It calls for empathy, compassion, and a commitment to creating positive change.

And you know what? This process of tidying up changes us. It's like polishing a rough stone, each rub, each moment of friction, revealing a little more of the shine underneath. The mess, the process of cleaning it, it's all part of our evolution, our journey towards becoming the best versions of ourselves.

— DAY 345 —

Either you control your day or the day controls you

H AVE you ever had one of those days where it feels like everything is out of your control? Maybe you wake up late, spill coffee on your shirt, and get stuck in traffic on the way to work. By the time you arrive at your desk, you feel worn out and out of sorts, like you're already behind before the day has even begun. This is a stark reality, and it bounces back with an unsettling yet empowering truth: Either you control your day, or the day controls you.

Our lives are comprised of an assortment of days, each oscillating with potentialities and challenges. You might envision each dawn as an untouched canvas, an unscripted scene, or an unread chapter. The palette is teeming with colors, the stage brims with props, and the pen hovers above the page. Yet, who holds the brush, directs the scene, or scripts the narrative? That's right, it's you.

A day left unchecked unfolds like a loose kite not bound by its string. It soars and swoops on the whims of the wind, with no apparent direction or purpose. This is a day controlling you, propelling you into a reactive mode where you become a passive participant, swaying to its rhythm, responding to its demands.

Now imagine a different scenario. You rise with the sun, a clear plan etched in your mind. Your objectives defined, priorities sorted, and distractions sidelined. This is not a day waiting to engulf you but a day waiting to be harnessed by you. A day where you don't merely respond but engage. You become the proactive puppet master, pulling the strings, and setting the pace. This is you controlling the day.

In controlling your day, you exercise your autonomy, channel your focus, and cultivate your path. Like a seasoned sailor, you navigate through the day's ebbs and flows, seizing opportunities, averting distractions, and driving toward your chosen horizon. Each sunset then leaves in its wake not a mere smattering of random events but a day imbued with meaning.

Let's be clear, though; controlling your day doesn't mean scripting every second. It means being flexible and adaptable, it means setting the course but adjusting the sails when necessary. It's about owning your journey.

— DAY 346 —

Travel as much as you can

T RAVEL opens the door to a world of possibilities, offering us a fresh perspective on life. It allows us to step outside our comfort zones, challenge our assumptions, and broaden our horizons. As we navigate unfamiliar streets, interact with different cultures, and immerse ourselves in new environments, we gain a deeper understanding of the world and our place in it.

Think of travel as the most intimate conversation you could ever have with the world. It's an opportunity to listen to the whispers of cultures, taste the secrets hidden in diverse cuisines, and touch the heartbeat of history pulsating within century-old architecture. The more you travel, the more fluent you become in this global dialect, a language that surpasses boundaries and merges hearts. How amazing is that?

But that's not all. Traveling is also a fantastic reality check, a humbling encounter that brings you face-to-face with the world's vastness and your tiny existence within it. You realize how the mountain you've been making of your worries is but a pebble in the grand scheme of things. This revelation is a liberating experience.

Now, let's dive deeper. Ever noticed how we often walk through life wearing a blindfold, ignoring the richness that surrounds us? Travel pulls this blindfold off. It sharpens your senses, it makes you see the colors you've been missing, hear the melodies you've been ignoring, and feel the textures you've been overlooking. It's an awakening, a rebirth even.

Pack your bags, strap on your shoes, and set out. Venture beyond the horizon, beyond the comfort of the known. Travel across the world, scale mountains, sail across seas, delve into forests, and roam cities. With each step, uncover a world that's waiting to share its secrets, and in the process, unearth your own hidden depths.

Dear friend, travel as far as you can, as much as you can. For in the grand theatre of life, every journey enriches the threads that weave your personal story. And isn't that the most thrilling adventure there is?

— DAY 347 —

Stop trying to change the unchangeable

IN our quest for control and perfection, we often overlook the beauty and power of acceptance. Acceptance is not a surrender, nor is it a sign of weakness. It is an act of wisdom and strength, a conscious choice to embrace the truth of what is and release the struggle against what cannot be altered.

Take a second and think about it. How often have you found yourself tangled up in something that, no matter how hard you push, just won't change? Maybe it's a person you're trying to form into your ideal, a past mistake you're hoping to erase, or a future you're attempting to predict. We've all been there, haven't we? Trying to change the unchangeable.

It's like standing at the shore, demanding the ocean to stop its waves. The ocean is going to do its thing, regardless of our attempts to command it. So why do we insist on fighting such a futile battle? We stubbornly try to shape the world around us according to our wishes, and when it doesn't bend, we feel defeated, frustrated, or even desperate. It's not the world that needs to change; it's our approach.

Remember how your parents used to tell you that you can't control others, only yourself? Well, they were onto something. It's about adapting, evolving, not just surviving, but thriving.

Let me paint a picture for you. Imagine you're in a boxing ring with an opponent who's stronger and faster. Would you drain yourself trying to match their strength or adapt your strategy to use their power against them? The answer seems clear when you put it like that, doesn't it?

It's time we stop clashing with the unchangeable and start dancing with it. Let it lead sometimes, and use its momentum to drive our movements. It's about accepting, embracing, and learning to navigate around the immovable objects in our path.

The truth is, life is a mix of changeable and unchangeable elements, a dance we need to learn the steps to. Once we stop resisting and start moving with the rhythm, we can achieve a graceful flow and navigate life with a little more ease and a lot less friction.

— DAY 348 —

Be the parent you wished you had or had

PARENTING, a sacred journey of nurturing and guiding a young life, comes with both challenges and joys. Being the parent you longed for—a source of love, support, and guidance. Someone who listens, understands, and nurtures. It's a chance to break the cycle, to create a new narrative for the generations to come.

Let me take you back to your childhood, to those mornings filled with the smells of pancakes, to the nights covered in stories and lullabies. Picture your parent—or perhaps their absence—the joys, the disappointments, the unconditional love, or the lessons learned through tough love. Now, imagine a life where you are in their place, holding a miniature hand, guiding a new life through this labyrinth we call the world.

Parenthood is not just a change of roles but a transformation of self. It's a challenge to shape a person, to guide them, all the while battling our own flaws, fears, and past experiences. However, instead of approaching it with anxiety, let's see it as a golden opportunity, a second chance if you will.

Being a parent is like being handed a lump of clay, still soft, still impressionable. And in our hands lies the ability to shape that clay, to smooth out the rough edges, to fill in the gaps that were perhaps left unfilled in our own upbringing.

Remember those times when you wished your parent understood you better? Be that understanding parent. Remember the times when you wished for a bit more freedom? Be the parent who knows when to let go. Remember the times when you longed for an affectionate hug or an encouraging word? Be that warm, reassuring presence.

However, do not forget to celebrate the good parts too. The warmth, the sacrifices, the patience, the love—replicate them, amplify them. Draw from the wealth of your own experiences, both the good and the challenging ones.

So folks, buckle up! Let's not just raise kids; let's raise them better, stronger, and happier. After all, we're not just creating the next generation, but the future of the world, one child at a time.

— DAY 349 —

Life is a mirror reflecting your inner world

CONSIDER the mirror. Reflective, transparent, and unflinchingly honest, it takes no prisoners in its relentless pursuit of truth. It casts back an image, capturing the physical realm in all its glory and all its horror. Now, take this mirror and elevate it beyond its physical limitations. Imagine it as a metaphysical entity, its reflective surface reaching deep into our core, capturing not our physical image but our inner self, our soul, our very essence. This is the mirror that life holds up to us.

A mirror merely reflects, it doesn't pass judgment. Thus, life, as a mirror, faithfully reflects the images projected by our thoughts, emotions, and beliefs. Each interaction, each experience, and every single manifestation of life around us is but a reflection of the universe within us. This statement is not poetic whimsy but a truth grounded in the fundamental laws of existence.

Our inner dialogue, the thoughts and beliefs we hold, the emotions we feel, the expectations we have from ourselves and the world; all have energetic vibrations that we radiate out into the universe. Life, the ever-faithful mirror, absorbs these vibrations and reflects situations, circumstances, and relationships that match the same frequency. If we are vibrating with happiness, peace, and love, life mirrors this back to us through joyful experiences, peaceful moments, and loving relationships.

However, if our inner world is a storm of negativity, if our thoughts are tangled with worry, if our hearts are heavy with bitterness, life will hold no quarter. It will reflect these back to us through adversities, through distress, through encounters tinged with acrimony.

Our existence, then, is a dance with the mirror of life. A dance where every move we make, every thought we harbor, every emotion we experience, finds a way to express itself on the dance floor of our existence. Understanding this dance and recognizing the mirror can lead to profound changes in our lives.

By consciously cultivating positivity, love, and compassion within us, we change our dance steps. We change the energy we release, and life, the faithful mirror, reflects these changes back to us, transforming our life experience.

— DAY 350 —

Attitude shapes success or failure

TWO individuals may face the same circumstances, encounter the same obstacles, and possess similar skills and talents. Yet, their attitudes will ultimately determine their paths. How we think, feel, and approach circumstances plays a huge role in the outcomes we generate.

Imagine you're standing on a high diving board, staring down into the pool. You're filled with anxiety, a sense of thrill, and maybe a bit of dread. You have a choice to make—to jump or to step back. Now, your attitude determines your next move and the splash it creates.

Think of life as that diving board. The difference between diving or retreating, between success or failure, is not necessarily the circumstances that confront us—it's how we approach them. You see, our attitude is the lens through which we view the world. It affects our perceptions, reactions, and interactions. It molds our decisions, propels our actions, and eventually sculpts our reality.

Let's say you want to start a business. If you approach it with a can-do attitude, seeing challenges as opportunities for growth, you set yourself up for success. Even if the business fails, you haven't. You've learned, grown, become stronger and wiser. In contrast, if you approach it with a fear of failure, seeing obstacles as insurmountable, you're setting yourself up for defeat. Even if the business succeeds, have you really succeeded? Or have you just added to your fear, creating a life of "what ifs" and "if onlys"?

This is the power of attitude. It's the sculptor of our lives. And just like any artist, we can choose what we create. We can shape our attitude, shape our actions, shape our outcomes. We can choose to see failures as stepping stones to success, and challenges as avenues for growth.

Are you ready to take the plunge, to shape your attitude, your success, and your life story? Remember, it's all in the attitude. Your journey towards success or failure doesn't kick off with a step; it kicks off with a mindset. Your mindset. Make your choice, shape it intentionally, and live it with passion. Because in the grand painting of life, your attitude is the brush that paints it all.

— DAY 351 —

Overthinking hinders progress

OVERTHINKING—we've all been there. It's like a whirlpool that engulfs our minds, trapping us in a never-ending cycle of analysis and doubt. We analyze every decision, every possibility, and every outcome until we're paralyzed by indecision.

Life's journey often presents us with challenging situations that require prompt action. However, sometimes, we find ourselves tangled in the cobwebs of our thoughts, analyzing every possible outcome, every potential risk, and every feasible solution. We tend to believe that by analyzing every detail and playing out every scenario, we are better preparing ourselves to handle the task at hand. But more often than not, we end up doing nothing. This is the paradox of overthinking.

Overthinking is like an aggressive weed in the garden of our minds, rapidly spreading and choking the healthy plants of decision-making and progress. It's a thief, robbing us of our time and emotional energy, and more importantly, our ability to act. And what's life, if not a series of actions?

Let's imagine you're a musician. You've been working on a piece for months. You want to make it perfect, so you keep tweaking, adding, removing, and revising. Weeks turn into months, months into years, and the piece remains unreleased. While the pursuit of perfection is admirable, there's a point where it hinders progress, suppresses creativity, and prevents us from sharing our talents with the world.

Overthinking is a clear sign of underdoing. Yes, you read that right. It's when we hesitate to step into the unknown, to take risks and make mistakes, that we start overthinking. We conjure up fears that only exist in our minds, ignoring the fact that it's okay to stumble, to falter, to fail even. It's through these experiences that we grow, evolve, and move forward.

Life, in all its complexity, doesn't come with a manual. It requires us to think on our feet, to adapt, to learn, and to act. Overthinking, with its whirlpool of "what ifs" and "should haves," inhibits this process. It's crucial to understand that thinking has its place, but it's action that breeds results.

— DAY 352 —

Success is no coincidence

W HAT is success? A climb to the peak of the corporate ladder? The acquisition of material wealth? Recognition, admiration, or perhaps a renowned legacy? The interpretations are manifold, as varied as the individuals envision it. However, in its universal essence, success is the realization of purpose, the manifestation of dreams, and the fulfillment of potential.

We might think it's all about luck or being in the right place at the right time, but that's not the case. Success is the result of intentional choices, steadfast dedication, and a burning desire to achieve something meaningful. It's about having a vision and taking consistent action to bring that vision to life.

To succeed is to shape landscape of dreams with elements of resilience, innovation, and tenacity. It is to sail the stormy seas of challenges, navigating through the tempest with the compass of self-belief, buoyed by the lifeboat of hard work. Success is the relentless pursuit of growth, the constant striving for improvement, and the courage to venture beyond the comfort zones.

Consider the biography of any successful person—inventors, athletes, entrepreneurs, artists. Their narratives are rife with instances of determination, hard work, persistence, and, above all, a steadfast belief in themselves. Did they find their success at the end of a rainbow, or was it the product of their blood, sweat, and tears?

For instance, consider the story of Airbnb. Its founders, Brian Chesky, Joe Gebbia, and Nathan Blecharczyk, faced skepticism and financial challenges, even resorting to selling cereal boxes to fund their venture. Despite these hurdles, their unwavering commitment to their innovative idea of home sharing transformed Airbnb into a global phenomenon. Their journey exemplifies how perseverance and belief in a vision can turn adversity into success.

And yet, the belief in the coincidental nature of success persists, often serving as a convenient excuse to avoid responsibility, justify inaction, and hide behind the veil of luck. But success cannot be wooed by idle dreams or wishful thinking. It demands action, persistence, and an unyielding will.

— DAY 353 —

Read

R EADING is not merely an activity; it is a gateway to endless possibilities. It is an opportunity to escape the boundaries of our own lives and submerge ourselves in new worlds, perspectives, and ideas. It is a journey of the mind, a way to expand our horizons and challenge our beliefs.

A child who reads is a child who is given the keys to the universe. A reader not only visits strange lands and meets the most fascinating characters, but also learns empathy, stepping into the shoes of those who are different, those who challenge our perceptions of "normality." They learn to suspend their disbelief, to question, to challenge, to explore. They build vocabulary, foster imagination, develop critical thinking skills, and learn about the world and their place within it. Reading is a gateway to empathy, to understanding, to a broader perspective.

Meanwhile, consider the adult who reads. In the words, phrases, ideas, and narratives, they find mirrors, windows, and doors. Mirrors that reflect their own experiences and validate their existence. Windows that offer glimpses of lives different from their own, expanding their horizons. Doors that open to new ideas, perspectives, and possibilities. Reading as an adult is an act of selfdiscovery and an exploration of humanity.

Reading, too, is a form of resistance. In a world consumed by instant gratification, where information is bite-sized and engagement is fleeting, to sit down with a book is a disruptive act. It demands patience, concentration, and dedication.

Finally, let's not forget that reading is a form of connection. In the solitary act of reading, we are paradoxically connected to the multitude. We are part of a silent, invisible fellowship of readers who, across time and space, have shared the same experience, lived within the same pages, walked the same literary paths.

Read. One simple word, yet it signifies an invitation to a journey of infinite possibilities, a command to engage deeply with our world, and a mantra that fosters growth, empathy, understanding, and connection.

— DAY 354 —

Your diet mirrors your self-view

E VERY bite we take, every sip we enjoy, narrates a silent yet profound story of our innermost beliefs about ourselves. For many, food is not merely about satiating hunger, but it's a reflection of their self-worth, discipline, aspirations, and sometimes, even their struggles. Beyond the simple act of consuming food, our dietary choices shape not only our physical health but also our mental and emotional well-being. It is a reminder that the fuel we provide our bodies has a profound impact on our overall vitality and the expression of our true selves.

The food we consume becomes the building blocks of our bodies, fueling every cell, organ, and system within us. It's a concept that goes beyond the physical, extending to our mental, emotional, and even spiritual well-being.

Imagine biting into a ripe, juicy apple. It's fresh, it's sweet, it's filled with vitamins. Now reflect upon this: the moment you eat that apple, its nutrients begin to mix with your cells. That apple is now a part of you. You've quite literally just become what you ate.

It's about how your food choices affect your mood, your energy levels, and even how you think. You know those days when you're feeling low, and all you want to do is eat ice cream? Then you do, and for a moment you feel better, but later you feel sluggish, maybe even a bit down again. That's your food influencing your mood.

And there's another layer to this food story. What you eat often reflects how you view yourself. Ever noticed when you're feeling good about yourself, you tend to reach for healthier options? But when you're down, the sugary, processed foods seem way more appealing. Your diet is like a mirror, reflecting your self-esteem, and your self-worth. It is not just some health guru's mantra.

It's a powerful insight into how our choices shape our bodies, our minds, and our feelings. Every bite is a chance to nourish your body, boost your mood, and show yourself some love. So, go on, and make a choice that will make your body feel good. Remember, you're not just eating food, you're eating your future. Now, isn't that food for thought?

— DAY 355 —

Hard choices, easy life

CONSIDER this: a fork in the road, two paths ahead. One is well-trodden, simple, and easy. The other is rough, steep, and strewn with obstacles. You've got a choice, but which way do you go? The easy way promises comfort, the hard way promises struggle. But I'll tell you a secret: it's the hard choices that make for an easy life.

Now, don't get me wrong. I'm not saying you have to suffer now to be happy later. Rather, think of it as a trade-off. Choosing the steep, rocky path instead of the well-worn trail might seem daunting, but it's this decision to face challenges head-on that shapes us, shapes us, and brings out the best in us.

Take a star athlete, for instance. Imagine the discipline, the grueling training sessions, and all those missed parties. Choosing the path of discipline and focus isn't a walk in the park. But hey, when they're standing on the podium, basking in the glory of their success, I bet they'd say it was worth every bead of sweat.

Or what about starting a new business or even ending a toxic relationship? Sure, these decisions can be terrifying and loaded with uncertainty. But man, when you come out on the other side, it's like breathing fresh air for the first time. You've got newfound freedom, emotional health, and a sense of achievement that no easy choice could ever give you.

But you know, life isn't always about the big decisions. Sometimes, it's the small daily choices that pile up over time, like choosing to exercise, eat healthily, or even make time for people you love. Sure, it might be hard to get off that comfy couch, but in the long run, these choices lead to a healthier, happier life.

Embrace the hard choices. Because, at the end of the day, it's the hard choices that form an easy life, a life that's a breathtaking panorama, not just a limited view. It's hard choices that give you stories to tell, not just days to live. Are you ready to choose the hard path?

— DAY 356 —

Why shouldn't it be you?

WE live in a world full of possibilities, where success knows no boundaries. Yet, many of us hesitate to take that leap of faith, doubting our abilities and questioning whether we're worthy of achieving greatness. You are just as capable as anyone else. There is no valid reason why it shouldn't be you who achieves your dreams.

So often, we're weighed down by self-doubt, haunted by the specter of failure, and inhibited by a deep-seated fear of disappointment. We view success as a remote island, accessible only to the privileged few while we're left stranded on the shores of mediocrity. But here's a question, a little seed of thought to plant in the fertile soil of your mind—Why shouldn't it be you who bridges the chasm between mediocrity and excellence?

Why shouldn't it be you who pens the next bestselling novel, discovers the next groundbreaking scientific theory, or pioneers the next revolutionary technological innovation? Why shouldn't it be you who stands atop the podium, bathing in the golden glow of success and accomplishment? After all, every successful person, every achiever, every dreamer-turned-doer, started where you are right now—on the edge of possibility, fueled by the fires of ambition.

What separates them from the rest is not some mystical gift, not some divine touch of genius, but a powerful mixture of perseverance, resilience, and steadfast self-belief. They dared to ask, "Why shouldn't it be me?" and answered with a resounding, "Why not indeed?"

Every wall that stands between you and your dreams, every barrier that seems insurmountable, can crumble under the power of your will. Each failure, each setback, and each stumbling block is but a stepping stone on the path to success. Your dreams are not castles in the air, but foundations waiting to be built upon.

Don't let fear hold you back. Take risks, try new things, and embrace the unknown. Embrace the journey, knowing that growth and transformation happen outside of your comfort zone. Believe in yourself and your abilities, for that belief is the foundation of your success.

— DAY 357 —

Pay yourself first

Y OU'RE on a plane and the flight attendant instructs you to put on your oxygen mask first before assisting others. At first, it may seem counterintuitive, as our instinct is often to help others before ourselves. But the rationale is simple: If you don't take care of yourself first, you won't be in a position to help anyone else. The same principle applies to your financial well-being.

Let's think about this in financial terms. When you get a paycheck, what's the first thing you do? Do you immediately pay your bills, buy groceries, cover your rent, and maybe treat your friends? If you're like most people, you probably do. And by the end of it all, there's often not much left for you. This is where the concept of "paying yourself first" comes into play.

The idea is simple: before you pay your bills or buy anything, you set aside a portion for yourself—you save it, invest it, or use it to improve your skills or well-being. It's a commitment to your future self, a commitment to growing your wealth and expanding your horizons. It's a commitment to ensuring your financial health and freedom.

Now, let's extrapolate this concept beyond just money. What if you "paid" yourself first with time, energy, or care? What if, instead of rushing into the demands of the day, you took a few moments each morning for meditation, a walk, or reading a book? What if you prioritized your mental and physical health, your personal growth, your dreams, and your passions?

Too often, we get caught up in the hustle and bustle of life, fulfilling responsibilities and meeting expectations of others, that we forget to care for ourselves. We forget that to be of value to others, we must first value ourselves.

This is the broader, deeper meaning of "pay yourself first." This isn't about being selfish; it's about being self-respectful. So give it a go. Because when it comes down to it, you're the most valuable investment you'll ever make. Trust me on this.

— DAY 358 —

There is no get-rich elevator in life

A vast majority of people live this way—always in search of shortcuts, hoping to find that elusive express elevator to success and wealth. But let me tell you a little secret: there is no get-rich elevator in life. What we have instead are the stairs and climbing them is what truly defines our journey to success. They are the result of hard work, persistence, and dedication over a long period of time.

In today's fast-paced and instant-gratification culture, it's easy to fall into the trap of looking for shortcuts to success. We're bombarded with messages that promise quick and easy wealth, often through questionable means such as get-rich-quick schemes or gambling.

Picture this: a grand, winding staircase, each step representing a challenge, a lesson, or an opportunity for growth. Now, imagine yourself at the bottom, looking up. It's daunting, isn't it? Every step you take, every ounce of effort you put in, brings you closer to your goals. And the view from the top? Absolutely breathtaking.

I can already hear you say, "What about those stories of overnight success? The lottery winners and the tech geniuses who make millions seemingly out of nowhere?" Well, let me tell you, those are the exceptions, not the rule. And even then, behind every so-called "overnight success" lies years of hard work, dedication, and persistence. It's just that we don't always see the whole picture.

In this light, the difficult staircase of life becomes not a burden, but a source of empowerment. As we ascend each step, we are gifted with invaluable lessons and experiences that shape our character and refine our abilities. This iterative process of growth and self-discovery is what ultimately propels us toward the pinnacle of our aspirations.

As we climb the staircase of success, we come to understand that the true value of our journey lies not in the wealth or accolades we accumulate, but in the person we become along the way.

— DAY 359 —

Time rental is not going to make you rich

THE construct of society often drives us towards the illusion that the only avenue to wealth is through renting our time. In the hustle and bustle of modern life, time seems to slip through our fingers like grains of sand. This might seem a little contradictory, especially if you've been told that the key to riches lies in working longer hours, and getting those big paychecks, right? But let's take a little detour today. After all, if time is so valuable, why not try to monetize it?

A conventional route is to secure a well-paying job, work for the stipulated hours, and receive a paycheck at the end of the month. It's predictable, secure, and most importantly, it's familiar. But pause and consider, in this cycle of time-for-money trade-off, what happens when you stop trading your time? The money stream dries up, doesn't it? Therein lies the crux of the problem.

This isn't to dismiss the importance of employment or the dignity of labor. It's about understanding the constraints of linear income, where your earnings are directly proportional to your hours worked.

However, shift your gaze to the richest people around the globe. You'll find a different story; their wealth is often not tied directly to their time. They build systems, create assets, invest, and innovate. These are avenues that generate wealth, even when they aren't actively engaged in them. It's about passive income, money that flows in whether you are clocked in or not.

Look at Steve Jobs, whose wealth didn't come from renting out his time but from creating assets like the iPhone and iPad, which continued to generate income long after their initial release. Similarly, consider George Lucas, whose fortune doesn't hinge on hourly wages but on the creation of the Star Wars franchise, an asset that has spawned movies, merchandise, and spin-offs, providing a continuous stream of wealth and income.

Your time is valuable, but if your wealth is solely dependent on it, you're on a hamster wheel. Breaking away from this model to create, invest, and build is where the path to true wealth lies. To put it in perspective, remember, no one ever got rich simply by renting out their time.

— DAY 360 —

You're replaceable

I N a world of billions of people, each with their unique talents and capabilities, it's essential to acknowledge that no one is truly irreplaceable. We all play different roles, contribute in various ways, and leave our mark on the world. But at the same time, we must recognize that the world will go on even when we're no longer a part of it.

Now, where's the comfort in being replaceable, you might ask. It sounds bleak, a bit of a downer, doesn't it? But imagine for a moment the weight off your shoulders when you realize that the world will indeed continue spinning, whether you're part of it or not. There's a sort of strange comfort in knowing that, don't you think?

We often romanticize our importance at work or home, believing that without us, things will fall apart. We wrap ourselves in the burden of being vital. But the reality is, someone else will always be there to step in. And guess what? That's not a bad thing!

This isn't about diminishing your worth or discounting your contributions. No, it's quite the opposite. It's about recognizing that your value doesn't hinge on being irreplaceable, but on being authentically you. It's about knowing that even if you are replaceable, what you bring to the table, your unique mixture of experiences, talent, and personality, is one of a kind.

Besides, knowing we're replaceable shakes us free from self-satisfaction. It nudges us to keep growing, learning, and evolving because standing still in a world that's always moving is just not an option, is it?

Being replaceable also has a beautiful way of putting things in perspective. We learn to value relationships more, realizing that we are all temporary actors in each other's life stories. It encourages kindness, and empathy, and reminds us to appreciate the here and now.

So, yes, we're replaceable. But being replaceable doesn't mean you're not valuable. It means you're a part of something larger, a constantly changing, endlessly evolving narrative. It means you can breathe, live, and enjoy your existence without the crushing weight of being the "only one."

— DAY 361 —

Anxiety fuels misery

A NXIETY is a common emotion that we all experience from time to time. It's like that annoying friend who always seems to show up uninvited and overstays their welcome. While anxiety can be a normal response to stress or uncertainty, excessive and prolonged anxiety can be detrimental to our mental and emotional well-being, leading to misery and suffering.

When we're anxious, our thoughts tend to be negative and catastrophic. We start imagining worst-case scenarios, and it's like a horror movie playing on repeat in our heads. We become consumed with fear and helplessness, and the more we focus on these negative thoughts, the more anxious we become.

This negative spiral of thoughts and emotions can lead to a sense of misery and suffering that can be difficult to shake off. We feel like we're stuck in a rut and that there's no way out. It's like being trapped in a dark tunnel with no light at the end.

Anxiety doesn't just affect us mentally and emotionally; it can also lead to physical symptoms such as headaches, nausea, and insomnia. These symptoms can further contribute to our misery and make it difficult for us to function on a day-to-day basis.

What can we do to break free from this cycle of anxiety and misery? Well, first of all, we need to acknowledge that anxiety is not a permanent state. It may feel overwhelming and all-consuming at times, but it's important to remember that it's a temporary feeling that will eventually pass.

One way to manage anxiety is through mindfulness practices such as meditation, deep breathing, and yoga. These practices can help us develop a greater awareness of our thoughts and emotions and learn to respond to them in a more positive and constructive way.

In conclusion, it's important to remember that anxiety is not a permanent state, and with the right tools and support, we can learn to manage and overcome our anxiety, leading to a greater sense of calm and well-being. So, let's take a deep breath, acknowledge our anxiety, and take the necessary steps to break free from the cycle of misery and suffering.

— DAY 362 —

Alcohol is a way of escaping reality

ALCOHOL is a substance that has been used for thousands of years for various reasons. It can be used to socialize, celebrate, and even for medicinal purposes. Human beings, for centuries, have been on a relentless quest for escape—escape from harsh realities, from despair, from the monotonous routine of life. One such attempted shortcut to temporary relief has often been alcohol.

When we use alcohol as a way of escaping reality, we're essentially avoiding the challenges and stresses of life. We're not dealing with the root cause of our problems, but rather, covering them up with alcohol-induced euphoria. It's like a *Band-Aid* solution that doesn't address the underlying issue.

Moreover, alcohol can have numerous negative effects on our physical, mental, and emotional well-being. It can weaken our judgment, lead to poor decision-making, and even cause addiction. What started as a temporary escape can quickly spiral out of control and become a long-term problem that affects every aspect of our lives.

Let's probe a little deeper and borrow wisdom from ancient Greek philosophy, notably from the Stoics. They believed that the path to true peace and tranquility lay not in avoiding reality, but in embracing it, accepting it, and working with it. They proposed that liberation wasn't found in the bottom of a bottle but within ourselves, in our perception, and our response to reality.

Consider this: instead of reaching for that glass, reach within. Channel your energy into decoding your reality, understanding it, and confronting it. Engage in dialogue with your fears, negotiate with your pain, and make peace with your past. Engulfed in this process, you'll discover your resilience, your courage, and your invincible spirit.

Alcohol may provide a temporary escape from reality, but it's not a sustainable solution. The truth is, using alcohol to escape reality is a bit like trying to outrun your own shadow. The momentary illusion might seem appealing, but the reality is, the true route to freedom lies not in evasion, but in acceptance. Not in blurry illusions, but in clear, courageous truth.

— DAY 363 —

Comfort is a cheap ticket to depression

COMFORT is something that we all crave in our lives. Comfort appears to be the ultimate goal in life; a haven of safety and contentment. However, upon closer examination, it becomes clear that excessive reliance on comfort can lead to stagnation, self-satisfaction, and ultimately, depression.

Human beings are creatures of progress. Our minds are wired to strive, to explore, to break boundaries. The early humans didn't survive and evolve by staying comfortable in their caves; they ventured out, took risks, and faced adversity. This intrinsic need to grow, to move forward, is part of our DNA. It's how we're designed.

Comfort, while pleasant, is the opposite of growth. In comfort, there's no challenge, no exploration, no room for progress. It's akin to a calm lake, quiet and peaceful, but stagnant. Over time, this stagnation begins to weigh on our psyche. A subtle unease sets in, a sense of dissatisfaction that lurks beneath the calm surface of comfort. This is the onset of stagnation depression—a mental state that arises from a prolonged period of unchallenged comfort.

Comfort also breeds self-satisfaction, a feeling of "good enough" that inhibits our drive to strive for more. This self-satisfaction is a silent killer of ambition. It's a subtle trap that lulls us into a false sense of contentment, suppressing our innate desire for growth and progress. As we settle into this state, our life becomes a monotonous cycle of the same, devoid of excitement or novelty. This lack of stimulation, over time, can foster a sense of emptiness, leading to depression.

This is not a call to abandon comfort entirely; rather, it's a prompt to examine the role of comfort in our lives. Comfort is a wonderful respite, a necessary pause in the hustle of life. But it's a rest stop, not a destination. Our journey, our growth, must continue beyond these pauses. When we become too comfortable, we may lose our sense of purpose and direction, and we may start to avoid challenges and growth.

— DAY 364 —

Life's a single-player game

L IFE is often compared to a game, with its ups and downs, challenges and rewards. Life is inherently a single-player game—we live with our individual interpretations of the world and our unique mindsets. We enter and leave the world alone, and our actions will be forgotten in a few generations.

Picture it this way: You're the main character of your story. Yes, you've got side characters who pop up, some stay for a while, others just a brief visit. But the spotlight is on you. Your triumphs, your losses, they're yours to experience. Others might cheer or console you, but they're spectators, even the closest ones.

Now, don't get me wrong. This isn't about becoming a lone wolf. We absolutely need the cheer squad, the wise sages, and even the villains in our lives. They enrich our experiences, they make our stories vivid and colorful. But, they don't live our stories for us.

Think about the last time you felt really ecstatic or downright devastated. You could explain your feelings to your friend, your partner, but they didn't really get it, did they? They empathized, of course, but they weren't in your shoes. They were living their own single-player game, just like you.

Realizing that life's a single-player game isn't a grim prospect. It's liberating! The thought that you're the one at the steering wheel of your life, gives you a sense of power. You're not a puppet being moved by others. You're the puppeteer.

And the best part? You don't have to stick to a script. You can be a Wall Street hotshot, or a free-spirited artist, or both. There's no set path. You're free to design your own unique game. Sure, society will try to set rules, but hey, you're the player here.

Envisioning life as a single-player game is not a teaching of isolation but a celebration of uniqueness and a testament to individual journeying. It is a call to travel the winding lanes of self-exploration, to dance to the rhythm of selfdiscovery, and to savor the taste of personal growth. It is an invitation to be the navigator, the sailor, and the ship, braving the tides of life's ocean, one wave at a time.

— DAY 365 —

Action is the antidote to fear

FEAR is a natural and ubiquitous part of the human experience. It can hold us back from pursuing our dreams, taking risks, and living life to the fullest. Fear can paralyze us and make us feel like we are trapped in a never-ending cycle of anxiety and uncertainty. But what if I told you that there is a cure for fear? An antidote that can free you from its grasp and empower you to take control of your life? That antidote is action.

Fear. It's that icy shiver crawling down your spine, that restless monster gnawing at the corners of your mind. We've all been there, haven't we? Frozen in place by this thing called fear, conjuring up worst-case scenarios, playing out each potential disaster in Technicolor. And the more we think about it, the more it grows, ballooning into this enormous entity that feels unbeatable. It's all in our heads, these nightmare scenarios that may never see the light of day.

Now, let's talk about action. Imagine you're at the edge of a cliff, heart pounding, looking down at the swirling waters below. You want to jump, but fear is holding you back. You can either stand there forever, locked in your terror, or you can leap. That leap? That's action.

The thing about action is, it's real. It's right here, right now. It's the moment your feet leave the cliff, the rush of wind in your hair, the exciting thrill of free fall. That's when fear loses its grip, replaced by the intense presence of the experience.

It doesn't matter if you belly-flop or dive gracefully. What matters is that you jumped. You acted. And that action, no matter how small, chips away at the towering wall of fear. It's like David meeting Goliath, armed with nothing but a slingshot. Except, in this story, you're David, and your slingshot? It's action. And trust me, it's more powerful than you think.

Action, my friends, is learning, growing, and expanding your horizons. It's staring fear in the face and saying, "Move over, buddy. I've got things to do." Every step forward, every leap, every dive, brings us closer to our potential, to the things we want to achieve.

— DAY 366 —

You are the captain of your destiny

L IFE'S a lot like sailing a ship through uncharted waters. One moment you're cruising along, basking in the warm sunlight, and the next, you're battling the tempest, feeling the full force of nature's fury. In this extraordinary voyage of self-discovery, you are not merely a passive passenger but the master of your fate.

Let's close our eyes and picture ourselves aboard a grand vessel. This ship is our life. The sails are our goals, the helm our decisions, the compass our values, and the unpredictable sea is the world around us. We are the captain, and the journey is our destiny.

As captains, we are tasked with navigating through calm and stormy seas alike, under the clear azure sky or in the middle of a black storm. These are our circumstances—sometimes serene, often challenging. They may affect our journey, shape the course we take, but they never have the final say in where we end up. That power lies with us, the captains of our destinies.

As we stand at the helm, we steer our ship, our life, with decisions we make every day. Do we sail toward the horizon of our dreams or let the tides of selfsatisfaction carry us? The choice, as always, is ours to make. Our decisions are the rudder that directs our life's course, guiding us toward our envisioned destiny or away from it.

Our compass, the values we hold dear, ensures we don't lose ourselves in the vast expanse of the sea. They keep us on course, providing a sense of direction when the lighthouse of our goals seems too far away. Without our values, we risk becoming lost at sea, adrift and aimless.

As captains, we can't control the sea, but we can control how we navigate it. We can't predict the storms, but we can decide how we weather them.

So, stand tall at the helm, my friend. Navigate the sea of life with confidence and conviction. Set your sails, hold your course, weather the storms, and remember, no matter what, you are the captain of your destiny. Therein lies the magic of these words—they remind us of our power, our ability to chart our course, to steer our ship toward the horizon of our dreams.

— NOTES —

[1] Wikipedia contributors, "Mu¨nchhausen trilemma — Wikipedia, the free encyclopedia." https://en.wikipedia.org/w/index.php?title=M%C3%BCnchhausen trilemma&oldid=1158287248, 2023.

[2] B. Headey, *Hedonic Adaptation*, pp. 2831–2833. Dordrecht: Springer Netherlands, 2014.

[3] S. McMains and S. Kastner, "Interactions of top-down and bottom-up mechanisms in human visual cortex," *Journal of Neuroscience*, vol. 31, no. 2, pp. 587–597, 2011.

[4] Wikipedia contributors, "Carol dweck — Wikipedia, the free encyclopedia," 2023.

[5] https://www.nih.gov/news-events/nih-research-matters/weekend-catch-cant-counter-chronic-sleep-deprivation, 2020.

[6] R. Rastogi, "Statistical analysis for effect of positive thinking on stress management and creative problem solving for adolescents," 03 2018.

THANK YOU

T HANK you for taking the time to read my book. I hope that the ideas and insights presented in these pages have been valuable to you and that they have inspired you to make positive changes in your life.

As an author, there is nothing more rewarding than knowing that my work has positively impacted someone's life. Whether you were looking to improve your health, mindset, relationships, or career, I hope this book has provided you with the guidance and inspiration you needed to move forward.

I greatly appreciate your time reading my book and would love to hear your thoughts. Your feedback is iinvaluable to me, as it helps me improve my work and better cater to my readers. Please consider leaving a review from the QR code below, whether you enjoyed the book or found areas that need improvement.

Scan and leave a review on Amazon here!

ALSO BY HONEROD

www.honerod.com